RANDALL E. DECKER

PATTERNS OF
EXPOSITION 6

LITTLE, BROWN AND COMPANY
BOSTON   TORONTO

Published simultaneously in Canada
by Little, Brown & Company (Canada) Limited

PRINTED IN THE UNITED STATES OF AMERICA

PATTERNS OF
EXPOSITION 6

To the Instructor

Patterns of Exposition 6 retains the basic principles and the general format of our five former editions. Use of the book continues to expand (the publisher tells me that *Patterns 5* is the most widely adopted composition anthology in the country) and we continue to poll instructor-users for evaluations of the selections and about the need for basic changes in the framework. In preparing this edition more user questionnaires were mailed out and returned than ever before. We also reviewed the responses of hundreds of students who returned questionnaires like the one at the back of this book. Although obviously we are unable to comply with all requests, many suggestions have been incorporated into this new edition, and all have been seriously considered and fully appreciated.

One of these, persistent in recent years and now grown into popular demand, is for a few selections of argumentation. Many instructors want just enough examples of that form to be able to illustrate the differences between it and exposition, or to use as a brief introduction to their next semester's work. Our difficulty, of course, has been in justifying such selections in a book about exposition. (Description and narration are included only because they are useful *aids* in explaining.) But we also know that our job is to provide a textbook most useful to most teachers using it — so this time we decided to include some examples of argument and persuasion.

But we faced another problem: the fact that there is no sharp, indelible line between exposition and argumentation. Almost the only reason for categorizing writing types at all, of course, is to provide a convenient means of teaching the special methods involved, however much they may overlap — a fact that is also true of our "patterns of exposition." Between argument and exposition the differences are solely dependent on the nature of the subject and the author's purpose; but between the extremes of obviously pure explanation and of courtroom-type efforts to convince, most other writings are less distinct in purpose, perhaps even to the authors. (For that matter, we could easily justify classifying some of our "expository" selections as argument — e.g., Mitford, B. Lawrence, Jefferson.)

To make room for additional selections in the last section without unduly expanding the volume, we eliminated one essay from each of four lesser-used "patterns" sections. "Further Readings," all of which can now be shown to have *some elements* of argument or persuasion, have been arranged, roughly (and no doubt debatably), in order of ascending logical intensity. They are presented without suggestions or questions, so that instructors may use them without difficulty however they like — as an approach to further study of argument, or simply as additional readings for discussion and writing. In the instructor's manual, however, is a brief discussion of the special techniques and hazards of argument, as well as a few suggestions for using the various selections. In this way, we believe, no one need be discomfited by the slight changes in the book itself.

But throughout *Patterns of Exposition 6* we have tried, as always, to make possible the convenient use of all materials in whatever ways instructors think best for their own classes. Only complete essays or free-standing units of larger works have been included. With their inevitable overlap of patterns, they are more complicated than excerpts illustrating single principles, but they are also more realistic examples of exposition and more useful for other classroom purposes. Versatility is one important standard in choosing materials.

The total number of selections remains the same. Twenty-three of those best liked in the previous edition have been retained; twenty are new, and several of these are anthologized here for the first time anywhere.

Their arrangement is but one of many workable orders; the instructor can easily develop another if he so desires. To make such variations convenient, we have nearly always placed interessay questions at the end of sequences, where they can be quickly detected and, if not suitable, easily eliminated or modified.

We have tried to vary the study questions — and undoubtedly have included far more than any one teacher will want — from the purely objective to those calling for some serious self-examination by the students. (The booklet, *Instructor's Manual to Accompany Patterns of Exposition 6,* is available, placing further materials at the instructor's disposal.)

Suggestions for writing assignments to be developed from ideas in the essays are located immediately after each selection. But for classes in which the instructor prefers writing to be done according to the expository pattern under study at the time, regardless of subject matter, topic suggestions are located at the end of each section.

"A Guide to Terms," where matters from *Abstract* to *Unity* are briefly discussed, refers whenever possible to the essays themselves for illustrations. To permit unity and easy access, it is located at the back of the book, but there are continuing cross-references to it in the study questions.

In all respects — in size, content, arrangement, format — we have tried to keep *Patterns of Exposition 6* uncluttered and easy to use.

The editor wishes to express appreciation for the helpful criticism and suggestions provided by his friends and colleagues, especially L. David Allen, Richard Benston, Richard Bier, Samuel Blate, Marie Bohmbach, Sr. Don Bowens, Delores Bowyer, Julia Brent, Daniel Brislane, Janet Carnesi, James Clapsaddle, Betty Clark, Sharon Cleland, Lawrence J. Clipper, Pat Collins, Gary Collison, Lois M. Craig, MaryAnn Deibel, Louise Dibble, Lee F. Dickerson, Julia Dietche, Antoinette Empringham, Elmer Evans, Douglas C. Fricke, Peggy Gaddy, Joan Gage, Frank Gaspar, Silas H. Garrison, G. Dale Gleason, Katherine Gitter, Frederick Goldberg, E. Grant, James Hanlon, William A. Harrison III, Frederic B. Irvin, Linda V. Itzoe, Nobuko T. Keith, John Thomas Kelly, J. F. Kobler, Natalie A. Kuhlman, Richard E. Lander, T. N. Lane, Russ Larson, Charles S. Lausheim, David Light, Judi McAdo, Paul J. McCarthy, Russell Mills, Ronald Newman, Hannelore Noble, Henry Norris, Cheryl J. Plumb, Kathy J. Rosengren, Gregory Ross, Clifton Snider, Anthony Spatola, Roger P. Wallens, Robert H. Watrous, Colleen Wells, and Amberys R. Whittle. He would also like to thank Douglas Cope and certainly the many cooperative members of the Little, Brown staff, especially Jan Beatty, Charles Christensen, Elizabeth Philipps, and Andrea Pozgay.

PUBLISHER'S NOTE

We maintain an unusual revision policy on *Patterns of Exposition*. It is revised every two years to ensure that its popular framework is always well stocked with fresh selections. However, for those who do not like to change texts so frequently, the previous edition does *not* go out of print. Thus, two editions of *Patterns of Exposition* are available at all times.

Table of Contents

MON. IN CLASS (USE OF EXAMPLES)

BY FRIDAY

xi

Introduction

Exposition is one of the four basic forms of communication, more important to most people than any of the others — narration, description, or argumentation (including persuasion). The novelist and to some extent the sports reporter use narration and description; the lawyer, the salesman, the preacher become skilled in logical argument and persuasion. But these persons are in specialized fields, prepared by specialized training. People in such professions, like the rest of us, are also frequent users of exposition in one way or another.

Exposition means explanation, simply an *exposing* of information or ideas. Its primary function is not to tell a story or relate a happening, although exposition often *uses* narration as one of many techniques. Its primary function is not to create vivid pictures for the reader, although description, too, may at times be a valuable technique of exposition. The primary function of exposition is not to convince or persuade, although, conversely, logical argument and persuasion frequently use exposition as one of their techniques. But the primary function of exposition itself is merely *to explain*.

Even beyond our increasing need for informally written and spoken explanations, we use the processes of written exposition throughout college — in reports, term papers, essay examinations. Most of us use exposition throughout our working lives — in letters, in memoranda, in business and professional reports. Hence there are practical reasons why most college composition courses are devoted primarily to study and practice in exposition. And these, of course, are the reasons this book concentrates on patterns of expository writing and other techniques commonly used. (An exception is the last part, "Further Readings," which offers a wider variety of composition forms and subject matter.)

There is nothing new about the ten basic patterns of exposition; we have been using most of them since we first tried to explain why some types of birds fly south in the winter. But mature writing depends partly on the author's being able to use *deliberately* whichever techniques will do the job best, with the least chance of misunderstanding. We study them to get a clearer view of their functions and possibilities, with the aim of being able to use them more effectively in our own writing.

We examine and practice these techniques separately, realizing they are seldom used separately in practical writing. After all, when we observe and practice for hours a skill involved in tennis or golf, we are not assuming that an entire game will be made up of serving or putting. In writing, we know there is no reason why a process analysis should not be used to assist comparison in some explanations, why illustration might not be valuably aided in certain developments by narration. In good writing, if the patterns do not overlap, it is simply because one alone is sufficient for the purpose.

But besides the study of writing techniques in a college anthology, we have a right to expect real benefit from the reading itself. Reading and thinking about new ideas or experiences is an excellent way to widen horizons, to broaden our interests — and that is an important phase of becoming educated. In general, each set of essays in this book progresses in complexity and depth. Challenges help our understanding to reach an ever higher level.

The manner of approaching each reading, or the study of it, may be suggested by the instructor. If not, a worthwhile system for the student to give at least a fair trial is this:

1. For the first reading relax. Read the selection casually, as you would some magazine article, for whatever enjoyment or new ideas you can get without straining. Do not stop to look up new words unless the sentences in which they are used are meaningless until you do. But have a pencil in hand and mark all words you are doubtful about, then go on.

2. When finished with the first reading, put the book down; for a few minutes think over what you have read.

3. Then use the dictionary to help you understand the words you have marked. Do not make the mistake of finding the first or

the shortest definition and trying to memorize it. Instead, look at the various meanings, and for the word's uses as noun, verb, and modifier. *Think* about them. Pronounce the word. Use it in a few sentences. Identify it with similar words you already know. Then see how the author has used it.

4. After you understand all the words, read and think briefly about the assigned questions and remarks following the selection. (The paragraphs in each selection are numbered for easy reference.)

5. Then reread the essay, pausing sometimes to think and to *question,* underlining important ideas, marking sentences or phrases that seem to you especially interesting, misleading, amusing, or well expressed.

6. Then return to the questions at the end. You will probably find that you have already provided most of the answers. If not, give them further thought, referring again to the essay and to "A Guide to Terms" or earlier explanations wherever necessary for thorough understanding.

7. Next, try to *evaluate* the selection. What was the author trying to explain? Did he succeed in explaining? Was his endeavor worthwhile?

Useful as these selections can be, however, they are not intended as models for imitation by students. Each was written, as all expository projects should be, to give a particular audience a particular explanation. The style of some is much too informal for most college writing. Other styles, perhaps from a slower and more sedate age than ours, would be too stately for today. Pure imitation is not the purpose of our study.

But each of the selections does demonstrate one or more of the *patterns* of exposition, which are as useful now as ever. Each can provide, too, some profitable study of other sound principles of writing — principles of effective sentences and paragraphs, mature diction, forceful introductions and closings. The consideration of all these principles, instead of being handled in separate sections, is a continuing study within the basic framework of the expository patterns. The book is designed so that instructors and students can use it in several ways.

PATTERNS OF
EXPOSITION 6

Illustrating Ideas by Use of *Example*

The use of examples to illustrate an idea under discussion is the most common, and frequently most efficient, pattern of exposition. It is a method we use almost instinctively; for instance, instead of talking in generalities about the qualities of a good city manager, we cite Harry Hibbons as an example. We may go further and illustrate Harry's virtues by a specific account of his handling of a crucial situation during the last power shortage or hurricane disaster. In this way we put our abstract ideas into concrete form — a process that is always an aid to clarity. (As a matter of fact, with the "for instance" in this very paragraph, examples are employed to illustrate even the *use* of example.)

Lack of clear illustrations may leave the reader with only a hazy conception of the points the writer has tried to make. Even worse, the reader may try to supply examples from his own knowledge or experience, and these might do the job poorly or even lead him to an impression different from that intended by the author. Since the writer is the one trying to communicate, clarity is primarily his responsibility.

Not only do good examples put into clear, concrete form what otherwise might remain vague and abstract, but the writing also becomes more interesting, with a better chance of holding the reader's attention. With something specific to be visualized, a statement also becomes more convincing — but convincing within certain limitations. If we use the Volvo as an example of Swedish workmanship, the reader is probably aware that this car may not be entirely typical. Although isolated examples will not hold up well in logical argument, for ordinary purposes of explanation the Volvo example could make its point convincingly enough.

As in the selection and use of all materials for composition, of course, the successful writer selects and uses examples cautiously, always keeping in mind the nature of his reader-audience and his own specific purpose for communicating. To be effective, each example must be pertinent, respecting the chief qualities of the generality it illustrates. Its function as an example must be either instantly obvious to the reader or fully enough developed so that he learns exactly what it illustrates, and how. Sometimes, however, illustration may be provided best by something other than a real-life example — a fictional anecdote, an analogy, or perhaps a parable that demonstrates the general idea. Here even greater care is needed to be sure these examples are both precise and clear.

Illustration is sometimes used alone as the basic means of development; but it also frequently assists other basic techniques, such as comparison and contrast. In either of its functions, the author may find his purpose best served by one well-developed example, possibly with full background information and descriptive details. But sometimes citing several shorter examples is best, particularly if the author is attempting to show a trend or a prevalence. In more difficult explanations, of course, a careful combination of the two techniques — using both one well-developed example and several shorter examples — may be worth the extra time and effort required.

Whichever method is used, the writer is following at least one sound principle of writing: he is trying to make the general more specific, the abstract more concrete.

ALDOUS HUXLEY

ALDOUS HUXLEY (1894–1963) was a British novelist, essayist, and poet. After receiving his education at Oxford University, Aldous Huxley worked in England as writer, editor, and drama critic. After 1937 he lived in California, continuing a diversified career, which included writing screenplays. Among his scores of famous books are *Brave New World* (1932), *After Many a Summer Dies the Swan* (1939), *Ape and Essence* (1948), *Genius and the Goddess* (1955), *On Art and Artists* (1960), and *Literature and Science* (1963).

Waterworks and Kings

"Waterworks and Kings" was published in *The Olive Tree* (1936), a collection of Huxley's essays. In it he uses a somewhat unusual technique, presenting his major illustration first without explanation, and then proceeding only gradually to develop his central theme. This is a method we could aptly call the "pyramid" form, as it starts with a specific point at the top and then gradually broadens to full meaning at the bottom (i.e., the end) of the essay.

In the chancelleries of eighteenth-century Europe nobody bothered very much about Hesse. Its hostility was not a menace, its friendship brought no positive advantages. Hesse was only one of the lesser German states — a tenth-rate Power.

1

Tenth-rate: and yet, on the outskirts of Kassel, which was the capital of this absurdly unimportant principality, there stands a palace large and splendid enough to house a full-blown emperor. And from the main façade of this palace there rises to the very top of the neighbouring mountain one of the most magnificent architectural gardens in the world. This garden, which is like a straight wide corridor of formal stone-work driven through the hillside for-

2

est, climbs up to a nondescript building in the grandest Roman
manner, almost as large as a cathedral and surmounted by a colossal bronze statue of Hercules. Between Hercules at the top and the
palace at the bottom lies an immense series of terraces, with foun-
tains and cascades, pools, grottos, spouting tritons, dolphins, nereids
and all the other mythological fauna of an eighteenth-century
water-garden. The spectacle, when the waters are flowing, is magnificent. There must be the best part of two miles of neoclassic
cataract and elegantly canalized foam. The waterworks at Versailles
are tame and trivial in comparison.

It was Whit Sunday when I was at Kassel. With almost the   3
entire population of the town I had climbed up to the shrine of
Hercules on the hilltop. Standing there in the shadow of the god,
with the waters in full splash below me and the sunshine brilliant
on the green dome of the palace at the long cataract's foot, I found
myself prosaically speculating about ways and means and motives.
How could a mere prince of Hesse run to such imperial splendours?
And why, having somehow raised the money, should he elect to
spend it in so fantastically wasteful a fashion? And, finally, why
did the Hessians ever put up with his extravagance? The money,
after all, was theirs; seeing it all squandered on a house and garden,
why didn't they rise up against their silly, irresponsible tyrant?

The answer to these last questions was being provided, even   4
as I asked them, by the good citizens of Kassel around me. *Schön,
herrlich, prachtvoll* [roughly: beautiful, magnificent, splendid] —
their admiration exploded emphatically on every side. Without any
doubt, they were thoroughly enjoying themselves. In six generations, humanity cannot undergo any fundamental change. There is
no reason to suppose that the Hessians of 1750 were greatly different from those of 1932. Whenever the prince allowed his subjects
to visit his waterworks, they came and, I have no doubt, admired
and enjoyed their admiration just as much as their descendants do
today. The psychology of revolutionaries is apt to be a trifle crude.
The magnificent display of wealth does not necessarily, as they
imagine, excite a passion of envy in the hearts of the poor. Given
a reasonable amount of prosperity, it excites, more often, nothing
but pleasure. The Hessians did not rise up and kill their prince for
having wasted so much money on his house and garden; on the
contrary, they were probably grateful to him for having realized
in solid stone and rainbow-flashing water their own vague day-

dreams of a fairy-tale magnificence. One of the functions of royalty is to provide people with a vicarious, but none the less real, fulfilment of their wishes. Kings who make a fine show are popular, and the people not only forgive, but actually commend, extravagances which, to the good Marxian, must seem merely criminal. Wise kings always ear-marked a certain percentage of their income for display. Palaces and waterworks were good publicity for kingship, just as an impressive office building is good publicity for a business corporation. Business, indeed, has inherited many of the responsibilities of royalty. It shares with the State and the municipality the important duty of providing the common people with vicarious wish-fulfilments. Kings no longer build palaces; but newspapers and insurance companies do. Popular restaurants are as richly marbled as the mausoleum of the Escorial; hotels are more splendid than Versailles. In every society there must always be some person or some organization whose task it is to realize the day-dreams of the masses. Life in a perfectly sensible, utilitarian community would be intolerably dreary. Occasional explosions of magnificent folly are as essential to human well-being as a sewage system. More so, probably. Sanitary plumbing, it is significant to note, is a very recent invention; the splendours of kingship are as old as civilization itself.

Meanings and Values

1a. What is the author's central theme?
 b. At what point does he make clear its broadest meaning?

2a. What is the "psychology of revolutionaries" that Huxley thinks is refuted by the show-loving nature of people?
 b. How important to the soundness of this idea is his qualification "given a reasonable amount of prosperity" (par. 4)?

3. What is the significance of the late invention of plumbing, and the slow spread of its use by common people, in view of the thousands of years these same people paid taxes to support the "splendours of kingship"?

4a. What are "vicarious wish-fulfilments" (par. 4)?
 b. Do you agree that government, even down to the city level, has "an important duty of providing the common people" with these fulfillments — even though it is obviously done with their own money? Explain your views.

5. Supply as widely-varying examples as possible of local government's actual functioning in this respect. (Try to find examples other than the obvious ones of public buildings.)

6a. To what extent, if any, do U.S. presidents also need the publicity of a "splendid show" for the common people?
   b. Cite examples in at least two recent presidencies which will tend to illustrate that Huxley's theory is, or is not, universally valid.
   c. If these recent examples do not support Huxley's theories, what sides of the issue do you think he has failed to consider?

Expository Techniques

1a. Besides the fully developed example of Hesse, where does the author make further use of examples to illustrate his central theme?
   b. How might these have been made still more specific, if the essay had been written for a local audience? (See Guide to Terms: *Specific/General*.)
   c. List five additional examples which could have been compiled to show "prevalence."

2. Is this a formal or informal essay? Why? (Guide: *Essay*.)

3a. Does your answer to question 2 justify the author's introduction, which does not let us know the real theme, or central idea, of his essay? Explain.
   b. Why is this method inappropriate to most college writing? (Guide: *Introductions*.)

4. Explain why the first paragraph is needed to show the full significance of the second.

5a. Is there either a stated or implied topic sentence which would cover all ingredients of paragraph 4? (Guide: *Unity*.) If so, what is it?
   b. Show why such a topic sentence would (or does) indicate that this paragraph, despite its length, has unity.

6a. If paragraph 4 were divided into two shorter ones, where would be the logical place?
   b. Try to supply topic sentences for each of these paragraphs, to see if you now have two unified paragraphs.
   c. If both paragraphing methods discussed above permit unity, is there any advantage to the latter?

Diction and Vocabulary

1. Explain the following references: Hercules (par. 2); Versailles (2, 4); Escorial (4).

2. There is a rather subtle connotation (Guide: *Connotation/Denotation*) in "elegantly canalized foam" (par. 2) and "the waters in full splash below me" (3). Describe the connotation and explain its significance, if any, to the central theme.

3. If not already familiar with the following words, study their meanings as given in the dictionary and as used in this essay: chancelleries (par. 1); principality, façade, nondescript, surmounted, colossal, cascades, grottos, dolphins, nereids, neo-classic, canalized (2); Whit Sunday, prosaically, imperial (3); realized, vicarious, commend, municipality, mausoleum, utilitarian (4).

Suggestions for Writing and Discussion

1. If you had to choose between having a sewage system and "occasional explosions of magnificent folly," which would you choose? Why?

2. Select one of the following standard activities of many American communities and explain the reasons for and against spending public money for that purpose. (Do not argue for either side.)
   a. Fourth of July fireworks.
   b. Elaborate parades.
   c. Municipal Christmas decorations.
   d. Extensive landscaping of public property.

3. Would a row of large Quonset huts, well equipped for classes, library, and laboratories, be as satisfactory to you for your college or former high school as the more expensive buildings now in use or being planned? Explain why or why not.

4. What practical, economic values, if any, are derived from the construction of expensive public and private buildings? Explain fully.

5. Richard B. Sheridan (British dramatist, 1751–1816) observed that there is "no other passion so strongly rooted in the human heart as envy." Explain the reasons why you agree or disagree, and show the practical importance of being aware of this human tendency.

(NOTE: Suggestions for topics requiring development by use of EXAMPLE are on page 33, at the end of this section.)

GEORGE PLIMPTON

GEORGE PLIMPTON (b. 1927) is the founding editor of *The Paris Review*. He is best known for his books detailing his experiences as an amateur participating in professional sports: in football, *Paper Lion;* baseball, *Out of My League;* and golf, *The Bogey Man*. In addition, Plimpton has edited *Writers at Work*, three volumes of collected interviews with authors (1958, 1963, 1967), and written *The Rabbit's Umbrella*, a children's book. His articles have appeared in many magazines, including *Vogue, Esquire,* and *Horizon*. His most recent books are *Mad Duck and Bears* (1974), *Hank Aaron: One for the Record* (1974), *Plimpton Pugilist* (1976), and *One More July: A Football Dialogue with Bill Curry* (1977).

The American Tradition of Winning

"The American Tradition of Winning" examines the contemporary mania of sports fans for victory at any price — even, it seems to the author, the sacrifice of rational behavior. Unlike Huxley in the preceding essay, with its one fully developed example to make more specific the central theme (as always, a generality), Plimpton uses shorter examples liberally in developing his.

Involvement with sports, as participant or observer in the stands, is supposed to provide a healthy uplift . . . largely by identification with winning. Chief Justice Warren once offered a pertinent observation: "At the breakfast table," he said, "I always open the newspaper to the sports page first. The sports page records people's accomplishments. The front page has nothing but man's failures." 1

I have never been comfortable with that comment — since in fact the sports page lists far more failures, losers, and also-rans than any other page in a newspaper short of the stock market listings on a Black Friday. 2

Reprinted courtesy *Mainliner* Magazine carried aboard United Airlines; © 1976 East/West Network, Inc.

The reason for this is obvious enough: for every winner there 3
is a loser; in the case of tournaments, with rafts of contestants
entered, only one winner can emerge. Since there are so many
losers, sport has not been a release at the breakfast table, but a
type of daily agony. The fan looks at the paper in the morning and
he probably starts off his day (unless he possesses the magnanimity
of a Chief Justice) by feeling punk. Imagine being a Washington
Capitals hockey fan. At this writing the team has lost 26 straight
games!

The problem, of course, is that these things are taken very 4
seriously. It was not always so. Back in the 1870s, in the infancy
of football, President White of Cornell once rather testily denied
the request of an undergraduate football squad to travel to the
Midwest to play a Michigan team. "I will not permit 30 men to
travel 400 miles," he said, "merely to agitate a bag of wind." One
can scarcely imagine what the good president would have said, and
the height to which his eyebrows would have arched, had his undergraduate student body turned up with the team and requested
to travel out there simply to *watch* a bag of wind being agitated.

Since then a near-symbiotic relationship has developed be- 5
tween the player and the fan in the stands watching him — that
phrase, "I just die with the Chiefs (or the Rams, or the Mets, or
whatever)" . . . the fan's forefinger raised to denote that his team
(and he) are Number One, the "we did it, we did it," and the self-
satisfied smiles on the faces of people coming down the stadium
ramps after their teams have won. We seem to require the personal
assurance of an idol's triumph in the highly dramatic situation that
sports provides — and a loser too, someone to jeer at and feel superior to . . . the substitute scapegoat for the tyrant down the hall
who has the key to the executive washroom.

All of this is probably natural enough, and understandable — 6
but then the fan in his intensity for a win begins to take on the
same desperate excesses that sometimes the athlete must indulge in
to play at his best. His team loses and he crumples up the sports
page and throws it at the family cat. In the stands the fan becomes
as competitive as a man striving for a championship.

Unfortunately, the champion is so often driven by a set of 7
impulses and persuasions that are not necessarily desirable or
attractive. Billie Jean King, who drove herself to championships
with 40/200 vision, a bad set of knees and a famous tendency to

eat too much ice cream, has said that many topflight tennis players have never become true winners because they are *afraid* to be ... to accept the ugliness of those responsibilities — not only the grim determination to become the champion, but also the enmity and jealousy that comes with attaining the top. Her close pal Rosemary Casals called off their friendship ostensibly because she could not accept the idea of being friendly with someone whose position she coveted.

Sad and interesting — friendships disbanded, everything put aside to win. But then surely it is the athlete's prerogative to do so: the choice is personal; reputation, livelihood, the future, and so forth are obvious determinants. 8

It is difficult, however, to understand how such intensity applies to a *fan* (unless he has bet his wife and that family cat on the outcome of a game). Yet the honest emphasis on supporting a winner has become an obsession to such a point (witness the Soviet hockey series in which the visitors' anthem was booed, obscenities in Russian held aloft on signs, objects thrown and generally a type of bellicosity in the air that awed witnesses felt was almost palpable) that editorial writers surveying the national character, get fidgety and begin worrying once again about the win-at-all-cost grip that seizes American fans and so often makes them louts. 9

I remember John Gordy, the All-Pro Detroit offensive guard, talking about it: "The snowballs come down with rocks in them. I've seen these guys who are sedate businessmen, and they've got a Caddy out in the parking lot, and a big house in Grosse Pointe to drive home to, and a wine cellar, and all they have to worry about are their.golf handicaps — and I've seen these guys hanging over the runways with the hair hanging down into their eyes, and their faces blood-red, screaming insults, like you were a bug and they wanted to exterminate you. ... When something like that happens to you, and the pain, and all the grief of losing, you come off the field and you want to get to your family, and you hurry through the tunnel to get away from the crowd, and you hear them screaming at you, and you think about where you can go to eat in a place where nobody knows you, and all the time you're wondering how you can be *hated* so much for going out there and trying your best." 10

What seems to be missing is a sense of perspective — an appreciation that there is much more of a feast going on at an athletic 11 contest besides the matter of winning. One would hope for vision that is panoramic rather than focussed, so that the occasion itself can be relished . . . the skills, the pageantry, the incidentals (Marianne Moore, the poet laureate of the Brooklyn Dodgers, was entranced by the behavior of the Ebbets Field pigeons). . . .

Jim Murray, the great West Coast sports columnist, addressed one of his books to readers who did not need "larger-than-life heroics all the time. They can take their sport with a squirt of humor and a twist of irreverence." 12

In the spirit of this attitude I remember some years back, in the heat of a hectic football game at Harvard Stadium, a pigeon (Marianne Moore would have exclaimed in delight!) landed on the four-yard line — turning as soon as he put down and setting out toward the goal line with great determination, his neck bobbing in his haste. But then indecision, or perhaps something startling in the grass, diverted his attention, and he stopped a foot or two short. He revolved, peering here and there . . . and suddenly that immense crowd focussed on him, neighbors nudging each other and remarking on the pigeon's vacillation just at the brink of the goal line: megaphones went up, cries of "Go, bird, go!" erupted from one side of the stadium and, "Hold that pigeon!" from the Harvard side. 13

Odd, I cannot remember whether he crossed the line or not, but I recall that the vast good-natured attention given the bird seemed from that point on to infuse the crowd's reaction to the game itself — chauvinism muted, skills enjoyed. A sudden sensibility reflected, if only for a time, President White of Cornell's long-past suspicion of undue emphasis on "agitating a bag of wind." 14

Meanings and Values

1a. How is it that a player could serve as scapegoat for "the tyrant down the hall" (par. 5)?

b. For what larger generality, stated or implied, is "the tyrant" a subtle example?

2. What, if anything, do you find ironical about the attitude described by the author and, in paragraph 10, by John Gordy? (See Guide to Terms: *Irony*.)

3. Do you find emotional behavior at a school game more, or less, understandable than that at a large professional game? Explain the difference, if any.

4. Explain how the tone of this writing reflects the author's attitude toward his subject. (Guide: *Style/Tone.*)

5. If you have already read the Huxley essay, can you find any relationship between the themes of the two authors? Explain fully.

Expository Techniques

1a. Cite five good uses of example in this selection and show how each is used to illustrate a generality.
 b. How, if at all, does the use of these examples improve the writing?

2a. What is Plimpton's central theme? (Guide: *Unity.*)
 b. Does the writing have good unity? Why, or why not?

3a. What kind of rhetorical device is used to introduce the writing? (Guide: *Introductions.*)
 b. Is it successful? Why, or why not?

4a. Which of the common methods of closing has the author used? (Guide: *Closings.*)
 b. What is the advantage, if any, of such a closing?

Diction and Vocabulary

1a. Cite one colloquialism each in the second and third paragraphs. (Guide: *Colloquial Expressions.*)
 b. Why are these expressions appropriate, or inappropriate, to this particular essay?

2. Consider each of the following words, using your dictionary as necessary to make sure of their meanings as used by the author: symbiotic (par. 5); ostensibly (7); prerogative (8); bellicosity, palpable, louts (9); perspective (11); vacillation (13); infuse, chauvinism (14).

Suggestions for Writing and Discussion

1. How do you account for the "perspective" that leads many sports fans to become so emotional about games — and about players they will never know personally? Why do other regular spectators take sports much less seriously?

2. In what fields other than sports do many people seem to find "personal assurance [in] an idol's triumph" (par. 5)? Does such idolization indicate to you a basic human need, or perhaps a lack in the make-up or everyday lives of some people? How else would you account for it?

3. Describe, as if to one who had never seen a game (of football, basketball, baseball, or hockey), the "pageantry" (par. 11) of such an occasion.

(NOTE: Suggestions for topics requiring development by use of EXAMPLE are on page 33, at the end of this section.)

JAMES THURBER

JAMES THURBER (1894–1961) was a writer and cartoonist whose essays, short stories, and line drawings have helped enliven and illuminate American life for half a century. He joined the staff of *The New Yorker* in 1925, and most of his writings were first published in that magazine. Some of his collections are *Is Sex Necessary?* (1929, with E. B. White), *The Owl in the Attic* (1931), *Let Your Mind Alone!* (1937), *The Thurber Carnival* (1945), *The Thurber Album* (1952), and *Thurber Country* (1953). His more recent books are *Alarms and Diversions* (1957), *The Years with Ross* (1959), and *Lanterns and Lances* (1961).

Courtship Through the Ages

"Courtship Through the Ages" was first published in 1939 by *The New Yorker*, and was included the same year in Thurber's book *My World — and Welcome to It*. Although it would be misleading to call any one selection "typical" of writing as varied as Thurber's, this one is at least representative of the kind of humor that made him famous. It also serves, for us, to illustrate example usage to show a "prevalence."

Surely nothing in the astonishing scheme of life can have non-   1
plussed Nature so much as the fact that none of the females of any of the species she created really cared very much for the male, as such. For the past ten million years Nature has been busily inventing ways to make the male attractive to the female, but the whole business of courtship, from the marine annelids up to man, still lumbers heavily along, like a complicated musical comedy. I have

been reading the sad and absorbing story in Volume 6 (Cole to Dama) of the *Encyclopaedia Britannica.* In this volume you can learn all about cricket, cotton, costume designing, crocodiles, crown jewels, and Coleridge, but none of these subjects is so interesting as the Courtship of Animals, which recounts the sorrowful lengths to which all males must go to arouse the interest of a lady.

We all know, I think, that Nature gave man whiskers and a mustache with the quaint idea in mind that these would prove attractive to the female. We all know that, far from attracting her, whiskers and mustaches only made her nervous and gloomy, so that man had to go in for somersaults, tilting with lances, and performing feats of parlor magic to win her attention; he also had to bring her candy, flowers, and the furs of animals. It is common knowledge that in spite of all these "love displays" the male is constantly being turned down, insulted, or thrown out of the house. It is rather comforting, then, to discover that the peacock, for all his gorgeous plumage, does not have a particularly easy time in courtship; none of the males in the world do. The first peahen, it turned out, was only faintly stirred by her suitor's beautiful train. She would often go quietly to sleep while he was whisking it around. The *Britannica* tells us that the peacock actually had to learn a certain little trick to wake her up and revive her interest: he had to learn to vibrate his quills so as to make a rustling sound. In ancient times man himself, observing the ways of the peacock, probably tried vibrating his whiskers to make a rustling sound; if so, it didn't get him anywhere. He had to go in for something else; so, among other things, he went in for gifts. It is not unlikely that he got this idea from certain flies and birds who were making no headway at all with rustling sounds.

One of the flies of the family Empidae, who had tried everything, finally hit on something pretty special. He contrived to make a glistening transparent balloon which was even larger than himself. Into this he would put sweetmeats and tidbits and he would carry the whole elaborate envelope through the air to the lady of his choice. This amused her for a time, but she finally got bored with it. She demanded silly little colorful presents, something that you couldn't eat but that would look nice around the house. So the male Empis had to go around gathering flower petals and pieces of bright paper to put into his balloon. On a courtship flight

a male Empis cuts quite a figure now, but he can hardly be said
to be happy. He never knows how soon the female will demand
heavier presents, such as Roman coins and gold collar buttons.
It seems probable that one day the courtship of the Empidae will
fall down, as man's occasionally does, of its own weight.

The bowerbird is another creature that spends so much time   4
courting the female that he never gets any work done. If all the
male bowerbirds became nervous wrecks within the next ten or
fifteen years, it would not surprise me. The female bowerbird
insists that a playground be built for her with a specially constructed bower at the entrance. This bower is much more elaborate
than an ordinary nest and is harder to build; it costs a lot more,
too. The female will not come to the playground until the male
has filled it up with a great many gifts: silvery leaves, red leaves,
rose petals, shells, beads, berries, bones, dice, buttons, cigar bands,
Christmas seals, and the Lord knows what else. When the female
finally condescends to visit the playground, she is in a coy and
silly mood and has to be chased in and out of the bower and up
and down the playground before she will quit giggling and stand
still long enough even to shake hands. The male bird is, of course,
pretty well done in before the chase starts, because he has worn
himself out hunting for eyeglass lenses and begonia blossoms. I
imagine that many a bowerbird, after chasing a female for two or
three hours, says the hell with it and goes home to bed. Next day,
of course, he telephones someone else and the same trying ritual
is gone through with again. A male bowerbird is as exhausted as
a night-club habitué before he is out of his twenties.

The male fiddler crab has a somewhat easier time, but it can   5
hardly be said that he is sitting pretty. He has one enormously
large and powerful claw, usually brilliantly colored, and you might
suppose that all he had to do was reach out and grab some passing
cutie. The very earliest fiddler crabs may have tried this, but, if
so, they got slapped for their pains. A female fiddler crab will not
tolerate any caveman stuff; she never has and she doesn't intend
to start now. To attract a female, a fiddler crab has to stand on
tiptoe and brandish his claw in the air. If any female in the neighborhood is interested — and you'd be surprised how many are not
— she comes over and engages him in light badinage, for which
he is not in the mood. As many as a hundred females may pass
the time of day with him and go on about their business. By night-

fall of an average courting day, a fiddler crab who has been standing on tiptoe for eight or ten hours waving a heavy claw in the
air is in pretty sad shape. As in the case of the males of all species,
however, he gets out of bed next morning, dashes some water on
his face, and tries again.

The next time you encounter a male web-spinning spider, stop   6
and reflect that he is too busy worrying about his love life to have
any desire to bite you. Male web-spinning spiders have a tougher
life than any other males in the animal kingdom. This is because
the female web-spinning spiders have very poor eyesight. If a male
lands on a female's web, she kills him before he has time to lay
down his cane and gloves, mistaking him for a fly or a bumblebee
who has tumbled into her trap. Before the species figured out
what to do about this, millions of males were murdered by ladies
they called on. It is the nature of spiders to perform a little dance
in front of the female, but before a male spinner could get near
enough for the female to see who he was and what he was up
to, she would lash out at him with a flat-iron or a pair of garden
shears. One night, nobody knows when, a very bright male spinner
lay awake worrying about calling on a lady who had been killing
suitors right and left. It came to him that this business of dancing
as a love display wasn't getting anybody anywhere except the
grave. He decided to go in for web-twitching, or strand-vibrating.
The next day he tried it on one of the nearsighted girls. Instead
of dropping in on her suddenly, he stayed outside the web and
began monkeying with one of its strands. He twitched it up and
down and in and out with such a lilting rhythm that the female
was charmed. The serenade worked beautifully; the female let
him live. The *Britannica*'s spider-watchers, however, report that
this system is not always successful. Once in a while, even now,
a female will fire three bullets into a suitor or run him through
with a kitchen knife. She keeps threatening him from the moment
he strikes the first low notes on the outside strings, but usually
by the time he has got up to the high notes played around the
center of the web, he is going to town and she spares his life.

Even the butterfly, as handsome a fellow as he is, can't always   7
win a mate merely by fluttering around and showing off. Many
butterflies have to have scent scales on their wings. Hepialus carries a powder puff in a perfumed pouch. He throws perfume at the
ladies when they pass. The male tree cricket, Oecanthus, goes

Hepialus one better by carrying a tiny bottle of wine with him and giving drinks to such doxies as he has designs on. One of the male snails throws darts to entertain the girls. So it goes, through the long list of animals, from the bristle worm and his rudimentary dance steps to man and his gift of diamonds and sapphires. The golden-eye drake raises a jet of water with his feet as he flies over a lake; Hepialus has his powder puff, Oecanthus his wine bottle, man his etchings. It is a bright and melancholy story, the age-old desire of the male for the female, the age-old desire of the female to be amused and entertained. Of all the creatures on earth, the only males who could be figured as putting any irony into their courtship are the grebes and certain other diving birds. Every now and then a courting grebe slips quietly down to the bottom of a lake and then, with a mighty "Whoosh!," pops out suddenly a few feet from his girl friend, splashing water all over her. She seems to be persuaded that this is a purely loving display, but I like to think that the grebe always has a faint hope of drowning her or scaring her to death.

I will close this investigation into the mournful burdens of the male with the *Britannica*'s story about a certain Argus pheasant. It appears that the Argus displays himself in front of a female who stands perfectly still without moving a feather. . . . The male Argus the *Britannica* tells about was confined in a cage with a female of another species, a female who kept moving around, emptying ash-trays and fussing with lampshades all the time the male was showing off his talents. Finally, in disgust, he stalked away and began displaying in front of his water trough. He reminds me of a certain male (Homo sapiens) of my acquaintance who one night after dinner asked his wife to put down her detective magazine so that he could read a poem of which he was very fond. She sat quietly enough until he was well into the middle of the thing, intoning with great ardor and intensity. Then suddenly there came a sharp, disconcerting *slap!* It turned out that all during the male's display, the female had been intent on a circling mosquito and had finally trapped it between the palms of her hands. The male in this case did not stalk away and display in front of a water trough; he went over to Tim's and had a flock of drinks and recited the poem to the fellas. I am sure they all told bitter stories of their own about how their displays had been interrupted by females. I am also sure that they all ended up singing "Honey, Honey, Bless Your Heart."

Meanings and Values

1a. Clarify the meaning of "irony of situation" by using at least one example from this essay. (See Guide to Terms: *Irony*.)

 b. Use at least three examples to illustrate the meaning of "verbal irony."

2. Thurber's writing is sometimes said to have nearly universal appeal — not only because of the humor, but also because of his subjects and his attitude toward them. What appeals would this subject have to various types of people you know?

3a. The author's themes are ordinarily deeper than they may appear to be on the surface, and they are sometimes quite serious. How seriously is he concerned about the mating foolishness of human males? How can you tell?

 b. Explain the relation of this matter of attitude to that of tone in writing. (Guide: *Style/Tone*.)

 c. Describe Thurber's tone in this essay, using no more than two or three descriptive words.

4. How much literal truth, if any, is in the allegation that "none of the females . . . really cared very much for the male, as such" (par. 1)?

5. Do you think we are really laughing at the animals themselves when we go to the zoo? If not, what do we laugh at? Explain carefully.

Expository Techniques

1. How does the author remind us with each new example, without making an issue of it, that he is describing people as well as (perhaps even more than) wildlife?

2. List the general ways in which humor is achieved in this selection and illustrate each with a specific example.

3. Briefly explain why some people would classify these examples as personification, whereas others would not. (Guide: *Figures of Speech*.)

4a. Which of the common transitional devices is (or are) used to bridge between paragraphs 2 and 3? (Guide: *Transition*.)

 b. Between 3 and 4?

 c. Between 4 and 5?

 d. How do such matters relate to coherence? (Guide: *Coherence*.)

Diction and Vocabulary

1. Which, if any, of the ways listed in answering question 2 of "Expository Techniques" are matters of diction? Why? (Guide: *Diction*.)

2. If you are not already familiar with the following words as used in this essay, study their meanings as given in the dictionary; nonplussed, lumbers (par. 1); condescends, habitué (4); brandish, badinage (5); doxies (7); intoning, disconcerting (8).

Suggestions for Writing and Discussion

1. Explain fully, using specific examples, the real reasons for amusement at a zoo (or, for some people, a barnyard).

2. How do young men today try to impress the young woman they are interested in?

3. Examine the possibility that women are interested in male "displays" because such reactions have been "programmed" into them from their earliest childhood.

4. If you are familiar with the aims and methods of the women's liberation movement, how do you think its more radical members would react to Thurber's impressions of courtship?

(NOTE: Suggestions for topics requiring development by use of EXAMPLE are on page 33, at the end of this section.)

LAURENCE J. PETER and RAYMOND HULL

LAURENCE J. PETER was born in Canada in 1919 and received his Ed.D. from Washington State University. Based on his wide experience as a teacher, counselor, school psychologist, prison instructor, consultant, and university professor, he has written numerous articles for professional journals. His books include *Prescriptive Teaching* (1965), *Teaching System: Vol. 1, Individual Instruction* (1972), *The Peter Prescription* (1972), *Competencies for Teaching*, 4 vols. (1975), and *The Peter Plan* (1977). Peter is now associate professor of education, director of the Evelyn Frieden Center for Prescriptive Teaching, and coordinator of programs for emotionally disturbed children at the University of Southern California.

RAYMOND HULL, also born in 1919, the son of an English Methodist minister, has lived in British Columbia since 1947. He has been a prolific writer of television and stage plays, and his published works cover a wide range, including such subjects as surveying, meat curing, weaving, wine and beer making, and public speaking. Hull's articles have been featured in *Punch, Maclean's, Esquire,* and other magazines.

The Peter Principle

"The Peter Principle," as it follows, combines the first two chapters of the book by that name, which was published in 1969. It is a clear and orderly illustration of the use of developed examples to give concrete form to an abstract central theme.

When I was a boy I was taught that the men upstairs knew what they were doing. I was told, "Peter, the more you know, the further you go." So I stayed in school until I graduated from college and then went forth into the world clutching firmly these ideas and my new teaching certificate. During the first year of teaching

I was upset to find that a number of teachers, school principals, supervisors and superintendents appeared to be unaware of their professional responsibilities and incompetent in executing their duties. For example my principal's main concerns were that all window shades be at the same level, that classrooms should be quiet and that no one step on or near the rose beds. The superintendent's main concerns were that no minority group, no matter how fanatical, should ever be offended and that all official forms be submitted on time. The children's education appeared farthest from the administrator mind.

At first I thought this was a special weakness of the school   2
system in which I taught so I applied for certification in another province. I filled out the special forms, enclosed the required documents and complied willingly with all the red tape. Several weeks later, back came my application and all the documents!

No, there was nothing wrong with my credentials; the forms   3
were correctly filled out; an official departmental stamp showed that they had been received in good order. But an accompanying letter said, "The new regulations require that such forms cannot be accepted by the Department of Education unless they have been registered at the Post Office to ensure safe delivery. Will you please remail the forms to the Department, making sure to register them this time?"

I began to suspect that the local school system did not have a   4
monopoly on incompetence.

As I looked further afield, I saw that every organization con-   5
tained a number of persons who could not do their jobs.

A UNIVERSAL PHENOMENON

Occupational incompetence is everywhere. Have you noticed it?   6
Probably we all have noticed it.

We see indecisive politicians posing as resolute statesmen and   7
the "authoritative source" who blames his misinformation on "situational imponderables." Limitless are the public servants who are indolent and insolent; military commanders whose behavioral timidity belies their dreadnaught rhetoric, and governors whose innate servility prevents their actually governing. In our sophistication, we virtually shrug aside the immoral cleric, corrupt judge, incoherent attorney, author who cannot write and English teacher who

cannot spell. At universities we see proclamations authored by administrators whose own office communications are hopelessly muddled; and droning lectures from inaudible or incomprehensible instructors.

Seeing incompetence at all levels of every hierarchy — political, legal, educational and industrial — I hypothesized that the cause was some inherent feature of the rules governing the placement of employees. Thus began my serious study of the ways in which employees move upward through a hierarchy, and of what happens to them after promotion. [8]

For my scientific data hundreds of case histories were collected. Here are three typical examples. [9]

Municipal Government File, Case No. 17. J. S. Minion[1] was a maintenance foreman in the public works department of Excelsior City. He was a favorite of the senior officials at City Hall. They all praised his unfailing affability. [10]

"I like Minion," said the superintendent of works. "He has good judgment and is always pleasant and agreeable." [11]

This behavior was appropriate for Minion's position: he was not supposed to make policy, so he had no need to disagree with his superiors. [12]

The superintendent of works retired and Minion succeeded him. Minion continued to agree with everyone. He passed to his foreman every suggestion that came from above. The resulting conflicts in policy, and the continual changing of plans, soon demoralized the department. Complaints poured in from the Mayor and other officials, from taxpayers and from the maintenance-workers' union. [13]

Minion still says "Yes" to everyone, and carries messages briskly back and forth between his superiors and his subordinates. Nominally a superintendent, he actually does the work of a messenger. The maintenance department regularly exceeds its budget, yet fails to fulfill its program of work. In short, Minion, a competent foreman, became an incompetent superintendent. [14]

Service Industries File, Case No. 3. E. Tinker was exceptionally zealous and intelligent as an apprentice at G. Reece Auto Repair [15]

---

[1] Some names have been changed, in order to protect the guilty.

Inc., and soon rose to journeyman mechanic. In this job he showed outstanding ability in diagnosing obscure faults, and endless patience in correcting them. He was promoted to foreman of the repair shop.

But here his love of things mechanical and his perfectionism became liabilities. He will undertake any job that he thinks looks interesting, no matter how busy the shop may be. "We'll work it in somehow," he says. [16]

He will not let a job go until he is fully satisfied with it. [17]

He meddles constantly. He is seldom to be found at his desk. He is usually up to his elbows in a dismantled motor and while the man who should be doing the work stands watching, other workmen sit around waiting to be assigned new tasks. As a result the shop is always overcrowded with work, always in a muddle, and delivery times are often missed. [18]

Tinker cannot understand that the average customer cares little about perfection — he wants his car back on time! He cannot understand that most of his men are less interested in motors than in their pay checks. So Tinker cannot get on with his customers or with his subordinates. He was a competent mechanic, but is now an incompetent foreman. [19]

Military File, Case No. 8. Consider the case of the late renowned General A. Goodwin. His hearty, informal manner, his racy style of speech, his scorn for petty regulations and his undoubted personal bravery made him the idol of his men. He led them to many well-deserved victories. [20]

When Goodwin was promoted to field marshall he had to deal, not with ordinary soldiers, but with politicians and allied generalissimos. [21]

He would not conform to the necessary protocol. He could not turn his tongue to the conventional courtesies and flatteries. He quarreled with all the dignitaries and took to lying for days at a time, drunk and sulking, in his trailer. The conduct of the war slipped out of his hands into those of his subordinates. He had been promoted to a position that he was incompetent to fill. [22]

AN IMPORTANT CLUE!

In time I saw that all such cases had a common feature. The employee had been promoted from a position of competence to a [23] position of incompetence. I saw that, sooner or later, this could happen to every employee in every hierarchy.

Hypothetical Case File, Case No. 1. Suppose you own a pill-rolling 24 factory, Perfect Pill Incorporated. Your foreman pill roller dies of a perforated ulcer. You need a replacement. You naturally look among your rank-and-file pill rollers.

Miss Oval, Mrs. Cylinder, Mr. Ellipse and Mr. Cube all show 25 various degrees of incompetence. They will naturally be ineligible for promotion. You will choose — other things being equal — your most competent pill roller, Mr. Sphere, and promote him to foreman.

Now suppose Mr. Sphere proves competent as foreman. Later, 26 when your general foreman, Legree, moves up to Works Manager, Sphere will be eligible to take his place.

If, on the other hand, Sphere is an incompetent foreman, he 27 will get no more promotion. He has reached what I call his "level of incompetence." He will stay there till the end of his career.

Some employees, like Ellipse and Cube, reach a level of incom- 28 petence in the lowest grade and are never promoted. Some, like Sphere (assuming he is not a satisfactory foreman), reach it after one promotion.

E. Tinker, the automobile repair-shop foreman, reached his 29 level of incompetence on the third stage of the hierarchy. General Goodwin reached his level of incompetence at the very top of the hierarchy.

So my analysis of hundreds of cases of occupational incom- 30 petence led me on to formulate *The Peter Principle:*

In a Hierarchy Every Employee Tends
to Rise to His Level of Incompetence

A NEW SCIENCE!

Having formulated the Principle, I discovered that I had inad- 31 vertently founded a new science, hierarchiology, the study of hierarchies.

The term "hierarchy" was originally used to describe the 32 system of church government by priests graded into ranks. The contemporary meaning includes any organization whose members or employees are arranged in order of rank, grade or class.

Hierarchiology, although a relatively recent discipline, appears 33 to have great applicability to the fields of public and private administration.

THIS MEANS YOU!

My Principle is the key to an understanding of all hierarchal systems, and therefore to an understanding of the whole structure of civilization. A few eccentrics try to avoid getting involved with hierarchies, but everyone in business, industry, trade-unionism, politics, government, the armed forces, religion and education is so involved. All of them are controlled by the Peter Principle. 34

Many of them, to be sure, may win a promotion or two, moving from one level of competence to a higher level of competence. But competence in that new position qualifies them for still another promotion. For each individual, for _you_, for _me_, the final promotion is from a level of competence to a level of incompetence.[2] 35

So, given enough time — and assuming the existence of enough ranks in the hierarchy — each employee rises to, and remains at, his level of incompetence. Peter's Corollary states: 36

In time, every post tends to be occupied by an employee who is incompetent to carry out its duties. 37

WHO TURNS THE WHEELS?

You will rarely find, of course, a system in which _every_ employee has reached his level of incompetence. In most instances, something is being done to further the ostensible purposes for which the hierarchy exists. 38

Work is accomplished by those employees who have not yet reached their level of incompetence. 39

*   *   *

A study of a typical hierarchy, the Excelsior City school system, will show how the Peter Principle works within the teaching profession. Study this example and understand how hierarchiology operates within every establishment. 40

---

[2] The phenomena of "percussive sublimation" (commonly referred to as "being kicked upstairs") and of "the lateral arabesque" are not, as the casual observer might think, exceptions to the Principle. They are only pseudo-promotions. . . .

Let us begin with the rank-and-file classroom teachers. I group   41
them, for this analysis, into three classes: competent, moderately
competent and incompetent.

Distribution theory predicts, and experience confirms, that   42
teachers will be distributed unevenly in these classes: the majority
in the moderately competent class, minorities in the competent and
incompetent classes. This graph illustrates the distribution:

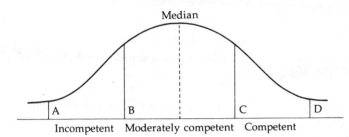

Incompetent   Moderately competent   Competent

THE CASE OF THE CONFORMIST

An incompetent teacher is ineligible for promotion. Dorothea D.   43
Ditto, for example, had been an extremely conforming student in
college. Her assignments were either plagiarisms from textbooks
and journals, or transcriptions of the professors' lectures. She always did exactly as she was told, no more, no less. *She was considered to be a competent student.* She graduated with honors
from the Excelsior Teachers' College.

When she became a teacher, she taught exactly as she herself   44
had been taught. She followed precisely the textbook, the curriculum guide and the bell schedule.

Her work goes fairly well, except when no rule or precedent is   45
available. For example, when a water pipe burst and flooded the
classroom floor, Miss Ditto kept on teaching until the principal
rushed in and rescued the class.

"Miss Ditto!" he cried. "In the Name of the Superintendent!   46
There are three inches of water on this floor. Why is your class
still here?"

She replied. "I didn't hear the emergency bell signal. I pay   47
attention to those things. You know I do. I'm certain you didn't
sound the bell." Flummoxed before the power of her awesome
non sequitur, the principal invoked a provision of the school code

giving him emergency powers in an extraordinary circumstance
and led her sopping class from the building.

So, although she never breaks a rule or disobeys an order, she   48
is often in trouble, and will never gain promotion. Competent as
a student, *she has reached her level of incompetence as a classroom teacher, and will therefore remain in that position throughout her teaching career.*

THE ELIGIBLE MAJORITY

Most beginning teachers are moderately competent or competent   49
— see the area from B to D on the graph — and *they will all be
eligible for promotion.* Here is one such case.

A Latent Weakness. Mr. N. Beeker had been a competent student,   50
and became a popular science teacher. His lessons and lab periods
were inspiring. His students were co-operative and kept the laboratory in order. Mr. Beeker was not good at paper work, but
this weakness was offset, in the judgment of his superiors, by his
success as a teacher.

Beeker was promoted to head of the science department where   51
he now had to order all science supplies and keep extensive records. *His incompetence is evident!* For three years running he has
ordered new Bunsen burners, but no tubing for connecting them.
As the old tubing deteriorates, fewer and fewer burners are oper-
able, although new ones accumulate on the shelves.

Beeker is not being considered for further promotion. *His ulti-*   52
mate position is one for which he is incompetent.

Higher up the Hierarchy. B. Lunt had been a competent student,   53
teacher and department head, and was promoted to assistant principal. In this post he got on well with teachers, students and
parents, and was intellectually competent. He gained a further
promotion to the rank of principal.

Till now, he had never dealt directly with school-board mem-   54
bers, or with the district superintendent of education. It soon appeared that he lacked the required finesse to work with these high
officials. *He kept the superintendent waiting* while he settled a
dispute between two children. Taking a class for a teacher who
was ill, *he missed a curriculum revision committee meeting* called
by the assistant superintendent.

He worked so hard at running his school that *he had no en-*   55
ergy for running community organizations. He declined offers to
become program chairman of the Parent-Teacher Association, president of the Community Betterment League and consultant to the
Committee for Decency in Literature.

His school lost community support and he fell out of favor   56
with the superintendent. Lunt came to be regarded, by the public
and by his superiors, as an incompetent principal. When the assistant superintendent's post became vacant, the school board declined to give it to Lunt. He remains, and will remain till he retires,
unhappy and incompetent as a principal.

The Autocrat. R. Driver, having proved his competence as student,   57
teacher, department head, assistant principal and principal, was
promoted to assistant superintendent. Previously he had only to
interpret the school board's policy and have it efficiently carried
out in his school. Now, as assistant superintendent, he must par-
ticipate in the policy discussions of the board, using democratic
procedures.

But Driver dislikes democratic procedures. He insists on his   58
status as an expert. He lectures the board members much as he
used to lecture his students when he was a classroom teacher. He
tries to dominate the board as he dominated his staff when he was
a principal.

The board now considers Driver an incompetent assistant su-   59
perintendent. He will receive no further promotion.

Soon Parted. G. Spender was a competent student, English teacher,   60
department head, assistant principal and principal. He then worked
competently for six years as an assistant superintendent — patriotic, diplomatic, suave and well liked. He was promoted to superintendent. Here he was obliged to enter the field of school finance,
in which he soon found himself at a loss.

From the start of his teaching career, Spender had never both-   61
ered his head about money. His wife handled his pay check, paid
all household accounts and gave him pocket money each week.

Now Spender's incompetence in the area of finance is re-   62
vealed. He purchased a large number of teaching machines from a
fly-by-night company which went bankrupt without producing any
programs to fit the machines. He had every classroom in the city
equipped with television, although the only programs available in

the area were for secondary schools. Spender has found his level of incompetence.

ANOTHER PROMOTION MECHANISM

The foregoing examples are typical of what are called "line pro-   63
motions." There is another mode of upward movement: the "staff
promotion." The case of Miss T. Totland is typical.

Miss Totland, who had been a competent student and an out-   64
standing primary teacher, was promoted to primary supervisor.
She now has to teach, not children, but teachers. Yet *she still uses
the techniques which worked so well with small children.*

Addressing teachers, singly or in groups, she speaks slowly   65
and distinctly. She uses mostly words of one or two syllables. She
explains each point several times in different ways, to be sure it is
understood. She always wears a bright smile.

Teachers dislike what they call her false cheerfulness and her   66
patronizing attitude. Their resentment is so sharp that, instead of
trying to carry out her suggestions, they spend much time devising
excuses for *not* doing what she recommends.

Miss Totland has proved herself incompetent in communicat-   67
ing with primary teachers. She is therefore ineligible for further
promotion, *and will remain as primary supervisor, at her level of
incompetence.*

YOU BE THE JUDGE

You can find similar examples in any hierarchy. Look around you   68
where you work, and pick out the people who have reached their
level of incompetence. You will see that in every hierarchy *the
cream rises until it sours.* Look in the mirror and ask whether . . .

Meanings and Values

1a. Has it been your experience that incompetence is really widespread
    enough to make this selection worthwhile?
  b. Support your answer, either way, by examples from your own or
    your family's experience. (You will not be *proving* anything —
    merely supporting an observation.)
 2. Does it seem feasible to you that our highly successful, complex
    industrial and educational systems were devised and are run either
    by incompetent top executives and engineers or by underlings in
    the hierarchy? Why, or why not?

3. To what extent are people in elective public office subject to the Peter Principle?

4. Clarify the distinction between "line" and "staff" promotions, as referred to in paragraph 63.

5. Specify at least two ways in which an understanding of the Peter Principle might be of value.

6. Why do people permit themselves to be promoted to levels of incompetence?

Expository Techniques

1. Show how at least two of the standard methods of introduction are used for this exposition. (See Guide to Terms: *Introductions*.)

2a. Where do the authors first give a simple statement of their central theme? (Guide: *Unity*.)

 b. How, if at all, is the statement qualified? (Guide: *Qualification*.)

 c. Do all portions of the essay serve as "tributaries" into the central theme, thus giving unity to the writing? If not, what are the exceptions?

3a. Several short, undeveloped examples are used in paragraph 1 to show a "prevalence." What is the generality they support?

 b. What generality does the list of short examples in paragraph 7 support?

4a. A brief comparison between the examples of paragraph 1 and those of paragraph 7 can be used to show that examples, like words, can achieve differing degrees of specificity. (Guide: *Specific/General*.) Which of the two sets is more general?

 b. Is one set then necessarily more, or less, effective than the other? Explain.

5. Paragraphs 2 and 3 comprise a more fully developed example. Which paragraph contains the generalization it supports?

6. All the authors' case file reports, themselves fully developed examples, also *use* example. Analyze any one of these reports for its basic structure, its use of this kind of interior example, and the effectiveness of presentation.

7a. Of the "hundreds of case histories" (par. 9) at the authors' disposal, why do you think cases 17, 3, and 8 were chosen to use as examples?

 b. Were these good choices?

8a. How is the series of developed examples beginning in paragraph 43 organized?

 b. How is this organization superior, or inferior, to a less structured, more casual arrangement?

 c. Can you think of some other order that would have been as effective? Explain.

  d. What advantage is derived from the similar formats and endings of these examples?

Diction and Vocabulary

1. If you are not familiar with the meanings of any of the following words, consult your dictionary: phenomenon (subheading before par. 6); indolent, dreadnaught, innate, servility, incoherent, inaudible (7); hypothesized, inherent (8); succeeded, demoralized (13); protocol (22); inadvertently (31); eccentrics (34); corollary (36); ostensible (38); plagiarisms (43); flummoxed, *non sequitur* (47); latent (50).

Suggestions for Writing and Discussion

1. How is it possible, if at all in this complex society, to avoid getting involved with hierarchies (par. 34), other than in occasional dealings with them in the necessary conduct of personal affairs? Consider such pertinent matters as methods, penalties, rewards.

2. If one's work is necessarily involved in a hierarchy, what practical methods would you suggest for reaching and remaining on the highest level of *competence,* thereby defying the Peter Principle?

3. From your own knowledge, select an example of incompetence dissimilar to any of those discussed in this essay. Show as well as you can the way in which a person passed his highest level of competence and, if possible, the results of the mistake for himself and others.

4. If you have reason to doubt the Peter Principle's rather broad claims, show the nature of and justification for your doubts. You should not try to "prove" the principle wrong unless you have at least as much ammunition as the authors do. Remember that they do qualify most of their major generalizations.

Writing Suggestions for Section 1
Illustration by Example

Use one of the following statements or another suggested by them as your central theme. Develop it into a unified composition, using examples from history, current events, or personal experience to illustrate your ideas. Be sure to have your reader-audience clearly in mind, as well as your specific purpose for the communication.

1. Successful businesses keep employees at their highest level of *competence*.
2. Laws holding parents responsible for their children's crimes would (or would not) result in serious injustices.
3. You can't always tell a nonconformist just by the way he looks.
4. Not all women want to be liberated.
5. One thing is certain about styles: they cannot stay the same.
6. Good sportsmanship is far more than shaking hands with the winner.
7. Religion in the United States is not dying.
8. Democracy is not always the best form of government.
9. Colonialism was not entirely bad.
10. Nearly anyone can have a creative hobby.
11. The general quality of television commercials may be improving (or deteriorating).
12. "Some books are to be tasted; others swallowed; and some few to be chewed and digested." (*Francis Bacon*, English scientist-author, 1561–1626.)

Analyzing a Subject by *Classification*

People naturally like to sort and classify things. The untidiest urchin, moving into a new dresser of his own, will put his handkerchiefs together, socks and underwear in separate stacks, and perhaps his toads and snails (temporarily) into a drawer of their own. He may classify animals as those with legs, those with wings, and those with neither. As he gets older, he finds that schoolteachers have ways of classifying *him*, not only into a reading group but, periodically, into an "A" or "F" category, or somewhere in between. On errands to the grocery store, he discovers the macaroni in the same department as noodles, the pork chops somewhere near the ham. In reading the local newspaper, he observes that its staff has done some classifying for him, putting most of the comics together and seldom mixing sports stories with the news of bridal showers. Eventually he finds courses neatly classified in the college catalogue, and he knows enough not to look for biology courses under "Social Science." (Examples again — used to illustrate a "prevalence.")

However, our main interest in classification here is its use as a structural pattern for explanatory writing. Many subjects about which either student or graduate may need to write will remain a hodgepodge of facts and opinions unless he can find some system of analyzing the material, dividing the subject into categories, and classifying individual elements into those categories. Here we have the distinction usually made between the rhetorical terms *division* and *classification* — for example, dividing "meat" into pork, beef, mutton, and fowl, then classifying ham and pork chops into the category of "pork." But this distinction is one we need scarcely pause for here; once the need for analysis is recognized, the dividing and classifying become inevitable companions and result in the single scheme of "classification" itself, as we have been discussing it. The original division into parts merely sets up the system which, if well chosen, best serves our purpose.

Obviously, no single system of classification is best for all purposes. Our untidy urchin may at some point classify girls according to athletic prowess, then later by size or shape or hair color. Other people may need entirely different systems of classification: the music instructor classifies girls as sopranos, altos, contraltos; the psychologist, according to their behavioral patterns; the sociologist, according to their ethnic origins.

Whatever the purpose, for the more formal uses of classification ("formal," that is, to the extent of most academic and on-the-job writing), we should be careful to use a logical system that is complete and that follows a consistent principle throughout. It would not be logical to divide Protestantism into the categories of Methodist, Baptist, and Lutheran, because the system would be incomplete and misleading. But in classifying Protestants attending some special conference — a different matter entirely — such a limited system might be both complete and logical. In any case, the writer must be careful that classes do not overlap: to classify the persons at the conference as Methodists, Baptists, Lutherans, and clergy would be illogical, because some are undoubtedly both Lutheran, for instance, and "clergy."

In dividing and classifying we are really using the basic process of outlining. Moreover, if we are dealing with classifiable *ideas,* the resulting pattern *is* our outline, which has been our aim all along — a basic organizational plan.

This process of classification frequently does, in fact, organize much less tangible things than the examples mentioned. We might wish to find some orderly basis for discussing the South's post–Civil War problems. Division might give us three primary categories of information: economic, political, and social. But for a full-scale consideration of these, the major divisions themselves may be subdivided for still more orderly explanation: the economic information may be further divided into agriculture and industry. Now it is possible to isolate and clarify such strictly industrial matters as shortage of investment capital, disrupted transportation systems, and lack of power development.

Any plan like this seems almost absurdly obvious, of course — *after* the planning is done. It appears less obvious, however, to the inexperienced writer who is dealing with a jumble of information he must explain to someone else. This is when he should be aware of the patterns at his disposal, and one of the most useful of these, alone or combined with others, is classification.

ERIC BERNE

ERIC BERNE (1910–1970) was a graduate of McGill University's School of Medicine. A psychiatrist, he wrote extensively in that field, lectured at various universities, and served on the psychiatric staff of Mount Sinai Hospital in New York City. He later engaged in private practice and research in California. His books include *Games People Play* (1964), *The Happy Valley* (1968), and *Sex in Human Loving* (1970).

Can People Be Judged by Their Appearance?

"Can People Be Judged by Their Appearance?" was originally published in Berne's *The Mind in Action* (1947) and was later included in a revised edition of his book, *A Layman's Guide to Psychiatry and Psychoanalysis.* This explanation of one theory of basic human types is an example of a scientific subject made readable for nonscientists. Using division and classification as his primary pattern of development, Berne also relies to varying extents on most of the other expository patterns: illustration, comparison and contrast, process analysis, cause and effect, definition, and description.

Everyone knows that a human being, like a chicken, comes from   1
an egg. At a very early stage, the human embryo forms a three-layered tube, the inside layer of which grows into the stomach and lungs, the middle layer into bones, muscles, joints, and blood vessels, and the outside layer into the skin and nervous system.

Usually these three grow about equally, so that the average   2
human being is a fair mixture of brains, muscles, and inward organs. In some eggs, however, one layer grows more than the others, and when the angels have finished putting the child to-

gether, he may have more gut than brain, or more brain than muscle. When this happens, the individual's activities will often be mostly with the overgrown layer.

We can thus say that while the average human being is a mixture, some people are mainly "digestion-minded," some "muscle-minded," and some "brain-minded," and correspondingly digestion-bodied, muscle-bodied, or brain-bodied. The digestion-bodied people look thick; the muscle-bodied people look wide; and the brain-bodied people look long. This does not mean the taller a man is the brainier he will be. It means that if a man, even a short man, looks long rather than wide or thick, he will often be more concerned about what goes on in his mind than about what he does or what he eats; but the key factor is slenderness and not height. On the other hand, a man who gives the impression of being thick rather than long or wide will usually be more interested in a good steak than in a good idea or a good long walk. 3

Medical men use Greek words to describe these types of bodybuild. For the man whose body shape mostly depends on the inside layer of the egg, they use the word *endomorph*. If it depends mostly upon the middle layer, they call him a *mesomorph*. If it depends upon the outside layer, they call him an *ectomorph*. We can see the same roots in our English words "enter," medium," and "exit," which might just as easily have been spelled "ender," "mesium," and "ectit." 4

Since the inside skin of the human egg, or endoderm, forms the inner organs of the belly, the viscera, the endomorph is usually belly-minded; since the middle skin forms the body tissues, or soma, the mesomorph is usually muscle-minded; and since the outside skin forms the brain, or cerebrum, the ectomorph is usually brain-minded. Translating this into Greek, we have the viscerotonic endomorph, the somatotonic mesomorph, and the cerebrotonic ectomorph. 5

Words are beautiful things to a cerebrotonic, but a viscerotonic knows you cannot eat a menu no matter what language it is printed in, and a somatotonic knows you cannot increase your chest expansion by reading a dictionary. So it is advisable to leave these words and see what kinds of people they actually apply to, remembering again that most individuals are fairly equal mixtures and that what we have to say concerns only the extremes. Up to the present, these types have been thoroughly studied only in the male sex. 6

Viscerotonic Endomorph. If a man is definitely a thick type rather   7
than a broad or long type, he is likely to be round and soft, with
a big chest but a bigger belly. He would rather eat than breathe
comfortably. He is likely to have a wide face, short, thick neck,
big thighs and upper arms, and small hands and feet. He has over-
developed breasts and looks as though he were blown up a little
like a balloon. His skin is soft and smooth, and when he gets bald,
as he does usually quite early, he loses the hair in the middle of his
head first.

The short, jolly, thickset, red-faced politician with a cigar in   8
his mouth, who always looks as though he were about to have a
stroke, is the best example of this type. The reason he often makes
a good politician is that he likes people, banquets, baths, and sleep;
he is easygoing, soothing, and his feelings are easy to understand.

His abdomen is big because he has lots of intestines. He likes   9
to take in things. He likes to take in food, and affection and approval as well. Going to a banquet with people who like him is his
idea of a fine time. It is important for a psychiatrist to understand
the natures of such men when they come to him for advice.

Somatotonic Mesomorph. If a man is definitely a broad type rather   10
than a thick or long type, he is likely to be rugged and have lots
of muscle. He is apt to have big forearms and legs, and his chest
and belly are well formed and firm, with the chest bigger than the
belly. He would rather breathe than eat. He has a bony head, big
shoulders, and a square jaw. His skin is thick, coarse, and elastic,
and tans easily. If he gets bald, it usually starts on the front of the
head.

Dick Tracy, Li'l Abner, and other men of action belong to this   11
type. Such people make good lifeguards and construction workers.
They like to put out energy. They have lots of muscles and they
like to use them. They go in for adventure, exercise, fighting, and
getting the upper hand. They are bold and unrestrained, and love
to master the people and things around them. If the psychiatrist
knows the things which give such people satisfaction, he is able
to understand why they may be unhappy in certain situations.

Cerebrotonic Ectomorph. The man who is definitely a long type is   12
likely to have thin bones and muscles. His shoulders are apt to sag
and he has a flat belly with a dropped stomach, and long, weak

legs. His neck and fingers are long, and his face is shaped like a long egg. His skin is thin, dry, and pale, and he rarely gets bald. He looks like an absent-minded professor and often is one.

Though such people are jumpy, they like to keep their energy 13 and don't fancy moving around much. They would rather sit quietly by themselves and keep out of difficulties. Trouble upsets them, and they run away from it. Their friends don't understand them very well. They move jerkily and feel jerkily. The psychiatrist who understands how easily they become anxious is often able to help them get along better in the sociable and aggressive world of endomorphs and mesomorphs.

In the special cases where people definitely belong to one type 14 or another, then, one can tell a good deal about their personalities from their appearance. When the human mind is engaged in one of its struggles with itself or with the world outside, the individual's way of handling the struggle will be partly determined by his type. If he is a viscerotonic he will often want to go to a party where he can eat and drink and be in good company at a time when he might be better off attending to business; the somatotonic will want to go out and do something about it, master the situation, even if what he does is foolish and not properly figured out, while the cerebrotonic will go off by himself and think it over, when perhaps he would be better off doing something about it or seeking good company to try to forget it.

Since these personality characteristics depend on the growth 15 of the layers of the little egg from which the person developed, they are very difficult to change. Nevertheless, it is important for the individual to know about these types, so that he can have at least an inkling of what to expect from those around him, and can make allowances for the different kinds of human nature, and so that he can become aware of and learn to control his own natural tendencies, which may sometimes guide him into making the same mistakes over and over again in handling his difficulties.

Meanings and Values

1. Consider men you have known who fit, or nearly fit, into one or another of the three categories of build.

    a. Do they also have the traits described by Berne in paragraphs 8, 9, 11, and 13? Or do you know, perhaps, a "thick" man who hates banquets, a "wide" man who writes poetry, or a "long" man who bullies people?

    b. If so, should we assume that these are learned characteristics? Explain.

2. Illustrate clearly how an understanding of basic types of people can be important to the layman.

3. In view of the fact that so many of a person's characteristics are determined before he is born, what room does the author leave for the possibility of altering or controlling these natural tendencies?

4. If you have read "The Peter Principle" in Section 1, show by use of a clear example how an understanding of Berne's theory might benefit an individual in his personal application of the Peter Principle.

Expository Techniques

1a. Most people, according to the author, are not classifiable in the categories he discusses. Is the classification system then faulty, since it does not include everyone?

    b. Explain the difference, if any, between this system and the faulty classification of Protestants mentioned in the introduction to this section.

2. Study the general organization of this essay.

    a. Which paragraphs give an overall preview of Berne's classification system?

    b. Which paragraphs are devoted to explanations of individual categories?

    c. Where does the author bring the categories together again to show the importance of the whole analysis?

    d. Can you work out another plan that would have presented his material as meaningfully?

3. The author ends each detailed account of type characteristics with a statement of why the psychiatrist needs to know these things (pars. 9, 11, 13). Why is this a valuable technique, even though the essay was not written for psychiatrists?

4. Show the value of the parallel structures in paragraphs 4 and 5. (See Guide to Terms: *Parallel Structure*.)

5. In your opinion, do Berne's occasional attempts at humor — e.g., "the angels" and "cannot eat a menu" — benefit or detract from his explanation? Why?

Diction and Vocabulary

1a. Are the numerous Greek words as bothersome as you expected them to be when you first glanced at the essay? Why, or why not?
  b. Do you think the author expects us really to master them? If not, why did he use them?

2. Aside from the Greek words, you probably found no words with which you were not already familiar. Is this a result of the type of subject matter, the author's concern for his audience, or something else? Explain.

Suggestions for Writing and Discussion

1. At the time this essay was written, the types had been "thoroughly studied only in the male sex." Even if the same general traits were characteristic of women, might tradition and social pressures tend to modify the natural tendencies more in women than in men (e.g., women are "not supposed" to go around flexing their muscles or getting into fist fights)? Explain any differences that you would expect.

2. Using examples for illustration, show that basic nature can be changed — or, if you prefer, that such change is very difficult or impossible.

3. Show the practical importance — especially for success in your future career — of understanding people and why they act as they do.

4. Develop the thesis that people of opposite types can sometimes get along more congenially than those of the same type.

(NOTE: Suggestions for topics requiring development by use of CLASSIFI-CATION are on page 66, at the end of this section.)

DONALD HALL

DONALD HALL, educator and writer, was born in Connecticut in 1928. He earned a B.A. degree from Harvard University and a B.Litt. degree at Oxford, later doing postgraduate work at Stanford University. This versatile author has written about universities for *The Atlantic Monthly*, about baseball for *Playboy*, about the sculptor Henry Moore for *The New Yorker*. Besides his six books of poems, he has written two children's books, a collection of limericks, a biography, literary criticism, short stories in *Esquire* and *The New Yorker*, a best-selling freshman composition text, and two plays, one of which ran off Broadway. Until recently Hall taught creative writing, literature, and freshman English at the University of Michigan. He now lives on the old family farm in Danbury, New Hampshire, where he continues to write, and sometimes emerges to give a poetry reading or to teach a class at Dartmouth or Colby-Sawyer college.

Reading Tastes and Habits

"Reading Tastes and Habits" is a piece of purely subjective writing, and as such is nearly as likely to provoke disagreement as favor. Hall's problem was simple: having asserted that some reading is simply narcotic and of no value in itself, he was faced with the task of telling us *which* reading, as well as what other kinds he believes do have value. The project, of course, demands some clear system of division/classification.

Everywhere one meets the idea that reading is an activity desirable in itself. It is understandable that publishers and librarians — and even writers — should promote this assumption, but it is strange that the idea should have general currency. People surround the idea of reading with piety, and do not take into account the purpose of reading or the value of what is being read. Teachers and parents praise the child who reads, and praise themselves, whether the text be *The Reader's Digest* or *Moby Dick*. The advent of TV has increased the false values ascribed to reading, since TV provides a vulgar alternative. But this piety is silly; and most reading is no more cultural nor intellectual nor imaginative than shooting pool or watching *What's My Line*.

It is worth asking how the act of reading became something 2 to value in itself, as opposed for instance to the act of conversation or the act of taking a walk. Mass literacy is a recent phenomenon, and I suggest that the aura which decorates reading is a relic of the importance of reading to our great-great-grandparents. Literacy used to be a mark of social distinction, separating a small portion of humanity from the rest. The farm laborer who was ambitious for his children did not daydream that they would become school-teachers or doctors; he daydreamed that they would learn to read, and that a world would therefore open up to them in which they did not have to labor in the fields fourteen hours a day for six days a week in order to buy salt and cotton. On the next rank of society, ample time for reading meant that the reader was free from the necessity to spend most of his waking hours making a living of any kind. This sort of attitude shades into the contemporary man's boast of his wife's cultural activities. When he says that his wife is interested in books and music and pictures, he is not only en-closing the arts in a delicate female world; he is saying that he is rich enough to provide her with the leisure to do nothing. Reading is an inactivity, and therefore a badge of social class. Of course, these reasons for the piety attached to reading are never acknowl-edged. They show themselves in the shape of our attitudes toward books; reading gives off an air of gentility.

It seems to me possible to name four kinds of reading, each 3 with a characteristic manner and purpose. The first is reading for information — reading to learn about a trade, or politics, or how to accomplish something. We read a newspaper this way, or most textbooks, or directions on how to assemble a bicycle. With most of this sort of material, the reader can learn to scan the page quickly, coming up with what he needs and ignoring what is irrele-vant to him, like the rhythm of the sentence, or the play of meta-phor. Courses in speed reading can help us read for this purpose, training the eye to jump quickly across the page. If we read *The*

New York Times with the attention we should give a novel or a poem, we will have time for nothing else, and our mind will be cluttered with clichés and dead metaphor. Quick eye-reading is a necessity to anyone who wants to keep up with what's happening, or learn much of what has happened in the past. The amount of reflection, which interrupts and slows down the reading, depends on the material.

But it is not the same activity as reading literature. There ought to be another word. If we read a work of literature properly, we read slowly, and we hear all the words. If our lips do not actually move, it's only laziness. The muscles in our throats move, and come together when we see the word "squeeze." We hear the sounds so accurately that if a syllable is missing in a line of poetry we hear the lack, though we may not know what we are lacking. In prose we accept the rhythms, and hear the adjacent sounds. We also register a track of feeling through the metaphors and associations of words. Careless writing prevents this sort of attention, and becomes offensive. But the great writers reward this attention. Only by the full exercise of our powers to receive language can we absorb their intelligence and their imagination. This kind of reading goes through the ear — though the eye takes in the print, and decodes it into sound — to the throat and the understanding, and it can never be quick. It is slow and sensual, a deep pleasure that begins with touch and ends with the sort of comprehension that we associate with dream. 4

Too many intellectuals read in order to reduce images to abstractions. With a philosopher one reads slowly, as if it were literature, but much time must be spent with the eyes turned away from the pages, reflecting on the text. To read literature this way is to turn it into something it is not — to concepts clothed in character, or philosophy sugar-coated. I think that most literary intellectuals read this way, including the brighter Professors of English, with the result that they miss literature completely, and concern themselves with a minor discipline called the history of ideas. I remember a course in Chaucer at my University in which the final exam largely required the identification of a hundred or more fragments of Chaucer, none as long as a line. If you liked poetry, and read Chaucer through a couple of times slowly, you found yourself knowing them all. If you were a literary intellectual, well-informed 5 about the great chain of being, chances are you had a difficult time. To read literature is to be intimately involved with the words on the page, and never to think of them as the embodiments of ideas which can be expressed in other terms. On the other hand, intellectual writing — closer to mathematics on a continuum that has at its opposite pole lyric poetry — requires intellectual reading, which is slow because it is reflective and because the reader must pause to evaluate concepts.

But most of the reading which is praised for itself is neither 6 literary nor intellectual. It is narcotic. Novels, stories and biographies — historical sagas, monthly regurgitations of book clubs, four- and five-thousand word daydreams of the magazines — these are the opium of the suburbs. The drug is not harmful except to the addict himself, and is no more injurious to him than Johnny Carson or a bridge club, but it is nothing to be proud of. This reading is the automated daydream, the mild trip of the housewife and the tired businessman, interested not in experience and feeling but in turning off the possibilities of experience and feeling. Great literature, if we read it well, opens us up to the world, and makes us more sensitive to it, as if we acquired eyes that could see through things and ears that could hear smaller sounds. But by narcotic reading, one can reduce great literature to the level of *The Valley of the Dolls*. One can read *Anna Karenina* passively and inattentively, and float down the river of lethargy as if one were reading a confession magazine: "I Spurned My Husband for a Count."

I think that everyone reads for narcosis occasionally, and per- 7 haps most consistently in late adolescence, when great readers are born. I remember reading to shut the world out, away at a school where I did not want to be; I invented a word to name my disease: "bibliolepsy," on the analogy of narcolepsy. But after a while the books became a window on the world, and not a screen against it. This change doesn't always happen. I think that late adolescent narcotic reading accounts for some of the badness of English departments. As a college student, the boy loves reading and majors in English because he would be reading anyway. Deciding on a career, he takes up English teaching for the same reason. Then in graduate school he is trained to be a scholar, which is painful and irrelevant, and finds he must write papers and publish them to be a Professor — and at about this time he no longer requires reading

for narcosis, and he is left with nothing but a Ph.D. and the prospect of fifty years of teaching literature; and he does not even like
literature.

Narcotic reading survives the impact of television, because   8
this type of reading has even less reality than melodrama; that is,
the reader is in control: once the characters reach into the reader's
feelings, he is able to stop reading, or glance away, or superimpose
his own daydream. The trouble with television is that it writes its
own script. Literature is often valued precisely because of its distance from the tangible. Some readers prefer looking into the text
of a play to seeing it performed. Reading a play, it is possible to
stage it oneself by an imaginative act; but it is also possible to
remove it from real people. Here is Virginia Woolf, who was lavish
in her praise of the act of reading, talking about reading a play
rather than seeing it: "Certainly there is a good deal to be said for
reading *Twelfth Night* in the book if the book can be read in a
garden, with no sound but the thud of an apple falling to the earth,
or of the wind ruffling the branches of the trees." She sets her own
stage; the play is called *Virginia Woolf Reads Twelfth Night in a
Garden*. Piety moves into narcissism, and the high metaphors of
Shakespeare's lines dwindle into the flowers of an English garden;
actors in ruffles wither, while the wind ruffles branches.

Meanings and Values

1. Why is this essay classifiable as subjective writing? (See headnotes
   and Guide to Terms: *Objective/Subjective*.)

2a. What kind of people would be apt to read something like this piece
   on their own?

 b. As which of the four kinds of reading does the author apparently
   intend his own essay to be viewed?

3. Does it seem to you that the remarks about Virginia Woolf (par. 8)
   are entirely merited? Explain.

4. Do you agree that reading is not justifiable in itself? Why, or why
   not?

5a. What inconsistency do you see, if any, between the author's criti-
   cisms in paragraph 1 and the account of his own early reading in
   paragraph 7?

 b. If you find any such inconsistency, does it seriously damage credibility?

6a. Which of the four kinds of reading does Hall seem to prefer as an adult?
  b. Show how this preference is reflected in the tone. (Guide: *Style/ Tone.*)

7a. Use examples of your own (e.g., newspaper, lyric poetry, philosophy, detective stories) to show how writings that would ordinarily be used in one or another of the categories would probably be read in differing ways by different kinds of readers.
  b. If you have read the Berne selection preceding this one, match the extremes of his three types of men with the kind of reading each would be most likely to prefer. Explain why, using examples as necessary.

Expository Techniques

1a. How well does Hall's system of division/classification meet the requirements of logic and completeness?
  b. Does the fact that reading matter of any category may be treated differently by different people make the system itself less valid? Explain.

2. Cite three paragraphs in which Hall uses examples to make the general more specific. (Guide: *Specific/General.*)

3a. In paragraph 6 the author calls stories and novels "the opium of the suburbs." What reason have we to doubt that he intends to include *all* stories and novels?
  b. Demonstrate how a simple use of qualification could have prevented this misrepresentation. (Guide: *Qualification.*)
  c. If you find other statements that could have benefited by qualification, show how this could have been achieved.

4. This author frequently employs sarcasm as a means of emphasis. (Guide: *Emphasis.*) Cite at least three examples of this technique and comment on their effectiveness.

5. What closing techniques does Hall use? (Guide: *Closings.*)

Diction and Vocabulary

1. In what sense does TV provide a "vulgar alternative" to reading (par. 1)?

2a. Select three of the author's best metaphors by which to demonstrate how style may be affected by figurative language. (Guide: *Figures of Speech.*)
  b. Cite three examples in which his nonfigurative diction clearly becomes an important element of his style. (Giude: *Style/Tone.*)

3. Consult the dictionary as needed for an understanding of the following words, as used in this essay: currency (par. 1); concepts, embodiments (5); sagas, regurgitations, lethargy (6); narcolepsy (7); narcissism (8).

Suggestions for Writing and Discussion

1. Discuss the tendency of some people to "enclose the arts in a delicate female world" (par. 2) — e.g., the reasons for that attitude, or your own experiences in the face of it.
2. Explain how it is that our minds can become "cluttered with clichés and dead metaphors" (par. 3), using examples from current newspapers to illustrate their prevalence.
3. If you believe that any reading is better than no reading at all (in general, or for any particular type of person), explain why your views differ from Hall's.

(NOTE: Suggestions for topics requiring development by use of CLASSIFICATION are on page 66, at the end of this section.)

ERICH FROMM

Symbolic Language

"Symbolic Language" (editor's title) is a part of "Symbolic Language of Dreams," Fromm's contribution to the book *Language: An Enquiry into Its Meaning and Function*. In one respect the entire selection is an extended definition (which we will study in detail in Section 7), but the process the author uses in defining the term "symbolism" is basically analysis by classification. Illustration and comparison are also used effectively throughout the exposition.

One of the current definitions of a symbol is that it is "something that stands for something else." The definition is too general to be useful, unless we can be more specific with regard to the crucial question concerning the nature of the connection between symbol and that which it symbolizes. . . .

We can differentiate between three kinds of symbols: the *conventional*, the *accidental*, and the *universal* symbol.

The *conventional* symbol is the best known of the three, since we employ it in everyday language. If we see the word "table" or

Reprinted by permission from pp. 188–193 of "Symbolic Language of Dreams" by Erich Fromm in *Language: An Enquiry Into Its Meaning and Function*, edited by Ruth Nanda Anshen. Copyright © 1957 by Harper & Row, Publishers, Inc.

hear the sound "table," the letters *t-a-b-l-e* stand for something else. They stand for the thing "table" that we see, touch, and use. What is the connection between the *word* "table" and the *thing* "table"? Is there any inherent relationship between them? Obviously not. The *thing* table has nothing to do with the *sound* table, and the only reason the word symbolizes the thing is the convention of calling this particular thing by a name. We learn this connection as children by the repeated experience of hearing the word in reference to the thing until a lasting association is formed so that we don't have to think to find the right word.

There are some words, however, in which the association is   4
not only conventional. When we say "phooey," for instance, we make with our lips a movement of dispelling the air quickly. By this quick expulsion of air we imitate and thus express our intention to expel something, to get it out of our system. In this case, as in some others, the symbol has an inherent connection with the feeling it symbolizes. But even if we assume that originally many or even all words had their origins in some such inherent connection between symbol and the symbolized, most words no longer have this meaning for us when we learn a language.

Words are not the only illustration for conventional symbols,   5
although they are the most frequent and best-known ones. Pictures also can be conventional symbols. A flag, for instance, may stand for a specific country, and yet there is no intrinsic connection between the specific colors and the country for which they stand. They have been accepted as denoting that particular country, and we translate the visual impression of the flag into the concept of that country, again on conventional grounds. Some pictorial symbols are not entirely conventional; for example, the cross. The cross can be merely a conventional symbol of the Christian Church and in that respect no different from a flag. But the specific content of the cross referring to Jesus' death or, beyond that, to the interpenetration of the material and spiritual planes, puts the connection between the symbol and what it symbolizes beyond the level of mere conventional symbols.

The opposite to the conventional symbol is the *accidental*   6
symbol, although they have one thing in common: there is no intrinsic relationship between the symbol and that which it symbolizes. Let us assume that someone has had a saddening experience in a certain city; when he hears the name of that city, he will easily

connect the name with a mood of sadness, just as he would connect it with a mood of joy had his experience been a happy one. Quite obviously there is nothing in the nature of the city that is either sad or joyful. It is the individual experience connected with the city that makes it a symbol of a mood. The same reaction could occur in connection with a house, a street, a certain dress, certain scenery, or anything once connected with a specific mood. . . . The connection between the symbol and the experience symbolized is entirely accidental.

In contrast to the conventional symbol, the accidental symbol 7 cannot be shared by anyone else except as we relate the events connected with the symbol. For this reason accidental symbols are rarely used in myths, fairy tales, or works of art written in symbolic language because they are not communicable unless the writer adds a lengthy comment to each symbol he uses. In dreams, however, accidental symbols are frequent, and Freud by his method of free association devised a method for understanding their meaning.

The *universal* symbol is one in which there is an intrinsic re- 8 lationship between the symbol and that which it represents. Take, for instance, the symbol of fire. We are fascinated by certain qualities of fire in a fireplace. First of all, by its aliveness. It changes continuously, it moves all the time, and yet there is constancy in it. It remains the same without being the same. It gives the impression of power, of energy, of grace and lightness. It is as if it were dancing, and had an inexhaustible source of energy. When we use fire as a symbol, we describe the *inner experience* characterized by the same elements which we notice in the sensory experience of fire — the mood of energy, lightness, movement, grace, gaiety, sometimes one, sometimes another of these elements being predominant in the feeling.

Similar in some ways and different in others is the symbol of 9 water — of the ocean or of the stream. Here, too, we find the blending of change and constant movement and yet of permanence. We also feel the quality of aliveness, continuity, and energy. But there is a difference; where fire is adventurous, quick, exciting, water is quiet, slow, and steady. Fire has an element of surprise; water an element of predictability. Water symbolizes the mood of aliveness, too, but one which is "heavier," "slower," and more comforting than exciting. . . .

The universal symbol is the only one in which the relation-   10
ship between the symbol and that which is symbolized is not co-
incidental but intrinsic. It is rooted in the experience of the affinity
between an emotion or thought, on the one hand, and a sensory
experience, on the other. It can be called universal because it is
shared by all men, in contrast not only to the accidental symbol,
which is by its very nature entirely personal, but also to the conventional symbol, which is restricted to a group of people sharing
the same convention. The universal symbol is rooted in the properties of our body, our senses, and our mind, which are common
to all men and, therefore, not restricted to individuals or to specific groups. Indeed, *the language of the universal symbol is the
one common tongue developed by the human race,* a language
which it forgot before it succeeded in developing a universal conventional language.

There is no need to speak of a racial inheritance in order to   11
explain the universal character of symbols. Every human being
sharing the essential features of bodily and mental equipment with
the rest of mankind is capable of speaking and understanding the
symbolic language that is based upon these common properties.
Just as we do not need to learn to cry when we are sad or to get
red in the face when we are angry, and just as these reactions are
not restricted to any particular race or group of people, symbolic
language does not have to be learned and is not restricted to any
segment of the human race. Evidence for this is to be found in the
fact that symbolic language as it is employed in myths and dreams
is found in all cultures, in the so-called primitive as well as such
developed cultures as those of Egypt and Greece. Furthermore, the
symbols used in these various cultures are strikingly similar since
they all go back to the basic sensory as well as emotional experiences shared by men of all cultures. Dreams of people living in the
United States, India, or China today, as well as those which are
reported to us from Greece, Palestine, or Egypt 3000 years ago, are
essentially the same in content and structure.

The foregoing statement needs qualification, however. Some   12
symbols differ in meaning according to the difference in their realistic significance in various cultures. For instance, the function
and consequently the meaning of the sun is different in northern
countries and in tropical countries. In northern countries, where
water is plentiful, all growth depends on sufficient sunshine. The
sun is the warm, life-giving, protecting, loving power. In the Near

East, where the heat of the sun is much more powerful, the sun is a dangerous and even threatening power from which man must protect himself, while water is felt to be the source of all life and the main condition for growth. We may speak of *dialects of universal symbolic language,* which are determined by those differences in natural conditions which cause certain symbols to have a different meaning in different regions of the earth.

Different from these "symbol dialects" is the fact that many   13 symbols have more than one meaning in accordance with various kinds of experiences which can be connected with one and the same natural phenomenon. Let us take the symbol of fire again. If we watch fire in the fireplace, which is a source of pleasure and comfort, it is expressive of a mood of aliveness, warmth, and pleasure. But if we see a building or forest on fire, it conveys to us an experience of threat and terror, of the powerlessness of man against the elements of nature. Fire, then, can be the symbolic representation of inner aliveness and happiness as well as of fear, powerlessness, or of one's own destructive tendencies. The same holds true of the symbol of water. Water can be a most destructive force when it is whipped up by a storm or when a swollen river floods its banks. Therefore, it can be the symbolic expression of horror and chaos as well as of comfort and peace.

Another illustration of the same principle is a symbol of a   14 valley. The valley enclosed between mountains can arouse in us the feeling of security and comfort, of protection against all dangers from the outside. But the protecting mountains can also mean isolating walls which do not permit us to get out of the valley and thus the valley can become a symbol of imprisonment.

The particular meaning of the symbol in any given place can   15 only be determined from the whole context in which the symbol appears, and in terms of the predominant experiences of the person using the symbol. . . .

Meanings and Values

1. Explain the difference between the use of the cross as a conventional symbol and its use as a universal symbol, clarifying the distinction with examples.

2. What symbols other than words and flags can be classified as purely conventional symbols?

3. Into which of the three categories would you place the symbolic

uses of colors? For instance, are the symbolic sadness of black, the purity of white, and the violence of red merely agreed-upon (conventional) meanings, or peculiar to our own individual experiences (accidental) — or is there some natural connection between the colors themselves and what they could mean to people universally?

4a. Using the colors black, white, and red as examples, demonstrate the fact that words can have more than one symbolic meaning.
  b. How universal can we assume these additional color-meanings to be?
  c. If you were communicating by the use of one of these colors, how would the reader or listener know which symbolic meaning you intended? Explain your answer by illustration.

5a. Does the author make a clear enough distinction between symbolic "dialects" and symbols with "more than one meaning in accordance with various kinds of experiences" (pars. 12, 13)?
  b. Study this difference and then clarify with additional examples of your own.

6. Select two of your own accidental symbols and explain why you classify them as such.

7. In "Guide to Terms" read the section on connotations of words (*Connotation/Denotation*).
  a. Then explain, in your own way, the relationship between symbolism and connotation.
  b. Why is an understanding of how symbolism works a valuable aid in getting the most from word connotations?
  c. People in what professions especially need this assistance?

8. Select as many of the following as you are directed, list their various symbolic meanings, and classify each as conventional, accidental, or universal: a sunset; a sunrise; the color blue; the color yellow; the moon; notes of the musical scale; a white dove; a snake; a cat; a buzzard; the revolving, candy-striped cylinder in front of a shop; champagne; the swastika; a wedding ring; roast turkey; cupid with bow; a bee; a torch; the four-leaf clover; a sword; a lighthouse; the oak tree; an eagle; a key; a covered wagon; the cornucopia; mortar and pestle; the White House; an orchid.

9a. If you have read Huxley's essay in Section 1, explain how the waterworks served as a symbol for the Hessians.
  b. Is a king himself (or a queen) in any sense a symbol? If so, how would you classify the symbolism?

10. If you have read "Reading Tastes and Habits" (this section), in which type of reading would we be most likely to encounter universal symbolism? Why?

Expository Techniques

1a. What method of introduction does Fromm use? (Guide: *Introductions*.)
 b. Can we assume anything about the essay's basic organization after reading the second paragraph?
 c. About the methods to be used in development?
 d. In an essay of this kind, why is the basic organization important to know as soon as possible?

2a. Does the fact that symbols may belong to more than one of Fromm's categories make his system weak?
 b. What is the important difference, if any, between this system and the illustration (in the introduction to this section) of the man who was both a Lutheran and a minister?

3. Would you classify this essay as formal or informal? Why? (Guide: *Essay*.)

4a. If you had trouble understanding the meaning of any of Fromm's sentences (aside from difficulty caused by unfamiliar words), study these sentences again and determine the cause of the communication block.
 b. How, if at all, could they have been written to avoid this block?

5. List the transitional devices used to form helpful bridges between paragraphs. (Guide: *Transition*.)

6. How would you describe the tone of "Symbolic Language"? Why? (Guide: *Style/Tone*.)

Diction and Vocabulary

1. If you were not previously familiar with the words *inherent* and *intrinsic*, did their repeated use annoy you? Now more familiar with their meanings, can you better understand why Fromm chose them — or can you think of "simpler" words that would have conveyed his meaning just as well? Explain.

2. Use the dictionary as necessary to understand how the author uses the following words: crucial (par. 1); differentiate (2); inherent (3, 4); dispelling, expulsion (4); intrinsic (5, 6, 8, 10); denoting, concept, interpenetration (5); affinity, sensory (10); context (15).

Suggestions for Writing and Discussion

1. Explain the source and meaning (either to you personally, or to your family) of one of your accidental symbols. Show what significant

effect this symbolic meaning has had on your behavior or on some important decision.

2. Select one of the symbols listed in question 8 of "Meanings and Values" — or a group of related symbols from the list, if you prefer — and analyze fully the nature of their symbolism: the sources, the various meanings and uses, and their significance in everyday affairs or unusual occasions.

3. Select one occupation (other than fiction or poetry writing) in which an understanding of symbolism is especially important, and explain why, illustrating your ideas by the use of examples.

(NOTE: Suggestions for topics requiring development by CLASSIFICATION are on page 66, at the end of this section.)

JAMES DAVID BARBER

JAMES DAVID BARBER was born in Charleston, West Virginia, in 1930. He received his B.A. and M.A. degrees from the University of Chicago and holds a Ph.D. degree in political science from Yale University. Barber has served in various capacities on the faculties of Stetson, Yale, and Columbia universities, and he is a frequent guest lecturer at other universities throughout the country. At present he is Professor and Chairman of the Political Science Department at Duke University. Barber has contributed steadily to both scholarly and popular periodicals and has written and edited several important books in his field.

Four Types of President

"Four Types of President" (editor's title) is selected from Barber's most widely known book, *Presidential Character: Predicting Performance in the White House.* In this piece he attempts to explain, by division and classification, a much more complex subject than those of the other authors of this section; the resulting system, however, is admirably simple. Also worth a beginning writer's study are the distinctive elements of Barber's style.

Who the President is at a given time can make a profound difference in the whole thrust and direction of national politics. Since we have only one President at a time, we can never prove this by comparison, but even the most superficial speculation confirms the commonsense view that the man himself weighs heavily among other historical factors. A Wilson re-elected in 1920, a Hoover in 1932, a John F. Kennedy in 1964 would, it seems very likely, have guided the body politic along rather different paths from those

1

their actual successors chose. Or try to imagine a Theodore Roosevelt ensconced behind today's "bully pulpit" of a Presidency, or Lyndon Johnson as President in the age of McKinley. Only someone mesmerized by the lures of historical inevitability can suppose that it would have made little or no difference to government policy had Alf Landon replaced FDR in 1936, had Dewey beaten Truman in 1948, or Adlai Stevenson reigned through the 1950s. Not only would these alternative Presidents have advocated different policies — they would have approached the office from very different psychological angles. It stretches credibility to think that Eugene McCarthy would have run the institution the way Lyndon Johnson did.

The first baseline in defining Presidential types is *activity-passivity*. How much energy does the man invest in his Presidency? Lyndon Johnson went at his day like a human cyclone, coming to rest long after the sun went down. Calvin Coolidge often slept eleven hours a night and still needed a nap in the middle of the day. In between the Presidents array themselves on the high or low side of the activity line.

The second baseline is *positive-negative affect* toward one's activity — that is, how he feels about what he does. Relatively speaking, does he seem to experience his political life as happy or sad, enjoyable or discouraging, positive or negative in its main effect. The feeling I am after here is not grim satisfaction in a job well done, not some philosophical conclusion. The idea is this: is he someone who, on the surfaces we can see, gives forth the feeling that he has *fun* in political life? Franklin Roosevelt's Secretary of War, Henry L. Stimson wrote that the Roosevelts "not only understood the *use* of power, they knew the *enjoyment* of power, too. . . . Whether a man is burdened by power or enjoys power; whether he is trapped by responsibility or made free by it; whether he is moved by other people and outer forces or moves them — that is the essence of leadership."

The positive-negative baseline, then, is a general symptom of the fit between the man and his experience, a kind of register of *felt* satisfaction.

Why might we expect these two simple dimensions to outline the main character types? Because they stand for two central features of anyone's orientation toward life. In nearly every study of personality, some form of the active-passive contrast is critical; the general tendency to act or be acted upon is evident in such concepts as dominance-submission, extraversion-introversion, aggression-timidity, attack-defense, fight-flight, engagement-withdrawal, approach-avoidance. In everyday life we sense quickly the general energy output of the people we deal with. Similarly we catch on fairly quickly to the affect dimension — whether the person seems to be optimistic or pessimistic, hopeful or skeptical, happy or sad. The two baselines are clear and they are also independent of one another: all of us know people who are very active but seem discouraged, others who are quite passive but seem happy, and so forth. The activity baseline refers to what one does, the affect baseline to how one feels about what he does.

Both are crude clues to character. They are leads into four basic character patterns long familiar in psychological research. In summary form, these are the main configurations:

Active-positive: There is a congruence, a consistency, between much activity and the enjoyment of it, indicating relatively high self-esteem and relative success in relating to the environment. The man shows an orientation toward productiveness as a value and an ability to use his styles flexibly, adaptively, suiting the dance to the music. He sees himself as developing over time toward relatively well-defined personal goals — growing toward his image of himself as he might yet be. There is an emphasis on rational mastery, on using the brain to move the feet. This may get him into trouble; he may fail to take account of the irrational in politics. Not everyone he deals with sees things his way and he may find it hard to understand why.

Active-negative: The contradiction here is between relatively intense effort and relatively low emotional reward for that effort. The activity has a compulsive quality, as if the man were trying to make up for something or to escape from anxiety into hard work. He seems ambitious, striving upward, power-seeking. His stance toward the environment is aggressive and he has a persistent problem in managing his aggressive feelings. His self-image is vague and discontinuous. Life is a hard struggle to achieve and hold power, hampered by the condemnations of a perfectionistic conscience. Active-negative types pour energy into the political system, but it is an energy distorted from within.

Passive-positive: This is the receptive, compliant, other-directed   9
character whose life is a search for affection as a reward for being
agreeable and cooperative rather than personally assertive. The
contradiction is between low self-esteem (on grounds of being un-
lovable, unattractive) and a superficial optimism. A hopeful attitude helps dispel doubt and elicits encouragement from others.
Passive-positive types help soften the harsh edges of politics. But
their dependence and the fragility of their hopes and enjoyments
make disappointment in politics likely.

Passive-negative: The factors are consistent — but how are we to   10
account for the man's *political* role-taking? Why is someone who
does little in politics and enjoys it less there at all? The answer lies
in the passive-negative's character-rooted orientation toward doing
dutiful service; this compensates for low self-esteem based on a
sense of uselessness. Passive-negative types are in politics because
they think they ought to be. They may be well adapted to certain
nonpolitical roles, but they lack the experience and flexibility to
perform effectively as political leaders. Their tendency is to with-
draw, to escape from the conflict and uncertainty of politics by
emphasizing vague principles (especially prohibitions) and proce-
dural arrangements. They become guardians of the right and
proper way, above the sordid politicking of lesser men.

Active-positive Presidents want most to achieve results. Ac-   11
tive-negatives aim to get and keep power. Passive-positives are
after love. Passive-negatives emphasize their civic virtue. The relation of activity to enjoyment in a President thus tends to outline a
cluster of characteristics, to set apart the adapted from the compulsive, compliant, and withdrawn types.

The first four Presidents of the United States, conveniently,   12
ran through this gamut of character types. (Remember, we are
talking about tendencies, broad directions; no individual man exactly fits a category.) George Washington — clearly the most important President in the pantheon — established the fundamental
legitimacy of an American government at a time when this was a
matter in considerable question. Washington's dignity, judiciousness, his aloof air of reserve and dedication to duty fit the passive-
negative or withdrawing type best. Washington did not seek inno-
vation, he sought stability. He longed to retire to Mount Vernon,

but fortunately was persuaded to stay on through a second term, in which, by rising above the political conflict between Hamilton and Jefferson and inspiring confidence in his own integrity, he gave the nation time to develop the organized means for peaceful change.

John Adams followed, a dour New England Puritan, much 13
given to work and worry, an impatient and irascible man — an active-negative President, a compulsive type. Adams was far more partisan than Washington; the survival of the system through his Presidency demonstrated that the nation could tolerate, for a time, domination by one of its nascent political parties. As President, an angry Adams brought the United States to the brink of war with France, and presided over the new nation's first experiment in political repression: the Alien and Sedition Acts, forbidding, among other things, unlawful combinations "with intent to oppose any measure or measures of the government of the United States," or "any false, scandalous, and malicious writing or writings against the United States, or the President of the United States, with intent to defame . . . or to bring them or either of them, into contempt or disrepute."

Then came Jefferson. He too had his troubles and failures — 14
in the design of national defense, for example. As for his Presidential character (only one element in success or failure), Jefferson was clearly active-positive. A child of the Enlightenment, he applied his reason to organizing connections with Congress aimed at strengthening the more popular forces. A man of catholic interests and delightful humor, Jefferson combined a clear and open vision of what the country could be with a profound political sense, expressed in his famous phrase, "Every difference of opinion is not a difference of principle."

The fourth President was James Madison, "Little Jemmy," the 15
constitutional philosopher thrown into the White House at a time of great international turmoil. Madison comes closest to the passive-positive, or compliant, type; he suffered from irresolution, tried to compromise his way out, and gave in too readily to the "warhawks" urging combat with Britain. The nation drifted into war, and Madison wound up ineptly commanding his collection of amateur generals in the streets of Washington. General Jackson's victory at New Orleans saved the Madison administration's historical reputation; but he left the Presidency with the United States close to bankruptcy and secession.

These four Presidents — like all Presidents — were persons 16
trying to cope with the roles they had won by using the equipment
they had built over a lifetime. The President is not some shapeless
organism in a flood of novelties, but a man with a memory in a
system with a history. Like all of us, he draws on his past to shape
his future. The pathetic hope that the White House will turn a
Caligula into a Marcus Aurelius is as naive as the fear that ultimate
power inevitably corrupts. The problem is to understand — and to
state understandably — what in the personal past foreshadows the
Presidential future.

Meanings and Values

1. Is this selection more nearly objective or subjective writing? Why?
    (See Guide to Terms: *Objective/Subjective.*)
2. What seems to be the author's opinion of "historical inevitability"
    (par. 1)? Justify your answer.
3. What have been some of the most important "historical factors"
    (par. 1) which have combined with the character of recent presi-
    dents to shape their conduct in office?
4a. How, if at all, could a person be "made free" by responsibility
    (par. 3)?
  b. Does Stimson's statement constitute a paradox? Why, or why not?
    (Guide: *Paradox.*)
5. Why was the "fundamental legitimacy of an American government"
    in question (par. 12), even after the Revolutionary War was won?
6a. In paragraph 5, Barber makes clear that his classification system
    applies to ordinary people, not just to presidents. If you have also
    read Berne's system of classifying types of people, do you find any
    parallels between the two?
  b. If you do, show the parallels. If not, are they then contradictory to
    each other? Why, or why not?

Expository Techniques

1a. If this seems to be a more complicated classification system than
    the others in this section, try to determine why.
  b. Devise, if you can, a simpler way to present the material. Is yours
    more, or less, effective? Why?
2. In paragraph 12, Barber says that no individual man exactly fits a
    category. Must we therefore conclude that it is not a complete and
    logical system? Why, or why not?

3a. Cite the paragraphs in which the author uses examples as an expository technique.
  b. Do the examples improve the effectiveness of the writing, or merely slow down the reading? Why?

4a. Cite examples of parallel structure in at least two paragraphs. (Guide: *Parallel Structure.*)
  b. How is their use a matter of syntax and of style? (Guide: *Syntax, Style/Tone.*)

5. What other qualities of Barber's writing are relevant to style? Use examples to illustrate.

6a. What is the apparent purpose of paragraph 11 and the last sentence of paragraph 5?
  b. Would you use this technique if you were doing similar writing? Why, or why not?

Diction and Vocabulary

1a. Which, if any, of your answers to question 5 of "Expository Techniques" are also matters of diction? (Guide: *Diction.*)
  b. If none of them are, why did you not consider diction a distinctive element of Barber's style? (Guide: *Style/Tone.*)

2a. Why are the baselines "crude" clues to character (par. 6)?
  b. Are they therefore not valid? Why, or why not?

3a. The author uses two qualifications in the final sentence of paragraph 7. What are they? (Guide: *Qualification.*)
  b. What is gained by their use?

4a. How might the careless reader misunderstand the meaning of "His stance toward the environment is aggressive . . ." (par. 8)?
  b. In view of the author's apparent purpose and reader-audience, is there any reason to believe he would be concerned about this possible ambiguity? Explain.
  c. How, if at all, is this a matter of connotation? (Guide: *Connotation/Denotation.*)

5a. What are the meanings, both literal and figurative, of the allusions in paragraph 16? (Guide: *Figure of Speech.*)
  b. Cite at least one example each of simile and metaphor in paragraph 2 or 7.

6. Consult the dictionary as needed for full understanding of the following words: ensconced, mesmerized (par. 1); array (2); essence (3); configurations (6); congruence (7); discontinuous (8); dispel, elicits (9); compliant (9, 15); gamut, pantheon, judiciousness (12); dour, irascible, nascent, defame (13); catholic (14); irresolution, ineptly (15).

Suggestions for Writing and Discussion

1. Analyze your own character patterns and determine which category they best fit. For what practical purposes might such analysis be used?

2. How can we reliably analyze and categorize a candidate's character during the fakery of a presidential campaign?

3. To what extent should we consider the national situation or "other historical factors" at the time of election, in relation to the candidates' character types?

4. If Barber's meaning of "character" differs from your own — e.g., if it is more or less concerned with integrity — explain the differences.

5. Where do the three most recent presidents best fit into Barber's classification system? Justify your answer.

Writing Suggestions for Section 2
Classification

Use division and classification (into at least three categories) as your basic method of analyzing one of the following subjects from one interesting point of view. (Your instructor may have good reason to place limitations on your choice of subject.) Narrow the topic as necessary to enable you to do a thorough job.

1. College students.
2. College teachers.
3. Athletes.
4. Coaches.
5. Salespeople.
6. Hunters (or fishermen).
7. Parents.
8. Marijuana users.
9. Policemen.
10. Summer (or part-time) jobs.
11. Sailing vessels.
12. Horses (or other animals).
13. Television programs.
14. Motivations for study.
15. Methods of studying for exams.
16. Lies.
17. Selling techniques.
18. Tastes in clothes.
19. Contemporary music.
20. Love.
21. Immorality.
22. Attitudes toward life.

3

Explaining by Means of
Comparison and *Contrast*

One of the first expository methods we used as children was *comparison*, noticing similarities of objects, qualities, and actions, or *contrast*, noticing their differences. We compared the color of the new puppies with that of their mother, contrasted our father's height with our own. Then the process became more complicated, and we employ it frequently in college essay examinations or term papers when we compare or contrast forms of government, reproductive systems of animals, or ethical philosophies of man. Later, in the business or professional worlds, we may prepare important reports based on comparison and contrast — between kinds of equipment for purchase, the personnel policies of different departments, or precedents in legal matters. Nearly everyone uses the process, though he may not be aware of this, many times a day — in choosing a head of lettuce, in deciding what to wear to school, in selecting a house or a friend or a religion.

In the more formal scholastic and professional uses of comparison and contrast, however, an ordered plan is needed to avoid having a mere list of characteristics or a frustrating jumble of similarities and differences. If the author wants to avoid communication blocks that will prevent his "getting through" to his reader, he will observe a few basic principles of selection and development. These principles apply mostly to comparisons between two subjects only; if three or more are to be considered, the usual method is to compare or contrast them in pairs.

A *logical* comparison or contrast can be made only between subjects of the same general type. (Analogy, a special form of comparison used for another purpose, is discussed in the next section.) For example, contrasting a pine and a maple could be useful or meaningful, but little would be gained, except exercise in sentence construction, by contrasting the pine and the pansy.

Of course, logical but informal comparisons that are merely incidental to the basic structure, and hence follow no special pattern, may be made in any writing. Several of the preceding selections make limited use of comparison and contrast, and Donald Hall (Sec. 2) relies heavily on the process in his fifth paragraph to distinguish between two of his types of reading. But once committed to a formal, full-scale analysis by comparison and contrast, the careful writer ordinarily gives the subjects similar treatment. Points used for one should also be used for the other, and usually in the same order. All pertinent points should be explored — pertinent, that is, to the purpose of the comparison.

The purpose and the complexity of materials will usually indicate their arrangement and use. Sometimes the purpose is merely to point out *what* the likenesses and differences are, sometimes it is to show the *superiority* of one thing over another — or possibly to convince the reader of the superiority, as this is also a technique of argumentation. The purpose may be to explain the *unfamiliar* (wedding customs in Ethiopia) by comparing to the *familiar* (wedding customs in Kansas). Or it may be to explain or emphasize some other type of *central idea,* as in most of the essays in this section.

One of the two basic methods of comparison is to present all the information on the two subjects, one at a time, and to summarize by combining their most important similarities and differences. This method may be desirable if there are few points to compare, or if the individual points are less important than the overall picture they present. Therefore, this procedure might be a satisfactory means of showing the relative difficulty of two college courses, or comparing two viewpoints concerning an automobile accident. (Of course, as in all other matters of expository arrangement, the last subject discussed is in the most emphatic position.)

However, if there are several points of comparison to be considered, or if the points are of individual importance, alternation of the material would be a better arrangement. Hence, in a detailed comparison of Oak Valley and Elm Hill hospitals, we might compare their sizes, locations, surgical facilities, staffs, and so on, always in the same order. To tell all about Oak Valley and then all about Elm Hill would create a serious communication block, requiring the reader constantly to call on his memory of what was cited earlier, or to turn back to the first group of facts again and again in order to make the meaningful comparisons that the author should have made for him.

Often the subject matter or the purpose itself will suggest a more casual treatment, or some combination or variation of the two basic methods. We might present the complete information on the first subject, then summarize it point by point within the complete information on the second. In other circumstances (as in "The Spider and the Wasp" in Section 5), it may be desirable simply to set up the thesis of likeness or difference, and then to explain a *process* that demonstrates this thesis. And, although expository comparisons and contrasts are frequently handled together, it is sometimes best to present all similarities first, then all differences — or vice versa, depending on the emphasis desired.

In any basic use of "comparison" (conveniently, the term is most often used in a general sense to cover both comparison and contrast), the important thing is to have a plan that suits the purpose and material thoughtfully worked out in advance.

MARK TWAIN

Mark Twain was the pen name of Samuel Clemens (1835–1910). He was born in Missouri and became the first author of importance to emerge from "beyond the Mississippi." Although best known for bringing humor, realism, and western local color to American fiction, Mark Twain wanted to be remembered as a philosopher and social critic. Still widely read, in most languages and in all parts of the world, are his numerous short stories (his "tall tales," in particular), autobiographical accounts, and novels, especially *Adventures of Huckleberry Finn* (1884). Ernest Hemingway called the latter "the best book we've had," an appraisal with which many critics agree.

Two Ways of Seeing a River

"Two Ways of Seeing a River" (editor's title) is from Mark Twain's "Old Times on the Mississippi," which was later expanded and published in book form as *Life on the Mississippi* (1883). It is autobiographical. The prose of this selection is vivid, as in all of Mark Twain's writing, but considerably more reflective in tone than most.

Now when I had mastered the language of this water and had come to know every trifling feature that bordered the great river as familiarly as I knew the letters of the alphabet, I had made a valuable acquisition. But I had lost something, too. I had lost something which could never be restored to me while I lived. All the grace, the beauty, the poetry, had gone out of the majestic river! I still kept in mind a certain wonderful sunset which I witnessed when steamboating was new to me. A broad expanse of the river was turned to blood; in the middle distance the red hue brightened into gold, through which a solitary log came floating, black and conspicuous; in one place a long, slanting mark lay sparkling upon the water; in another the surface was broken by boiling, tumbling rings, that were as many-tinted as an opal; where the ruddy flush was faintest, was a smooth spot that was covered with graceful circles and radiating lines, ever so delicately traced; the shore on our left was densely wooded and the somber shadow that fell from this forest was broken in one place by a long, ruffled trail that shone like silver; and high above the forest wall a clean-stemmed dead tree waved a single leafy bough that glowed like a flame in the unobstructed splendor that was flowing from the sun. There were graceful curves, reflected images, woody heights, soft distances, and over the whole scene, far and near, the dissolving lights drifted steadily, enriching it every passing moment with new marvels of coloring.

I stood like one bewitched. I drank it in, in a speechless rapture. The world was new to me and I had never seen anything like this at home. But as I have said, a day came when I began to cease from noting the glories and the charms which the moon and the sun and the twilight wrought upon the river's face; another day came when I ceased altogether to note them. Then, if that sunset scene had been repeated, I should have looked upon it without rapture, and should have commented upon it inwardly after this fashion: "This sun means that we are going to have wind to-morrow; that floating log means that the river is rising, small thanks to it; that slanting mark on the water refers to a bluff reef which is going to kill somebody's steamboat one of these nights, if it keeps on stretching out like that; those tumbling 'boils' show a dissolving bar and a changing channel there; the lines and circles in the slick water over yonder are a warning that that troublesome place is shoaling up dangerously; that silver streak in the shadow of the forest is the 'break' from a new snag and he has located himself in the very best place he could have found to fish for steamboats; that tall dead tree, with a single living branch, is not going to last long, and then how is a body ever going to get through this blind place at night without the friendly old landmark?"

No, the romance and beauty were all gone from the river. All the value any feature of it had for me now was the amount of usefulness it could furnish toward compassing the safe piloting of a steamboat. Since those days, I have pitied doctors from my heart. What does the lovely flush in a beauty's cheek mean to a doctor but a "break" that ripples above some deadly disease? Are not all her visible charms sown thick with what are to him the signs and symbols of hidden decay? Does he ever see her beauty at all, or doesn't he simply view her professionally and comment upon her unwholesome condition all to himself? And doesn't he sometimes wonder whether he has gained most or lost most by learning his trade?

Meanings and Values

1. No selection could better illustrate the intimate relationship of several skills with which students of writing should be familiar, especially the potentials in "point of view" (and attitude), "style," "tone."
   a. What is the point of view in paragraph 1? (See Guide to Terms: *Point of View.*)
   b. Where, and how, does it change in paragraph 2?
   c. Why is the shift important to the author's contrast?
   d. Show how the noticeable change of tone is related to this change in point of view. (Guide: *Style/Tone.*)
   e. Specifically, what changes in style accompany the shift in tone and attitude?
   f. How effectively do they all relate to the central theme itself? (Remember that such effects seldom just "happen"; the writer *makes* them happen.)

2a. Is the first paragraph primarily objective or subjective? (Guide: *Objective/Subjective.*)
   b. How about the latter part of paragraph 2?
   c. Are your answers to "a" and "b" related to point of view? If so, how?

3a. Does the author permit himself to engage in sentimentality? (Guide: *Sentimentality.*) If so, how could it have been avoided without damage to his theme's development?
   b. If not, what restraints does the author use?

4. Do you think the last sentence refers only to doctors? Why, or why not?

5. List other vocations in which you assume (or perhaps have occasion to know) that the beauty and romance eventually give way to practical realities; state briefly, for each, why this hardening should be expected.

Expository Techniques

1a. Where do you find a second comparison or contrast? Which is it?
   b. Is the comparison/contrast made within itself, with something external, or both? Explain.

   c. Is this part of the writing closely enough related to the major contrast to justify its use? Why, or why not?

2a. In developing the numerous points of the major contrast, would an alternating, point-to-point system have been better? Why, or why not?

   b. Show how the author uses organization within the groups to assist in the overall contrast.

3a. What is the most noteworthy feature of syntax in paragraphs 1 and 2? (Guide: *Syntax.*)

   b. How effectively does it perform the function intended?

4. What is gained by the apparently deliberate decision to use rhetorical questions only toward the end? (Guide: *Rhetorical Question.*)

Diction and Vocabulary

1. Why would the colloquialism in the last sentence of paragraph 2 have been inappropriate in the first paragraph? (Guide: *Colloquial Expressions.*)

2a. Compare the quality of metaphors in the quotation of paragraph 2 with the quality of those preceding it. (Guide: *Figures of Speech.*)

   b. Is the difference justified? Why, or why not?

Suggestions for Writing and Discussion

1. Select for further development one of the vocations in your answer to question 5 of "Meanings and Values." How would one's attitude be apt to change from the beginning romantic appeal?

2. Show how, if at all, Mark Twain's contrast might be used to show parallels to life itself — e.g., differences in the idealism and attitudes of youth and maturity.

3. Explore the possibility, citing examples if possible, of being able to retain *both* the "rapture" and the "usefulness."

(NOTE: Suggestions for topics requiring development by use of COMPARISON and CONTRAST are on page 93, at the end of this section.)

MEG GREENFIELD

MEG GREENFIELD, born in Seattle in 1930, earned a B.A. degree
summa cum laude at Smith College and was a Fulbright scholar
at Cambridge University in England. She worked for *Reporter*
from 1957 to 1968, the last three years as the Washington
editor. She joined *The Washington Post* as an editorial writer
in 1968 and in 1970 advanced to the position of editorial page
editor. Greenfield is a columnist for *Newsweek* and sometimes
free-lances as a literary critic. She is a member of the American Society of Newspaper Editors.

Uncle Tom's Roots

"Uncle Tom's Roots," first published in *Newsweek*, is a detailed, point-by-point analysis by comparison and contrast.
This essay may also be classified as literary criticism; as such
it will almost inevitably express a highly subjective viewpoint.
In such writing, however, we still have the right to expect the
author to be fair, lucid, and convincing — qualities that Greenfield is well able to supply.

The last publishing event in this country that was in any way   1
comparable to the phenomenon of "Roots" occurred in 1851. It
was the publication, first as a serial and then as a book, of "Uncle
Tom's Cabin" by Harriet Beecher Stowe. In fact, there are so many
parallels between the two books — as well as between their recep-
tions — that we could do worse than to give Mrs. Stowe a chance
to answer the question about "Roots" that seems to be on everybody's mind: What does it all *mean?* I think she can tell us.

Before we go further, I should say that I share the view of the   2
late critic Edmund Wilson that "Uncle Tom's Cabin" does not deserve the general contempt in which it is nowadays held. Yes, it has

From *Newsweek*, February 14, 1977, p. 100. Copyright 1977 by Newsweek, Inc.
All rights reserved. Reprinted by permission.

stunning lapses into inaccuracy, sentimentality and tub-thumping propaganda. But it also has a grandeur of conception and what Wilson called a "certain eruptive force" that overwhelm these deficiencies. I would say precisely the same thing about "Roots." For the most part, Alex Haley's blacks strike me as being every bit as sentimentalized as Mrs. Stowe's in their unrelieved virtue down through the generations. But all that only heightens — as it is meant to — our rage at their treatment.

Mrs. Stowe's book was originally going to be called "Uncle   3
Tom's Cabin; or, The Man That Was a Thing." Her subtitle was changed (to "Life Among the Lowly"), but the original expressed her real intention: to make vivid the individual, personal cruelties of the slave system, especially as it tore families apart, and to expose the monumental insensitivity of those who countenanced it. And, as a deeply religious woman, she would also demonstrate, in what she regarded as Uncle Tom's near-perfect Christianity, the superiority of the oppressed to the oppressor — an amazing capacity on the part of the enslaved blacks to preserve their souls.

That is not very different from the thrust of "Roots," and   4
there are actually some very similar episodes in the two books. Kunta Kinte's devastation by the sale of his daughter — it is the end of him — put me forcibly in mind of the awful silent reaction of the slave Lucy, in "Uncle Tom's Cabin," when she learns that her child has been sold. Of Lucy, who would that night take her life by drowning, Mrs. Stowe wrote: "The shot had passed too straight and direct through the heart for a cry or a tear."

There is an emotional truth in these moments that seems to   5
me to transcend the *untruths* of characterization of both Lucy and Kunta Kinte, their implausible, idealized aspects. And in the current controversy over the fidelity of "Roots" to history and nature, I think the book's defenders ought to stipulate as much. "Roots" is romantic and melodramatic, its characters are in many ways unconvincing and unreal. But none of that disturbs its larger human truth.

The same can be said of the argument over the factual accu-   6
racy of "Roots," an argument also reminiscent of that generated by "Uncle Tom's Cabin." As a feat of research and imagination, Mrs. Stowe's enterprise was not unlike Haley's, although one was seeking his historical identity, while the other was seeking to arouse the sensibilities of her countrymen. Mrs. Stowe had had a

few encounters with the system she wrote about. But like Haley
she undertook prodigious study with a view to re-creating reality.
Her biographer, Forrest Wilson, cites, for instance, a letter she
wrote to the abolitionist, Frederick Douglass, asking for help in
portraying the reality of life on a cotton plantation: "I have before
me an able paper written by a Southern planter, in which the details and modus operandi are given from his point of sight. I am
anxious to have something from another standpoint."

Her scrupulous efforts remind me of Haley's. Both sought to   7
achieve verisimilitude. But both, inevitably, made errors of fact.
And both also bent reality for the sake of their message, painting
things sharper and simpler than they really were. Mrs. Stowe was
so disturbed by the charges of inaccuracy that she eventually
gathered up supporting research material and published it for her
critics to inspect. But that, like the insistence of the defenders of
"Roots" that Haley has portrayed life as it was actually lived,
seems to me to have missed the point. On the larger historical
truth, both win hands down. The detail and background are there
to enhance this truth — but they are not the issue. Haley's book,
like Mrs. Stowe's, is a work of historical imagination and re-creation. It is fiction, though people tend to forget that.

You could say that this forgetfulness is a tribute to the emo-   8
tional power of Haley's re-creation of events, to his skill as a
melodramatist — a skill he shares with Mrs. Stowe. The public
response to "Uncle Tom's Cabin" — pre-television, pre-abolition
and all — was like the response to "Roots." It was an unexpected
and unaccountable wildfire thing.

Contemporary observers tell us how families read aloud (and   9
wept over) each installment of Mrs. Stowe's saga, how copies of
the magazine in which it appeared were passed from household to
household, how printing presses were going 24 hours a day to
keep the book available. Uncle Tom and Liza and Simon Legree,
et al., joined the national vocabulary overnight, just as Kizzy and
Chicken George and Massa Waller have done. Mrs. Stowe did for
the audience of the magazine that serialized her more or less what
Alex Haley did for ABC's. She was commended by Dickens and
Tolstoy and George Sand. She was translated into Finnish.

And, of course, as is also the case with Haley, her work was   10
oversimplified, exploited and cheapened in the enthusiasm that en-
sued. One reason people have so low an opinion of her book is

that they know it only from the vulgarized dramas that were made from it. In fact, Forrest Wilson tells us, within months of the first magazine installment people were singing Uncle Tom songs and a manufacturer had put out a card game called "Uncle Tom and Little Eva," whose action was "the continual separation and reunion of families."

"Roots," one likes to think, won't come to that. We are more 11 sophisticated and more somber. Blacks and whites alike are earnestly trying to sort out the meaning and message of "Roots," noting its incorporation of black history into the American experience in a novel way, wondering why it has had the impact it has on themselves and other people.

Overnight, it has become part of the national folklore, this 12 saga with its enormous power to move, and we all seem mystified by that. Mrs. Stowe would not have been. She knew what she was about, and she anticipated Haley. She wished, she wrote to her editor on the eve of publication, to present slavery "in the most lifelike and graphic manner possible. There is no arguing with *pictures,* and everybody is impressed by them, whether they mean to be or not."

Meanings and Values

1a. The author seems to have two purposes in this essay. Which becomes evident in the first paragraph?
 b. Which in the second?
 c. How well does she succeed in fulfilling the expectations thus invited?

2a. What is the author's point of view in relation to her subject? (See Guide to Terms: *Point of View.*)
 b. How is the tone affected by her point of view? (Guide: *Style/Tone.*)
 c. How does it help establish the degree of objectivity or subjectivity? Explain. (Guide: *Objective/Subjective.*)

3. Does it seem to you that Greenfield tends to dismiss the books' weaknesses too lightly? Cite examples to justify your answer.

4. Do you agree that we are "more sophisticated and more somber" than were Mrs. Stowe's readers (par. 11)? Why, or why not?

5a. Explain the significance, both obvious and subtle, of Greenfield's title.
 b. How effective is it? Why?

Expository Techniques

1a. Does the beginning perform the three necessary functions of a good introduction? Explain any inadequacies. (Guide: *Introductions*.)
  b. If it also indicates the essay's plan of organization, what is it?
2a. What is the advantage, in this piece, of the alternating method of presentation?
  b. Cite two examples of contrast.
  c. How many paragraphs contain comparisons?
3. Comment on Greenfield's choice of details to be used as examples in paragraph 9. (Obviously such materials do not just select themselves: Greenfield had many from which to choose.)
4. Does any part of this selection not serve as a tributary into the central theme, thus damaging the unity of composition? Be prepared to justify your answer. (Guide: *Unity*.)

Diction and Vocabulary

1. Does the author apparently use the words "sentimentality" and "melodrama" (pars. 2, 5) in the same sense that we do in this book? Explain as necessary. (Guide: *Sentimentality*.)
2. Lavish book illustrations were unknown in Mrs. Stowe's day. What is the meaning of "pictures" in the last sentence?
3. Use the dictionary as necessary to acquaint yourself with the following words as they are used in this selection: countenanced (par. 3); transcend, implausible (5); prodigious, modus operandi (6); scrupulous, verisimilitude, enhance (7); contemporary, et al. (9); saga (9, 12); vulgarized (10); graphic (12).

Suggestions for Writing and Discussion

1. Some people believe they see a strong tendency in Western society to sentimentalize the "superiority of the oppressed to the oppressor" (par. 3). Discuss this viewpoint — either objectively or subjectively, as directed by your instructor.
2. The American blacks, of course, were not the first (nor the last) people in history to be held as slaves. After doing suitable research on the subject, organize and present the information on one or more such instances of slavery. You may, if appropriate, make points of comparison between those and American slavery.
3. If you have read both *Roots* and the Hall essay (Sec. 2), in which of his four categories would you place your own reading of the novel? Which others might have been possible? How?

(NOTE: Suggestions for topics requiring development by use of COMPARISON and CONTRAST are on page 93, at the end of this section.)

BRUCE CATTON

BRUCE CATTON, born in Michigan in 1899, is a Civil War specialist whose early career included reporting for various newspapers. In 1954 he received both the Pulitzer Prize for historical work and the National Book Award. He has served as director of information for the United States Department of Commerce and has written many books, including *Mr. Lincoln's Army* (1951), *Glory Road* (1952), *A Stillness at Appomattox* (1953), *The Hallowed Ground* (1956), *America Goes to War* (1958), *The Coming Fury* (1961), *Terrible Swift Sword* (1963), *Never Call Retreat* (1966), *Waiting for the Morning Train: An American Boyhood* (1972), and *Gettysburg: The Final Fury* (1974). For five years, Catton edited *American Heritage*.

Grant and Lee: A Study in Contrasts

"Grant and Lee: A Study in Contrasts" was written as a chapter of *The American Story*, a collection of essays by noted historians. In this study, as in most of his other writing, Catton does more than recount the facts of history: he shows the significance within them. It is a carefully constructed essay, using contrast and comparison as the entire framework for his explanation.

When Ulysses S. Grant and Robert E. Lee met in the parlor of a 1 modest house at Appomattox Court House, Virginia, on April 9, 1865, to work out the terms for the surrender of Lee's Army of Northern Virginia, a great chapter in American life came to a close, and a great new chapter began.

These men were bringing the Civil War to its virtual finish. 2 To be sure, other armies had yet to surrender, and for a few days the fugitive Confederate government would struggle desperately

From *The American Story*, ed. Earl Schenk Miers. © 1956 by Broadcast Music, Inc. Reprinted by permission of the copyright holder.

and vainly, trying to find some way to go on living now that its chief support was gone. But in effect it was all over when Grant and Lee signed the papers. And the little room where they wrote out the terms was the scene of one of the poignant, dramatic contrasts in American history.

They were two strong men, these oddly different generals, and 3 they represented the strengths of two conflicting currents that, through them, had come into final collision.

Back of Robert E. Lee was the notion that the old aristocratic 4 concept might somehow survive and be dominant in American life.

Lee was tidewater Virginia, and in his background were fam- 5 ily, culture, and tradition . . . the age of chivalry transplanted to a New World which was making its own legends and its own myths. He embodied a way of life that had come down through the age of knighthood and the English country squire. America was a land that was beginning all over again, dedicated to nothing much more complicated than the rather hazy belief that all men had equal rights and should have an equal chance in the world. In such a land Lee stood for the feeling that it was somehow of advantage to human society to have a pronounced inequality in the social structure. There should be a leisure class, backed by ownership of land; in turn, society itself should be keyed to the land as the chief source of wealth and influence. It would bring forth (according to this ideal) a class of men with a strong sense of obligation to the community; men who lived not to gain advantage for themselves, but to meet the solemn obligations which had been laid on them by the very fact that they were privileged. From them the country would get its leadership; to them it could look for the higher values — of thought, of conduct, of personal deportment — to give it strength and virtue.

Lee embodied the noblest elements of this aristocratic ideal. 6 Through him, the landed nobility justified itself. For four years, the Southern states had fought a desperate war to uphold the ideals for which Lee stood. In the end, it almost seemed as if the Confederacy fought for Lee; as if he himself was the Confederacy . . . the best thing that the way of life for which the Confederacy stood could ever have to offer. He had passed into legend before Appomattox. Thousands of tired, underfed, poorly clothed Confederate soldiers, long since past the simple enthusiasm of the early days of the struggle, somehow considered Lee the symbol of everything for which they had been willing to die. But they could not quite put this feeling into words. If the Lost Cause, sanctified by so much heroism and so many deaths, had a living justification, its justification was General Lee.

Grant, the son of a tanner on the Western frontier, was every-   7
thing Lee was not. He had come up the hard way and embodied nothing in particular except the eternal toughness and sinewy fiber of the men who grew up beyond the mountains. He was one of a body of men who owed reverence and obeisance to no one, who were self-reliant to a fault, who cared hardly anything for the past but who had a sharp eye for the future.

These frontier men were the precise opposites of the tidewater   8
aristocrats. Back of them, in the great surge that had taken people over the Alleghenies and into the opening Western country, there was a deep, implicit dissatisfaction with a past that had settled into grooves. They stood for democracy, not from any reasoned con-clusion about the proper ordering of human society, but simply because they had grown up in the middle of democracy and knew how it worked. Their society might have privileges, but they would be privileges each man had won for himself. Forms and patterns meant nothing. No man was born to anything, except perhaps to a chance to show how far he could rise. Life was competition.

Yet along with this feeling had come a deep sense of belong-   9
ing to a national community. The Westerner who developed a farm, opened a shop, or set up in business as a trader, could hope to prosper only as his own community prospered — and his com-munity ran from the Atlantic to the Pacific and from Canada down to Mexico. If the land was settled, with towns and highways and accessible markets, he could better himself. He saw his fate in terms of the nation's own destiny. As its horizons expanded, so did his. He had, in other words, an acute dollars-and-cents stake in the continued growth and development of his country.

And that, perhaps, is where the contrast between Grant and   10
Lee becomes most striking. The Virginia aristocrat, inevitably, saw himself in relation to his own region. He lived in a static society which could endure almost anything except change. Instinctively, his first loyalty would go to the locality in which that society existed. He would fight to the limit of endurance to defend it, be-cause in defending it he was defending everything that gave his own life its deepest meaning.

The Westerner, on the other hand, would fight with an equal   11
tenacity for the broader concept of society. He fought so because
everything he lived by was tied to growth, expansion, and a constantly widening horizon. What he lived by would survive or fall
with the nation itself. He could not possibly stand by unmoved in
the face of an attempt to destroy the Union. He would combat it
with everything he had, because he could only see it as an effort
to cut the ground out from under his feet.

So Grant and Lee were in complete contrast, representing two   12
diametrically opposed elements in American life. Grant was the
modern man emerging; beyond him, ready to come on the stage,
was the great age of steel and machinery, of crowded cities and a
restless burgeoning vitality. Lee might have ridden down from the
old age of chivalry, lance in hand, silken banner fluttering over his
head. Each man was the perfect champion of his cause, drawing
both his strengths and his weaknesses from the people he led.

Yet it was not all contrast, after all. Different as they were —   13
in background, in personality, in underlying aspiration — these
two great soldiers had much in common. Under everything else,
they were marvelous fighters. Furthermore, their fighting qualities
were really very much alike.

Each man had, to begin with, the great virtue of utter tenacity   14
and fidelity. Grant fought his way down the Mississippi Valley in
spite of acute personal discouragement and profound military
handicaps. Lee hung on in the trenches at Petersburg after hope
itself had died. In each man there was an indomitable quality . . .
the born fighter's refusal to give up as long as he can still remain
on his feet and lift his two fists.

Daring and resourcefulness they had, too; the ability to think   15
faster and move faster than the enemy. These were the qualities
which gave Lee the dazzling campaigns of Second Manassas and
Chancellorsville and won Vicksburg for Grant.

Lastly, and perhaps greatest of all, there was the ability, at the   16
end, to turn quickly from war to peace once the fighting was over.
Out of the way these two men behaved at Appomattox came the
possibility of a peace of reconciliation. It was a possibility not
wholly realized, in the years to come, but which did, in the end,
help the two sections to become one nation again . . . after a war
whose bitterness might have seemed to make such a reunion wholly
impossible. No part of either man's life became him more than the

part he played in their brief meeting in the McLean house at Appomattox. Their behavior there put all succeeding generations of Americans in their debt. Two great Americans, Grant and Lee — very different, yet under everything very much alike. Their encounter at Appomattox was one of the great moments of American history.

Meanings and Values

1a. Clarify the assertions that through Lee "the landed nobility justified itself" and that "if the Lost Cause . . . had a living justification," it was General Lee (par. 6).
  b. Why are these assertions pertinent to the central theme?
2a. Does it seem reasonable that "thousands of tired, underfed, poorly clothed Confederate soldiers" (par. 6) had been willing to fight for the aristocratic system in which they would never have had even a chance to be aristocrats? Why, or why not?
  b. Can you think of more likely reasons why they were willing to fight?
3. Under any circumstances today might such a social structure as the South's be best for a country? Explain.
4a. What countries of the world have recently been so torn by internal war and bitterness that reunion has seemed, or still seems, impossible?
  b. Do you see any basic differences between the trouble in those countries and that in America at the time of the Civil War?
5a. The author calls Lee a symbol (par. 6). Was Grant also a symbol? If so, of what?
  b. How would you classify this kind of symbolism? (See Fromm, "Symbolic Language," or Guide to Terms: *Symbol*.)

Expository Techniques

1. Make an informal list of paragraph numbers from 3 to 16, and note by each whether the paragraph is devoted primarily to Lee, to Grant, or to direct comparison or contrast of the two. This chart will show you Catton's basic pattern of development. (Notice, for instance, how the broad information of paragraphs 4–6 and 7–9 seems almost to "funnel" down through the narrower summaries in 10 and 11 and into paragraph 12, where the converging elements meet and the contrast is made specific.)
2. What new technique of development is started in paragraph 13?

3a. What is gained, or lost, by using one sentence for paragraph 3?
 b. For paragraph 4?
4a. How many paragraphs does the introduction comprise?
 b. How successfully does it fulfill the three basic requirements of a good introduction? (Guide: *Introductions.*)
5. Show how Catton has constructed the beginning of each paragraph so that there is a smooth transition from the one preceding it. (Guide: *Transition.*)
6. The author's conclusion is really only the explanation of one of his integral points — and this method, if not carefully planned, runs the risk of ending too abruptly and leaving the reader unsatisfied. How has Catton avoided this hazard? (Guide: *Closings.*)
7a. What seems to be the author's attitude toward Grant and Lee?
 b. Show how his tone reflects this attitude. (Guide: *Style/Tone.*)

Diction and Vocabulary

1. Why would a use of colloquialisms have been inconsistent with the tone of this writing?
2a. List or mark all metaphors in paragraphs 1, 3, 5, 7–11, 16. (Guide: *Figures of Speech.*)
 b. Comment on their general effectiveness.
3. If you are not already familiar with the following words, study their meanings as given in the dictionary and as used in this essay: virtual, poignant (par. 2); concept (4); sinewy, obeisance (7); implicit (8); tenacity (11); diametrically, burgeoning (12); aspiration (13); fidelity, profound, indomitable (14); succeeding (16).
4. Explain how the word "poignant" aptly describes this contrast of two men (par. 2).

Suggestions for Writing and Discussion

1. Find, by minor research, an incident in the life of Grant or Lee which will, in suitable essay form, illustrate one of Catton's points.
2. Select some other dramatic moment in history and show its long-range significance.
3. Select some important moment in your life and show its long-range significance.
4. Explain how someone you know symbolizes a philosophy or way of life.

(NOTE: Suggestions for topics requiring development by use of COMPARISON and CONTRAST are on page 93, at the end of this section.)

ANNE ROIPHE

ANNE RICHARDSON ROIPHE (born 1935) is a native New Yorker.
After graduating from Sarah Lawrence she pursued further
studies in Munich, Germany. Upon her return to the United
States Roiphe worked for a public relations firm and did research for Forbes. Her first novel, *Digging Out*, published in
1968, was met with great enthusiasm. She has since published
Up The Sandbox (1971), which was made into a movie, *Long
Division* (1973), and *Torch Song* (1977). Her articles appear
frequently in *Vogue* and *The New York Times Magazine*.
Roiphe and her husband live in New York City with their
family.

Confessions of a Female Chauvinist Sow

"Confessions of a Female Chauvinist Sow" first appeared in
the magazine *New York*. This is an informal essay (which
some would classify as "familiar"), and the author uses personal examples liberally to illustrate her central theme. It is
a theme, however, that depends directly on comparison and
contrast for its primary development.

I once married a man I thought was totally unlike my father and   1
I imagined a whole new world of freedom emerging. Five years
later it was clear even to me — floating face down in a wash of
despair — that I had simply chosen a replica of my handsome
daddy-true. The updated version spoke English like an angel but —
good God! —underneath he was my father exactly: wonderful,
but not the right man for me.

Most people I know have at one time or another been fouled   2
up by their childhood experiences. Patterns tend to sink into the
unconscious only to reappear, disguised, unseen, like marionette
strings, pulling us this way or that. Whatever ails people — keeps

Reprinted by permission of Brandt & Brandt from *New York* Magazine (October 30, 1972). Copyright © 1972 by Anne Roiphe.

them up at night, tossing and turning — also ails movements no matter how historically huge or politically important. The women's movement cannot remake consciousness, or reshape the future, without acknowledging and shedding all the unnecessary and ugly baggage of the past. It's easy enough now to see where men have kept us out of clubs, baseball games, graduate schools; its easy enough to recognize the hidden directions that limit Sis to cake-baking and Junior to bridge-building; it's now possible for even Miss America herself to identify what *they* have done to us, and, of course, *they* have and *they* did and *they* are. . . . But along the way we also developed our own hidden prejudices, class assumptions and an anti-male humor and collection of expectations that gave us, like all oppressed groups, a secret sense of superiority (co-existing with a poor self-image — it's not news that people can believe two contradictory things at once).

Listen to any group that suffers materially and socially. They   3
have a lexicon with which they tease the enemy: ofay, goy, honky gringo. "Poor pale devils," said Malcolm X loud enough for us to hear, although blacks had joked about that to each other for years. Behind some of the women's liberation thinking lurk the rumors, the prejudices, the defense systems of generations of oppressed women whispering in the kitchen together, presenting one face to their menfolk and another to their card clubs, their mothers and sisters. All this is natural enough but potentially dangerous in a revolutionary situation in which you hope to create a future that does not mirror the past. The hidden anti-male feelings, a result of the old system, will foul us up if they are allowed to persist.

During my teen years I never left the house on my Saturday   4
night dates without my mother slipping me a few extra dollars — mad money, it was called. I'll explain what it was for the benefit of the new generation in which people just sleep with each other: the fellow was supposed to bring me home, lead me safely through the asphalt jungle, protect me from slithering snakes, rapists and the like. But my mother and I knew young men were apt to drink too much, to slosh down so many rye-and-gingers that some hero might well lead me in front of an oncoming bus, smash his daddy's car into Tiffany's window or, less gallantly, throw up on my new dress. Mad money was for getting home on your own, no matter what form of insanity your date happened to evidence. Mad money was also a wallflower's rope ladder; if the guy you came with

suddenly fancied someone else, well, you didn't have to stay there and suffer, you could go home. Boys were fickle and likely to be unkind; my mother and I knew that, as surely as we knew they tried to make you do things in the dark they wouldn't respect you for afterwards, and in fact would spread the word and spoil your rep. Boys liked to be flattered; if you made them feel important they would eat out of your hand. So talk to them about their interests, don't alarm them with displays of intelligence — we all knew that, we groups of girls talking into the wee hours of the night in a kind of easy companionship we thought impossible with boys. Boys were prone to have a good time, get you pregnant, and then pretend they didn't know your name when you came knocking on their door for finances or comfort. In short, we believed boys were less moral than we were. They appeared to be hypocritical, self-seeking, exploitative, untrustworthy and very likely to be showing off their precious masculinity. I never had a girl friend I thought would be unkind or embarrass me in public. I never expected a girl to lie to me about her marks or sports skill or how good she was in bed. Altogether — without anyone's directly coming out and saying so — I gathered that men were sexy, powerful, very interesting, but not very nice, not very moral, humane and tender, like us. Girls played fairly while men, unfortunately, reserved their honor for the battlefield.

Why are there laws insisting on alimony and child support?   5
Well, everyone knows that men don't have an instinct to protect their young and, given half a chance, with the moon in the right phase, they will run off and disappear. Everyone assumes a mother will not let her child starve, yet it is necessary to legislate that a father must not do so. We are taught to accept the idea that men are less than decent; their charms may be manifold but their characters are riddled with faults. To this day I never blink if I hear that a man has gone to find his fortune in South America, having left his pregnant wife, his blind mother and taken the family car. I still gasp in horror when I hear of a woman leaving her asthmatic infant for a rock group in Taos because I can't seem to avoid the assumption that men are naturally heels and women the ordained carriers of what little is moral in our dubious civilization.

My mother never gave me mad money thinking I would ditch   6
a fellow for some other guy or that I would pass out drunk on the floor. She knew I would be considerate of my companion because,

after all, I was more mature than the boys that gathered about. Why was I more mature? Women just are people-oriented; they learn to be empathetic at an early age. Most English students (students interested in humanity, not artifacts) are women. Men and boys — so the myth goes — conceal their feelings and lose interest in anybody else's. Everyone knows that even little boys can tell the difference between one kind of a car and another — proof that their souls are mechanical, their attention directed to the non-human.

I remember shivering in the cold vestibule of a famous men's athletic club. Women and girls are not permitted inside the club's door. What are they doing in there, I asked? They're naked, said my mother, they're sweating, jumping up and down a lot, telling each other dirty jokes and bragging about their stock market exploits. Why can't we go in? I asked. Well, my mother told me, they're afraid we'd laugh at them. 7

The prejudices of childhood are hard to outgrow. I confess that every time my business takes me past that club, I shudder. Images of large bellies resting on massage tables and flaccid penises rising and falling with the Dow Jones average flash through my head. There it is, chauvinism waving its cancerous tentacles from the depths of my psyche. 8

Minorities automatically feel superior to the oppressor because, after all, they are not hurting anybody. In fact, they feel morally better. The old canard that women need love, men need sex — believed for too long by both sexes — attributes moral and spiritual superiority to women and makes of men beasts whose urges send them prowling into the night. This false division of good and bad, placing deforming pressures on everyone, doesn't have to contaminate the future. We know that the assumptions we make about each other become a part of the cultural air we breathe and, in fact, become social truths. Women who want equality must be prepared to give it and to believe in it, and in order to do that it is not enough to state that you are as good as any man, but also it must be stated that he is as good as you and both will be humans together. If we want men to share in the care of the family in a new way, we must assume them as capable of consistent loving tenderness as we. 9

I rummage about and find in my thinking all kinds of anti-male prejudices. Some are just jokes and others I will have a hard 10 time abandoning. First, I share an emotional conviction with many sisters that women given power would not create wars. Intellectually I know that's ridiculous; great queens have waged war before; the likes of Lurleen Wallace, Pat Nixon and Mrs. General Lavelle can be depended upon in the future to guiltlessly condemn to death other people's children in the name of some ideal of their own. Little girls, of course, don't take toy guns out of their hip pockets and say "Pow, pow" to all their neighbors and friends like the average well-adjusted little boy. However, if we gave little girls the six-shooters, we would soon have double the pretend body count.

Aggression is not, as I secretly think, a male-sex-linked characteristic: brutality is masculine only by virtue of opportunity. True, there are 1,000 Jack the Rippers for every Lizzie Borden, but that surely is the result of social forms. Women as a group are indeed more masochistic than men. The practical result of this division is that women seem nicer and kinder, but when the world changes, women will have a fuller opportunity to be just as rotten as men and there will be fewer claims of female moral superiority. [11]

Now that I am entering early middle age, I hear many women complaining of husbands and ex-husbands who are attracted to younger females. This strikes the older woman as unfair, of course. But I remember a time when I thought all boys around my age and grade were creeps and bores. I wanted to go out with an older man: a senior or, miraculously, a college man. I had a certain contempt for my coevals, not realizing that the freshman in college I thought so desirable, was some older girl's creep. Some women never lose that contempt for men of their own age. That isn't fair either and may be one reason why some sensible men of middle years find solace in young women. [12]

I remember coming home from school one day to find my mother's card game dissolved in hysterical laughter. The cards were floating in black rivers of running mascara. What was so funny? A woman named Helen was lying on a couch pretending to be her husband with a cold. She was issuing demands for orange juice, aspirin, suggesting a call to a specialist, complaining of neglect, of fate's cruel finger, of heat, of cold, of sharp pains on the bridge of the nose that might indicate brain involvement. What was so funny? The ladies explained to me that all men behave just like that with colds, they are reduced to temper tantrums by simple [13] nasal congestion, men cannot stand any little physical discomfort — on and on the laughter went.

The point of this vignette is the nature of the laughter — us   14
laughing at them, us feeling superior to them, us ridiculing them behind their backs. If they were doing it to us we'd call it male chauvinist pigness; if we do it to them, it is inescapably female chauvinist sowness and, whatever its roots, it leads to the same isolation. Boys are messy, boys are mean, boys are rough, boys are stupid and have sloppy handwriting. A cacophony of childhood memories rushes through my head, balanced, of course, by all the well-documented feelings of inferiority and envy. But the important thing, the hard thing, is to wipe the slate clean, to start again without the meanness of the past. That's why it's so important that the women's movement not become anti-male and allow its most prejudiced spokesmen total leadership. The much-chewed-over abortion issue illustrates this. The women's-liberation position, insisting on a woman's right to determine her own body's destiny, leads in fanatical extreme to a kind of emotional immaculate conception in which the father is not judged even half-responsible — he has no rights, and no consideration is to be given to his concern for either the woman or the fetus.

Woman, who once was abandoned and disgraced by an un-   15
wanted pregnancy, has recently arrived at a new pride of ownership or disposal. She has traveled in a straight line that still excludes her sexual partner from an equal share in the wanted or unwanted pregnancy. A better style of life may develop from an assumption that men are as human as we. Why not ask the child's father if he would like to bring up the child? Why not share decisions, when possible, with the male? If we cut them out, assuming an old-style indifference on their part, we perpetrate the ugly divisiveness that has characterized relations between the sexes so far.

Hard as it is for many of us to believe, women are not really   16
superior to men in intelligence or humanity — they are only equal.

Meanings and Values

  1a. How would you describe the author's point of view in this selection? (See Guide to Terms: *Point of View*.)
    b. How did the tone help determine your answer? (Guide: *Style/Tone*.)

2. In the last sentence of paragraph 2 is an example of irony. (Guide: *Irony*.)
   a. What kind is it?
   b. Could it also be used to illustrate the meaning of "paradox"? (Guide: *Paradox*.) Why, or why not?
3a. Exactly what is the "myth" with which Roiphe is primarily concerned?
   b. Is it explained more by comparison or by contrast?
   c. Which aspects of it, if any, do young women of your acquaintance still seem to believe? Explain.
4. Show the special significance, in relation to the theme, of the author's mother's last answer in paragraph 7.
5. How is it possible, if at all, to "guiltlessly" condemn to death other people's children (par. 10)?

Expository Techniques

1. The central theme of this essay becomes clear more slowly than in most expository writings. (Guide: *Unity*.)
   a. At what point did you first become aware of it?
   b. Where is it first clearly stated?
   c. Is this statement specific or general? (Guide: *Specific/General*.)
   d. What is the primary function of the rest of the essay?
2a. Is the further development accomplished more by comparison or contrast? Explain.
   b. Cite paragraphs by which your answer to 2a can best be illustrated.
   c. Which pattern of exposition previously studied does the author use more freely in her comparison/contrast? How effectively?
3. Which of the standard means of introducing an exposition are used in this essay? (Guide: *Introductions*.)
4a. In paragraphs 6 and 7 can be found examples of both rhetorical and non-rhetorical questions. (Guide: *Rhetorical Question*.) Identify one of each and show the difference.
   b. Cite one further question used as a rhetorical device.
5a. Cite two examples of parallel structure in paragraph 14. (Guide: *Parallel Structure*.)
   b. What advantage, if any, is gained by use of this technique?
6. How effective is the brief closing paragraph? (Guide: *Closings*.) Why?

Diction and Vocabulary

1a. What is the significance of the word "sow," as used in the title?
   b. How, if at all, is this significance a matter of connotation? (Guide: *Connotation/Denotation*.)

2a. Cite five figures of speech that you consider particularly effective. (Guide: *Figures of Speech*.)

b. Indicate the kind of each.

3a. Which, if any, of the author's figures of speech could also be classed as a cliché. (Guide: *Clichés*.)

b. If any, is its use justified here? Why, or why not?

4. Would you consider any of the author's expressions colloquial? (Guide: *Colloquial Expressions*.) If so, which?

5. Explain briefly how your answers to questions 2–4 are related to matters of style. (Guide: *Style/Tone*.)

6. Use the dictionary as necessary to understand the meanings of the following words: lexicon (par. 3); empathetic, artifacts (6); flaccid (8); chauvinism (8, 14); canard (9); masochistic (11); coevals, solace (12); vignette, cacophony (14).

Suggestions for Writing and Discussion

1. Show by use of examples that it is also possible in other matters to "believe two contradictory things at once" (par. 2).

2. Has it been your observation that girls are less likely than boys to embarrass one in public or to lie about such things as grades or sexual prowess (par. 4)? Explain the difference, if any.

3. What justification is there for laws forcing men to pay alimony and/or child support (par. 5)?

4. Is there any *natural* reason that mothers are less apt to desert their children than fathers? In your estimation, is one desertion more reprehensible than the other? Explain.

5. Explore the author's assertion (par. 11) that women are more masochistic than men.

6. If applicable, select any one aspect of Roiphe's "myth" about men-women differences and show why you still consider the difference more fact than myth.

Writing Suggestions for Section 3
Comparison and Contrast

Base your central theme on one of the following, and develop your composition primarily by use of comparison and/or contrast. Use examples liberally for clarity and concreteness, chosen always with your purpose and reader-audience in mind.

1. Two kinds of home life.
2. The sea at two different times.
3. The innate qualifications needed for success in two careers.
4. The natural temperaments of two acquaintances.
5. Two poets.
6. The teaching techniques of two instructors or former teachers.
7. Two methods of parental handling of teenage problems.
8. Two family attitudes toward the practice of religion.
9. Two "moods" of the same town at different times.
10. The personalities (or atmospheres) of two cities or towns of similar size.
11. Two acquaintances who exemplify different ways of serving humanity.
12. Two acquaintances who seem to symbolize different philosophies of life.
13. Two different attitudes toward the same thing or activity: one "practical," the other romantic or aesthetic.
14. The beliefs and practices of two religions or denominations concerning *one* aspect of religion.
15. Two courses on the same subject: one in high school and one in college.
16. The differing styles of two players of some sport or game.
17. The hazards of frontier life and those of today.
18. The views of two recent presidents concerning the trappings of high office.

4

Using *Analogy* as an Expository Device

Analogy is a special form of comparison that is used for a specific purpose: to explain something abstract or difficult to understand by showing its similarity to something concrete or easy to understand. A much less commonly used technique than logical comparison (and contrast), analogy is, nonetheless, a highly efficient means of explaining some difficult concepts or of giving added force to the explanations.

Logical comparison is made between two members of the same general class, usually assuming the same kind of interest in the subject matter of both. But in analogy we are really concerned only with the subject matter of one, using a second just to help explain the first. The two subjects, quite incomparable in most respects, are never of the same general class; if they are, we then have logical comparison, not analogy.

If the analogy is to be effective, the writer should be able to assume that his reader is familiar enough with the easier subject, or can quickly be made so, that it really helps explain the more difficult one. A common example is the explanation of the human circulatory system, which we may have trouble comprehending, by comparing the heart and arteries with a pump forcing water through the pipes of a plumbing system. This analogy has been carried further to liken the effect of cholesterol deposits on the inner walls of the arteries to mineral deposits that accumulate inside water pipes and eventually close them entirely. Although there is little logical similarity between a steel pipe and a human artery, the *analogical* similarity would be apparent to most readers — but the analogy might cause even greater confusion for any who did not know about pumps.

Distinguishing between analogy and metaphor is sometimes difficult. The difference is basically in their purpose: the function of a metaphor is merely *to describe*, to create a brief, vivid image for the reader; the function of analogy is primarily one of exposition, *to explain*, rather than to describe. In this sense, however, the function of a metaphor is actually *to suggest* an analogy: instead of showing the similarities of the heart and the pump, a metaphor might simply refer to "that faithful pump inside my chest," implying enough of a comparison to serve its purpose as description. (We can see here why some people refer to analogy as "extended" metaphor.) The analogist, when trying to explain the wide selection of college subjects and the need for balance in a course of study, could use the easily understood principle of a cafeteria, which serves Jell-O and lemon meringue pie, as well as meat and potatoes. If his purpose had been only to create an image, to describe, he might have referred simply to the bewildering variety in "the cafeteria of college courses" — and that would have been a metaphor.

Sometimes related metaphors, however, through continued use to explain an abstract concept, can in effect work together to *build* a kind of analogy. You may already have seen this process at work in Donald Hall's "Reading Tastes and Habits" (Sec. 2), in his explanation of the fourth type of reading. (For still another example of the more conventional type of analogy, see the explanation of *Unity*, in Guide to Terms.)

But as useful as analogy can be in exposition, it is a risky technique to use in logical argument. It should never be offered anywhere as *proof*. The two subjects of any analogy, although similar in one or more ways useful for illustration, are basically too unlike for any reliable conclusions to be drawn from their similarity.

ALVIN TOFFLER

ALVIN TOFFLER (born 1928), a native of New York City and graduate of New York University, has been a Washington correspondent for various newspapers and magazines. His freelance articles still appear regularly in professional journals and in numerous magazines, most often in *Seventeen* and *Saturday Evening Post*. At one time he was an associate editor of *Fortune*. Toffler has served on the faculty of the New School for Social Research and has lectured at Cornell and other universities. In addition to *Future Shock*, his most famous book, he has written *The Culture Consumers* (1964), and has edited *Schoolhouse in the City* (1968), *The Futurists* (1972), *Learning for Tomorrow* (1974), and *The Eco-Spasm Report: Why Our Economy Is Running Out of Control* (1975).

Modular Man

"Modular Man" (editor's title) is from the chapter "The Cost of Involvement" in Toffler's best-seller *Future Shock*, published in 1970. Here he has used simple analogy to help explain his concept of a personal problem imposed on city dwellers by increasing "urbanism."

Urbanism — the city dweller's way of life — has preoccupied sociology since the turn of the century. Max Weber pointed out the obvious fact that people in cities cannot know all their neighbors as intimately as it was possible for them to do in small communities. Georg Simmel carried this idea one step further when he declared, rather quaintly, that if the urban individual reacted emotionally to each and every person with whom he came into contact, or cluttered his mind with information about them, he would be "completely atomized internally and would fall into an unthinkable mental condition."   1

Louis Wirth, in turn, noted the fragmented nature of urban   2 relationships. "Characteristically, urbanites meet one another in highly segmental roles . . ." he wrote, "Their dependence upon others is confined to a highly fractionalized aspect of the other's round of activity." Rather than becoming deeply involved with the total personality of every individual we meet, he explained, we necessarily maintain superficial and partial contact with some. We are interested only in the efficiency of the shoe salesman in meeting our needs; we couldn't care less that his wife is an alcoholic.

What this means is that we form limited involvement relationships with most of the people around us. Consciously or not we define our relationships with most people in functional terms. So long as we do not become involved with the shoe salesman's problems at home, or his more general hopes, dreams and frustrations, he is, for us, fully interchangeable with any other salesman of equal competence. In effect, we have applied the modular principle to human relationships. We have created the disposable person: Modular Man.

Rather than entangling ourselves with the whole man, we plug into a module of his personality. Each personality can be imagined as a unique configuration of thousands of such modules. Thus no whole person is interchangeable with any other. But certain modules are. Since we are seeking only to buy a pair of shoes, and not the friendship, love or hate of the salesman, it is not necessary for us to tap into or engage with all the other modules that form his personality. Our relationship is safely limited. There is limited liability on both sides. The relationship entails certain accepted forms of behavior and communication. Both sides understand, consciously or otherwise, the limitations and laws. Difficulties arise only when one or another party oversteps the tacitly understood limits, when he attempts to connect up with some module not relevant to the function at hand.

Today a vast sociological and psychological literature is devoted to the alienation presumed to flow from this fragmentation of relationships. Much of the rhetoric of existentialism and the student revolt decries this fragmentation. It is said that we are not sufficiently "involved" with our fellow man. Millions of young people go about seeking "total involvement."

Before leaping to the popular conclusion that modularization is all bad, however, it might be well to look more closely at the matter. Theologian Harvey Cox, echoing Simmel, has pointed out that in an urban environment the attempt to "involve" oneself fully with everyone can lead only to self-destruction and emotional emptiness. Urban man, he writes, "must have more or less impersonal relationships with most of the people with whom he comes in contact precisely in order to choose certain friendships to nourish and cultivate ... His life represents a point touched by dozens of systems and hundreds of people. His capacity to know some of them better necessitates his minimizing the depth of his relationship to many others. Listening to the postman gossip becomes for the urban man an act of sheer graciousness, since he probably has no interest in the people the postman wants to talk about."

Moreover, before lamenting modularization, it is necessary to ask ourselves whether we really would prefer to return to the traditional condition of man in which each individual presumably related to the whole personality of a few people rather than to the personality modules of many. Traditional man has been so sentimentalized, so cloyingly romanticized, that we frequently overlook the consequences of such a return. The very same writers who lament fragmentation also demand freedom — yet overlook the un-freedom of people bound together in totalistic relationships. For any relationship implies mutual demands and expectations. The more intimately involved a relationship, the greater the pressure the parties exert on one another to fulfill these expectations. The tighter and more totalistic the relationship, the more modules, so to speak, are brought into play, and the more numerous are the demands we make.

In a modular relationship, the demands are strictly bounded. So long as the shoe salesman performs his rather limited service for us, thereby fulfilling our rather limited expectations, we do not insist that he believe in our God, or that he be tidy at home, or share our political values, or enjoy the same kind of food or music that we do. We leave him free in all other matters — as he leaves us free to be atheist or Jew, heterosexual or homosexual, John Bircher or Communist. This is not true of the total relationship and cannot be. To a certain point, fragmentation and freedom go together.

All of us seem to need some totalistic relationships in our lives. But to decry the fact that we cannot have *only* such relationships is nonsense. And to prefer a society in which the individual has holistic relationships with a few, *rather than* modular relationships with many, is to wish for a return to the imprisonment of the past — a past when individuals may have been more tightly bound to one another, but when they were also more tightly regimented by social conventions, sexual mores, political and religious restrictions.

This is not to say that modular relationships entail no risks or   10
that this is the best of all possible worlds. There are, in fact, profound risks in the situation. . . . Until now, however, the entire public and professional discussion of these issues has been badly out of focus.

Meanings and Values

1a. Explain further, using examples, the "limitations and laws" which "both sides" understand in typical urban contact with other people (par. 4).
 b. Just what happens when one of the parties oversteps the limits?

2. Why is it necessary to limit relationships with most people to know a few others well (par. 6) — e.g., is this merely a matter of the limitation of time?

3a. How is it that "traditional man" has become romanticized (par. 7)?
 b. Is there anything ironical in thus overlooking the "un-freedom" of people totally involved with each other? (See Guide to Terms: *Irony*.) Explain.

4. Use the three-point system of evaluation to measure the success of this selection. (Guide: *Evaluation*.)

Expository Techniques

1a. Where does Toffler's analogy begin?
 b. Why can it not qualify as logical comparison?
 c. Why not as metaphor?
 d. How successfully does it fulfill the basic purpose of analogy?

2a. Cite two examples each of loose and periodic sentences. (Guide: *Emphasis*.)
 b. In what way is the use of these a matter of emphasis?
 c. How, if at all, is such usage related to syntax? (Guide: *Syntax*.)

3a. Illustrate the meaning of "parallel structure" by examples from paragraph 8. (Guide: *Parallel Structure*.)
 b. If the use of such structures is also a matter of syntax, explain how.

4a. How does Toffler make the highly generalized statement of Louis Wirth more specific (par. 2)? (Guide: *Specific/General*.)
 b. In which paragraphs is this specific put to still further uses?

Diction and Vocabulary

1a. The word "modular" has in very recent years taken on new meaning in everyday parlance. Supply as many examples as possible of this newer usage. (The word itself could be used, of course, to illustrate the fact that our language is in a constant state of change.)

   b. How appropriate is the word to the purposes of this analogy?

2. If not already familiar with the following words as they are used in this selection, consult your dictionary for their meanings: configuration, entails, tacitly (4); existentialism (5); cloyingly (7).

Suggestions for Writing and Discussion

1. Explain fully, using examples as necessary, what may happen to the urban dweller who gets too involved with too many "total personalities."

2. Trace the process by which an increasing intimacy of relationship between two people (preferably *not* romantic) increases the pressures on each other (par. 7).

3. Do you agree that all of us need some totalistic relationships in our lives (par. 9)? How can this be, with the inevitable result of restriction on our own freedom?

4. Where may we still find situations in which individuals are "tightly bound to one another" within a group (par. 9), with modular relationships severely limited? If you have had experience in such a situation, explain its effect on freedom.

5. Discuss some of the most apparent "profound risks" entailed in modular relationships (par. 10).

(NOTE: Suggestions for topics requiring development by use of ANALOGY are on page 121 at the end of this section.)

JAMES RETTIE

JAMES RETTIE was an employee of the National Forest Service's experimental station at Upper Darby, Pennsylvania in 1948 when he adapted this fable from a United States Department of Agriculture pamphlet entitled "To Hold This Soil." At the time, he was a member of The Society of the Friends of the Land and an ardent conservationist.

But a Watch in the Night

"But a Watch in the Night"[1] is a highly innovative analogy and serves to illustrate, among other things, the extreme versatility of this pattern of exposition. The analogy itself (a "scientific fable," as the author has called it) is composed almost entirely of narration (a pattern to be studied further in Section 9). While Rettie has taken numerous creative liberties not often available to the student in ordinary college writing, he apparently was very much aware of the same goal we all need to keep in mind when writing: the desired effect, for *his* purposes, on *his* reader-audience.

Out beyond our solar system there is a planet called Copernicus. 1
It came into existence some four or five billion years before the

"But a Watch in the Night" by James C. Rettie from *Forever the Land*, edited by Russell and Kate Lord. Copyright 1950 by Harper & Row, Publishers, Inc. Reprinted by permission of the publishers.

[1] From the Bible, Psalm 90, apparently either slightly altered or using a translation other than the King James version, which reads:

Lord, thou hast been our dwelling place
In all generations.
Before the mountains were brought forth,
Or ever thou hadst formed the earth and the world,
Even from everlasting to everlasting, thou art God.
Thou turnest man to destruction;
And sayest, "Return, ye children of men."
For a thousand years in thy sight
Are but as yesterday when it is past,
And as a watch in the night. . . .

birth of our Earth. In due course of time it became inhabited by a race of intelligent men.

About 750 million years ago the Copernicans had developed the motion picture machine to a point well in advance of the stage that we have reached. Most of the cameras that we now use in motion picture work are geared to take twenty-four pictures per second on a continuous strip of film. When such film is run through a projector, it throws a series of images on the screen and these change with a rapidity that gives the visual impression of normal movement. If a motion is too swift for the human eye to see it in detail, it can be captured and artificially slowed down by means of the slow-motion camera. This one is geared to take many more shots per second — ninety-six or even more than that. When the slow-motion film is projected at the normal speed of twenty-four pictures per second, we can see just how the jumping horse goes over a hurdle. 2

What about motion that is too slow to be seen by the human eye? That problem has been solved by the use of the time-lapse camera. In this one, the shutter is geared to take only one shot per second, or one per minute, or even one per hour — depending upon the kind of movement that is being photographed. When the time-lapse film is projected at the normal speed of twenty-four pictures per second, it is possible to see a bean sprout growing up out of the ground. Time-lapse films are useful in the study of many types of motion too slow to be observed by the unaided, human eye. 3

The Copernicans, it seems, had time-lapse cameras some 757 million years ago and they also had superpowered telescopes that gave them a clear view of what was happening upon this Earth. They decided to make a film record of the life history of Earth and to make it on the scale of one picture per year. The photography has been in progress during the last 757 million years. 4

In the near future, a Copernican interstellar expedition will arrive upon our Earth and bring with it a copy of the time-lapse film. Arrangements will be made for showing the entire film in one continuous run. This will begin at midnight of New Year's eve and continue day and night without a single stop until midnight of December 31. The rate of projection will be twenty-four pictures per second. Time on the screen will thus seem to move at the rate of twenty-four years per second; 1,440 years per minute; 86,400 years per hour; approximately two million years per day; and 62 million years per month. The normal life-span of individual man 5 will occupy about three seconds. The full period of Earth history that will be unfolded on the screen (some 757 million years) will extend from what the geologists call Pre-Cambrian times up to the present. This will, by no means, cover the full time-span of the Earth's geological history but it will embrace the period since the advent of living organisms.

During the months of January, February and March the pic-   6
ture will be desolate and dreary. The shape of the land masses and the oceans will bear little or no resemblance to those that we know. The violence of geological erosion will be much in evidence. Rains will pour down on the land and promptly go booming down to the seas. There will be no clear streams anywhere except where the rains fall upon hard rock. Everywhere on the steeper ground the stream channels will be filled with boulders hurled down by rushing waters. Raging torrents and dry stream beds will keep alternating in quick succession. High mountains will seem to melt like so much butter in the sun. The shifting of land into the seas, later to be thrust up as new mountains, will be going on at a grand scale.

Early in April there will be some indication of the presence of   7
single-celled living organisms in some of the warmer and sheltered coastal waters. By the end of the month it will be noticed that some of these organisms have become multicellular. A few of them, including the Trilobites, will be encased in hard shells.

Toward the end of May, the first vertebrates will appear, but   8
they will still be aquatic creatures. In June about 60 percent of the land area that we know as North America will be under water. One broad channel will occupy the space where the Rocky Mountains now stand. Great deposits of limestone will be forming under some of the shallower seas. Oil and gas deposits will be in process of formation — also under shallow seas. On land there will still be no sign of vegetation. Erosion will be rampant, tearing loose particles and chunks of rock and grinding them into sand and silt to be spewed out by the streams into bays and estuaries.

About the middle of July the first land plants will appear and   9
take up the tremendous job of soil building. Slowly, very slowly, the mat of vegetation will spread, always battling for its life against the power of erosion. Almost foot by foot, the plant life will advance, lacing down with its root structures whatever pulverized rock material it can find. Leaves and stems will be giving added protection against the loss of the soil foothold. The increasing veg-

etation will pave the way for the land animals that will live upon it.

Early in August the seas will be teeming with fish. This will 10 be what geologists call the Devonian period. Some of the races of these fish will be breathing by means of lung tissue instead of through gill tissues. Before the month is over, some of the lung fish will go ashore and take on a crude lizard-like appearance. Here are the first amphibians.

In early September the insects will put in their appearance. 11 Some will look like huge dragon flies and will have a wingspread of 24 inches. Large portions of the land masses will now be covered with heavy vegetation that will include the primitive spore-propagating trees. Layer upon layer of this plant growth will build up, later to appear as the coal deposits. About the middle of this month, there will be evidence of the first seed-bearing plants and the first reptiles. Heretofore, the land animals will have been amphibians that could reproduce their kind only by depositing a soft egg mass in quiet waters. The reptiles will be shown to be freed from the aquatic bond because they can reproduce by means of a shelled egg in which the embryo and its nurturing liquids are sealed in and thus protected from destructive evaporation. Before September is over, the first dinosaurs will be seen — creatures destined to dominate the animal realm for about 140 million years and then to disappear.

In October there will be series of mountain uplifts along what 12 is now the eastern coast of the United States. A creature with feathered limbs — half bird and half reptile in appearance — will take itself into the air. Some small and rather unpretentious animals will be seen to bring forth their young in a form that is a miniature replica of the parents and to feed these young on milk secreted by mammary glands in the female parent. The emergence of this mammalian form of animal life will be recognized as one of the great events in geologic time. October will also witness the high water mark of the dinosaurs — creatures ranging in size from that of the modern goat to monsters like Brontosaurus that weighed some 40 tons. Most of them will be placid vegetarians, but a few will be hideous-looking carnivores, like Allosaurus and Tyrannosaurus. Some of the herbivorous dinosaurs will be clad in bony armor for protection against their flesh-eating comrades.

November will bring pictures of a sea extending from the Gulf 13 of Mexico to the Arctic in space now occupied by the Rocky Mountains. A few of the reptiles will take to the air on bat-like wings. One of these, called Pteranodon, will have a wingspread of 15 feet. There will be a rapid development of the modern flowering plants, modern trees, and modern insects. The dinosaurs will disappear. Toward the end of the month there will be a tremendous land disturbance in which the Rocky Mountains will rise out of the sea to assume a dominating place in the North American landscape.

As the picture runs on into December it will show the mammals in command of the animal life. Seed-bearing trees and grasses will have covered most of the land with a heavy mantle of vegetation. Only the areas newly thrust up from the sea will be barren. Most of the streams will be crystal clear. The turmoil of geologic erosion will be confined to localized areas. About December 25 will begin the cutting of the Grand Canyon of the Colorado River. Grinding down through layer after layer of sedimentary strata, this stream will finally expose deposits laid down in Pre-Cambrian times. Thus in the walls of that canyon will appear geological formations dating from recent times to the period when the earth had no living organisms upon it.

The picture will run on through the latter days of December and even up to its final day with still no sign of mankind. The spectators will become alarmed in the fear that man has somehow been left out. But not so; sometime about noon on December 31 (one million years ago) will appear a stooped, massive creature of man-like proportions. This will be Pithecanthropus, the Java ape man. For tools and weapons he will have nothing but crude stone and wooden clubs. His children will live a precarious existence threatened on the one side by hostile animals and on the other by tremendous climatic changes. Ice sheets — in places 4000 feet deep — will form in the northern parts of North America and Eurasia. Four times this glacial ice will push southward to cover half the continents. With each advance the plant and animal life will be swept under or pushed southward. With each recession of the ice, life will struggle to reestablish itself in the wake of the retreating glaciers. The wooly mammoth, the musk ox, and the caribou all will fight to maintain themselves near the ice line. Sometimes they will be caught and put into cold storage — skin, flesh, blood, bones and all.

The picture will run on through supper time with still very little evidence of man's presence on the Earth. It will be about 11 o'clock when Neanderthal man appears. Another half hour will go by before the appearance of Cro-Magnon man living in caves and painting crude animal pictures on the walls of his dwelling. Fifteen minutes more will bring Neolithic man, knowing how to chip stone and thus produce sharp cutting edges for spears and tools. In a few minutes more it will appear that man has domesticated the dog, the sheep and, possibly, other animals. He will then begin the use of milk. He will also learn the arts of basket weaving and the making of pottery and dugout canoes.

The dawn of civilization will not come until about five or six 17 minutes before the end of the picture. The story of the Egyptians, the Babylonians, the Greeks, and the Romans will unroll during the fourth, the third and the second minute before the end. At 58 minutes and 43 seconds past 11:00 P.M. (just 1 minute and 17 seconds before the end) will come the beginning of the Christian era. Columbus will discover the new world 20 seconds before the end. The Declaration of Independence will be signed just 7 seconds before the final curtain comes down.

In those few moments of geologic time will be the story of all 18 that has happened since we became a nation. And what a story it will be! A human swarm will sweep across the face of the continent and take it away from the . . . red men. They will change it far more radically than it has ever been changed before in a comparable time. The great virgin forests will be seen going down before ax and fire. The soil, covered for aeons by its protective mantle of trees and grasses, will be laid bare to the ravages of water and wind erosion. Streams that had been flowing clear will, once again, take up a load of silt and push it toward the seas. Humus and mineral salts, both vital elements of productive soil, will be seen to vanish at a terrifying rate. The railroads and highways and cities that will spring up may divert attention, but they cannot cover up the blight of man's recent activities. In great sections of Asia, it will be seen that man must utilize cow dung and every scrap of available straw or grass for fuel to cook his food. The forests that once provided wood for this purpose will be gone without a trace. The use of these agricultural wastes for fuel, in place of returning them to the land, will be leading to increasing soil impoverishment. Here and there will be seen a dust storm darkening the landscape over an area a thousand miles across. Man-creatures will be shown counting their wealth in terms of bits of printed paper representing other bits of a scarce but comparatively useless yellow metal that is kept buried in strong vaults. Meanwhile, the soil, the only real wealth that can keep mankind alive on the face of this Earth is savagely being cut loose from its ancient moorings and washed into the seven seas.

We have just arrived upon this Earth. How long will we stay?   19

Meanings and Values

1a. What is the significance of the quotation, as it is used in the title of this essay?
 b. Is the title itself an allusion? Why, or why not? (See Guide to Terms: *Figures of Speech*.)
 c. Explain why you personally do, or do not, like the title.

2a. What do you find ironical in the latter part of paragraph 18? (Guide: *Irony*.)
 b. What kind of irony is it?

3a. Compare the effectiveness of Rettie's unique handling of the soil-loss problem with the methods commonly used for environmental propaganda.
 b. Could he have enlarged it effectively to include other environmental problems? Why, or why not?

Expository Techniques

1a. In what respects does "But a Watch in the Night" qualify as analogy?
 b. Why could the author not have achieved his purpose as well by showing us more simply, in actual year-spans, the brevity of human existence on earth, rather than by this condensed movie version?

2a. The author devotes five paragraphs just to setting up his analogy. In what way, or ways, might this slow beginning be justified?
 b. Does the analogy benefit by such a detailed explanation of the camera's capabilities? How, or why not?
 c. Why do you suppose Rettie created a fictional planet?
 d. Should he have told us at some point that the whole thing is make-believe? Why, or why not?

3a. Why do you think the author took the trouble to work out the rate of projection to fit exactly into one year?
 b. What is gained, or lost, by learning as early as paragraph 5 that the normal life span of individual man would occupy only about three seconds?

4a. What did you believe at first to be the central theme? (Guide: *Unity.*)
   b. How did your impression of the theme become modified in paragraph 5?
   c. In view of the overall essay, state what you now believe to have been the author's theme.
   d. Does the composition have unity—i.e., do all parts serve as tributaries, however indirect, into the central theme?

5a. Explain fully, in terms of "emphasis," why this slow unfolding of real theme helps, or hinders, in achieving the author's apparent purpose. (Guide: *Emphasis.*)
   b. This is a more "creative" piece than most expositions. Why would such a slow unfolding be inappropriate to most college and workaday writing?

6. What advantage is gained, if any, by the parallel beginnings of most paragraphs? (Guide: *Parallel Structures.*)

7a. What criteria did Rettie apparently use in selecting, from among thousands, the details to be included in the various time periods?
   b. Would it have been better to use some other criteria? Why, or why not?

8a. A rhetorical question is used here in a highly strategic position. Where is it? (Guide: *Rhetorical Question.*)
   b. How effective is its use?

Diction and Vocabulary

1a. The naming of the planet makes use, rather indirectly, of an allusion. To what does it refer? (Guide: *Figures of Speech.*)
   b. Why is it appropriate, or inappropriate, for this piece?

2a. What kind of figure of speech do you find in paragraph 6?
   b. In paragraph 17 is a figure of speech that is also a cliché. What is it? (Guide: *Figures of Speech, Cliché.*)
   c. What kind of figure of speech is it?
   d. Why is it also classifiable as a cliché?

Suggestions for Writing and Discussion

1. What practical steps could be taken now to prevent the rest of our "only real wealth" from being washed into the sea? What are the chances of such steps being taken seriously enough, soon enough?

2. Assuming that our food-production technology continues to advance

rapidly, is it conceivable that mankind might manage to survive without much soil? Discuss this possibility.

3. If you are particularly interested in the Bible, for either literary or religious reasons, discuss more fully the meanings of the part of Psalm 90 quoted in the introduction. If you like, you may enlarge your discussion to include the entire psalm.

(NOTE: Suggestions for topics requiring development by use of ANALOGY are on page 121 at the end of this section.)

TOM WOLFE

Tom Wolfe grew up in Richmond, Virginia, was graduated
from Washington and Lee University, and took his doctorate
at Yale. After working for several years as a reporter for *The
Washington Post,* he joined the staff of the New York *Herald
Tribune* in 1962. He has won two Washington Newspaper
Guild Awards, one for humor and the other for foreign news.
Wolfe has been a regular contributor to *New York, Esquire,*
and other magazines. His books include *The Kandy-Kolored
Tangerine-Flake Streamline Baby* (1965), *The Electric Kool-
Aid Acid Test* (1968), *Radical Chic and Mau-mauing the
Flak Catchers* (1970), *The New Journalism* (1973), *The Painted
Word* (1975), and *The Right Stuff* (1977).

O Rotten Gotham—
Sliding Down into the Behavioral Sink

"O Rotten Gotham — Sliding Down into the Behavioral Sink,"
as used here, is excerpted from a longer selection by that title
in Wolfe's book *The Pump House Gang* (1968). Here, as he
frequently does, the author investigates an important aspect
of modern life — seriously, but in his characteristic and seem-
ingly freewheeling style. It is a style that is sometimes ridi-
culed by scholars but is far more often admired. (Wolfe, as the
serious student can discover for himself, is always in complete
control of his materials and methods, using them to create certain effects, to reinforce his ideas.) In this piece his analogy is
particularly noteworthy for the extensive usage he is able to
get from it.

I just spent two days with Edward T. Hall, an anthropologist, 1
watching thousands of my fellow New Yorkers short-circuiting

themselves into hot little twitching death balls with jolts of their own adrenalin. Dr. Hall says it is overcrowding that does it. Overcrowding gets the adrenalin going, and the adrenalin gets them queer, autistic, sadistic, barren, batty, sloppy, hot-in-the-pants, chancred-on-the-flankers, leering, puling, numb — the usual in New York, in other words, and God knows what else. Dr. Hall has the theory that overcrowding has already thrown New York into a state of behavioral sink. Behavioral sink is a term from ethology, which is the study of how animals relate to their environment. Among animals, the sink winds up with a "population collapse" or "massive die-off." O rotten Gotham.

It got to be easy to look at New Yorkers as animals, especially looking down from some place like a balcony at Grand Central at the rush hour Friday afternoon. The floor was filled with the poor white humans, running around, dodging, blinking their eyes, making a sound like a pen full of starlings or rats or something.

"Listen to them skid," says Dr. Hall.

He was right. The poor old etiolate animals were out there skidding on their rubber soles. You could hear it once he pointed it out. They stop short to keep from hitting somebody or because they are disoriented and they suddenly stop and look around, and they skid on their rubber-soled shoes, and a screech goes up. They pour out onto the floor down the escalators from the Pan-Am Building, from 42nd Street, from Lexington Avenue, up out of subways, down into subways, railroad trains, up into helicopters —

"You can also hear the helicopters all the way down here," says Dr. Hall. The sound of the helicopters using the roof of the Pan-Am Building nearly fifty stories up beats right through. "If it weren't for this ceiling" — he is referring to the very high ceiling in Grand Central — "this place would be unbearable with this kind of crowding. And yet they'll probably never 'waste' space like this again."

They screech! And the adrenal glands in all those poor white animals enlarge, micrometer by micrometer, to the size of cantaloupes. Dr. Hall pulls a Minox camera out of a holster he has on his belt and starts shooting away at the human scurry. The Sink!

Dr. Hall has the Minox up to his eye — he is a slender man, calm, 52 years old, young-looking, an anthropologist who has worked with Navajos, Hopis, Spanish-Americans, Negroes, Trukese. He was the most important anthropologist in the government during the crucial years of the foreign aid program, the 1950's. He directed both the Point Four training program and the Human Relations Area Files. He wrote *The Silent Language* and *The Hidden Dimension*, two books that are picking up the kind of "underground" following his friend Marshall McLuhan started picking up about five years ago. He teaches at the Illinois Institute of Technology, lives with his wife, Mildred, in a high-ceilinged town house on one of the last great residential streets in downtown Chicago, Astor Street; he has a grown son and daughter, loves good food, good wine, the relaxed, civilized life — but comes to New York with a Minox at his eye to record! — perfect —The Sink.

We really got down in there by walking down into the Lexington Avenue line subway stop under Grand Central. We inhaled those nice big fluffy fumes of human sweat, urine, effluvia, and sebaceous secretions. One old female human was already stroked out on the upper level, on a stretcher, with two policemen standing by. The other humans barely looked at her. They rushed into line. They bellied each other, haunch to paunch, down the stairs. Human heads shone through the gratings. The species North European tried to create bubbles of space around themselves, about a foot and a half in diameter — 8

"See, he's reacting against the line," says Dr. Hall. 9

— but the species Mediterranean presses on in. The hell with 10 bubbles of space. The species North European resents that, this male human behind him presses forward toward the booth ... *breathing* on him, he's disgusted, he pulls out of the line entirely, the species Mediterranean resents him for resenting it, and neither of them realizes what the hell they are getting irritable about exactly. And in all of them the old adrenals grow another micrometer.

Dr. Hall whips out the Minox. Too perfect! The bottom of 11 The Sink.

It is the sheer overcrowding, such as occurs in the business 12 sections of Manhattan five days a week and in Harlem, Bedford-Stuyvesant, southeast Bronx every day — sheer overcrowding is converting New Yorkers into animals in a sink pen. Dr. Hall's argument runs as follows: all animals, including birds, seem to have a built-in, inherited requirement to have a certain amount of territory, space, to lead their lives in. Even if they have all the food they need, and there are no predatory animals threatening them, they cannot tolerate crowding beyond a certain point. No more than two hundred wild Norway rats can survive on a quarter acre of ground, for example, even when they are given all the food they can eat. They just die off.

But why? To find out, ethologists have run experiments on all 13 sorts of animals, from stickleback crabs to Sika deer. In one major experiment, an ethologist named John Calhoun put some domesticated white Norway rats in a pen with four sections to it, connected by ramps. Calhoun knew from previous experiments that the rats tend to split up into groups of ten to twelve and that the pen, therefore, would hold forty to forty-eight rats comfortably, assuming they formed four equal groups. He allowed them to reproduce until there were eighty rats, balanced between male and female, but did not let it get any more crowded. He kept them supplied with plenty of food, water, and nesting materials. In other words, all their more obvious needs were taken care of. A less obvious need — space —was not. To the human eye, the pen did not even look especially crowded. But to the rats, it was crowded beyond endurance.

The entire colony was soon plunged into a profound be- 14 havioral sink. "The sink," said Calhoun, "is the outcome of any behavioral process that collects animals together in unusually great numbers. The unhealthy connotations of the term are not accidental: a behavioral sink does act to aggravate all forms of pathology that can be found within a group."

For a start, long before the rat population reached eighty, a 15 status hierarchy had developed in the pen. Two dominant male rats took over the two end sections, acquired harems of eight to ten females each, and forced the rest of the rats into the two middle pens. All the overcrowding took place in the middle pens. That was where the "sink" hit. The aristocrat rats at the end grew bigger, sleeker, healthier, and more secure the whole time.

In The Sink, meanwhile, nest building, courting, sex behavior, 16 reproduction, social organization, health — all of it went to pieces. Normally, Norway rats have a mating ritual in which the male chases the female, the female ducks down into a burrow and sticks her head up to watch the male. He performs a little dance outside the burrow, then she comes out, and he mounts her, usually for a few seconds. When The Sink set in, however, no more than three males — the dominant males in the middle sections — kept up the

old customs. The rest tried everything from satyrism to homosexuality or else gave up on sex altogether. Some of the subordinate
males spent all their time chasing females. Three or four might
chase one female at the same time, and instead of stopping at the
burrow entrance for the ritual, they would charge right in. Once
mounted, they would hold on for minutes instead of the usual
seconds.

Homosexuality rose sharply. So did bisexuality. Some males   17
would mount anything — males, females, babies, senescent rats,
anything. Still other males dropped sexual activity altogether,
wouldn't fight and, in fact, would hardly move except when the
other rats slept. Occasionally a female from the aristocrat rats'
harems would come over the ramps and into the middle sections to
sample life in The Sink. When she had had enough, she would run
back up the ramp. Sink males would give chase up to the top of the
ramp, which is to say, to the very edge of the aristocratic preserve.
But one glance from one of the king rats would stop them cold and
they would return to The Sink.

The slumming females from the harems had their adventures   18
and then returned to a placid, healthy life. Females in The Sink,
however, were ravaged, physically and psychologically. Pregnant
rats had trouble continuing pregnancy. The rate of miscarriages
increased significantly, and females started dying from tumors and
other disorders of the mammary glands, sex organs, uterus, ovaries,
and Fallopian tubes. Typically, their kidneys, livers, and adrenals
were also enlarged or diseased or showed other signs associated
with stress.

Child-rearing became totally disorganized. The females lost   19
the interest or the stamina to build nests and did not keep them up
if they did build them. In the general filth and confusion, they
would not put themselves out to save offspring they were momen-
tarily separated from. Frantic, even sadistic competition among the
males were going on all around them and rendering their lives
chaotic. The males began unprovoked and senseless assaults upon
one another, often in the form of tail-biting. Ordinarily, rats will
suppress this kind of behavior when it crops up. In The Sink, male
rats gave up all policing and just looked out for themselves. The
"pecking order" among males in The Sink was never stable. Normally, male rats set up a three-class structure. Under the pressure
of overcrowding, however, they broke up into all sorts of unstable

subclasses, cliques, packs — and constantly pushed, probed, explored, tested one another's power. Anyone was fair game, except for the aristocrats in the end pens.

Calhoun kept the population down to eighty, so that the next 20 stage, "population collapse" or "massive die-off," did not occur. But the autopsies showed that the pattern — as in the diseases among the female rats — was already there.

The classic study of die-off was John J. Christian's study of 21 Sika deer on James Island in the Chesapeake Bay, west of Cambridge, Maryland. Four or five of the deer had been released on the island, which was 280 acres and uninhabited, in 1916. By 1955 they had bred freely into a herd of 280 to 300. The population density was only about one deer per acre at this point, but Christian knew that this was already too high for the Sikas' inborn space requirements, and something would give before long. For two years the number of deer remained 280 to 300. But suddenly, in 1958, over half the deer died; 161 carcasses were recovered. In 1959 more deer died and the population steadied at about 80.

In two years, two-thirds of the herd had died. Why? It was 22 not starvation. In fact, all the deer collected were in excellent condition, with well-developed muscles, shining coats, and fat deposits between the muscles. In practically all the deer, however, the adrenal glands had enlarged by 50 percent. Christian concluded that the die-off was due to "shock following severe metabolic disturbance, probably as a result of prolonged adrenocortical hyperactivity. . . . There was no evidence of infection, starvation, or other obvious cause to explain the mass mortality." In other words, the constant stress of overpopulation, plus the normal stress of the cold of the winter, had kept the adrenalin flowing so constantly in the deer that their systems were depleted of blood sugar and they died of shock.

Well, the white humans are still skidding and darting across 23 the floor of Grand Central. Dr. Hall listens a moment longer to the skidding and the darting noises, and then says, "You know, I've been on commuter trains here after everyone has been through one of these rushes, and I'll tell you, there is enough acid flowing in the stomachs in every car to dissolve the rails underneath."

Just a little invisible acid bath for the linings to round off the 24 day. The ulcers the acids cause, of course, are the one disease people have already been taught to associate with the stress of city life.

But overcrowding, as Dr. Hall sees it, raises a lot more hell with the body than just ulcers. In everyday life in New York — just the usual, getting to work, working in massively congested areas like 42nd Street between Fifth Avenue and Lexington, especially now that the Pan-Am Building is set in there, working in cubicles such as those in the editorial offices at Time-Life, Inc., which Dr. Hall cites as typical of New York's poor handling of space, working in cubicles with low ceilings and, often, no access to a window, while construction crews all over Manhattan drive everybody up the Masonite wall with air-pressure generators with noises up to the boil-a-brain decibel level, then rushing to get home, piling into subways and trains, fighting for time and for space, the usual day in New York — the whole now-normal thing keeps shooting jolts of adrenalin into the body, breaking down the body's defenses and winding up with the work-a-daddy human animal stroked out at the breakfast table with his head apoplexed like a cauliflower out of his $6.95 semi-spread Pima-cotton shirt, and nosed over into a plate of No-Kloresto egg substitute, signing off with the black thrombosis, cancer, kidney, liver, or stomach failure, and the adrenals ooze to a halt, the size of eggplants in July.

One of the people whose work Dr. Hall is interested in on this   25
score is Rene Dubos at the Rockefeller Institute. Dubos's work indicates that specific organisms, such as the tuberculosis bacillus or a pneumonia virus, can seldom be considered "the cause" of a disease. The germ or virus, apparently, has to work in combination with other things that have already broken the body down in some way — such as the old adrenal hyperactivity. Dr. Hall would like to see some autopsy studies made to record the size of adrenal glands in New York, especially of people crowded into slums and people who go through the full rush-hour-work-rush-hour cycle every day. He is afraid that until there is some clinical, statistical data on how overcrowding actually ravages the human body, no one will be willing to do anything about it. Even in so obvious a thing as air pollution, the pattern is familiar. Until people can actually see the smoke or smell the sulphur or feel the sting in their eyes, politicians will not get excited about it, even though it is well known that many of the lethal substances polluting the air are invisible and odorless. For one thing, most politicians are like the aristocrat rats. They are insulated from The Sink by practically sultanic buffers — limousines, chauffeurs, secretaries, aides-de-

camp, doormen, shuttered houses, high-floor apartments. They almost never ride subways, fight rush hours, much less live in the slums or work in the Pan-Am Building.

Meanings and Values

1a. Who are members of the "species Mediterranean"?
 b. Who belong to the "species North European"?
 c. What could account for their difference in space requirements (pars. 8–10)?

2. Is this writing primarily objective or subjective? (See Guide to Terms: *Objective/Subjective*.) Why?

3a. Do you get the impression that the author is being unkind, "making fun" of the harried New Yorkers?
 b. How, if at all, does he prevent such an impression?

4a. Compare Wolfe's style, tone, and point of view with those of Huxley (Sec. 1), Fromm (Sec. 2), or Catton (Sec. 3). (Guide: *Style/ Tone, Point of View*.)
 b. Do these features make one author less effective than the other in achieving his purposes? Explain.

5a. If you have read "Modular Man," do you think Toffler or Wolfe sees more hope for urban humans? Why?
 b. What, if anything, do attitude and tone have to do with your answer above?

Expository Techniques

1a. Using whatever criteria we have available for judging the success of analogy, appraise the effectiveness of this one.
 b. Does the author work it *too* hard? Be prepared to defend your answer.

2. What are the benefits of the frequent return to what Dr. Hall is doing or saying (e.g., in pars. 3, 5, 7, 9, 11, 23)?

3. Paragraph 12 has a useful function beyond the simple information it imparts — a sort of organic relation to the coming development. Explain how this is accomplished.

4. How is the switch to Sika deer (par. 21) prepared for, and bumpy transition avoided?

5. The preceding three questions have been related in some manner to the problems of transition. How, if at all, are such problems also matters of coherence? (Guide: *Coherence*.)

6. Wolfe is adept at creating just the effect he wants, and the careful

student of writing can detect a subtle change of style and pace with each change of subpurpose. (Guide: *Style/Tone*.)

a. Analyze stylistic differences, with resulting effects, between the description of chaos at Grand Central and the information about Dr. Hall in paragraph 7.

b. Analyze such differences between the Grand Central scene and the account of the laboratory experiment with rats.

c. Analyze the differences between the Grand Central scene and the final paragraph.

7. Explain how the style of the more descriptive portions is also a matter of emphasis. (Guide: *Emphasis*.)

8a. Illustrate as many as possible of the elements of effective syntax (itself a matter of style) by examples from this selection. (Guide: *Syntax*.)

b. What is gained or lost by the unusual length and design of the last sentence of paragraph 24? (We can be sure that it did not "just happen" to Wolfe — and equally sure that one of such length would be disastrous in most writing.)

Diction and Vocabulary

1. What is the significance of the word "Gotham"?

2a. Why do you think the author refers (deliberately, no doubt) to "my fellow New Yorkers" in the first sentence?

b. What soon could have been the effect if he had not taken such a step?

3. Why does he consistently, after paragraph 2, refer to the people as "poor white humans," "poor human animals," etc?

4. In paragraph 14 he refers to the connotations of the word "sink." What are its possible connotations? (Guide: *Connotation/Denotation*.)

5. Cite examples of verbal irony to be found in paragraphs 5, 8, 24. (Guide: *Irony*.)

6. Which of the elements of style mentioned in your answer to question 4a of "Meanings and Values" are also matters of diction?

7. Consult your dictionary as needed for full understanding of the following words: autistic, puling (par. 1); etiolate (4); effluvia, sebaceous (8); pathology (14); satyrism (16); senescent (17); decibel, thrombosis (24); lethal (25).

Suggestions for Writing and Discussion

1. Carrying Wolfe's analogy still further, trace the steps by which a

rise in serious crime must result from the overcrowding of "poor human animals."

2. If you are familiar with another city, particularly during rush hours, which appears to you much like New York in this respect, describe it.

3. If you are familiar with some area of high density population that has solved its problem of overcrowding, explain the solution.

4. What practical steps can the *individual* take, if forced to live and/or work in overcrowded conditions, to avoid becoming the victim of his own adrenals?

Writing Suggestions for Section 4
Analogy

(In any normal situation, of course, the analogy is chosen to help explain a theme-idea that already exists — such as those in the first group below. But for classroom training, which even at best is bound to be somewhat artificial, it is sometimes permissible to work from the other direction, to develop a theme that fits some preselected analogy-symbol. Your instructor will indicate which of the groups he prefers you to use.)

1. State a central theme about one of the following general topics or a suitable one of your own, and develop it into a composition by use of an analogy of your own choosing.

   a. A well-organized school system or business establishment.
   b. Starting a new kind of business or other enterprise.
   c. The long-range value of programs for underprivileged children.
   d. The complexity of narcotics control.
   e. The need for cooperation between management and labor.
   f. Today's intense competition for success.
   g. Women's liberation in a "man's world."
   h. The results of ignorance.
   i. The dangers of propaganda.

2. Select an analogy-symbol from the following list and fashion a worthwhile theme that it can illustrate. Develop your composition as instructed.

   a. A freeway at commuting time.
   b. Building a road through a wilderness.
   c. Building a bridge across a river.
   d. A merry-go-round.
   e. A wedding.
   f. A car-wash.
   g. Flood-destruction of a levee.
   h. The tending of a young orchard.
   i. An animal predator stalking prey.
   j. A medical clinic.
   k. A juggling act.
   l. An oasis.

5

Explaining Through *Process Analysis*

Process analysis explains how the steps of an operation lead to its completion. Although in one narrow sense it may be considered a kind of narration, process analysis has an important difference in purpose, and hence in approach. Other narration is mostly concerned with the story itself, or with a general concept illustrated by it, but process tells of methods that end in specified results. We might narrate a story about a rifle — its purchase, its role in colorful episodes, perhaps its eventual retirement from active service. (We could, for other purposes, *define* "rifle," or *classify* the types of rifles, no doubt *compare* and *contrast* these types and *illustrate* by examples.) But to show how a rifle works, or how it is manufactured, or how it should be cared for — this is process, and it sometimes becomes the basic pattern of an exposition.

Most writers are especially concerned with two kinds of process, both of them apparent in the preceding example of rifles: the directional, which explains how to *do* something (how to shoot a gun or how to clean it); and the informational, which explains how something is or was *done* (how guns are manufactured). The directional process can range from the instructions on a shampoo bottle to a detailed plan showing how to make the United Nations more effective, and will often contain detailed justification for individual steps or for the process itself. The informational process, on the other hand, might explain the steps of a wide variety of operations or actions or mental processes, with no how-to-do-it purpose at all — how someone went about choosing a college or how the planet Earth was formed. Informational process analysis has been seen in earlier selections: Peter and Hull explained how the Peter Principle works, Wolfe how the experiment with Norway rats was conducted.

Most process analyses are explained in simple, chronological steps. Indeed, the exact order is sometimes of greatest importance, as in a recipe. But occasionally there are problems in organization. The step-by-step format may need to be interrupted for descriptions, definitions, or other explanatory asides. And, still more of a problem, some processes defy a strict chronological treatment, because several things occur simultaneously. To explain the operating process of a gasoline engine, for example, the writer would be unable to convey at once everything that happens at the same time. Some way must be found to present the material in *general* stages, organized as subdivisions, so that the reader can see the step-by-step process through the confusion of interacting relationships.

Another difficulty in explaining by process analysis is estimating what knowledge the reader may already have. Presuming too little background may quickly result in boredom or even irritation, with a resulting communication block; presuming too much will almost certainly leave him bewildered. Like a chain dependent on its weakest link for its strength, the entire process analysis can fail because of just one unclear point that makes the rest unintelligible.

PETER ELBOW

Peter Elbow, born in 1935, was educated at Williams College and at Oxford, Harvard, and Brandeis universities. Now a member of the faculty at Evergreen State College, he previously taught at the Massachusetts Institute of Technology and Franconia College. He has had extensive experience directing writing programs in universities and for community groups. His articles have appeared in such publications as *College English*, the *Journal of General Education*, and *Change* magazine.

Freewriting

"Freewriting" (editor's title) is from Elbow's book *Writing without Teachers*. It is a simple example of "do-it-yourself" process — a process not all teachers of English will endorse. But the author's ample justification for the basics of his plan at least provides some solid grounds for agreement or disagreement.

The most effective way I know to improve your writing is to do   1 freewriting exercises regularly. At least three times a week. They are sometimes called "automatic writing," "babbling," or "jabbering" exercises. The idea is simply to write for ten minutes (later on, perhaps fifteen or twenty). Don't stop for anything. Go quickly without rushing. Never stop to look back, to cross something out, to wonder how to spell something, to wonder what word or thought to use, or to think about what you are doing. If you can't think of a word or a spelling, just use a squiggle or else write, "I can't think of it." Just put down something. The easiest thing is just to put down whatever is in your mind. If you get stuck it's fine to write "I can't think what to say, I can't think what to say" as many times

From *Writing without Teachers* by Peter Elbow. Copyright © 1973 by Oxford University Press, Inc. Reprinted by permission.

as you want; or repeat the last word you wrote over and over again; or anything else. The only requirement is that you *never* stop.

What happens to a freewriting exercise is important. It must 2 be a piece of writing which, even if someone reads it, doesn't send any ripples back to you. It is like writing something and putting it in a bottle in the sea. The teacherless class helps your writing by providing maximum feedback. Freewritings help you by providing no feedback at all. When I assign one, I invite the writer to let me read it, but also tell him to keep it if he prefers. I read it quickly and make no comments at all and I do not speak with him about it. The main thing is that a freewriting must never be evaluated in any way; in fact there must be no discussion or comment at all.

Here is an example of a fairly coherent exercise (sometimes 3 they are very incoherent, which is fine):

I think I'll write what's on my mind, but the only thing on my mind right now is what to write for ten minutes. I've never done this before and I'm not prepared in any way — the sky is cloudy today, how's that? now I'm afraid I won't be able to think of what to write when I get to the end of the sentence — well, here I am at the end of the sentence — here I am again, again, again, again, at least I'm still writing — Now I ask is there some reason to be happy that I'm still writing — ah yes! Here comes the question again — What am I getting out of this? What point is there in it? It's almost obscene to always ask it but I seem to question everything that way and I was gonna say something else pertaining to that but I got so busy writing down the first part that I forgot what I was leading into. This is kind of fun oh don't stop writing — cars and trucks speeding by somewhere out the window, pens clittering across peoples' papers. The sky is still cloudy — is it symbolic that I should be mentioning it? Huh? I dunno. Maybe I should try colors, blue, red, dirty words — wait a minute — no can't do that, orange, yellow, arm tired, green pink violet magenta lavender red brown black green — now that I can't think of any more colors — just about done — relief? maybe.

Freewriting may seem crazy but actually it makes simple 4 sense. Think of the difference between speaking and writing. Writing has the advantage of permitting more editing. But that's its downfall too. Almost everybody interposes a massive and complicated series of editings between the time words start to be born into consciousness and when they finally come off the end of the pencil or typewriter onto the page. This is partly because schooling makes us obsessed with the "mistakes" we make in writing. Many people are constantly thinking about spelling and grammar as they try to write. I am always thinking about the awkwardness, wordiness, and general mushiness of my natural verbal product as I try to write down words.

But it's not just "mistakes" or "bad writing" we edit as we write. We also edit unacceptable thoughts and feelings, as we do in speaking. In writing there is more time to do it so the editing is heavier: when speaking, there's someone right there waiting for a reply and he'll get bored or think we're crazy if we don't come out with *something*. Most of the time in speaking, we settle for the catch-as-catch-can way in which the words tumble out. In writing, however, there's a chance to try to get them right. But the opportunity to get them right is a terrible burden: you can work for two hours trying to get a paragraph "right" and discover it's not right at all. And then give up.

Editing, *in itself,* is not the problem. Editing is usually necessary if we want to end up with something satisfactory. The problem is that editing goes on *at the same time* as producing. The editor is, as it were, constantly looking over the shoulder of the producer and constantly fiddling with what he's doing while he's in the middle of trying to do it. No wonder the producer gets nervous, jumpy, inhibited, and finally can't be coherent. It's an unnecessary burden to try to think of words and also worry at the same time whether they're the right words.

The main thing about freewriting is that it is *nonediting.* It is an exercise in bringing together the process of producing words and putting them down on the page. Practiced regularly, it undoes the ingrained habit of editing at the same time you are trying to produce. It will make writing less blocked because words will come more easily. You will use up more paper, but chew up fewer pencils.

Next time you write, notice how often you stop yourself from writing down something you were going to write down. Or else cross it out after it's written. "Naturally," you say, "it wasn't any good." But think for a moment about the occasions when you spoke well. Seldom was it because you first got the beginning just right. Usually it was a matter of a halting or even garbled beginning, but you kept going and your speech finally became coherent and even powerful. There is a lesson here for writing: trying to get the beginning just right is a formula for failure — and probably a secret tactic to make yourself give up writing. Make some words, whatever they are, and then grab hold of that line and reel in as hard as you can. Afterwards you can throw away lousy beginnings and make new ones. This is the quickest way to get into good writing.

The habit of compulsive, premature editing doesn't just make   9 writing hard. It also makes writing dead. Your voice is damped out by all the interruptions, changes, and hesitations between the consciousness and the page. In your natural way of producing words there is a sound, a texture, a rhythm — a voice — which is the main source of power in your writing. I don't know how it works, but this voice is the force that will make a reader listen to you, the energy that drives the meanings through his thick skull. Maybe you don't *like* your voice; maybe people have made fun of it. But it's the only voice you've got. It's your only source of power. You better get back into it, no matter what you think of it. If you keep writing in it, it may change into something you like better. But if you abandon it, you'll likely never have a voice and never be heard.

Meanings and Values

1. If "freewriting" is a novel idea to you, did the advice to ignore mistakes and nonsense seem paradoxical at first? Why, or why not? (See Guide to Terms: *Paradox*.)

2. Does it seem to you that it might be more valuable to get some sort of idea in mind before you even start to write? Explain.

3. Why is it important that there be no discussion or comment at all about the freewriting result (par. 2)?

4. If you can, explain the meaning of the second and third sentences of paragraph 2.

Expository Techniques

1a. To which of the two basic types of process analysis does this belong?

b. Should the author have given more attention to a step-by-step explanation? Why, or why not?

c. A large proportion of the selection seems devoted to justification of the process. Is this emphasis warranted? Explain.

2. Cite passages where other patterns of exposition are used.

3. Would you classify this writing as formal or informal? Why? (Guide: *Essay*.)

Diction and Vocabulary

1. Which portions of your answer to question 3 of "Expository Techniques" are matters of diction or syntax? Why? (Guide: *Diction, Syntax*.)

2. Explain how Elbow is using the word "voice" (par. 9) in a figurative sense. (Guide: *Figures of Speech*.)

Suggestions for Writing and Discussion

1. Develop a thoughtful explanation of how it could be that struggling with an introduction is really a "secret tactic" (par. 8).

2. If you believe that freewriting is a useless practice, or possibly even a dangerous one, develop a reasonable defense of your own views, answering Elbow's assertions as completely as possible.

(NOTE: Suggestions for topics requiring development by PROCESS ANALYSIS are on page 153, at the end of this section.)

ROBERT M. PIRSIG

ROBERT M. PIRSIG was born in Minneapolis in 1928. He received both B.A. and M.A. degrees at the University of Minnesota and has been a Guggenheim Fellow since 1974. His first important book, *Zen and the Art of Motorcycle Maintenance* (1974), was quickly acclaimed by most reviewers — e.g., in *The New York Times:* "Profoundly important ... full of insights into our most perplexing contemporary dilemmas ... intellectual entertainment of the highest order." It was also rated on various best-seller lists, including those of college bookstores. Pirsig's next book, he says, will be about boats and sailing.

Mechanics' Logic

"Mechanics' Logic" (editor's title), from *Zen and the Art of Motorcycle Maintenance*, analyzes a much more complex process than that of the preceding selection. Although no doubt a worthwhile subject, it is also one that could easily be dry and uninteresting to more readers than not — perhaps even too "difficult" for the average non-logician. The fact that it is readable and even interesting for many laymen is a tribute to the author's skill — and discovering the techniques by which he achieves this success can provide one of the most rewarding experiences of its study.

Two kinds of logic are used [in motorcycle maintenance], inductive 1 and deductive. Inductive inferences start with observations of the machine and arrive at general conclusions. For example, if the cycle goes over a bump and the engine misfires, and then goes over another bump and the engine misfires, and then goes over another bump and the engine misfires, and then goes over a long smooth stretch of road and there is no misfiring, and then goes over a fourth bump and the engine misfires again, one can logically conclude that the misfiring is caused by the bumps. That is induction: reasoning from particular experiences to general truths.

Deductive inferences do the reverse. They start with general 2 knowledge and predict a specific observation. For example, if, from reading the hierarchy of facts about the machine, the mechanic knows the horn of the cycle is powered exclusively by electricity from the battery, then he can logically infer that if the battery is dead the horn will not work. That is deduction.

Solution of problems too complicated for common sense to 3 solve is achieved by long strings of mixed inductive and deductive inferences that weave back and forth between the observed machine and the mental hierarchy of the machine found in the manuals. The correct program for this interweaving is formalized as scientific method.

Actually I've never seen a cycle-maintenance problem complex 4 enough really to require full-scale formal scientific method. Repair problems are not that hard. When I think of formal scientific method an image sometimes comes to mind of an enormous juggernaut, a huge bulldozer — slow, tedious, lumbering, laborious, but invincible. It takes twice as long, five times as long, maybe a dozen times as long as informal mechanic's techniques, but you know in the end you're going to *get* it. There's no fault isolation problem in motorcycle maintenance that can stand up to it. When you've hit a really tough one, tried everything, racked your brain and nothing works, and you know that this time Nature has really decided to be difficult, you say, "Okay, Nature, that's the end of the *nice* guy," and you crank up the formal scientific method.

For this you keep a lab notebook. Everything gets written 5 down, formally, so that you know at all times where you are, where you've been, where you're going and where you want to get. In scientific work and electronics technology this is necessary because otherwise the problems get so complex you get lost in them and confused and forget what you know and what you don't know and have to give up. In cycle maintenance things are not that involved, but when confusion starts it's a good idea to hold it down by making everything formal and exact. Sometimes just the act of writing down the problems straightens out your head as to what they really are.

The logical statements entered into the notebook are broken 6
down into six categories: (1) statement of the problem, (2) hypotheses as to the cause of the problem, (3) experiments designed to test
each hypothesis, (4) predicted results of the experiments, (5) observed results of the experiments and (6) conclusions from the results of the experiments. This is not different from the formal
arrangement of many college and high-school lab notebooks but
the purpose here is no longer just busywork. The purpose now is
precise guidance of thoughts that will fail if they are not accurate.

The real purpose of scientific method is to make sure Nature 7
hasn't misled you into thinking you know something you don't actually know. There's not a mechanic or scientist or technician alive
who hasn't suffered from that one so much that he's not instinctively on guard. That's the main reason why so much scientific and
mechanical information sounds so dull and so cautious. If you get
careless or go romanticizing scientific information, giving it a flour-
ish here and there, Nature will soon make a complete fool out of
you. It does it often enough anyway even when you don't give it
opportunities. One must be extremely careful and rigidly logical
when dealing with Nature: one logical slip and an entire scientific
edifice comes tumbling down. One false deduction about the machine and you can get hung up indefinitely.

In Part One of formal scientific method, which is the state- 8
ment of the problem, the main skill is in stating absolutely no more
than you are positive you know. It is much better to enter a statement "Solve Problem: Why doesn't cycle work?" which sounds
dumb but is correct, than it is to enter a statement "Solve Problem:
What is wrong with the electrical system?" when you don't absolutely *know* the trouble is *in* the electrical system. What you
should state is "Solve Problem: What is wrong with cycle?" and
then state as the first entry of Part Two: "Hypothesis Number
One: The trouble is in the electrical system." You think of as many
hypotheses as you can, then you design experiments to test them
to see which are true and which are false.

This careful approach to the beginning questions keeps you 9
from taking a major wrong turn which might cause you weeks of
extra work or can even hang you up completely. Scientific questions often have a surface appearance of dumbness for this reason.
They are asked in order to prevent dumb mistakes later on.

Part Three, that part of formal scientific method called experi- 10 mentation, is sometimes thought of by romantics as all of science itself because that's the only part with much visual surface. They see lots of test tubes and bizarre equipment and people running around making discoveries. They do not see the experiment as part of a larger intellectual process and so they often confuse experiments with demonstrations, which look the same. A man conducting a gee-whiz science show with fifty thousand dollars' worth of Frankenstein equipment is not doing anything scientific if he knows beforehand what the results of his efforts are going to be. A motorcycle mechanic, on the other hand, who honks the horn to see if the battery works is informally conducting a true scientific experiment. He is testing a hypothesis by putting the question to Nature. The TV scientist who mutters sadly, "The experiment is a failure; we have failed to achieve what we had hoped for," is suffering mainly from a bad scriptwriter. An experiment is never a failure solely because it fails to achieve predicted results. An experiment is a failure only when it also fails adequately to test the hypothesis in question, when the data it produces don't prove anything one way or another.

Skill at this point consists of using experiments that test only   11 the hypothesis in question, nothing less, nothing more. If the horn honks, and the mechanic concludes that the whole electrical system is working, he is in deep trouble. He has reached an illogical conclusion. The honking horn only tells him that the battery and horn are working. To design an experiment properly he has to think very rigidly in terms of what directly causes what. This you know from the hierarchy. The horn doesn't make the cycle go. Neither does the battery, except in a very indirect way. The point at which the electrical system *directly* causes the engine to fire is at the spark plugs, and if you don't test here, at the output of the electrical system, you will never really know whether the failure is electrical or not.

To test properly the mechanic removes the plug and lays it   12 against the engine so that the base around the plug is electrically grounded, kicks the starter lever and watches the spark-plug gap for a blue spark. If there isn't any he can conclude one of two things: (a) there is an electrical failure or (b) his experiment is sloppy. If he is experienced he will try it a few more times, checking connections, trying every way he can think of to get that plug to fire. Then, if he can't get it to fire, he finally concludes that *a* is correct, there's an electrical failure, and the experiment is over. He has proved that his hypothesis is correct.

In the final category, conclusions, skill comes in stating no   13
more than the experiment has proved. It hasn't proved that when he fixes the electrical system the motorcycle will start. There may be other things wrong. But he does know that the motorcycle isn't going to run until the electrical system is working and he sets up the next formal question: "Solve problem: what is wrong with the electrical system?"

He then sets up hypotheses for these and tests them. By ask-   14
ing the right questions and choosing the right tests and drawing the right conclusions the mechanic works his way down the echelons of the motorcycle hierarchy until he has found the exact specific cause or causes of the engine failure, and then he changes them so that they no longer cause the failure.

An untrained observer will see only physical labor and often   15
get the idea that physical labor is mainly what the mechanic does. Actually the physical labor is the smallest and easiest part of what the mechanic does. By far the greatest part of his work is careful observation and precise thinking. That is why mechanics sometimes seem so taciturn and withdrawn when performing tests. They don't like it when you talk to them because they are concentrating on mental images, hierarchies, and not really looking at you or the physical motorcycle at all. They are using the experiment as part of a program to expand their hierarchy of knowledge of the faulty motorcycle and compare it to the correct hierarchy in their mind. They are looking at underlying form.

Meanings and Values

1. For even nonmechanics, what potential value can you see in understanding the "scientific method" and the importance of logic?
2. Where would you place this piece on an objective/subjective continuum? Why? (See Guide to Terms: *Objective/Subjective*.)
3a. Do you suppose most master mechanics realize they are using a time-honored scientific method?
  b. If many do not consciously take the six steps in solving their problems, would this fact make Pirsig's thesis less valid? Why, or why not?
4. Judge the success of "Mechanics' Logic" by applying our three-step evaluation method. (Guide: *Evaluation*.)

5. If you have read the Hall selection (Sec. 2) for what kinds of reading might differing people use "Mechanics' Logic"? Consider your answer carefully and explain your reasons for it.

Expository Techniques

1a. On first impression, which of the two basic types of process analysis did you assume this to be? Why?
  b. Considering the reader-audience Pirsig evidently had in mind, which of the two types would he have intended it to be? Why?
  c. Has he made his exposition understandable, as nearly as you can tell, to most types of readers? If not, what would be the exceptions?
  d. Should he have included more justification for his rather laborious process? Why, or why not?
2. Pirsig uses examples to make his general statements more specific. Select three of the best of these and explain why you think they are well chosen or well presented, or both.
3a. Cite one use of analogy, however minor.
  b. Why is it not a simple metaphor? (Guide: *Figure of Speech*.)
  c. How effective is it, in the job it has to do?
4a. How is paragraph 9, dealing as it does with two different parts of the process, saved from gross disunity? (Guide: *Unity*.)
  b. Would it have been better divided into two paragraphs? Why, or why not?

Diction and Vocabulary

1a. Cite as many colloquial expressions as possible. (Guide: *Colloquial Expressions*.)
  b. Does this informal usage damage or improve the general tone of the writing? Analyze your reasons for this answer. (Guide: *Style/Tone*.)
2a. Cite one example of allusion. (Guide: *Figures of Speech*.)
  b. Is its choice appropriate? Why, or why not?
3a. In what sense does Pirsig use the word "Nature"?
  b. Why is it capitalized?
4a. If you have read "The Peter Principle" (Section 1), differentiate between the meanings of "hierarchy," as used here and in that selection.
  b. Are both used correctly?
5. If you are not familiar with the meanings of the following words, as used in this selection, consult your dictionary: hypothesis (pars. 6, 11, 12, 14); edifice (7); bizarre (10); echelons (14); taciturn (15).

Suggestions for Writing and Discussion

1. Show how to apply Pirsig's six-step method to some problem in another field of endeavor with which you are familiar. Keep your subject narrow enough that it can be developed thoroughly.

2. Is it true that some people simply are not practical enough (logical enough?) to be good mechanics? Is the deficiency, if any, a matter of natural talent or training, or both? Can it be overcome? Use any of the four patterns of exposition previously studied that will support your thesis.

3. If you have read *Zen and the Art of Motorcycle Maintenance*, you are no doubt aware that the book is only incidentally about motorcycles. What then is it about? You may decide to prepare a critical review of the book, tailored to whatever aspects or length you and your instructor prefer.

(NOTE: Suggestions for topics requiring development by PROCESS ANALYSIS are on page 153, at the end of this section.)

ALEXANDER PETRUNKEVITCH

ALEXANDER PETRUNKEVITCH (1875–1964) was a Russian-born zoologist who taught at several leading American universities and received honors from others. He was one of the world's foremost authorities on spiders, and his first important book, published in 1911, was *Index Catalogue of Spiders of North, Central, and South America*. He later achieved distinction for his writings on zoological subjects as well as for his translations of English poetry into Russian and Russian poetry into English. Two of his other books are *Choice and Responsibility* (1947) and *Principles of Classification* (1952).

The Spider and the Wasp

"The Spider and the Wasp" was first published in the August 1952 issue of *Scientific American*. This essay should be particularly interesting to students of composition because it demonstrates not only exposition of natural process but also semiscientific writing that has been made understandable, perhaps even fascinating, for completely nonscientific readers. It is also a good illustration of the successful interweaving of several expository techniques.

In the feeding and safeguarding of their progeny insects and spiders exhibit some interesting analogies to reasoning and some crass examples of blind instinct. The case I propose to describe here is that of the tarantula spiders and their archenemy, the digger wasps of the genus Pepsis. It is a classic example of what looks like intelligence pitted against instinct — a strange situation in which the victim, though fully able to defend itself, submits unwittingly to its destruction. 1

Most tarantulas live in the tropics, but several species occur in the temperate zone and a few are common in the southern U.S. 2

Some varieties are large and have powerful fangs with which they can inflict a deep wound. These formidable looking spiders do not, however, attack man; you can hold one in your hand, if you are gentle, without being bitten. Their bite is dangerous only to insects and small mammals such as mice; for man it is no worse than a hornet's sting.

Tarantulas customarily live in deep cylindrical burrows, from which they emerge at dusk and into which they retire at dawn. Mature males wander about after dark in search of females and occasionally stray into houses. After mating, the male dies in a few weeks, but a female lives much longer and can mate several years in succession. In a Paris museum is a tropical specimen which is said to have been living in captivity for 25 years.

A fertilized female tarantula lays from 200 to 400 eggs at a time; thus it is possible for a single tarantula to produce several thousand young. She takes no care of them beyond weaving a cocoon of silk to enclose the eggs. After they hatch, the young walk away, find convenient places in which to dig their burrows and spend the rest of their lives in solitude. The eyesight of tarantulas is poor, being limited to a sensing of change in the intensity of light and to the perception of moving objects. They apparently have little or no sense of hearing, for a hungry tarantula will pay no attention to a loudly chirping cricket placed in its cage unless the insect happens to touch one of its legs.

But all spiders, and especially hairy ones, have an extremely delicate sense of touch. Laboratory experiments prove that tarantulas can distinguish three types of touch: pressure against the body wall, stroking of the body hair, and riffling of certain very fine hairs on the legs called trichobothria. Pressure against the body, by the finger or the end of a pencil, causes the tarantula to move off slowly for a short distance. The touch excites no defensive response unless the approach is from above where the spider can see the motion, in which case it rises on its hind legs, lifts its front legs, opens its fangs and holds this threatening posture as long as the object continues to move.

The entire body of a tarantula, especially its legs, is thickly clothed with hair. Some of it is short and wooly, some long and stiff. Touching this body hair produces one of two distinct reactions. When the spider is hungry, it responds with an immediate and swift attack. At the touch of a cricket's antennae the tarantula seizes the insect so swiftly that a motion picture taken at the rate of 64 frames per second shows only the result and not the process of capture. But when the spider is not hungry, the stimulation of its hairs merely causes it to shake the touched limb. An insect can walk under its hairy belly unharmed.

The trichobothria, very fine hairs growing from disklike mem-   7
branes on the legs, are sensitive only to air movement. A light breeze makes them vibrate slowly, without disturbing the common hair. When one blows gently on the trichobothria, the tarantula reacts with a quick jerk of its four front legs. If the front and hind legs are stimulated at the same time, the spider makes a sudden jump. This reaction is quite independent of the state of its appetite.

These three tactile responses — to pressure on the body wall,   ·8
to moving of the common hair, and to flexing of the trichobothria — are so different from one another that there is no possibility of confusing them. They serve the tarantula adequately for most of its needs and enable it to avoid most annoyances and dangers. But they fail the spider completely when it meets its deadly enemy, the digger wasp Pepsis.

These solitary wasps are beautiful and formidable creatures.   9
Most species are either a deep shiny blue all over, or deep blue with rusty wings. The largest have a wing span of about four inches. They live on nectar. When excited, they give off a pungent odor — a warning that they are ready to attack. The sting is much worse than that of a bee or common wasp, and the pain and swelling last longer. In the adult stage the wasp lives only a few months. The female produces but a few eggs, one at a time at intervals of two or three days. For each egg the mother must provide one adult tarantula, alive but paralyzed. The mother wasp attaches the egg to the paralyzed spider's abdomen. Upon hatching from the egg, the larva is many hundreds of times smaller than its living but helpless victim. It eats no other food and drinks no water. By the time it has finished its single Gargantuan meal and become ready for wasphood, nothing remains of the tarantula but its indigestible chitinous skeleton.

The mother wasp goes tarantula-hunting when the egg in her   10
ovary is almost ready to be laid. Flying low over the ground late on a sunny afternoon, the wasp looks for its victim or for the mouth of a tarantula burrow, a round hole edged by a bit of silk.

The sex of the spider makes no difference, but the mother is highly discriminating as to species. Each species of Pepsis requires a certain species of tarantula, and the wasp will not attack the wrong species. In a cage with a tarantula which is not its normal prey, the wasp avoids the spider and is usually killed by it in the night.

Yet when a wasp finds the correct species, it is the other way about. To identify the species the wasp apparently must explore the spider with her antennae. The tarantula shows an amazing tolerance to this exploration. The wasp crawls under it and walks over it without evoking any hostile response. The molestation is so great and so persistent that the tarantula often rises on all eight legs, as if it were on stilts. It may stand this way for several minutes. Meanwhile the wasp, having satisfied itself that the victim is of the right species, moves off a few inches to dig the spider's grave. Working vigorously with legs and jaws, it excavates a hole 8 to 10 inches deep with a diameter slightly larger than the spider's girth. Now and again the wasp pops out of the hole to make sure that the spider is still there. 11

When the grave is finished, the wasp returns to the tarantula to complete her ghastly enterprise. First she feels it all over once more with her antennae. Then her behavior becomes more aggressive. She bends her abdomen, protruding her sting, and searches for the soft membrane at the point where the spider's legs join its body — the only spot where she can penetrate the horny skeleton. From time to time, as the exasperated spider slowly shifts ground, the wasp turns on her back and slides along with the aid of her wings, trying to get under the tarantula for a shot at the vital spot. During all this maneuvering, which can last for several minutes, the tarantula makes no move to save itself. Finally the wasp corners it against some obstruction and grasps one of its legs in her powerful jaws. Now at last the harassed spider tries a desperate but vain defense. The two contestants roll over and over on the ground. It is a terrifying sight and the outcome is always the same. The wasp finally manages to thrust her sting into the soft spot and holds it there for a few seconds while she pumps in the poison. Almost immediately the tarantula falls paralyzed on its back. Its legs stop twitching; its heart stops beating. Yet it is not dead, as is shown by the fact that if taken from the wasp it can be restored to some sensitivity by being kept in a moist chamber for several months. 12

After paralyzing the tarantula, the wasp cleans herself by 13 dragging her body along the ground and rubbing her feet, sucks the drop of blood oozing from the wound in the spider's abdomen, then grabs a leg of the flabby, helpless animal in her jaws and drags it down to the bottom of the grave. She stays there for many minutes, sometimes for several hours, and what she does all that time in the dark we do not know. Eventually she lays her egg and attaches it to the side of the spider's abdomen with a sticky secretion. Then she emerges, fills the grave with soil carried bit by bit in her jaws, and finally tramples the ground all around to hide any trace of the grave from prowlers. Then she flies away, leaving her descendant safely started in life.

In all this the behavior of the wasp evidently is qualitatively 14 different from that of the spider. The wasp acts like an intelligent animal. This is not to say that instinct plays no part or that she reasons as man does. But her actions are to the point; they are not automatic and can be modified to fit the situation. We do not know for certain how she identifies the tarantula — probably it is by some olfactory or chemo-tactile sense — but she does it purposefully and does not blindly tackle a wrong species.

On the other hand, the tarantula's behavior shows only con- 15 fusion. Evidently the wasp's pawing gives it no pleasure, for it tries to move away. That the wasp is not simulating sexual stimulation is certain because male and female tarantulas react in the same way to its advances. That the spider is not anesthetized by some odorless secretion is easily shown by blowing lightly at the tarantula and making it jump suddenly. What, then, makes the tarantula behave as stupidly as it does?

No clear, simple answer is available. Possibly the stimulation 16 by the wasp's antennae is masked by a heavier pressure on the spider's body, so that it reacts as when prodded by a pencil. But the explanation may be much more complex. Initiative in attack is not in the nature of tarantulas; most species fight only when cornered so that escape is impossible. Their inherited patterns of behavior apparently prompt them to avoid problems rather than attack them. For example, spiders' always weave their webs in three dimensions, and when a spider finds that there is insufficient space to attach certain threads in the third dimension, it leaves the place and seeks another, instead of finishing the web in a single plane. This urge to escape seems to arise under all circumstances, in all phases of life, and to take the place of reasoning. For a spider to change the pattern of its web is as impossible as for an inexperienced man to build a bridge across a chasm obstructing his way.

In a way the instinctive urge to escape is not only easier but often more efficient than reasoning. The tarantula does exactly what is most efficient in all cases except in an encounter with a ruthless and determined attacker dependent for the existence of her own species on killing as many tarantulas as she can lay eggs. Perhaps in this case the spider follows its usual pattern of trying to escape, instead of seizing and killing the wasp, because it is not aware of its danger. In any case, the survival of the tarantula species as a whole is protected by the fact that the spider is much more fertile than the wasp.   17

Meanings and Values

1. Briefly summarize the "qualitative" differences between the behavior of the tarantula and that of the wasp.
2. What is the likelihood that some humans also have inherited patterns of behavior that "prompt them to avoid problems rather than attack them" (par. 16)? Use concrete examples, if possible, to support your view.
3. What parallels to the tarantula-wasp relationship can you find in the history of nations? Be specific and explain.
4a. Describe the type, or types, of readers to whom you think *Scientific American* is meant to appeal. (Do not jump to conclusions: if not familiar with the magazine, you may have to browse through a few issues.)
  b. If you were the editor, why would you have chosen (or not chosen) to publish this piece?

Expository Techniques

1a. Where does the author state his central theme?
  b. Is this a desirable location? Why, or why not?
2a. What is the primary function of the process analysis in relation to the central theme?
  b. How successfully does it accomplish its purpose?
3. In paragraph 9 the author goes from pure description of the wasp into the narrative account that involves both wasp and spider. How does he arrange the content itself to provide smooth and natural

transition, hence ensuring coherence? (See Guide to Terms: *Transition* and *Coherence*.)

4. The author also usually arranges his subject materials to help achieve effective *inter*paragraph transitions so that one gets an echo of the last part of one paragraph when reading the topic sentence of the next. List or mark the uses of this transitional device.

5. Effective coherence also depends to a great extent on smooth sentence-to-sentence transitions. In describing events in a time sequence, it is sometimes hard to avoid a dull list that runs on "and then . . . and then. . . ." List or mark the eight introductory devices showing time relationship in paragraph 12, and notice their variety.

6a. How many paragraphs constitute the closing?
  b. What function do they serve in addition to concluding the selection?

7. This essay utilizes, to varying extents, the expository patterns of cause and effect, definition, induction, and description. It can also be used to illustrate three patterns we have already studied.
  a. What are the patterns?
  b. Explain their use in this essay.

Diction and Vocabulary

1. Do such informal expressions as "pops out of the hole" (par. 11), "for a shot at the vital spot," and "pumps in the poison" (12) help or hinder the essay's success? Why?

2. Consider such expressions as "beautiful and formidable creatures" (par. 9), "ghastly enterprise," and "terrifying sight" (12).
  a. Are these expressions objective or subjective? (Guide: *Objective/Subjective*.) Explain why.
  b. Why would they be, or not be, suitable in a scientific report?
  c. What useful purpose, if any, do they serve here?

3a. What do your answers to questions 1 and 2 indicate about the author's tone? (Guide: *Style/Tone*.)
  b. How would you describe his tone?
  c. Explain why it is, or is not, suitable to his subject matter and to his audience.

4. Any specialist writing on a technical subject for a lay audience (as much of *Scientific American*'s audience is) has a problem with professional terminology. Consider this author's use of "trichobothria" (par. 5), "chitinous" (9), "olfactory," and "chemo-tactile" (14).
  a. Does there seem to be an excessive use of technical language?
  b. Do you think these words could have been avoided without weakening scientific exactness? If so, how?
  c. Does their use create a communication block for the lay reader, or does the author succeed in avoiding this fault?

    d. Why has he bothered to define "trichobothria" — even repeating his definition — but not the others?

5. The use of "Gargantuan" (par. 9) is an allusion. (Guide: *Figures of Speech*.) Find the source to which the author alludes and explain the word's meaning in this essay.

6. Consult the dictionary as needed for a full understanding of the following words, especially as used in this essay: progeny, archenemy, classic (par. 1); formidable (2); perception (4); riffling (5); disklike (7); tactile (8); pungent, chitinous (9); discriminating (10); evoking, molestation (11); harassed (12); secretion (13); qualitatively, olfactory, chemo-tactile (14); ruthless (17).

Suggestions for Writing and Discussion

1. Use the tarantula-wasp relationship as the basis of an analogy to explain the relationship between two persons that you know.

2. Use analogy as suggested above to explain the historical relationship between two specific countries.

3. Using patterns of illustration and comparison, distinguish between intellectual and instinctive human behavior.

4. Compare or contrast man's motives for killing with those of animals. Some use of classification might also be helpful in this assignment.

(NOTE: Suggestions for topics requiring development by PROCESS ANALYSIS are on page 153, at the end of this section.)

JESSICA MITFORD

JESSICA MITFORD was born in 1917, the daughter of an English peer. Her brother was sent to Eton, but she and her six sisters were educated at home by their mother. At the age of nineteen Mitford left home, eventually making her way to the United States in 1939. Since 1944 she has been an American citizen, and is now living in San Francisco. She did not begin her writing career until she was 38. Her books are *Lifeitselfmanship* (1956); her autobiography, *Daughters and Rebels* (1960); the best-seller, *The American Way of Death* (1963); *The Trial of Dr. Spock* (1969); and *Kind and Unusual Punishment* (1973), a devastating study of the American penal system. Mitford's articles have appeared in *The Atlantic Monthly*, *Harper's*, and *McCall's*.

To Dispel Fears of Live Burial

"To Dispel Fears of Live Burial" (editor's title) is a portion of *The American Way of Death*, a book described in *The New York Times* as a "savagely witty and well-documented exposé." The "savagely witty" style, evident in this selection, does not obscure the fact of its being a tightly organized, step-by-step process analysis.

Embalming is indeed a most extraordinary procedure, and one 1 must wonder at the docility of Americans who each year pay hundreds of millions of dollars for its perpetuation, blissfully ignorant of what it is all about, what is done, how it is done. Not one in ten thousand has any idea of what actually takes place. Books on the subject are extremely hard to come by. They are not to be found in most libraries or bookshops.

In an era when huge television audiences watch surgical oper- 2 ations in the comfort of their living rooms, when, thanks to the

animated cartoon, the geography of the digestive system has become familiar territory even to the nursery school set, in a land
where the satisfaction of curiosity about almost all matters is a
national pastime, the secrecy surrounding embalming can, surely,
hardly be attributed to the inherent gruesomeness of the subject.
Custom in this regard has within this century suffered a complete
reversal. In the early days of American embalming, when it was
performed in the home of the deceased, it was almost mandatory
for some relative to stay by the embalmer's side and witness the
procedure. Today, family members who might wish to be in at-
tendance would certainly be dissuaded by the funeral director. All
others, except apprentices, are excluded by law from the preparation room.

A close look at what does actually take place may explain in   3
large measure the undertaker's intractable reticence concerning a
procedure that has become his major *raison d'être.* Is it possible
he fears that public information about embalming might lead patrons to wonder if they really want this service? If the funeral men
are loath to discuss the subject outside the trade, the reader may,
understandably, be equally loath to go on reading at this point. For
those who have the stomach for it, let us part the formaldehyde
curtain. . . .

The body is first laid out in the undertaker's morgue — or   4
rather, Mr. Jones is reposing in the preparation room — to be
readied to bid the world farewell.

The preparation room in any of the better funeral establish-   5
ments has the tiled and sterile look of a surgery, and indeed the
embalmer–restorative artist who does his chores there is beginning
to adopt the term "dermasurgeon" (appropriately corrupted by
some mortician-writers as "demisurgeon") to describe his calling.
His equipment, consisting of scalpels, scissors, augers, forceps,
clamps, needles, pumps, tubes, bowls and basins, is crudely imitative of the surgeon's as is his technique, acquired in a nine- or
twelve-month post-high-school course in an embalming school. He
is supplied by an advanced chemical industry with a bewildering
array of fluids, sprays, pastes, oils, powders, creams, to fix or
soften tissue, shrink or distend it as needed, dry it here, restore
the moisture there. There are cosmetics, waxes and paints to fill
and cover features, even plaster of Paris to replace entire limbs.
There are ingenious aids to prop and stabilize the cadaver: a Vari-

Pose Head Rest, the Edwards Arm and Hand Positioner, the Repose Block (to support the shoulders during the embalming), and the Throop Foot Positioner, which resembles an old-fashioned stocks.

Mr. John H. Eckels, president of the Eckels College of Mortuary Science, thus describes the first part of the embalming procedure: "In the hands of a skilled practitioner, this work may be done in a comparatively short time and without mutilating the body other than by slight incision — so slight that it scarcely would cause serious inconvenience if made upon a living person. It is necessary to remove the blood, and doing this not only helps in the disinfecting, but removes the principal cause of disfigurements due to discoloration."

Another textbook discusses the all-important time element: "The earlier this is done, the better, for every hour that elapses between death and embalming will add to the problems and complications encountered   ." Just how soon should one get going on the embalming? The author tells us, "On the basis of such scanty information made available to this profession through its rudimentary and haphazard system of technical research, we must conclude that the best results are to be obtained if the subject is embalmed before life is completely extinct — that is, before cellular death has occurred. In the average case, this would mean within an hour after somatic death." For those who feel that there is something a little rudimentary, not to say haphazard, about this advice, a comforting thought is offered by another writer. Speaking of fears entertained in early days of premature burial, he points out, "One of the effects of embalming by chemical injection, however, has been to dispel fears of live burial." How true; once the blood is removed, chances of live burial are indeed remote.

To return to Mr. Jones, the blood is drained out through the veins and replaced by embalming fluid pumped in through the arteries. As noted in *The Principles and Practices of Embalming*, "every operator has a favorite injection and drainage point — a fact which becomes a handicap only if he fails or refuses to forsake his favorites when conditions demand it." Typical favorites are the carotid artery, femoral artery, jugular vein, subclavian vein. There are various choices of embalming fluid. If Flextone is used, it will produce a "mild, flexible rigidity. The skin retains a velvety softness, the tissues are rubbery and pliable. Ideal for women and children." It may be blended with B. and G. Products Company's Lyf-Lyk tint, which is guaranteed to reproduce "nature's own skin texture . . . the velvety appearance of living tissue." Suntone comes in three separate tints: Suntan; Special Cosmetic Tint, a pink shade "especially indicated for young female subjects"; and Regular Cosmetic Tint, moderately pink.

About three to six gallons of a dyed and perfumed solution of   9
formaldehyde, glycerin, borax, phenol, alcohol and water is soon circulating through Mr. Jones, whose mouth has been sewn together with a "needle directed upward between the upper lip and gum and brought out through the left nostril," with the corners raised slightly "for a more pleasant expression." If he should be bucktoothed, his teeth are cleaned with Bon Ami and coated with colorless nail polish. His eyes, meanwhile, are closed with flesh-tinted eye caps and eye cement.

The next step is to have at Mr. Jones with a thing called a   10
trocar. This is a long, hollow needle attached to a tube. It is jabbed into the abdomen, poked around the entrails and chest cavity, the contents of which are pumped out and replaced with "cavity fluid." This done, and the hole in the abdomen sewn up, Mr. Jones's face is heavily creamed (to protect the skin from burns which may be caused by leakage of the chemicals), and he is covered with a sheet and left unmolested for a while. But not for long — there is more, much more, in store for him. He had been embalmed, but not yet restored, and the best time to start the restorative work is eight to ten hours after embalming, when the tissues have become firm and dry.

The object of all this attention to the corpse, it must be re-   11
membered, is to make it presentable for viewing in an attitude of healthy repose. "Our customs require the presentation of our dead in the semblance of normality . . . unmarred by the ravages of illness, disease or mutilation," says Mr. J. Sheridan Mayer in his *Restorative Art*. This is rather a large order since few people die in the full bloom of health, unravaged by illness and unmarked by some disfigurement. The funeral industry is equal to the challenge: "In some cases the gruesome appearance of a mutilated or disease-ridden subject may be quite discouraging. The task of restoration may seem impossible and shake the confidence of the embalmer. This is the time for intestinal fortitude and determination. Once the formative work is begun and affected tissues are cleaned or re-

moved, all doubts of success vanish. It is surprising and gratifying to discover the results which may be obtained."

The embalmer, having allowed an appropriate interval to 12 elapse, returns to the attack, but now he brings into play the skill and equipment of sculptor and cosmetician. Is a hand missing? Casting one in plaster of Paris is a simple matter. "For replacement purposes, only a cast of the back of the hand is necessary; this is within the ability of the average operator and is quite adequate." If a lip or two, a nose or an ear should be missing, the embalmer has at hand a variety of restorative waxes with which to model replacements. Pores and skin texture are simulated by stippling with a little brush, and over this cosmetics are laid on. Head off? Decapitation cases are rather routinely handled. Ragged edges are trimmed, and head joined to torso with a series of splints, wires and sutures. It is a good idea to have a little something at the neck — a scarf or high collar — when time for viewing comes. Swollen mouth? Cut out tissue as needed from inside the lips. If too much is removed, the surface contour can easily be restored by padding with cotton. Swollen necks and cheeks are reduced by removing tissue through vertical incisions made down each side of the neck. "When the deceased is casketed, the pillow will hide the suture incisions . . . as an extra precaution against leakage, the suture may be painted with liquid sealer."

The opposite condition is more likely to present itself — that 13 of emaciation. His hypodermic syringe now loaded with massage cream, the embalmer seeks out and fills the hollowed and sunken areas by injection. In this procedure the backs of the hands and fingers and the under-chin area should not be neglected.

Positioning the lips is a problem that recurrently challenges 14 the ingenuity of the embalmer. Closed too tightly, they tend to give a stern, even disapproving expression. Ideally, embalmers feel, the lips should give the impression of being ever so slightly parted, the upper lip protruding slightly for a more youthful appearance. This takes some engineering, however, as the lips tend to drift apart. Lip drift can sometimes be remedied by pushing one or two straight pins through the inner margin of the lower lip and then inserting them between the two front upper teeth. If Mr. Jones happens to have no teeth, the pins can just as easily be anchored in his Armstrong Face Former and Denture Replacer. Another method to maintain lip closure is to dislocate the lower jaw,

which is then held in its new position by a wire run through holes
which have been drilled through the upper and lower jaws at the
midline. As the French are fond of saying, *il faut souffrir pour être
belle.*[1]

If Mr. Jones has died of jaundice, the embalming fluid will   15
very likely turn him green. Does this deter the embalmer? Not if
he has intestinal fortitude. Masking pastes and cosmetics are heavily laid on, burial garments and casket interiors are color-correlated
with particular care, and Jones is displayed beneath rose-colored
lights. Friends will say, "How *well* he looks." Death by carbon
monoxide, on the other hand, can be rather a good thing from the
embalmer's viewpoint: "One advantage is the fact that this type
of discoloration is an exaggerated form of a natural pink colora-
tion." This is nice because the healthy glow is already present and
needs but little attention.

The patching and filling completed, Mr. Jones is now shaved,   16
washed and dressed. Cream-based cosmetic, available in pink, flesh,
suntan, brunette and blond, is applied to his hands and face, his
hair is shampooed and combed (and, in the case of Mrs. Jones, set),
his hands manicured. For the horny-handed son of toil special care
must be taken; cream should be applied to remove ingrained grime,
and the nails cleaned. "If he were not in the habit of having them
manicured in life, trimming and shaping is advised for better appearance — never questioned by kin."

Jones is now ready for casketing (this is the present participle   17
of the verb "to casket"). In this operation, his right shoulder
should be depressed slightly "to turn the body a bit to the right
and soften the appearance of lying flat on the back." Positioning
the hands is a matter of importance, and special rubber positioning
blocks may be used. The hands should be cupped slightly for a
more lifelike, relaxed appearance. Proper placement of the body
requires a delicate sense of balance. It should lie as high as possible
in the casket, yet not so high that the lid, when lowered, will hit
the nose. On the other hand, we are cautioned, placing the body
too low "creates the impression that the body is in a box."

Jones is next wheeled into the appointed slumber room where   18
a few last touches may be added — his favorite pipe placed in his
hand or, if he was a great reader, a book propped into position. (In

[1] You have to suffer if you want to be beautiful.

the case of little Master Jones a Teddy bear may be clutched.) Here he will hold open house for a few days, visiting hours 10 A.M. to 9 P.M.

Meanings and Values

1a. What is the author's tone? (See Guide to Terms: *Style/Tone*.)
 b. Try to analyze the effect this tone had, at first reading, on your impressions of the subject matter itself.
 c. Form a specific comparison between this effect of tone and the effect of "tone of voice" in spoken language.

2. Why was it formerly "almost mandatory" for some relative to witness the embalming procedure (par. 2)?

3a. Do you believe that public information about this procedure would cost mortuaries much embalming business (par. 3)? Why, or why not?
 b. Why *do* people subject their dead to such a process?

4. Use the three part system of evaluation to judge the success of this process analysis. (Guide: *Evaluation*.)

Expository Techniques

1a. What is the central theme? (Guide: *Unity*.)
 b. Which parts of the writing, if any, do not contribute to the theme, thus damaging unity?
 c. What other elements of the writing contribute to, or damage unity?

2a. Beginning with paragraph 4, list or mark the transitional devices that help to bridge between paragraphs. (Guide: *Transition*.)
 b. Briefly explain how coherence is aided by such interparagraph transitions.

3. In this selection, far more than in most, emphasis can best be studied in connection with style. In fact, the two are almost indistinguishable here, and few, if any, of the other methods of achieving emphasis are used at all. (Guide: *Emphasis* and *Style/Tone*.) Consider each of the following stylistic qualities (some may overlap; others are included in diction) and illustrate, by examples, how each does create emphasis.
 a. Number and selection of details — e.g., the equipment and "aids" (par. 5).
 b. Understatement — e.g., the "chances of live burial" (par. 7).
 c. Special use of quotations — e.g., "that the body is in a box" (par. 17).
 d. Sarcasm and/or other forms of irony. (Guide: *Irony*) — e.g., "How *well* he looks" (par. 15).

Diction and Vocabulary

1. Much of the essay's unique style (with resulting emphasis) results from qualities of diction. Use examples to illustrate the following. (Some may be identical to those of the preceding answer, but they need not be.)

a. Choice of common, low-key words to achieve sarcasm through understatement — e.g., "This is nice . . ." (par. 15).

b. Terms of violence — e.g., "returns to the attack" (par. 12).

c. Terms of the living — e.g., "will hold open house" (par. 18).

d. The continuing use of "Mr. Jones."

2a. Illustrate the meaning of "connotation" with examples of quotations from morticians. (Guide: *Connotation/Denotation.*)

b. Are these also examples of "euphemism"?

c. Show how the author uses these facts to her own advantage — i.e., again, to achieve emphasis.

3a. Comment briefly on the quality and appropriateness of the metaphor that ends the introduction. (Guide: *Figures of Speech.*)

b. Is this, in any sense, also an allusion? Why, or why not?

4. Use the dictionary as needed to understand the meanings of the following words: docility, perpetuation (par. 1); inherent, mandatory (2); intractable, reticence, *raison d'être* (3); ingenious (5); rudimentary, cellular, somatic (7); carotid artery, femoral artery, subclavian vein (8); semblance (11); simulated, stippling, sutures (12); emaciation (13); dispel (7, title).

Suggestions for Writing and Discussion

1. What evidence can you find that "the satisfaction of curiosity about almost all matters is a national pastime" (par. 2)? Is this a good thing or not? Why?

2. Burial customs differ widely from country to country, sometimes from area to area in this country. If you can, describe one of the more distinctive customs and, if possible, show its sources — e.g., nature of the climate, "old country" tradition.

3. What do you foresee as near and far-future trends or radical changes in American burial practices? Why?

4. You may wish to develop further your answers to question 3 of "Meanings and Values"; the rationale of a large majority of people who do use this mortuary "service" for their departed relatives.

5. If you like, explain your personal preferences and the reasons for them.

Writing Suggestions for Section 5
Process Analysis

1. From one of the following topics develop a central theme into an *informational* process analysis showing:

    a. How you selected a college.
    b. How you selected your future career or major field of study.
    c. How your family selected a home.
    d. How a potential riot was stopped.
    e. How religious faith is achieved.
    f. How gasoline is made.
    g. How the air in ———— becomes polluted.
    h. How lightning kills.
    i. How foreign policy is made.
    j. How political campaigns are financed.
    k. How ———— Church was rebuilt.
    l. How fruit blossoms are pollinated.

2. Select a specific reader-audience and write a *directional* process analysis on one of the following topics, showing:

    a. How to *do* any of the processes suggested by topics 1a–e. (This treatment will require a different viewpoint, completely objective, and may require a different organization.)
    b. How to overcome shyness.
    c. How to overcome stage fright.
    d. How to make the best use of study time.
    e. How to write a college composition.
    f. How to sell an ugly house.
    g. How to prepare livestock or any other entry for a fair.
    h. How to start a club (or some other kind of recurring activity).
    i. How to reduce the number of highway accidents in an area.
    j. How to survive a tornado (or other natural disaster).
    k. How to select a car.
    l. How to develop moral (or physical) courage.

6

Analyzing *Cause* and *Effect* Relationships

Unlike process analysis, which merely tells *how*, causal analysis seeks to explain *why*. The two may be combined, but they need not be — many people have driven a car successfully after being told how to do it, never knowing or caring why the thing moved when they turned a key and worked a pedal or two.

Some causes and effects are not very complicated; at least the need for their explanation requires only a simple statement. A car may sit in the garage for a while because its owner has no money for a license tag, and sometimes this is explanation enough. But frequently a much more thorough analysis is required, and this may even become the basic pattern of an exposition.

To explain fully the causes of a war or depression or election results the writer must seek not only *immediate* causes (the ones he encounters first) but also *ultimate* causes (the basic, underlying factors that help to explain the more apparent ones). The business or professional man, as well as the student, often has pressing need for this type of analysis. How else could he fully understand or report on a failing sales campaign, diminishing church membership, a local increase of traffic accidents, or teenage use of hard drugs? The immediate cause of a disastrous warehouse fire could be faulty electrical wiring, but this might be attributed in turn to the company's unwise economy measures, which might be traced even further to undue pressures on the management to show large profits. The written analysis might logically stop at any point, of course, depending entirely on its purpose and the reader-audience for which it is intended.

Similarly, both the immediate and ultimate *effects* of an action or situation may, or may not, need to be fully explored. If a 5 per-cent pay raise is granted, what will be the immediate effect on the cost of production, leading to what ultimate effects on prices and, in some cases, on the whole economy of a business, a town, or perhaps the entire nation?

In earlier selections of this book we have seen several examples of causal analysis. In Section 1, for instance, Peter and Hull are concerned with the ultimate causes of incompetence in public life, and, in Section 2, Barber with both immediate and ultimate effects of presidential character.

Causal analysis is one of the chief techniques of reasoning; and if the method is used at all, the reader must always have confidence in its thoroughness and logic. Here are some ways to avoid the most common faults in causal reasoning:

1. Never mistake the fact that something happens with or after another occurrence as evidence of a causal relationship — for example, that a black cat crossing the road caused the flat tire a few minutes later, or that a course in English composition caused a student's nervous breakdown that same semester.

2. Consider all possibly relevant factors before attributing causes. Perhaps studying English did result in a nervous breakdown, but the cause may also have been ill health, trouble at home, or the anguish of a love affair. (The composition course, by providing an "emotional" outlet, may even have helped *postpone* the breakdown!)

3. Support the analysis by more than mere assertions: offer evidence. It would not often be enough to *tell* why Shakespeare's wise Othello believed the villainous Iago — the dramatist's lines should be used as evidence, possibly supported by the opinions of at least one literary scholar. If explaining that capital punishment deters crime, do not expect the reader to take your word for it — give before-and-after statistics or the testimony of reliable authorities.

4. Be careful not to omit any links in the chain of causes or effects unless you are certain that the readers for whom the writing is intended will automatically make the right connections themselves — and this is frequently a dangerous assumption. To unwisely omit one or more of the links might leave the reader with only a vague, or even erroneous, impression of the causal connec-

tion, possibly invalidating all that follows and thus making the entire writing ineffective.

5. Be honest and objective. The writer (or thinker) who brings his old prejudices to the task of causal analysis, or who fails to see the probability of *multiple* causes or effects, is almost certain to distort his analysis or to make it so superficial, so thin, as to be almost worthless.

Ordinarily the method of causal analysis is either to work logically from the immediate cause (or effect) down toward the most basic, or to start with the basic and work up toward the immediate. But after he has at least analyzed the subject in his mind and decided what his purpose requires in the paragraph or entire composition, the writer will usually find that a satisfactory pattern suggests itself.

ARNOLD TOYNBEE

ARNOLD TOYNBEE (1889–1975) was a world-famous historian and author. Trained in the classics, a graduate of Oxford University, he served in the British Foreign Office during both world wars. Toynbee is best known for his monumental, twelve-volume *A Study of History*, which is a philosophical investigation of the origins, growth, and breakdown of world civilization. Although widely admired, he was also extremely controversial: some scholars believed that his theories were too arbitrary and fraught with errors, and that he placed too much reliance on religion as a regenerative force. Toynbee also wrote *Civilization on Trial* (1948) and *The World and the West* (1953).

Intellectual Suicide at Puberty

"Intellectual Suicide at Puberty" (editor's title) is from Toynbee's "Why I Dislike Western Civilization," published in 1964. Although you may very well disagree with one or more of his basic assumptions, the selection does make a point worth thoughtful consideration, as well as providing a short, clear example of development by cause/effect analysis.

Looking back into the past history of the West — a past which was 1
still present when I was a child — I admire the nineteenth-century
West's success in postponing the age of sexual awakening, of sexual experience and sexual infatuation far beyond the age of physical puberty. You may tell me that this was against nature; but to be human consists precisely in transcending nature — in overcoming the biological limitations that we have inherited from our prehuman ancestors.

All human societies overcome death by creating and maintain- 2

From *The New York Times*, May 10, 1964. © 1964 by The New York Times Company. Reprinted by permission.

ing institutions that are handed on from one generation to another. Sex is a still more awkward feature of our biological inheritance than death, and our nineteenth-century Western society handled sex with relative success. By postponing the age of sexual awakening, it prolonged the length of the period of education. It is this, together with the seventeenth-century Western achievement of learning to think for oneself instead of taking tradition on trust, that accounts for the West's preeminence in the world during the last few centuries.

Nineteenth-century Westerners condemned with justice the   3 Hindu institution of child-marriage, and they deplored, also with justice, the spectacle of an intellectually promising Moslem boy being allowed to commit intellectual suicide by sexual indulgence at the age of puberty. The twentieth-century West is now imitating the non-Western habits that the nineteenth-century West rightly — though perhaps self-righteously — condemned.

Our irrational contemporary Western impatience and our   4 blind adulation of speed for speed's sake are making havoc, today, of the education of our children. We force their growth as if they were chicks in a pullet factory. We drive them into a premature awareness of sex even before physical puberty has overtaken them. In fact, we deprive our children of the human right of having a childhood. This forcing of sex-consciousness started in the United States; it has spread to Britain, and who knows how many other Western countries this perverse system of miseducation is going to invade and demoralize?

Our whole present policy in the upbringing of the young is   5 paradoxical. While we are lowering the age of sexual awareness — and frequently the age of sexual experience, too — to a veritably Hindu degree, we are at the same time prolonging the length of education. We force our boys and girls to become sex-conscious at twelve or thirteen, and then we ask them to prolong their postgraduate studies till they are nearly thirty. How are they to be expected to give their minds to education during those last sixteen or seventeen sex-haunted years?

We are proud of ourselves for providing secondary education,   6 college education, postgraduate education for everybody. But we shall be plowing the sands if we do not simultaneously revert to our grandparents' practice of prolonging the age of sexual innocence. If we persist, in this vital matter, on our present Hindu

course, our brand-new would-be institutions for higher education
will become, in practice, little more than social clubs for sexual
mating.

Meanings and Values

1. Is this selection primarily objective or subjective? Justify your answer. (See Guide to Terms: *Objective/Subjective.*)
2. Judging by what you know of your own great-grandparents and/or their contemporaries, do you believe Toynbee's assertions about delayed sexual awakening in nineteenth century youths? Explain.
3. How, if at all, can sex be considered an "awkward feature of our biological inheritance" (par. 2)?
4. In what ways do we "force" our boys and girls to become sex-conscious (pars. 4, 5)? If you do not agree with the author, state your reasons.
5. Do you agree that sexual involvement is detrimental to intellectual development? Why, or why not?

Expository Techniques

1a. Does the author make any use of qualification? If so, where? (Guide: *Qualification.*)
 b. Would the credibility of his thesis be improved with greater use of qualification? If so, explain why and how.
2a. Where would you place this writing on a specific/general continuum? Why? (Guide: *Specific/General.*)
 b. Would the writing have been improved by greater specificity? Demonstrate how this could have been achieved.

Diction and Vocabulary

1. What is "the West," as used by Toynbee?
2. Cite one example each of simile and metaphor (Guide: *Figures of Speech.*)
3. What would be the difference between "rightly" and "self-righteously" condemning non-Western sexual practices (par. 3)?
4a. Does the author use the word "paradoxical" (par. 5) in the same sense as we do? (Guide: *Paradox.*)
 b. Is this particular "paradox" also classifiable as irony? Why, or why not? (Guide: *Irony.*)

5. Consult your dictionary as needed to determine meanings of the following words: transcending (par. 1); preeminence (2); adulation, perverse, demoralize (4).

Suggestions for Writing and Discussion

1. Explain how it is that, even aside from matters of sex, the Western adulation of speed is "making havoc" of our children's education (par. 4). Make your discussion as specific as possible by means of clear examples.

2. Present *both* sides of the question of whether or not early sexual indulgence is a way of committing "intellectual suicide" (par. 3).

(NOTE: Suggestions for topics requiring development by analysis of CAUSE and EFFECT are on page 180, at the end of this section.)

GAIL SHEEHY

GAIL SHEEHY (born 1937) is a native New Yorker. After graduating from the University of Vermont she was a department
store consumer representative, a fashion coordinator, newspaper fashion editor, and women's feature writer for the New
York *Herald Tribune.* Since 1968 Sheehy has been a contributing editor for *New York* magazine. Her articles have appeared in numerous magazines, including *McCall's, Cosmo-
politan, Holiday, Glamour, Good Housekeeping,* and *The New
York Times Magazine.* Her books are *Lovesounds* (1970),
Speed Is of the Essence (1971), *Panthermania* (1971), *Hustling*
(1973), and *Passages* (1976), which was on the nation's best-
seller lists for many months.

$70,000 a Year, Tax Free

"$70,000 a Year, Tax Free" (editor's title) was written for
NBC's "Comment" series, but the material was incorporated
into *Hustling.* Its brevity, due to time limitations on the original presentation, obviously precluded a really thorough
analysis of the topic. Observing how the author did use the
time at her disposal provides some of the value of studying
the selection here.

How many women do you know who can take home seventy thou-   1
sand dollars a year? A psychiatrist? She might take home half that.
A congresswoman? Shirley Chisholm's salary is forty-two-five.

No, the quickest way for a woman to get ahead in this coun-   2
try is to take up the oldest profession: prostitution.

As one veteran streetwalker explained to a runaway she was   3
breaking in: "You have no status, no power, and no way to get it
except by using your body. Why give it away? You're sitting on a
gold mine!"

And so, every summer, in New York City, the hue and cry 4
goes up: Crack down on prostitution! Close the massage parlors!
But why has New York become a boomtown for hustlers? Not
because of the increased use of drugs, as most people assume. It
began with a change in New York's penal code four years ago.
Loitering for the purpose of prostitution was reduced by former
Police Commissioner Leary from a misdemeanor to a violation.
Even girls found guilty on the more serious "pross collar" rarely
go to jail. Most judges let them go for a twenty-five to fifty dollar
fine — and a week to pay. It amounts to a license.

Word of this change spread with interest through the pimp 5
grapevine around the country: New York was wide open. Today,
you'd hardly guess which four states have the largest pipeline shipping prostitutes to New York: in order, they are Minnesota, Massachusetts, Michigan, and Ohio. There are lots of fair haired girls
from Minnesota with street names like Little Tiffany, and Marion
the Librarian. But why do they come? It couldn't be a more American phenomenon: The prostitute's dream is the most upward mobile, middle class, American pie dream of all.

Number one: she wants money — high-style clothes, a model 6
apartment, candy color wigs and her teeth capped.

Number two: she's looking for a "family." Most of the girls 7
have one or two children — illegitimate. On top of that, the girl is
often white and her illegitimate child is black. Back home in Minneapolis, she was already a social pariah, and she couldn't make a
go of living and working while dragging a baby from room to
rented room. So she comes to New York, looking for a new kind
of family — exactly what the pimp provides.

He puts up his stable of three or four girls in a high-rise 8
apartment, pays their rent, buys their clothes, foots their doctor
bills. Top woman in this "family" — the pimp's favorite, who
brings in the most money — is called his "wife." The rest are
known as "wife-in-laws." Remarkably enough, they all get along
quite well. The tie that really binds is the baby sitter — the girls
share one for seventy-five dollars a week and this is what frees
them to work.

As a midtown hooker from Virginia put it to me: "Most of 9
the girls are here doing it for their kids. I don't want my daughter
to have the kind of childhood I had. She's going to have the best!"

So now the prostitute has money, a family, a baby sitter. The 10
other thing she craves is "glamour and excitement," things she

probably dreamed of finding in a career as a model or actress. But those fields are fiercely competitive. Besides, as a prostitute sees it, models and actresses are treated like dress hangers or pieces of meat: they give their bodies away to advance their careers, while so-called straight women exchange sex for the financial security of marriage. A "working girl," as the prostitute refers to herself, is the only honest one: She sets the price, delivers the goods, and concludes her business within the hour — no romantic nonsense about it.

And finally, after she is on the street for a few months, the   11
pace of peeping and hiding, the game of stinging johns and ducking police vans becomes a way of life. It gets into the blood like gambler's fever.

The hooker with the heart of gold? That's a male myth. Many   12
of our street girls can be as vicious and money mad as any corporation president. Moreover, they can be less emotional than men in conducting acts of personal violence. The bulk of their business is not the dispensation of pleasure: it is to mug, rob, swindle, knife, and possibly, even murder their patrons. Police drags against them are about as effective as pacification programs in Vietnam. Apply police pressure to streetwalkers and robberies generally go up. If a girl doesn't bring in that fixed amount, two hundred and fifty a night, she'll go home to a beating from her pimp.

People are puzzled: why this boom in prostitution when   13
young America is bursting with sexual freedom? They forget about men over forty, men who learned their sexual fantasies from nudie calendars in the gas station. To be fun, the bedmate must be a no-no. "You can't fantasize about your wife or girlfriend," one man explained. "The woman has to be an unknown." And where is this illicit thrill of forbidden flesh still to be found? On the black market of course. Furthermore, the prostitute makes no emotional demands. She would never call his office the next day. It is her stock in trade to encourage men's sexual fantasies and exploit them. How else can a girl make seventy thousand dollars a year, tax free!

Meanings and Values

1a. Briefly summarize the author's reasons for a girl's becoming a prostitute.

b. Do you consider these ultimate or immediate causes — or would you classify them somewhere in between? Why?

2a. Why does the author consider these motivations as an "American pie dream" (par. 5)?
 b. To which of the causes, if any, does the description seem to you not to apply? Why?

3. Why does she assume that we'd "hardly guess" which four states have the largest pipelines into New York prostitution (par. 5)?

4. Do you see anything ironical in the prostitute's comments in paragraph 9? (See Guide to Terms: *Irony*.) If so, explain.

5a. How can perpetuation of the "male myth" (par. 12) be explained?
 b. Why would it be more difficult to "fantasize" about one's wife or girlfriend (par. 13)?

6a. Where would you locate this selection on an objective-to-subjective continuum? (Guide: *Objective/Subjective*.)
 b. Is the author guilty of any sentimentality? (Guide: *Sentimentality*.) If so, where?

7. If you have read the preceding selection by Toynbee, what effect, if any, do you think the West's changing attitudes toward "sexual awakening" would have had on the prevalence of prostitution? Why?

Expository Techniques

1a. In which paragraphs does the author explain why prostitution has increased greatly in New York City?
 b. Does this seem to be a thorough cause-and-effect analysis?
 c. Is it sufficient for the purpose? Why, or why not?

2a. In paragraphs 6–11 she outlines a different set of causes. Would they have been more effective for her purpose if she had gone deeper into the more ultimate causes?
 b. Why do you think she did not?
 c. What function is served by the first sentence of paragraph 10? Why would the author have considered it a useful device in this particular exposition?

3a. What is Sheehy's central theme? (Guide: *Unity*.)
 b. Do all portions of the essay serve as tributaries into this theme, thus giving unity to the writing? If not, what are the exceptions?

4a. Which of the standard techniques of introduction does this author use? (Guide: *Introductions*.)
 b. Why do they seem particularly well chosen, considering the basic purpose of this exposition?

5a. The last sentence is a good example of at least one standard technique of closing. (Guide: *Closings*.) What is it?

b. Suggest a different kind of closing and compare the relative effectiveness of the two.

6. Which of the patterns of exposition already studied does Sheehy employ in paragraph 10?

7. In your opinion, would any of her statements have benefited by further qualification? (Guide: *Qualification.*) If so, explain why.

Diction and Vocabulary

1. Illustrate the meaning of the following terms by use of one or more examples from this selection.
   a. Colloquialism. (Guide: *Colloquial Expressions.*)
   b. Simile. (Guide: *Figures of Speech.*)
   c. Cliché. (Guide: *Clichés.*)
2. What is a "social pariah" (par. 7)?
3. Considering this exposition's original purpose, why do you think the author used few, if any, "dictionary-type" words?

Suggestions for Writing and Discussion

1. The author says most people assume that the increase of prostitution is related to an increased use of drugs. How logical does this assumption appear to you? Explain.
2. Explore parallels in other, more legitimate fields in which motivation may be provided by the "upward mobile, middle class, American pie dream" (par. 5).
3. In view of the five reasons for a girl's becoming a prostitute — all seeming to be fairly common desires — why is it that even more girls do not engage in prostitution?
4. Which of her five reasons do you think would also apply to the thriving business (in some cities especially) of male prostitution? Are there other reasons that apply here?
5. How logical and/or just do you consider the move in many areas toward "equal guilt" laws, whereby the male is considered as guilty as the prostitute he employs?
6. Should there even *be* laws prohibiting prostitution?
7. The word "prostitution" is often used with broader meaning than in Sheehy's analysis — e.g., "prostitution of talent" or "prostitution of science." Select one such usage and examine motivations in terms of this author's "upward mobility" theories.

(Note: Suggestions for topics requiring development by analysis of CAUSE and EFFECT are on page 180, at the end of this section.)

DIANA ROBINSON

DIANA ROBINSON was born in England and received most of her education there, but her B.S. degree is from Empire State College, State University of New York. She has been a student of psychic phenomena for about twenty-three years, and a freelance writer on the subject for about nine. She has been a newspaper columnist and a book reviewer for *Fate* magazine. Following a two-year research project on ESP, she wrote a book (still unpublished), *Karma and Christianity in the Here and Now*. Robinson is the founder of Howard County Psychic Study group in Columbia, Maryland, has worked with the Extended Services Division of Rochester Institute of Technology, and has taught numerous adult courses for schools and organizations such as Pittsford Central School and YMCA, and the Rochester Museum School of Science and Man. She wrote ten of the articles in *The People's Almanac*.

Recharging Yourself Through Meditation

"Recharging Yourself Through Meditation" is a selection from the best selling *The People's Almanac* (1975). Developing a topic of considerable current interest, Robinson's piece utilizes, to some extent at least, nearly all of the patterns of exposition already studied, as well as that of definition (Sec. 7). The cause/effect analysis is therefore informally constructed, casually interwoven with various other techniques.

There are almost as many definitions of meditation as there are 1 people meditating. It has been described as a 4th state of consciousness (neither waking, sleeping, nor dreaming); as a way to recharge one's inner batteries; as a state of passive awareness, of "no mind." Some teachers regard meditation as the complement to prayer: "Prayer is when you talk to God; meditation is when you listen to God." Meditation teaches the conscious mind to be still. The mind must learn to be still and listen, whether it listens to God, to the subconscious, or to an outside influence. Which of these one listens to depends on one's point of view and on which of the many forms of meditation one is attempting.

Contemplative meditation is a preliminary exercise for begin-   2 ners in which one stares at an object, trying to focus the entire consciousness on it and on nothing else. In meditation "with seed," also known as concentrative meditation, one *mentally* focuses the mind on a visualized object, phrase, or part of the body. Meditation *without* seed is far more difficult, for here nothing is visualized; the mind becomes or tries to become, a blank. There is also "open" meditation, in which one tries to be totally aware of one's environment, the sounds, the sensations (roughness of a sweater on an arm, weight of one's body pressing down on a chair, etc.). The reverse of this is meditation involving total sensory withdrawal, tuning out the environment. Mantra meditation involves the continuous repetition of a sound. (Transcendental meditation is one version.) Although we think of a meditator as sitting motionless, there is moving meditation too. The renowned whirling dervishes of the Sufis are actually meditating as they whirl. Tai Chi Ch'Uan, an oriental discipline now becoming popular in the West, combines slow physical movements with the mental techniques of meditation.

Why do people meditate? Why leave a busy schedule to sit   3 silently, spending valuable time apparently doing nothing? Isn't this a flight from the world? Couldn't we spend our time more constructively? Doesn't it foster anti-intellectualism? Doesn't such passivity make us mentally flabby, unable to face reality let alone try to change and improve it?

Opponents of meditation ask these questions and then answer   4 them affirmatively themselves. Most who have had experience in meditation disagree. The latter will tell you that with meditation they are calmer, more able to cope with problems. Far from withdrawing from life, they meet it more exuberantly, are able to think more clearly about what should be done to improve it, and have more energy to do what needs doing. Yet until recently all this was subjective. We could not tell if people were really benefiting from meditation, or if it was just the brief rest from routine that made them feel so good.

With the explosion of Western interest in meditation came, inevitably, the scientists. They moved meditation into the laboratory, measured it, tested it, computerized it, and they found that the meditators were right. Meditation really did things for its advocates.

They *were* more relaxed. Galvanic skin response, which is higher when you are relaxed, has been known to quadruple during meditation, whereas it only doubles during a full night's sleep. Meditators have lower anxiety levels, so they become more tolerant. Their reaction times are faster, and their senses seem to be more alert. Oxygen consumption goes below sleep levels; the heartbeat and entire metabolism seem to slow during meditation. There is also evidence that meditation increases ESP scores and, perhaps most significant of all, it has helped drug users to get off drugs.

Of course these tests cannot be said to be typical of *all* meditators, or of all types of meditation. Some produce results very different from others. When a clicking sound is repeated near us, most people react sharply the 1st few times, then adapt to it by "tuning it out." In one test Zen meditators, who generally practice the awareness-of-environment type of meditation, did not adapt to the sound at all. They continued to react to each click as they did to the 1st. On the other hand, yoga meditators, given the same test, did not even react to the 1st click, presumably because much yoga meditation involves turning inward and tuning out the senses.

Much has been made of the connection between meditation and the alpha waves of the brain. Experienced meditators can usually emit strong alpha waves, and alpha from some parts of the brain does seem to evoke feelings of peace. However, some practitioners of Kriya yoga, who meditate on visions of deities, have been found to emit very fast beta waves, rather than the expected slower alpha. Thus not all meditation involves alpha, and it is certain that not all alpha waves involve meditation, so much research remains to be done in this area.

Exactly why meditation has the effects it does is not known for certain. It is suspected that in Western society people have become overintellectualized. The conscious mind rarely stops ticking, let alone pauses to try to commune with the subconscious. In meditation it is trained to quiet down, to tune out all external and internal noise. Then it can become aware of what is coming from the subconscious, enabling conscious and subconscious to work together in close harmony, with less internal friction and consequently less stress. Beginning meditators, once they have mastered the basic techniques, may find themselves overwhelmed with long-forgotten memories, often very emotional ones. Obviously this can be deeply disturbing, and those who stop meditating because of this may report that meditation is harmful or frightening. However, when these experiences have been worked through and accepted into consciousness (as in psychoanalysis), the meditations become very peaceful. Patience is the key.

Another effect of meditation is to de-automatize the meditator. 10 We all know that we become used to things. If we were perceiving the sky, a tree, a loved one's face for the 1st time, we would be full of wonder, but we are used to them, so our senses become jaded; we are automatized. The form of meditation that tunes out the senses helps us to de-automatize. While we meditate we are unaware of any sensory input. Then, meditation over, we reawaken to a world in which, hopefully, "all things are made new." The awareness-of-environment type of meditation helps us not to automatize at all, as with the Zen Buddhists who did not automatize to the clicks.

It is also possible that by tuning out all normal stimuli we may 11 be better able to sense weaker "signals." (The stars are always in the sky, but in the presence of the "everyday" sun we cannot sense them.) These signals may be from God (meditation is, after all, recommended by all major religions), or from the environment in the form of ESP, or perhaps from other sources, but they must surely help us to be more aware of our universe, and so of ourselves.

Meditation techniques abound. Some may be helpful, others 12 just a distraction. No one technique is essential, but here are a few that have been found useful. Some people achieve very satisfying meditative states without any of them.

The spine should be straight. The lotus and other cross-legged 13 positions are good, but you can just as well sit in a straight-backed chair, feet on the ground, hands on knees. Concentrative or contemplative meditations are best for beginners. Either stare at or visualize an object, perhaps one of spiritual significance, perhaps one that is just beautiful. An uplifting or soothing phrase will do. Or observe your breathing. Whatever, focus your whole attention on it; there is nothing else in the universe. . . . Thoughts will come and go. Let them go; let them float by like fluffy clouds that cannot really ruffle the clear blue of the sky beyond. Let them go, and return to your focus. Relax, be comfortable. Be still. At 1st, try for no longer than 10 minutes, preferably twice a day, preferably in the same place, preferably not just after a meal. Later you can meditate longer — 20 to 30 minutes is ideal. Unsupervised meditation for over an hour at a time can lead to problems and for most people is unnecessarily time-consuming. Meditation is beautiful, but it is a means to a more fulfilling life; it should not be an end in itself. Peace.

Meanings and Values

1a. Illustrate the difference between objective and subjective writing by citing passages from this essay. (See Guide to Terms: *Objective/ Subjective*.)
 b. Which of the two seems more to reflect the author's own attitude toward her subject matter? Why?
2. Use the three-part system of evaluation to judge the success of this cause/effect analysis. (Guide: *Evaluation*.)
3a. What may be the reasons that meditation is steadily gaining popularity in the West?
 b. Does it seem to you that urban dwellers or rural people would have more need for meditation? Why?
 c. If you have read the Toffler and/or Wolfe selections (Sec. 4), which of your answers to "a" and "b" were suggested by those pieces?

Expository Techniques

1a. Cite the paragraphs in which Robinson has discussed the effects of meditation.
 b. Are these concerned mostly with immediate or ultimate effects? Explain your answer.
2. Use two of Robinson's examples to demonstrate the merits of specific writing. (Guide: *Specific/General*.)
3a. Cite whatever uses you can find of the various other patterns of exposition.
 b. Would the essay be better off without any of them? Why, or why not?
4. Use examples of parallel structure from this selection to illustrate the meaning of the term and advantages of the technique. (Guide: *Parallel Structure*.)
5. How effective do you consider the single concluding word? Why?

Diction and Vocabulary

1. Is the "fluffy clouds" sentence in paragraph 13 a better example of analogy or simile? Why? (Guide: *Figures of Speech.*)

2a. How do you account for the nearly total lack of "difficult" words in this composition?

 b. Is its simple diction demeaning to sophisticated readers? Why, or why not?

Suggestions for Writing and Discussion

1. If people of modern Western society are more apt to be victims of automation and overintellectualization than people of earlier times or of other societies, what, other than meditation, can individuals do about it? Explain.

2. Expand on the quotation in paragraph 1 for a full comparison/contrast of "meditation" and "prayer."

3. If you believe the author's discussion is more concerned with immediate than ultimate effects, carry her thesis further to show what ultimate effects, if any, one could expect to derive from the immediate effects.

(NOTE: Suggestions for topics requiring development by analysis of CAUSE and EFFECT are on page 180, at the end of this section.)

WILLIAM H. MASTERS and VIRGINIA E. JOHNSON

WILLIAM H. MASTERS, born in Cleveland (1915), received his B.S. from Hamilton College and his M.D. from the University of Rochester. He has taught at Washington University School of Medicine and has served on various hospital staffs in the practice of obstetrics and gynecology, and on several professional councils and boards of directors. He is married to Virginia Johnson, with whom he directs the Reproductive Biology Research Foundation in St. Louis. Together they have written three famous studies: *Human Sexual Response* (1966), *Human Sexual Inadequacy* (1970), and (in association with Robert J. Levin) *The Pleasure Bond* (1975).

VIRGINIA E. JOHNSON was born in Missouri (1925) and was educated at Drury College, the University of Missouri, and Washington University. A psychologist, she has written for newspapers and conducted several radio programs. In addition to the accomplishments she has shared with Masters, she has served on the staff of Washington University School of Medicine and has been active in numerous professional societies.

Touching—and Being Touched

"Touching — and Being Touched," as it appears here, is the *Reader's Digest* condensation of an article originally prepared for *Redbook* magazine and later used in expanded form in *The Pleasure Bond.* It provides a means of studying a far more comprehensive analysis of cause and effect than either of the preceding selections has afforded, and it also shows how such an analysis may be effectively combined with other patterns of exposition.

Long before sexual attraction exists as anything more than natural curiosity about anatomical differences, most little boys and girls sense that the mysterious feelings drawing them into the adventure of mutual exploration are wrong. They have absorbed from the adult world the idea that touching the human body is indecent.

Reprinted by permission of Little, Brown and Company from *The Pleasure Bond: A New Look at Sexuality and Commitment* by William H. Masters and

173

"Don't touch!" is a childhood litany. Many parents set clear   2
examples. Apart from an occasional perfunctory embrace, they do
not so much as hold hands. The father will decide that his little
son or daughter is too old to nestle in his lap or be kissed. The
mother will stop giving baths to a still young child.

Such parents cannot permit the spontaneous physical expres-   3
sion of feelings — the stroking, snuggling and enfolding movements with which almost all living creatures seek the warmth and
reassurance that is virtually indistinguishable from life itself. Thus,
while still too young to understand why, children learn to restrain
the impulse to reach out to someone of the opposite sex.

As they grow older, the impulse to touch is expressed by teas-   4
ing. This leads to scuffling and wrestling, which, although ostensibly in conflict, give boys and girls a chance to experience close
physical contact. By adolescence they realize that parental prohibitions are merely temporary restraining orders. Most then begin
experimenting with kissing games, which escalate into necking and
petting.

Now the girls become the ones who say, "Don't touch," echo-   5
ing the lesson deeply ingrained in childhood: that sex is dirty, and
touching means sex — so it's hands off. Reaching out, which has
already been sharply limited as a spontaneous way of expressing
affection and solidarity, is now stripped of all significance except
that of sexual provocation. Thus the use of touch as a natural, uncomplicated way to express goodwill or friendship is forfeited.

Later, at the age of sexual experimentation, girls are more in-   6
clined to let themselves be touched than to do the touching. This
again is partly a result of cultural conditioning — passivity as the
proper female role, and the deeply embedded feeling that sexual
activity for her may be dishonorable. With the rationalization that
the boy is the initiator, the aggressor, who must bear full responsibility for what takes place between them, she struggles to free herself from feelings of guilt or discomfort, to free herself from the
tight, involuntary tensions of her body, to free herself to enjoy her
natural, physical response to being touched.

Virginia E. Johnson in association with Robert J. Levin. Copyright © 1972,
1974 by William H. Masters and Virginia E. Johnson. As condensed in the
December 1972 *Reader's Digest*.

Her reluctance to touch also may be based on a practical con- 7
sideration. In her early encounters with a boy she is likely to find
that he becomes too excited too soon — and additional stimulation
seems not only unnecessary but inadvisable.

Boys think of touch — which, at this stage, is closer to grop- 8
ing or grabbing than to caressing — as a sexual starter, or trigger.
The boy expects that once he places his hand on a girl's body, her
sexual motor will automatically shift into high gear. Her failure to
respond with an ardor to match his own may baffle him. He is
likely to try all the harder to overcome the girl's resistance, believing that she is just afraid of being aroused by his touch, and
that if he can force his way past her defenses, her resistance will
melt.

When these first, fumbling encounters produce not the antici- 9
pated delight but dismay or disappointment, most young people
question not their expectations but themselves — or each other. He
decides she is uptight because she didn't let him touch her in the
right place; she decides he is inept because he didn't know how to
touch her in the right way. They believe that if they just try again
— with a new partner — before too long they will surely master
the trick of sex. And the search continues, on a trial-and-error
basis.

In time, some young men and women find at least partial an- 10
swers to their questions. But even for them, success is usually
flawed by continuing inability to grasp the true function of touch.
Many still think of it exclusively as a means to an end — touching
for the purpose of having intercourse, a functional, wordless way
to communicate a willingness, a wish or a demand to make love.

Meanwhile, for other couples, who also consider touching to 11
be just a means to the same end, it becomes a means they enjoy
almost as much as the end itself. They have advanced past the
adolescent notion of touch-as-trigger to the more sophisticated
notion of touch-as-technique. In essence, they have adopted the
philosophy of the how-to-do-it sex manuals. Sex becomes a skill
that can be learned, and then applied wherever desired. Men and
women are taught not how to touch another human being but how
to manipulate another body.

This is a dead-end approach to the sexual relationship. Pre- 12
occupation with manipulative technique turns persons into objects,

and touching is turned into the science of stimulation. Instead of a sharing of private emotions, sex then comes perilously close to being an exchange of impersonal services.

For the man and woman who value each other as individuals 13 and who want the satisfactions of a sustained relationship, it is important to avoid the fundamental error of believing that touch serves only as a means to an end. In fact it is a primary form of communication, a silent voice that avoids the pitfalls of words while expressing the feelings of the moment. It bridges the physical separateness from which no one is spared, literally establishing a sense of solidarity between two individuals.

Touch most often carries its own message. It can be asexual, 14 used to represent personal attitudes or emotions, to give comfort, to reassure. It can be a sensual thing, exploring the texture of the skin, the suppleness of a muscle, the contours of the body, with no further goal than enjoyment of tactile perceptions. And yet such is the nature of the sense of touch, which can simultaneously give and receive impressions, that the very pleasure a woman experiences in stroking her husband's face, for example, is relayed back through her fingertips, giving him the pleasure of awareness of her pleasure in him.

This is the wellspring of emotion from which sexuality flows. 15 In reaching out spontaneously to communicate by touch, a husband and wife reaffirm their trust in each other and renew their commitment. They draw on this emotional reservoir when one turns to the other with physical desire. Because their touching has a continuity, and is part of an intimate dialogue that does not begin and end in bed, they feel secure. Whoever makes an overture knows the other will understand and respond, and the partner is secure in the knowledge that his response will be accepted, no matter how limited the degree of erotic arousal may naturally be at that moment.

Where no such security exists, two individuals in a sexual encounter may touch physically but remain out of touch emotionally. 16 When touch or submitting to touch takes place solely for the purpose of intercourse it can express neither warmth nor closeness. It is a signal without subtlety, a demand for service or a yielding to such a demand. And over the years the service deteriorates, until finally one of the partners can no longer, or will no longer, perform. In a sad and ironic echo of their childhood, a man and woman live out their later lives in married celibacy and "do not touch."

Today's young couples seem to be freer to express themselves, 17 in words and physically. Perhaps they will succeed in incorporating into their sexual lives a new philosophy of touch. Perhaps they do understand that touching — like seeing, hearing, tasting and smelling — nourishes the pleasure of being alive; that touching another human being satisfies the profound creature need not to feel alone; that being touched by another human being satisfies the need to be desired as a physical presence; and that in touching and being touched, one can experience not only the pleasure of being alive but also the joy of being a sexual creature — a joy that ultimately and inevitably, as a natural extension of life itself, expresses itself in the sexual embrace.

Meanings and Values

1a. Judging from your own experience and observations, does it still seem to be true that children absorb from the adult world the idea that touching the human body is indecent (par. 1)?

  b. Do you then think the author's note of optimism in paragraph 17 is justified, or not? Explain.

2. Can the explanation of boy-girl scuffling and wrestling (par. 4) help in any way to explain the penchant of most boys for scuffling and wrestling with each other? Show how, or why not.

3. What are the "pitfalls of words" mentioned in paragraph 13?

4. Use the three-point system of evaluation to judge the success of this selection. (See Guide to Terms: *Evaluation*.)

5. If you have read the Toynbee piece in this section, what relationship do you see, if any, between his theory of earlier "sexual awakening" and the central theme of Masters and Johnson? Explain.

Expository Techniques

1a. In the first paragraph is a generalization that is at least a partial statement of central theme. (Guide: *Unity*.) What is it?

  b. This generality, as it becomes more specific, also provides a sort of fulcrum for the cause/effect analysis that follows. Which paragraphs are devoted to the causes?

  c. What is the function of the last sentence of paragraph 3?

2a. As the analysis of effects proceeds, they are presented as an almost indistinguishable element of another pattern of exposition previously studied. What is it?

b. Select one paragraph by which to illustrate clearly this blending technique.

c. How effective is it?

3. A more localized (and more subtle) use of still another pattern of exposition may be found in paragraphs 6–9. What is it?

4. Illustrate the meaning of both immediate and ultimate effects by use of passages from this composition.

5. Cite five examples that show how, in addition to careful organization, the use of interparagraph transitional devices helps achieve good coherence. (Guide: *Coherence and Transition.*)

6a. Cite five examples of qualification. (Guide: *Qualification.*)

b. What effect, if any, does such qualifying have on the credibility of the authors' ideas?

c. Would credibility be still further increased by even greater, or stronger, use of qualification? If so, cite passages and give your reasons.

7. The long closing sentence, which provides a kind of capsulized summary, includes rather extensive use of parallel structure. (Guide: *Parallel Structure.*) What specific advantages, if any, are gained here by use of this technique?

Diction and Vocabulary

1a. In developing this subject, some less disciplined writers might have resorted to the use of "four-letter" words. Would such usage have helped, or hindered, the effectiveness?

b. How, if at all, would these authors' purpose and intended reader-audience have helped determine this matter of taste and style?

c. Is there any reader-audience for which a different decision would have been advisable?

2. Illustrate the meaning of metaphor by examples from paragraphs 8, 12, 15. (Guide: *Figures of Speech.*)

3. Why is the situation referred to at the end of paragraph 16 an *ironic* echo? (Guide: *Irony.*)

4. Do you see anything paradoxical in the expression "married celibacy" (par. 16)? (Guide: *Paradox.*) Why, or why not?

5. Use the dictionary as necessary to understand the following words and their meanings: litany, perfunctory (par. 2); virtually (3); ostensibly (4); inept (9); asexual, sensual, tactile (14); erotic (15); subtlety (16).

Suggestions for Writing and Discussion

1. What ill effects, if any, do some parents (and also some child psychologists) think may result from too prolonged nestling, kissing, or bathing of growing children? How can a parent know what *is* best?

2. Explain further, or show to be doubtful, the authors' observation that stroking, snuggling, and enfolding movements are "virtually indistinguishable from life itself" (par. 3).

3. In various cultures other than ours the use of touch between adults of the same sex "as a natural, uncomplicated way to express goodwill or friendship" (par. 5) is not taboo, does not imply homosexuality. Explore the possibilities of our own eventual change in this respect.

4. From the Masters/Johnson analysis could you go further to see any possible explanation for Americans' devotion to animal pets? Is this, for instance, an unconscious (if perhaps pathetic) attempt to "bridge the physical separateness" referred to in paragraph 13?

5. Use comparison and/or contrast to show how two families of your acquaintance handle, or have handled, the matter of touch in parent-child relationships. If possible, also compare the ultimate effects.

Writing Suggestions for Section 6
Analysis of Cause and Effect

Analyze the immediate and ultimate causes and/or effects of one of the following subjects, or another suggested by them. (Be careful that your analysis does not develop into a mere listing of superficial "reasons.")

1. The ethnic makeup of a neighborhood.
2. Some *minor* discovery or invention.
3. The popularity of some modern singer or other celebrity admired especially by young people.
4. The popularity of some fad of clothing or hair style.
5. The widespread fascination for antique cars (or guns, furniture, dishes, etc.).
6. The widespread enjoyment of fishing or hunting.
7. Student cheating.
8. One person's decision to join a "hippie" commune.
9. Too much pressure (on you or an acquaintance) for good school grades.
10. Your being a member of some minority ethnic or religious group.
11. Your association, as an outsider, with members of such a group.
12. The decision of some close acquaintance to enter the religious life.
13. Some unreasonable fear or anxiety that afflicts you or someone you know well.
14. Your need to conform.
15. Your tendency toward individualism.

7

Using *Definition* to Help Explain

Few writing faults can cause a more serious communication block between writer and reader than using key terms that can have various meanings or shades of meaning. To be useful rather than detrimental, such terms must be adequately defined.

Of the two basic types of definition, only one is our special concern as a pattern of exposition. But the other, the simpler form, is often useful to clarify meanings of concrete or noncontroversial terms. This simple process is similar to that used most in dictionaries: either providing a synonym (for example, cinema: a motion picture), or placing the word in a class and then showing how it differs from others of the same class (for example, metheglin: an alcoholic liquor made of fermented honey — here the general class is "liquor," and the differences between metheglin and other liquors are that it is "alcoholic" and "made of fermented honey").

More pertinent to our study of structural patterns, however, is *extended* definition, a technique that may be vitally important when using an abstract term or new expression. Barber (Sec. 2), for example, uses "character" to suit his own needs, but devotes a large share of the selection to explaining what it means to him. Elbow (Sec. 5) defines his term "freewriting" by explaining how it works, and Robinson's essay (Sec. 6), while analyzing the causes and effects of meditation, also develop a thorough extended definition of the term.

With many such abstract or coined terms, typical readers are too limited by their own experiences and opinions (and no two sets are identical) for the writer to expect understanding of the exact sense in which he uses the terms. He has a right, of course, to use such abstract words any way he chooses — as long as his readers know what that way is. The importance of making this meaning clear becomes crucial when the term is used as a key element of the overall explanation. And sometimes the term being defined is even more than a key element: it may be the subject itself. For instance, to define "The Peter Principle" (Sec. 1) was really the primary purpose of writing, even though the authors use examples almost exclusively as a *means* of defining; and classification really was only Fromm's primary *method* of defining symbolic language (Sec. 2).

Extended definition, unlike the simple, dictionary type, follows no set and formal pattern. Often the reader is not even aware of the process. Because it is an integral part of the overall subject, extended definition is written in the same tone as the rest of the exposition, usually with an attempt to interest the reader, as well as to inform him.

There are some expository techniques peculiar to definition alone. The purpose may be served by giving the background of the term. Or the definition may be clarified by negation, sometimes called "exclusion" or "differentiation," by showing what is *not* meant by the term. Still another way is to enumerate the characteristics of what is defined, sometimes isolating an essential one for special treatment.

To demonstrate the possibilities in these patterns, we can use the term "juvenile delinquency," which might need defining in some contexts since it certainly means different things to different people. (Where do we draw the line, for instance, between "boyish pranks" and delinquency, or between delinquent and nondelinquent experimentation with sex or marijuana?) We might show how attitudes toward juvenile crime have changed: "youthful high spirits" was the label for some of our grandfathers' activities that would be called "delinquency" today. Or we could use negation, eliminating any classes of juvenile wrongdoing not considered delinquency in the current discussion. Or we could simply list characteristics of the juvenile delinquent or isolate one of these — disrespect for authority or lack of consideration for other people — as a universal.

But perhaps the most dependable techniques for defining are the basic expository patterns already studied. The writer could illustrate his meaning of "juvenile delinquency" by giving *examples* from his own experience, from newspaper accounts, or from other sources. (Every one of the introductions to the ten sections of this book, each a definition, relies greatly on illustration by example, as does the Peter/Hull selection.) He could analyze the subject by *classification* of types or degrees of delinquency. He could use the process of *comparison* and *contrast,* perhaps between delinquent and nondelinquent youth. Showing the *causes* and *effects* of juvenile crime could help explain his attitude toward it, and hence its meaning for him. He might choose to use *analogy,* perhaps comparing the child to a young tree growing grotesque because of poor care and attention. Or a step-by-step analysis of the *process* by which a child becomes delinquent might, in some cases, help explain the intended meaning.

Few extended definitions would use all these methods, but the extent of their use must always depend on three factors: (1) the term itself, since some are more elusive and subject to misunderstanding than others; (2) the function the term is to serve in the writing, since it would be foolish to devote several pages to defining a term that serves only a casual or unimportant purpose; and (3) the prospective reader-audience, since the writer wants to avoid insulting the intelligence or background of his readers, yet wants to go far enough to be sure of their understanding.

But this, of course, is a basic challenge in any good writing — analyzing the prospective reader and writing for the best effect on *him.*

WOODY ALLEN

Woody Allen, born Allen Stewart Konigsberg in 1935, is a
well-known comedian of TV, movie, and Broadway fame.
While still in his teens, Allen wrote TV comedy for Gary
Moore, Art Carney, and Sid Caesar. Not until 1961 did Allen
himself become a performer. He has contributed pieces to
magazines including *Playboy* and *The New Yorker;* some of
these have been collected in his books *Getting Even* (1971)
and *Without Feathers* (1975). Allen is perhaps best known
now for the films he has written, directed, and starred in,
the latest being *Love and Death* (1975) and *Annie Hall* (1977).

A Brief, Yet Helpful, Guide
to Civil Disobedience

"A Brief, Yet Helpful, Guide to Civil Disobedience" first appeared in *The New York Times* in October 1972. As is true of
most of Allen's writing, it is a humorous "put-on" — selected
for inclusion here partially to lighten our way into "Definition," but also because the author uses that particular pattern
of exposition in unexpected ways that merit our attention.

In perpetrating a revolution, there are two requirements: someone   1
or something to revolt against and someone to actually show up
and do the revolting. Dress is usually casual and both parties may
be flexible about time and place but if either faction fails to attend,
the whole enterprise is likely to come off badly. In the Chinese
Revolution of 1650 neither party showed up and the deposit on the
hall was forfeited.

The people or parties revolted against are called the "oppres-   2
sors" and are easily recognized as they seem to be the ones having
all the fun. The "oppressors" generally get to wear suits, own land,

and play their radios late at night without being yelled at. Their job is to maintain the "status quo," a condition where everything remains the same although they may be willing to paint every two years.

When the "oppressors" become too strict, we have what is known as a police state wherein all dissent is forbidden as is chuckling, showing up in a bow tie, or referring to the mayor as "Fats." Civil liberties are greatly curtailed in a police state and freedom of speech is unheard of although one is allowed to mime to a record. Opinions critical of the government are not tolerated, particularly about their dancing. Freedom of the press is also curtailed and the ruling party "manages" the news, permitting the citizens to hear only acceptable political ideas and ball scores that will not cause unrest.

The groups who revolt are called the "oppressed" and can generally be seen milling about and grumbling or claiming to have headaches. (It should be noted that the oppressors never revolt and attempt to become the oppressed as that would entail a change of underwear.)

Some famous examples of revolutions are:

The French Revolution, in which the peasants seized power by force and quickly changed all locks on the palace doors so the nobles could not get back in. Then they had a large party and gorged themselves. When the nobles finally recaptured the palace they were forced to clean up and found many stains and cigarette burns.

The Russian Revolution, which simmered for years and suddenly erupted when the serfs finally realized that the Czar and the Tsar were the same person.

It should be noted that after a revolution is over, the "oppressed" frequently take over and begin acting like the "oppressors." Of course by then it is very hard to get them on the phone and money lent for cigarettes and gum during the fighting may as well be forgotten about.

Methods of Civil Disobedience:

Hunger strike. Here the oppressed goes without food until his demands are met. Insidious politicians will often leave biscuits within easy reach or perhaps some cheddar cheese but they must be resisted. If the party in power can get the striker to eat, they usually have little trouble putting down the insurrection. If they can get him to eat and also lift the check, they have won for sure. In Pakistan, a hunger strike was broken when the Government produced an exceptionally fine veal cordon bleu which the masses found was too appealing to turn down but such gourmet dishes are rare.

The problem with the hunger strike is that after several days one can get quite hungry, particularly since sound-trucks are paid to go through the street saying, "Um . . . what nice chicken — umm . . . some peas . . . umm. . . ."

A modified form of the Hunger Strike for those whose political convictions are not quite so radical is giving up chives. This small gesture, when used properly, can greatly influence a government and it is well known that Mahatma Gandhi's insistence on eating his salads untossed shamed the British Government into many concessions. Other things besides food one can give up are: whist, smiling, and standing on one foot and imitating a crane.

Sit-down Strike. Proceed to a designated spot and then sit down, but sit all the way down. Otherwise you are squatting, a position that makes no political point unless the government is also squatting. (This is rare, although a government will occasionally crouch in cold weather.) The trick is to remain seated until concessions are made but as in the Hunger Strike, the government will try subtle means of making the striker rise. They may say, "Okay, everybody up, we're closing." Or, "Can you get up for a minute, we'd just like to see how tall you are?"

Demonstration and Marches. The key point about a demonstration is that it must be seen. Hence the term, "demonstration." If a person demonstrates privately in his own home, this is not technically a demonstration but merely "acting silly," or "behaving like an ass."

A fine example of demonstration was The Boston Tea Party where outraged Americans disguised as Indians dumped British tea into the harbor. Later, Indians disguised as outraged Americans dumped actual British into the harbor. Following that, the British disguised as tea, dumped each other into the harbor. Finally, German mercenaries clad only in costumes from "The Trojan Women" leapt into the harbor for no apparent reason.

When demonstrating, it is good to carry a placard stating 16
one's position. Some suggested positions are: (1) lower taxes, (2)
raise taxes, and (3) stop grinning at Persians.

Miscellaneous Methods of Civil Disobedience: 17

Standing in front of City Hall and chanting the word "pud- 18
ding" until one's demands are met.

Tying up traffic by leading a flock of sheep into the shopping 19
area.

Phoning members of "the establishment" and singing "Bess, 20
You Is My Woman, Now" into the phone.

Dressing as a policeman and then skipping. 21

Pretending to be an artichoke but punching people as they 22
pass.

Meanings and Values

1. If you find this essay amusing, what do you think is its basic *source*
   of humor? If not, analyze briefly why (for you, at least) it misses
   its mark.

2. Writers often use humor, in widely varying degrees, as a vehicle to
   convey some more serious theme, to share some observation of the
   human condition. (Humor merely for humor's sake, of course, with
   no function at all except to make people laugh, is a perfectly legitimate art form in its own right!)

   a. What more serious purpose, if any, does this author apparently
      have, either in overall theme or in individual parts? Cite examples
      as needed to support your answer.

   b. What do you consider his *primary* purpose? His secondary pur-
      pose, if any?

   c. How successful was he in achieving these aims?

   3a. What is Allen's point of view in this essay? (See Guide to Terms:
       Point of View.)

   b. How, if at all, is this related to the tone of the writing? (Guide:
      Style/Tone.)

Expository Techniques

1. Despite the loose organization and humorous tone, the "definitions"
   in this essay still use some of the standard techniques of more

serious definition. Isolate as many of these as possible and cite examples for support.

2. In what respects is Allen's humorous style a matter of syntax? (Guide: *Syntax*.) Be specific, citing examples.

3. One important element of Allen's style of humor is his selection of details, the constant use of surprise. (Only the greenest beginner would assume that even apparently minor details in successful writing are apt to "just happen" — even to an old pro like Woody Allen. They are carefully selected, weighed, and *placed*.)
   a. Cite five good examples of this use of surprise details.
   b. Briefly analyze why this is, or is not, a successful technique.

Diction and Vocabulary

1. How, if at all, is Allen's humorous style a matter of diction? (Guide: *Diction*.) Provide examples to help clarify your ideas.

2. Use the dictionary as necessary to understand the meanings of the following words: perpetrating (par. 1); mime (3); entail (4); insidious, gourmet (10); mercenaries (15).

Suggestions for Writing and Discussion

1. Explore the possibility that humor in itself may have real and very practical value.

2. Use recent or historical examples to demonstrate that civil disobedience, while seldom totally successful, is sometimes an effective instrument of change.

(NOTE: Suggestions for topics requiring development by use of DEFINITION are on page 207, at the end of this section.)

MARGARET MEAD and RHODA METRAUX

MARGARET MEAD, born in Philadelphia in 1901, is a widely respected anthropologist and author. She was educated at Barnard College (B.A., 1923) and Columbia University (Ph.D., 1929). In the course of a distinguished career she has served in responsible positions, among them as associate curator and director of research programs at the American Museum of Natural History at Columbia University, where she was also professor of anthropology. Mead was in government service during World War II and has served as president of the American Anthropological Association and of the World Federation for Mental Health. She has written almost innumerable books and articles for both popular and professional magazines. One of her best known and still-popular books is *Male and Female* (1949), but most of her writing has been anthropological, based on many years of extensive field research in the Pacific islands.

RHODA METRAUX was born in Brooklyn in 1914 and is another noted anthropologist. She earned her B.A. degree at Vassar, did postgraduate study at Yale, and received her Ph.D. degree from Columbia. Metraux has directed numerous important research expeditions and is currently a Research Associate at the American Museum of Natural History. Most of her writing has been done for anthropological and other professional journals.

The Egalitarian Error

"The Egalitarian Error," unlike the preceding definition, which is primarily intended for fun, is a serious effort to define an abstract term which the authors believe is commonly and dangerously misused. It provides an extensive illustration of one of the standard techniques of definition discussed in the introduction to this section.

Almost all Americans want to be democratic, but many Americans   1
are confused about what, exactly, democracy means. How do you

know when someone is acting in a democratic — or an undemocratic — way? Recently several groups have spoken out with particular bitterness against the kind of democracy that means equal
opportunity for all, regardless of race or national origin. They act
as if all human beings did not belong to one species, as if some
races of mankind were inferior to others in their capacity to learn
what members of other races know and have invented. Other extremists attack religious groups — Jews or Catholics — or deny the
right of an individual to be an agnostic. One reason that these
extremists, who explicitly do not want to be democratic, can get
a hearing even though their views run counter to the Constitution
and our traditional values is that the people who *do* want to be
democratic are frequently so muddled.

For many Americans, democratic behavior necessitates an out-   2
right denial of any significant differences among human beings. In
their eyes it is undemocratic for anyone to refer, in the presence
of any other person, to differences in skin color, manners or religious beliefs. Whatever one's private thoughts may be, it is necessary always to act as if everyone were exactly alike.

Behavior of this kind developed partly as a reaction to those   3
who discriminated against or actively abused members of other
groups. But it is artificial, often hypocritical behavior, nonetheless,
and it dulls and flattens human relationships. If two people can't
talk easily and comfortably but must forever guard against some
slip of the tongue, some admission of what is in both persons'
minds, they are likely to talk as little as possible. This embarrassment about differences reaches a final absurdity when a Methodist
feels that he cannot take a guest on a tour of his garden because
he might have to identify a wild plant with a blue flower, called
the wandering Jew, or when a white lecturer feels he ought not to
mention the name of Conrad's beautiful story *The Nigger of the
"Narcissus."* But it is no less absurd when well-meaning people,
speaking of the physically handicapped, tell prospective employers:
"They don't want special consideration. Ask as much of them as
you do of everyone else, and fire them if they don't give satisfaction!"

Another version of false democracy is the need to deny the   4

1964, 1965, 1966, 1967, 1968, 1969, 1970 by Margaret Mead and Rhoda
Metraux.

existence of personal advantages. Inherited wealth, famous parents, a first-class mind, a rare voice, a beautiful face, an exceptional physical skill — any advantage has to be minimized or denied. Continually watched and measured, the man or woman who is rich or talented or well educated is likely to be called "undemocratic" whenever he does anything out of the ordinary — more or less of something than others do. If he wants acceptance, the person with a "superior" attribute, like the person with an "inferior" attribute, often feels obliged to take on a protective disguise, to act as if he were just like everybody else. One denies difference; the other minimizes it. And both believe, as they conform to these false standards, that they act in the name of democracy.

For many Americans, a related source of confusion is success.   5
As a people we Americans greatly prize success. And in our eyes success all too often means simply outdoing other people by virtue of achievement judged by some single scale — income or honors or headlines or trophies — and coming out at "the top." Only one person, as we see it, can be the best — can get the highest grades, be voted the most attractive girl or the boy most likely to succeed. Though we often rejoice in the success of people far removed from ourselves — in another profession, another community, or en-dowed with a talent that we do not covet — we tend to regard the success of people close at hand, within our own small group, as a threat. We fail to realize that there are many kinds of success, including the kind of success that lies within a person. We do not realize, for example, that there could be in the same class one hundred boys and girls — each of them a "success" in a different kind of way. Individuality is again lost in a refusal to recognize and cherish the differences among people.

The attitude that measures success by a single yardstick and   6
isolates the *one* winner and the kind of "democracy" that denies or minimizes differences among people are both deeply destructive. Imagine for a moment a family with two sons, one of whom is brilliant, attractive and athletic while the other is dull, unattractive and clumsy. Both boys attend the same high school. In the interest of the slower boy, the parents would want the school to set equally low standards for everyone. Lessons should be easy; no one should be forced to study dead languages or advanced mathematics in order to graduate. Athletics should be noncompetitive; every boy should have a chance to enjoy playing games. Everyone should be

invited to all the parties. As for special attention to gifted children,
this is not fair to the other children. An all-round education should
be geared to the average normal child.

But in the interest of the other boy, these same parents would   7
have quite opposite goals. After all, we need highly trained people;
the school should do the most it can for its best students. Funds
should be made available for advanced classes and special teachers,
for the best possible coach, the best athletic equipment. Young
people should be allowed to choose friends on their own level. The
aim of education should be to produce topflight students.

This is an extreme example, but it illustrates the completely   8
incompatible aims that can arise in this kind of "democracy." Must
our country shut its eyes to the needs of either its gifted or its less
gifted sons? It would be a good deal more sensible to admit, as
some schools do today, that children differ widely from one another, that all successes cannot be ranged on one single scale, that
there is room in a real democracy to help each child find his own
level and develop to his fullest potential.

Moving now to a wider scene, before World War I Ameri-   9
cans thought of themselves as occupying a unique place in the
world — and there was no question in most minds that this country
was a "success." True, Europeans might look down on us for our
lack of culture, but with a few notable, local exceptions, we simply
refused to compete on European terms. There was no country in
the world remotely like the one we were building. But since World
War II we have felt the impact of a country whose size and
strength and emphasis on national achievement more closely parallel our own. Today we are ahead of Russia, or Russia is ahead of
us. Nothing else matters. Instead of valuing and developing the
extraordinary assets and potential of our country for their own
sake, we are involved in a simple set of competitions for wealth
and power and dominance.

These are expensive and dangerous attitudes. When democ-   10
racy ceases to be a cherished way of life and becomes instead the
name of one team, we are using the word democracy to describe
behavior that places us and all other men in jeopardy.

Individually, nationally and, today, internationally, the mis-   11
reading of the phrase "all men are created equal" exacts a heavy
price. The attitudes that follow from our misconceptions may be

compatible with life in a country where land and rank and prestige are severely limited and the roads to success are few. But they are inappropriate in a land as rich, as filled with opportunities as our own. They are the price we pay for being *less* democratic than we claim to be.

"All men are created equal" does not mean that all men are the same. What it does mean is that each should be accorded full respect and full rights as a unique human being — full respect for his humanity *and* for his differences from other people.

12

Meanings and Values

1a. Do you think the authors exaggerate the American tendency to equalize people, regardless of ability or endeavor?
  b. Support your answer by use of examples and comparison/contrast wherever possible.

2a. At what stage in the lives of Americans are we most likely to encounter the "egalitarian error" and its effects? Be prepared to justify your answer.
  b. Why, if at all, is this a particularly unfortunate time?

3. Clarify the metaphorical concept that a misrepresentation of the democratic ideal "dulls and flattens human relationships" (par. 3).

4. If you have read "Waterworks and Kings" (Sec. 1), explain precisely why the contrasts between the prince in Huxley's essay and his people were, or were not, justifiable under the thesis presented here.

Expository Techniques

1. Which of the standard techniques for introducing an essay are used in this writing? (See Guide to Terms: *Introductions*.)

2a. The authors achieve their purpose largely by use of a single one of the techniques peculiar to definition. Which is it?
  b. In which paragraphs is this technique used?
  c. Explain how the use of this method was prescribed by the nature of the writing purpose itself.

3a. Which of the other basic patterns of exposition do the authors employ in creating their definition?
  b. Cite examples of each.

4. Explain fully why you consider paragraph 12 an effective, or ineffective, closing. (Guide: *Closings*.)

Diction and Vocabulary

1a. What is an anthropologist (headnote)?
  b. By the nature of their work, should anthropologists be any better qualified to speak with authority on the differences in people than most other scholars? Why, or why not?
2a. The word "egalitarian" is not used in the essay itself. What does it mean?
  b. Is its use in the title appropriate, in view of the subject matter itself? Why, or why not?
3. Demonstrate the meanings of "connotation" and "denotation" by use of the authors' view of "democracy" set forth in this essay. (Guide: *Connotation/Denotation*.)

Suggestions and Writing for Discussion

1. By using a thorough cause/effect analysis, show the ultimate results of some particular application of the "egalitarian error."
2. Discuss practical ways by which some American schools do (or could, or should) avoid the dangers of this false view of democracy.
3. Compare and/or contrast the old-time attitude toward royalty (still held, apparently, by many British) with the typical, and presumably more democratic, American tendency toward "hero worship."

(NOTE: Suggestions for topics requiring development by use of DEFINI- TION are on page 207, at the end of this section.)

BARBARA LAWRENCE

BARBARA LAWRENCE was born in Hanover, New Hampshire. After receiving a B.A. in French literature from Connecticut College she worked for some time as an editor on *McCall's, Redbook, Harper's Bazaar,* and *The New Yorker.* During this period she also took an M.A. in philosophy from New York University. Currently an associate professor of humanities at the State University of New York's College at Old Westbury, Lawrence has published criticism, poetry, and fiction in *Choice, Commonweal, Columbia Poetry, The New York Times,* and *The New Yorker.*

Four-Letter Words Can Hurt You

"Four-Letter Words Can Hurt You" first appeared in *The New York Times* and was later published in *Redbook.* In explaining precisely why she is offended by the "earthy, gut-honest" language often preferred by her students, Lawrence also provides a thoughtful, even scholarly, extended definition of "obscenity" itself. To accomplish her purpose, the author employs several of the patterns of exposition we have already studied.

Why should any words be called obscene? Don't they all describe natural human functions? Am I trying to tell them, my students demand, that the "strong, earthy, gut-honest" — or, if they are fans of Norman Mailer, the "rich, liberating, existential" — language they use to describe sexual activity isn't preferable to "phony-sounding, middle-class words like 'intercourse' and 'copulate'?" "Cop You Late!" they say with fancy inflections and gagging grimaces. "Now, what is *that* supposed to mean?"

Well, what is it supposed to mean? And why indeed should one group of words describing human functions and human organs

Reprinted by permission of the publisher from *The New York Times* (October 27, 1973). © 1973 by The New York Times Company.

be acceptable in ordinary conversation and another, describing presumably the same organs and functions, be tabooed — so much so,
in fact, that some of these words still cannot appear in print in
many parts of the English-speaking world?

The argument that these taboos exist only because of "sexual   3
hangups" (middle-class, middle-age, feminist), or even that they
are a result of class oppression (the contempt of the Norman con-
querors for the language of their Anglo-Saxon serfs), ignores a
much more likely explanation, it seems to me, and that is the
sources and functions of the words themselves.

The best known of the tabooed sexual verbs, for example,   4
comes from the German *ficken*, meaning "to strike"; combined,
according to Partridge's etymological dictionary *Origins*, with the
Latin sexual verb *futuere*; associated in turn with the Latin *fustis*,
"a staff or cudgel"; the Celtic *buc*, "a point, hence to pierce"; the
Irish *bot*, "the male member"; the Latin *battuere*, "to beat"; the
Gaelic *batair*, "a cudgeller"; the Early Irish *bualaim*, "I strike";
and so forth. It is one of what etymologists sometimes call "the
sadistic group of words for the man's part in copulation."

The brutality of this word, then, and its equivalents ("screw,"   5
"bang," etc.), is not an illusion of the middle class or a crotchet of
Women's Liberation. In their origins and imagery these words
carry undeniably painful, if not sadistic, implications, the object of
which is almost always female. Consider, for example, what a
"screw" actually does to the wood it penetrates; what a painful,
even mutilating, activity this kind of analogy suggests. "Screw" is
particularly interesting in this context, since the noun, according to
Partridge, comes from words meaning "groove," "nut," "ditch,"
"breeding sow," "scrofula" and "swelling," while the verb, besides
its explicit imagery, has antecedent associations to "write on,"
"scratch," "scarify," and so forth — a revealing fusion of a mechanical or painful action with an obviously denigrated object.

Not all obscene words, of course, are as implicitly sadistic or   6
denigrating to women as these, but all that I know seem to serve a
similar purpose: to reduce the human organism (especially the
female organism) and human functions (especially sexual and procreative) to their least organic, most mechanical dimension; to substitute a trivializing or deforming resemblance for the complex
human reality of what is being described.

Tabooed male descriptives, when they are not openly deni- 7
grating to women, often serve to divorce a male organ or function
from any significant interaction with the female. Take the word
"testes," for example, suggesting "witnesses" (from the Latin
testis) to the sexual and procreative strengths of the male organ;
and the obscene counterpart of this word, which suggests little
more than a mechanical shape. Or compare almost any of the
"rich," "liberating" sexual verbs, so fashionable today among male
writers, with that much-derided Latin word "copulate" ("to bind
or join together") or even that Anglo-Saxon phrase (which seems
to have had no trouble surviving the Norman Conquest) "make
love."

How arrogantly self-involved the tabooed words seem in com- 8
parison to either of the other terms, and how contemptuous of the
female partner. Understandably so, of course, if she is only a
"skirt," a "broad," a "chick," a "pussycat" or a "piece." If she is,
in other words, no more than her skirt, or what her skirt conceals;
no more than a breeder, or the broadest part of her; no more than
a piece of a human being or a "piece of tail."

The most severely tabooed of all the female descriptives, inci- 9
dentally, are those like a "piece of tail," which suggest (either
explicitly or through antecedents) that there is no significant difference between the female channel through which we are all conceived and born and the anal outlet common to both sexes — a
distinction that pornographers have always enjoyed obscuring.

This effort to deny women their biological identity, their in- 10
dividuality, their humanness, is such an important aspect of obscene
language that one can only marvel at how seldom, in an era preoccupied with definitions of obscenity, this fact is brought to our
attention. One problem, of course, is that many of the people in
the best position to do this (critics, teachers, writers) are so reluctant today to admit that they are angered or shocked by obscenity.
Bored, maybe, unimpressed, aesthetically displeased, but — no
matter how brutal or denigrating the material — never angered,
never shocked.

And yet how eloquently angered, how piously shocked many 11
of these same people become if denigrating language is used about
any minority group other than women; if the obscenities are racial
or ethnic, that is, rather than sexual. Words like "coon," "kike,"

"spic," "wop," after all, deform identity, deny individuality and humanness in almost exactly the same way that sexual vulgarisms and obscenities do.

No one that I know, least of all my students, would fail to   12
question the values of a society whose literature and entertainment rested heavily on racial or ethnic pejoratives. Are the values of a society whose literature and entertainment rest as heavily as ours on sexual pejoratives any less questionable?

Meanings and Values

1a. Explain the meaning of "irony" by use of at least one illustration from the latter part of this essay. (See Guide to Terms: *Irony*.)
 b. What kind of irony is it?

2a. Inasmuch as the writing itself includes many of the so-called "strong, earthy, gut-honest" words, could anyone logically call it obscene? Why, or why not?
 b. To what extent, if at all, does the author's point of view help determine your answer to "a"? (Guide: *Point of View*.)

3a. Compose, in your own words, a compact statement of Lawrence's central theme. (Guide: *Unity*.)
 b. Are all parts of the essay completely relevant to this theme? Justify your answer.
 c. Does the writing have unity?

4. Evaluate this composition by use of our three-question system. (Guide: *Evaluation*.)

5. If you have read the Masters and Johnson selection (Sec. 6), and realizing that the authors are educated people, does it seem surprising that they would refrain from use of the "gut-honest" words? Why, or why not?

Expository Techniques

1a. Where does the author first let us know what major term is to be defined?
 b. Can the resulting treatment qualify as *extended* definition? Why, or why not?

2a. Which of the methods "peculiar to definition alone" (see the introduction to this section) does the author employ in developing her major definition?
 b. Which of the regular patterns of exposition does she also use?

c. Explain your reasons and cite examples to justify your answers to "a" and "b."

3a. Cite five examples of the simpler, non-"extended" kind of definition.
 b. Are these sufficiently documented to fulfill their function? Cite examples to justify your answer to "a."

4a. Illustrate the difference between "specific" and "general" by use of passages from this writing. (Guide: *Specific/General.*)
 b. Does it seem to you that the author becomes too involved with achieving one or the other? Explain.

5a. Which of the standard techniques of introduction are used? (Guide: *Introductions.*)
 b. Which methods are used to close it? (Guide: *Closings.*)

Diction and Vocabulary

1a. How, if at all, is this discussion of words related to "connotation"? (Guide: *Connotation/Denotation.*)
 b. To what extent would connotations in this matter depend on setting and circumstances in which the words are used? Cite illustrations to clarify your answer.

2. In view of the fact that the author uses frankly many of the "gut-honest" words, why do you suppose she plainly avoids others, such as in paragraphs 4 and 7?

3. The author says that a "kind of analogy" is suggested by some of the words discussed (par. 5). If you have studied Section 4 of this book, does her use of the term "analogy" seem in conflict with what you believed it to mean? Explain.

4. Study the author's uses of the following words, consulting the dictionary as needed: existential, grimaces (par. 1); etymological, cudgel (4); sadistic (4–6); crotchet, scrofula, explicit, antecedent, scarify (5); denigrated (5–7, 10–11); aesthetically (10); pejoratives (12).

Suggestions for Writing and Discussion

1. What is the relationship, if any, between obscene language and pornography?

2. Why is it the so-called middle class that is so often accused of having sexual hangups — and hence all sorts of sex-related taboos?

3. Probably most people using obscene language (obscene, at least, by Lawrence's definition) are not aware of the etymology of the words. Can they, therefore, be accused of denigrating women — or, unlike in legal matters, is ignorance a suitable defense?

4. Does the author make a justifiable comparison between obscene words and ethnic pejoratives? Using illustrations for specificity, carry the comparison further to show why it is sound, or explain why you consider it a weak comparison.

(NOTE: Suggestions for topics requiring development by use of DEFINITION are on page 207, at the end of this section.)

D. H. LAWRENCE

> DAVID HERBERT LAWRENCE (1885–1930), British novelist, poet,
> essayist, and playwright, was for many years a controversial
> literary figure because of his frank and, for his time, obsessive
> treatment of sex in some of his novels. The son of a coal
> miner, Lawrence began his career as a schoolmaster and with
> the success of his first novel, *The White Peacock* (1911), he
> decided to live by writing. His books include *Sons and Lovers*
> (1913), *The Rainbow* (1915), *Women in Love* (1921), and *Lady
> Chatterly's Lover* (1928). Lawrence has been admired by many
> for his insightful and artistic power in prose. E. M. Forster
> referred to him as "the greatest imaginative novelist of our
> generation."

Pornography

> "Pornography" is excerpted from *Pornography and Obscen-
> ity*, first published in 1930. Providing us with one man's defi-
> nition of a still highly controversial term, this selection also
> illustrates the naturalness and vivid spontaneity of style char-
> acteristic of Lawrence's writing. Also interesting should be a
> comparison of the way another Lawrence, from a different era
> and background, and with a different point of view, defines a
> term which is very close to the "obscenity" that concerns
> Barbara Lawrence.

What is pornography to one man is the laughter of genius to 1
another.

The word itself, we are told, means "pertaining to harlots" — 2
the graph of the harlot. But nowadays, what is a harlot? If she
was a woman who took money from a man in return for going to
bed with him — really, most wives sold themselves, in the past,
and plenty of harlots gave themselves, when they felt like it, for

nothing. If a woman hasn't got a tiny streak of harlot in her, she's a dry stick as a rule. And probably most harlots had somewhere a streak of womanly generosity. Why be so cut and dried? The law is a dreary thing, and its judgments have nothing to do with life. . . .

One essay on pornography, I remember, comes to the con- 3
clusion that pornography in art is that which is calculated to arouse sexual desire, or sexual excitement. And stress is laid on the fact, whether the author or artist *intended to* arouse sexual feelings. It is the old vexed question of intention, become so dull today, when we know how strong and influential our unconscious intentions are. And why a man should be held guilty of his conscious intentions, and innocent of his unconscious intentions, I don't know, since every man is more made up of unconscious intentions than of conscious ones. I am what I am, not merely what I think I am.

However! We take it, I assume, that *pornography* is some- 4
thing base, something unpleasant. In short, we don't like it. And why don't we like it? Because it arouses sexual feelings?

I think not. No matter how hard we may pretend otherwise, 5
most of us rather like a moderate rousing of our sex. It warms us, stimulates us like sunshine on a grey day. After a century or two of Puritanism, this is still true of most people. Only the mob-habit of condemning any form of sex is too strong to let us admit it naturally. And there are, of course, many people who are genuinely repelled by the simplest and most natural stirrings of sexual feeling. But these people are perverts who have fallen into hatred of their fellow-men: thwarted, disappointed, unfulfilled people, of whom, alas, our civilisation contains so many. And they nearly always enjoy some unsimple and unnatural form of sex excitement, secretly.

Even quite advanced art critics would try to make us believe 6
that any picture or book which had "sex appeal" was *ipso facto* a bad book or picture. This is just canting hypocrisy. Half the great poems, pictures, music, stories of the whole world are great by virtue of the beauty of their sex appeal. Titian or Renoir, the Song of Solomon or *Jane Eyre*, Mozart or "Annie Laurie," the loveliness is all interwoven with sex appeal, sex stimulus, call it what you will. Even Michelangelo, who rather hated sex, can't help filling the Cornucopia with phallic acorns. Sex is a very powerful, beneficial

and necessary stimulus in human life, and we are all grateful when we feel its warm, natural flow through us, like a form of sunshine. . . .

Then what is pornography, after all this? It isn't sex appeal or 7 sex stimulus in art. It isn't even a deliberate intention on the part of the artist to arouse or excite sexual feelings. There's nothing wrong with sexual feelings in themselves, so long as they are straightforward and not sneaking or sly. The right sort of sex stimulus is invaluable to human daily life. Without it the world grows grey. I would give everybody the gay Renaissance stories to read, they would help to shake off a lot of grey self-importance, which is our modern civilised disease.

But even I would censor genuine pornography, rigorously. It 8 would not be very difficult. In the first place, genuine pornography is almost always underworld, it doesn't come into the open. In the second, you can recognise it by the insult it offers, invariably, to sex, and to the human spirit.

Pornography is the attempt to insult sex, to do dirt on it. This 9 is unpardonable. Take the very lowest instance, the picture postcard sold underhand, by the underworld, in most cities. What I have seen of them have been of an ugliness to make you cry. The insult to the human body, the insult to a vital human relationship! Ugly and cheap they make the human nudity, ugly and degraded they make the sexual act, trivial and cheap and nasty.

It is the same with the books they sell in the underworld. They 10 are either so ugly they make you ill, or so fatuous you can't imagine anybody but a cretin or a moron reading them, or writing them.

It is the same with the dirty limericks that people tell after 11 dinner, or the dirty stories one hears commercial travellers telling each other in a smoke-room. Occasionally there is a really funny one, that redeems a great deal. But usually they are just ugly and repellent, and the so-called "humour" is just a trick of doing dirt on sex.

Now the human nudity of a great many modern people is just 12 ugly and degraded, and the sexual act between modern people is just the same, merely ugly and degrading. But this is nothing to be proud of. It is the catastrophe of our civilisation. I am sure no other civilisation, not even the Roman, has showed such a vast proportion of ignominious and degraded nudity, and ugly, squalid dirty

sex. Because no other civilisation has driven sex into the underworld, and nudity to the w.c.

The intelligent young, thank heaven, seem determined to 13
alter in these two respects. They are rescuing their young nudity
from the stuffy, pornographical hole-and-corner underworld of
their elders, and they refuse to sneak about the sexual relation. This
is a change the elderly grey ones of course deplore, but it is in fact
a very great change for the better, and a real revolution.

But it is amazing how strong is the will in ordinary, vulgar 14
people, to do dirt on sex. It was one of my fond illusions, when I
was young, that the ordinary healthy-seeming sort of men in rail-
way carriages, or the smoke-room of an hotel or a pullman, were
healthy in their feelings and had a wholesome rough devil-may-
care attitude towards sex. All wrong! All wrong! Experience teaches
that common individuals of this sort have a disgusting attitude
towards sex, a disgusting contempt of it, a disgusting desire to
insult it. If such fellows have intercourse with a woman, they tri-
umphantly feel that they have done her dirt, and now she is lower,
cheaper, more contemptible than she was before.

It is individuals of this sort that tell dirty stories, carry in- 15
decent picture postcards, and know the indecent books. This is the
great pornographical class — the really common men-in-the-street
and women-in-the-street. They have as great a hate and contempt
of sex as the greyest Puritan, and when an appeal is made to them,
they are always on the side of the angels. They insist that a film-
heroine shall be a neuter, a sexless thing of washed-out purity.
They insist that real sex-feeling shall only be shown by the villain
or villainess, low lust. They find a Titian or a Renoir really indecent, and they don't want their wives and daughters to see it.

Why? Because they have the grey disease of sex-hatred, 16
coupled with the yellow disease of dirt-lust. The sex functions and
the excrementory functions in the human body work so close together, yet they are, so to speak, utterly different in direction. Sex
is a creative flow, the excrementory flow is towards dissolution,
de-creation, if we may use such a word. In the really healthy
human being the distinction between the two is instant, our pro-
foundest instincts are perhaps our instincts of opposition between
the two flows.

But in the degraded human being the deep instincts have gone 17
dead, and then the two flows become identical. *This* is the secret

of really vulgar and of pornographical people: the sex flow and the excrement flow is the same to them. It happens when the psyche deteriorates, and the profound controlling instincts collapse. Then sex is dirt and dirt is sex, and sexual excitement becomes a playing with dirt, and any sign of sex in a woman becomes a show of her dirt. This is the condition of the common, vulgar human being whose name is legion, and who lifts his voice and it is the *Vox populi, vox Dei*. And this is the source of all pornography.

Meanings and Values

1. Could this selection best serve to illustrate subjective or objective writing? (See Guide to Terms: *Objective/Subjective.*) Justify your answer, citing specific examples.
2. Would you classify it as formal or informal writing? (Guide: *Essay.*) Why?
3a. Do you think that a person should, in general, be held responsible for his "unconscious intentions" (par. 3)?
  b. Does the law do so?
4a. Does it seem to you that the author may be overgeneralizing in the last sentence of paragraph 5?
  b. If such forms of sex excitement are enjoyed "secretly," how could he know enough about the matter to make such a broad assertion?
5. What, if anything, is paradoxical in the fact that the type of men described early in paragraph 14 have the "grey disease" (par. 16)? (Guide: *Paradox.*)
6. What relationship, if any, do you see between this definition and that of Barbara Lawrence, in the preceding essay?

Expository Techniques

1a. In developing his definition of pornography, Lawrence uses negation, or exclusion. What is negated?
  b. Which paragraphs are devoted to negation?
  c. Why do you suppose he considers them important enough for so much attention? Do you agree?
2a. Which of the other methods of extended definition does he use?
  b. In which paragraphs may they be found?
3. In your estimation, are rhetorical questions overused in this selection? (Guide: *Rhetorical Question.*) Be prepared to justify your answer.

4a. Cite examples of as many as possible of the standard methods of achieving emphasis. (Guide: *Emphasis*.)
 b. What, to you, is the overall effect?

5. Several of the most noticeable features of Lawrence's style are also matters of syntax. (Guide: *Style/Tone* and *Syntax*.) Illustrate as many of these as possible by examples from the writing.

Diction and Vocabulary

1a. In the second paragraph is a metaphor that is also a cliché. (Guide: *Clichés*.) What is it?
 b. How, if at all, can we justify its use?

2. Cite at least two other examples of metaphor and one of simile. (Guide: *Figures of Speech*.)

3. What is the meaning of "w.c." (par. 12)?

4a. What is the meaning of *ipso facto* (par. 6)?
 b. Why is it italicized?

5. What is the meaning of *Vox populi, vox Dei* (par. 17)?

6a. In at least five paragraphs Lawrence uses a euphemism. (Guide: *Connotation/Denotation*.) What is it?
 b. In which paragraphs do you find it used?
 c. If sex-hatred is the "grey disease," why do you suppose he chose "yellow" to describe the disease of "dirt-lust"?

7. Consult your dictionary as necessary for the meaning of the following words: canting, phallic (par. 6); fatuous, cretin (10); ignominious (12).

Suggestions for Writing and Discussion

1. Select one or more of the artists or works of art listed in paragraph 6, analyze, and explain fully why you agree or disagree that "the loveliness is all interwoven with sex appeal [or] sex stimulus."

2. The "intelligent young" of 1930 (par. 13) are now the grey "establishment" of parents and grandparents against whom the intelligent young of the '60s and '70s have been staging a so-called sexual revolution. Trace the process by which such an ironic reversal came about. Do you believe this is an inevitable result of generation-aging — e.g., will *your* children and grandchildren also be engaging in sexual revolution?

3. Both of the author's "negated" definitions have been used repeatedly in the attempt to get a fair and workable *legal* distinction between pornography and nonpornography. Usually these attempts

failed, and no one felt that the problem had been really solved. How well would Lawrence's definition work as a legal definition — perhaps with some modification you can suggest?

4. What, if anything, do you think should be done about "hard-core" pornography?

Writing Suggestions for Section 7
Definition

Develop a composition for a specified purpose and audience, using whatever methods and expository patterns will help convey a clear understanding of your meaning of one of the following terms:

1. Country rock music.
2. Conscience.
3. Religion.
4. Bigotry.
5. Rationalization.
6. Empathy.
7. Altruism.
8. Hypocrisy.
9. Humor.
10. Sophistication.

11. Naiveté.
12. Cowardice.
13. Wisdom.
14. Integrity.
15. Morality.
16. Sin.
17. Social poise.
18. Intellectual (the person).
19. Pornography (if your opinions differ appreciably from D. H. Lawrence's).

8

Explaining with the Help of *Description*

Although usually classed as one of the four basic forms of prose, description is used nearly always as a supporting device of one of the other three. Exposition, as well as argument and narration, can be made more vivid, and hence more understandable, with this support. Most exposition does contain some elements of description, and at times description carries almost the entire burden of the explanation, becoming a basic pattern for the expository purpose.

Description is most useful in painting a word-picture of something concrete, such as a scene or a person. Its use is not restricted, however, to what we can perceive with our senses; we can also describe (or attempt to describe) an abstract concept, such as an emotion or quality or mood. But most attempts to describe fear, for instance, still resort to the physical — a "coldness around the heart," perhaps — and in such concrete ways communicate the abstract to the reader.

In its extreme forms, description is either *objective* or *impressionistic* (subjective), but most of its uses are somewhere between these extremes. Objective description is purely factual, uncolored by any feelings of the author; it is the type used for scientific papers and most business reports. But impressionistic description, as the term implies, at least tinges the purely factual with the author's personal impressions; instead of describing how something *is*, objectively, he describes how it *seems*, subjectively. Such a description might refer to the "blazing heat" of an August day. Somewhat less impressionistic would be "extreme heat." But the scientist would describe it precisely as "115 degrees Fahrenheit," and this would be purely objective reporting, unaffected by the impressions of the author. (No examples of the latter are included in this section, but many textbooks for other courses utilize the technique of pure objective description, as do encyclopedias. The Petrunkevitch essay in Section 5 provides some good examples of objective description, although not entirely unmixed with colorful impressionistic details.)

The first and most important job in any descriptive endeavor is the selection of details to be included. There are usually many from which to choose, and the writer must constantly keep in mind the kind of picture he wants to paint with words — for *his* purpose and *his* audience. Such a word-picture need not be entirely visual; in this respect the writer has more freedom than the artist, for he can use strokes that will add the dimension of sound, smell, and even touch. Such "strokes," if made to seem natural enough, can help create a vivid and effective image in the reader's mind.

Most successful impressionistic description focuses on a single *dominant impression*. Of the many descriptive details ordinarily available for use, the author selects those which will help create a mood or atmosphere or emphasize a feature or quality. But more than the materials themselves are involved, for even diction can often assist in creating the desired dominant impression. Sometimes syntax is also an important factor, as in the use of short, hurried sentences to help convey a sense of urgency or excitement.

Actual structuring of passages is perhaps less troublesome in description than that in most of the other patterns. But some kind of orderliness is needed for the sake of both readability and a realistic effect. (Neither objective nor impressionistic description can afford not to be realistic, in one manner or another.) In visual description, orderliness is usually achieved by presenting details as the eye would find them — that is as arranged in space. We could describe a person from head to toe, or vice versa, or begin with his most noticeable feature and work from there. A scenic description might move from near to far or from far to near, from left to right or from right to left. It might also start with a broad, overall view, gradually narrowing to a focal point, probably the most significant feature of the scene. These are fairly standard kinds of description; but as the types and occasions for using description vary widely, so do the possibilities for interesting treatment. In many cases, the writer is limited only by his own ingenuity.

But ingenuity should not be allowed to produce *excessive* description, an amazingly certain path to reader boredom. A few well-chosen details are better than profusion. Economy of words is desirable in any writing, and description is no exception. Appropriate use of figurative language and careful choices of strong nouns and verbs will help prevent the need for strings of modifiers, which are wasteful and can seem amateurish.

Even for the experienced writer, however, achieving good description remains a constant challenge; the beginner should not expect to attain this goal without working at it.

SHARON CURTIN

SHARON CURTIN, a native of Douglas, Wyoming, was raised in a family of ranchers and craftsmen. Curtin, a women's liberationist and political leftist, has worked as a nurse in New York and California but now devotes most of her time to writing and to operating a small farm in Virginia. Her current projects include a book about industrial development in the western Great Plains.

Aging in the Land of the Young

"Aging in the Land of the Young" is the first part of Curtin's article by that title, as it appeared in *The Atlantic* in July 1972. It is largely a carefully restructured composite of portions of her book *Nobody Ever Died of Old Age,* also published in 1972. It illustrates the subjective form of description, generally known as impressionistic.

Old men, old women, almost 20 million of them. They constitute   1
10 percent of the total population, and the percentage is steadily
growing. Some of them, like conspirators, walk all bent over, as if
hiding some precious secret, filled with self-protection. The body
seems to gather itself around those vital parts, folding shoulders,
arms, pelvis like a fading rose. Watch and you see how fragile old
people come to think they are.

Aging paints every action gray, lies heavy on every move-   2
ment, imprisons every thought. It governs each decision with a
ruthless and single-minded perversity. To age is to learn the feeling of no longer growing, of struggling to do old tasks, to remember familiar actions. The cells of the brain are destroyed with
thousands of unfelt tiny strokes, little pockets of clotted blood wip-

ing out memories and abilities without warning. The body seems slowly to give up, randomly stopping, sometimes starting again as if to torture and tease with the memory of lost strength. Hands become clumsy, frail transparencies, held together with knotted blue veins.

Sometimes it seems as if the distance between your feet and   3
the floor were constantly changing, as if you were walking on shifting and not quite solid ground. One foot down, slowly, carefully force the other foot forward. Sometimes you are a shuffler, not daring to lift your feet from the uncertain earth but forced to slide hesitantly forward in little whispering movements. Sometimes you are able to "step out," but this effort — in fact the pure exhilaration of easy movement — soon exhausts you.

The world becomes narrower as friends and family die or   4
move away. To climb stairs, to ride in a car, to walk to the corner, to talk on the telephone; each action seems to take away from the energy needed to stay alive. Everything is limited by the strength you hoard greedily. Your needs decrease, you require less food, less sleep, and finally less human contact; yet this little bit becomes more and more difficult. You fear that one day you will be reduced to the simple acts of breathing and taking nourishment. This is the ultimate stage you dread, the period of helplessness and hopelessness, when independence will be over.

There is nothing to prepare you for the experience of growing   5
old. Living is a process, an irreversible progression toward old age and eventual death. You see men of eighty still vital and straight as oaks; you see men of fifty reduced to gray shadows in the human landscape. The cellular clock differs for each one of us, and is profoundly affected by our own life experiences, our heredity, and perhaps most important, by the concepts of aging encountered in society and in oneself.

The aged live with enforced leisure, on fixed incomes, subject   6
to many chronic illnesses, and most of their money goes to keep a roof over their heads. They also live in a culture that worships youth.

A kind of cultural attitude makes me bigoted against old people; it make me think young is best; it makes me treat old people   7
like outcasts.

Hate that gray? Wash it away!   8

Wrinkle cream.   9

Monkey glands.   10
Face-lifting.   11
Look like a bride again.   12
Don't trust anyone over thirty.   13
I fear growing old.   14
Feel Young Again!   15

I am afraid to grow old — we're all afraid. In fact, the fear of   16
growing old is so great that every aged person is an insult and a
threat to the society. They remind us of our own death, that our
body won't always remain smooth and responsive, but will some-
day betray us by aging, wrinkling, faltering, failing. The ideal way
to age would be to grow slowly invisible, gradually disappearing,
without causing worry or discomfort to the young. In some ways
that does happen. Sitting in a small park across from a nursing
home one day, I noticed that the young mothers and their children
gathered on one side, and the old people from the home on the
other. Whenever a youngster would run over to the "wrong" side,
chasing a ball or just trying to cover all the available space, the
old people would lean forward and smile. But before any communication could be established, the mother would come over,
murmuring embarrassed apologies, and take her child back to the
"young" side.

Now, it seemed to me that the children didn't feel any par-   17
ticular fear and the old people didn't seem to be threatened by the
children. The division of space was drawn by the mothers. And the
mothers never looked at the old people who lined the other side of
the park like so many pigeons perched on the benches. These well-
dressed young matrons had a way of sliding their eyes over,
around, through the old people; they never looked at them directly.
The old people may as well have been invisible; they had no reality
for the youngsters, who were not permitted to speak to them, and
they offended the aesthetic eye of the mothers.

My early experiences were somewhat different; since I grew   18
up in a small town, my childhood had more of a nineteenth-century flavor. I knew a lot of old people, and considered some of
them friends. There was no culturally defined way for me to "relate" to old people, except the rules of courtesy which applied to
all adults. My grandparents were an integral and important part of
the family and of the community. I sometimes have a dreadful fear
that mine will be the last generation to know old people as friends,

to have a sense of what growing old means, to respect and understand man's mortality and his courage in the face of death. Mine may be the last generation to have a sense of living history, of stories passed from generation to generation, of identity established by family history.

Meanings and Values

1. What is the general tone of this writing? (See Guide to Terms: *Style/Tone.*)

2. If you find it depressing to read about aging, try to analyze why (especially in view of the fact that you are very likely many years from the stage of "a fading rose").

3. Why do you suppose it is more likely to be the mothers than the children who shun old people (pars. 16–17)?

4a. Has this author avoided the excesses of sentimentality? (Guide: *Sentimentality.*)
 b. If not, where does she fail? If she does avoid them, try to discover how.

Expository Techniques

1a. Why should this writing be classed as primarily impressionistic, rather than objective?
 b. What is the dominant impression?

2a. Analyze the role which selection of details plays in creating the dominant impression.
 b. Provide examples of the type of details that could have been included but were not.
 c. Are such omissions justifiable?

3a. Paragraph 5 ends the almost pure description to begin another phase of the writing. What is it?
 b. How has the author provided for a smooth transition between the two? (Guide: *Transition.*)

4a. What particular method of gaining emphasis has been used effectively in one portion of the selection? (Guide: *Emphasis.*)
 b. How might the material have been presented if emphasis were not desired?

5. Which previously studied patterns of exposition are also used in this writing? Cite paragraphs where each may be found.

Diction and Vocabulary

1a. The author sometimes changes person — e.g., "they" to "you" after paragraph 2. Analyze where the changes occur.
 b. What justification, if any, can you find for each change?

2a. Which two kinds of figure of speech do you find used liberally to achieve this description? (Guide: *Figures of Speech.*)
 b. Cite three or more examples of each.
 c. As nearly as you can tell, are any of them clichés? (Guide: *Clichés.*)

Suggestions for Writing and Discussion

1. If Curtin is correct in her fears expressed in the last two sentences, what could be the consequences for society in general?

2. Discuss the pro's and con's of placing senile old people in rest homes, rather than letting them live alone or taking them to live with the family. What other alternatives, if any, does the family have?

3. If you know some very old person who (apparently) is not as affected by aging as the ones the author describes, what seems to account for this difference?

4. If you are familiar with the Gray Power movement, or others like it, what exactly is it that they hope to accomplish?

5. If many people at age 60–65 are still efficient at their jobs, as is often argued, what practical reasons are there for forcing retirement at that age?

(NOTE: Suggestions for topics requiring development by use of DESCRIPTION are on page 229, at the end of this section.)

ISAAC ASIMOV

Isaac Asimov, born in Russia in 1920, came to this country at the age of three. He was educated at Columbia University, taking his doctorate in chemistry in 1948, and subsequently taught at the Boston University School of Medicine. Asimov has been a professional writer since the age of eighteen, publishing hundreds of books and articles that span the fields of anatomy, biology, chemistry, mathematics, astronomy, geography, and history. Perhaps best known for his science fiction, Asimov has also written children's books, college textbooks, prepared annotated editions of *Paradise Lost* and *Don Juan*, and, more recently, guides to Shakespeare and the Bible. Among his other recent books: *Caves of Steel, Earth Is Room Enough*, and *The Stars in Their Courses* (1976), and *Buy Jupiter and Other Stories* and *The Gods Themselves* (1977).

The Nightmare Life Without Fuel

"The Nightmare Life Without Fuel" was written when *Time* asked Asimov for his vision of an energy-poor society that might exist at the end of the twentieth century. The resulting portrait (published in April 1977), as Asimov himself noted, "need not prove to be accurate. It is a picture of the worst, of waste continuing, of oil running out, of nothing in its place, of world population continuing to rise. But then, that could happen, couldn't it?"

So it's 1997, and it's raining, and you'll have to walk to work again. 1
The subways are crowded, and any given train breaks down one morning out of five. The buses are gone, and on a day like today the bicycles slosh and slide. Besides, you have only a mile and a half to go, and you have boots, raincoat and rain hat. And it's not a very cold rain, so why not?

Lucky you have a job in demolition too. It's steady work. Slow 2
and dirty, but steady. The fading structures of a decaying city are

the great mineral mines and hardware shops of the nation. Break
them down and re-use the parts. Coal is too difficult to dig up and
transport to give us energy in the amounts we need, nuclear fission
is judged to be too dangerous, the technical breakthrough toward
nuclear fusion that we hoped for never took place, and solar batteries are too expensive to maintain on the earth's surface in sufficient quantity.

Anyone older than ten can remember automobiles. They   3
dwindled. At first the price of gasoline climbed — way up. Finally
only the well-to-do drove, and that was too clear an indication that
they were filthy rich, so any automobile that dared show itself on
a city street was overturned and burned. Rationing was introduced
to "equalize sacrifice," but every three months the ration was reduced. The cars just vanished and became part of the metal re-
source.

There are many advantages, if you want to look for them.   4
Our 1997 newspapers continually point them out. The air is cleaner
and there seem to be fewer clouds. Against most predictions, the
crime rate has dropped. With the police car too expensive (and too
easy a target), policemen are back on their beats. More important,
the streets are full. Legs are king in the cities of 1997, and people
walk everywhere far into the night. Even the parks are full, and
there is mutual protection in crowds.

If the weather isn't too cold, people sit out front. If it is hot,   5
the open air is the only air conditioning they get. And at least the
street lights still burn. Indoors, electricity is scarce, and few people
can afford to keep lights burning after supper.

As for the winter — well, it is inconvenient to be cold, with   6
most of what furnace fuel is allowed hoarded for the dawn; but
sweaters are popular indoor wear and showers are not an everyday
luxury. Lukewarm sponge baths will do, and if the air is not always
very fragrant in the human vicinity, the automobile fumes are
gone.

There is some consolation in the city that it is worse in the   7
suburbs. The suburbs were born with the auto, lived with the auto,
and are dying with the auto. One way out for the suburbanites is
to form associations that assign turns to the procurement and distribution of food. Pushcarts creak from house to house along the
posh suburban roads, and every bad snowstorm is a disaster. It

isn't easy to hoard enough food to last till the roads are open. There is not much in the way of refrigeration except for the snow-banks, and then the dogs must be fought off.

What energy is left cannot be directed into personal comfort. 8 The nation must survive until new energy sources are found, so it is the railroads and subways that are receiving major attention. The railroads must move the coal that is the immediate hope, and the subways can best move the people.

And then, of course, energy must be conserved for agricul- 9 ture. The great car factories make trucks and farm machinery al-most exclusively. We can huddle together when there is a lack of warmth, fan ourselves should there be no cooling breezes, sleep or make love at such times as there is a lack of light — but nothing will for long ameliorate a lack of food. The American population isn't going up much any more, but the food supply must be kept high even though the prices and difficulty of distribution force each American to eat less. Food is needed for export so that we can pay for some trickle of oil and for other resources.

The rest of the world, of course, is not as lucky as we are. 10 Some cynics say that it is the knowledge of this that helps keep America from despair. They're starving out there, because earth's population has continued to go up. The population on earth is 5.5 billion, and outside the United States and Europe, not more than one in five has enough to eat at any given time.

All the statistics point to a rapidly declining rate of population 11 increase, but that is coming about chiefly through a high infant mortality; the first and most helpless victims of starvation are babies, after their mothers have gone dry. A strong current of American opinion, as reflected in the newspapers (some of which still produce their daily eight pages of bad news), holds that it is just as well. It serves to reduce the population, doesn't it?

Others point out that it's more than just starvation. There are 12 those who manage to survive on barely enough to keep the body working, and that proves to be not enough for the brain. It is esti-mated that there are now nearly 2 billion people in the world who are alive but who are permanently brain-damaged by undernutri-tion, and the number is growing year by year. It has already oc-curred to some that it would be "realistic" to wipe them out quietly and rid the earth of an encumbering menace. The American news-

papers of 1997 do not report that this is actually being done anywhere, but some travelers bring back horror tales.

At least the armies are gone — no one can afford to keep those   13
expensive, energy-gobbling monstrosities. Some soldiers in uni-
form and with rifles are present in almost every still functioning
nation, but only the United States and the Soviet Union can maintain a few tanks, planes and ships — which they dare not move
for fear of biting into limited fuel reserves.

Energy continues to decline, and machines must be replaced   14
by human muscle and beasts of burden. People are working longer
hours and there is less leisure; but then, with electric lighting restricted, television for only three hours a night, movies three evenings a week, new books few and printed in small editions, what
is there to do with leisure? Work, sleep and eating are the great
trinity of 1997, and only the first two are guaranteed.

Where will it end? It must end in a return to the days before   15
1800, to the days before the fossil fuels powered a vast machine
industry and technology. It must end in subsistence farming and
in a world population reduced by starvation, disease and violence
to less than a billion.

And what can we do to prevent all this now?   16

Now? Almost nothing.   17

If we had started 20 years ago, that might have been another   18
matter. If we had only started 50 years ago, it would have been
easy.

Meanings and Values

1a. What is the fundamental irony in this particular view of life in
    1997? (See Guide to Terms: *Irony*.)
 b. Why is it ironical?

2a. How would you describe Asimov's point of view in this writing?
    (Guide: *Point of View*.)
 b. To what extent is the essay's objectivity or subjectivity affected by
    this point of view? (Guide: *Objective/Subjective*.)

3. If there is a dominant impression in this description, what is it?
   If none, why?

4. In any discussion of decline and loss, sentimentality is always a
   threat to good writing. Where, if at all, does Asimov lapse into
   sentimentality? Justify your answer. (Guide: *Sentimentality*.)

5. If you have read "But a Watch in the Night" (Sec. 4), what use might Rettie have made of Asimov's conception of life in 1997?

Expository Techniques

1a. What apparently was the author's purpose?
 b. What entirely different methods might he have used to achieve it?
 c. Would they have involved a different point of view? Explain. (Guide: *Point of View.*)
 d. Why would they probably be more, or less, effective than the method he did use?

2. Is this description basically objective or impressionistic? Why? (You may need to weigh your answer carefully — e.g., with regard to both style and effect.)

3. In which other category of patterns of exposition might this piece logically have been placed for study? Why?

4a. What adjective do you think best describes Asimov's tone? (Guide: *Style/Tone.*)
 b. How, if at all, is this tone related to syntax? (Guide: *Syntax.*)
 c. Does it tend to promote formal or informal writing? Use specific examples to support your answer. (Guide: *Essay.*)

5a. What is the advantage, if any, to having included the few "good" results of the shortages, along with the bad?
 b. Selection of details must have been a difficult task for such a broad subject in such limited space. What other details, if any, do you think might have made the essay more interesting or satisfying to read?
 c. Which of those the author did include would you have chosen to replace? Why?

6a. Select any three paragraphs which can effectively illustrate the relationship between topic sentence and paragraph unity. (Guide: *Unity.*)
 b. Use sentences from these paragraphs by which to show the meanings of "general" and "specific." (Guide: *Specific/General.*)
 c. Is the topic sentence of a paragraph more apt to be general or specific? Why?

Diction and Vocabulary

1. What is "subsistence farming" (par. 15)?

2. Analyze Asimov's diction and demonstrate as explicitly as possible the close relationship between diction and style. (Guide: *Diction* and *Style/Tone.*)

222

Suggestions for Writing and Discussion

1. Do you consider this writing entirely credible — or is the author merely "crying wolf"? Justify your answer.

2. Select a central theme and develop a well-organized composition or discussion suggested by one of the following questions:

a. What, to you, is the most alarming prospect visualized by Asimov?

b. Do you consider it likely that nuclear fission would still be "judged too dangerous" (par. 2) after several years of decline caused by lack of power?

c. Does it seem probable that the functioning nations of the world would let their armies go (par. 13), even in the face of such devastating shortages?

d. What *is* there to do with leisure time under the circumstances described in paragraph 14?

e. What would be the limiting factors if appreciable numbers of Americans were to try returning to subsistence farming (par. 15)?

f. What might we have done fifty years ago that would have made solutions easy (par. 18)?

g. What progress, if any, has been made since this essay was first published which will help prevent a 1997 as Asimov describes it?

(NOTE: Suggestions for topics requiring development by use of DESCRIPTION are on page 229, at the end of this section.)

DEEMS TAYLOR

Deems Taylor (1885–1966), a native New Yorker, was a noted composer and music critic. He wrote for several newspapers and magazines, later becoming well known as a radio commentator on the broadcasts of the New York Philharmonic Orchestra. Taylor composed both chamber music and larger works, including several operas. He wrote two books, *The Well-Tempered Listener* (1940) and *Some Enchanted Evenings* (1953).

The Monster

"The Monster" is a character analysis that understandably uses description almost exclusively to develop a lifelike portrait of the subject. To describe a unique character, Taylor selects a highly individual technique, and his writing makes an interesting study. Writers should always remember that the material itself, along with purpose and audience, can usually suggest the most effective methods to use.

He was an undersized little man, with a head too big for his body — a sickly little man. His nerves were bad. He had skin trouble. It was agony for him to wear anything next to his skin coarser than silk. And he had delusions of grandeur.

He was a monster of conceit. Never for one minute did he look at the world or at people, except in relation to himself. He was not only the most important person in the world, to himself; in his own eyes he was the only person who existed. He believed himself to be one of the greatest dramatists in the world, one of the greatest thinkers, and one of the greatest composers. To hear him talk he was Shakespeare, and Beethoven, and Plato, rolled into one. And

you would have had no difficulty in hearing him talk. He was one
of the most exhausting conversationalists that ever lived. An evening with him was an evening spent in listening to a monologue.
Sometimes he was brilliant; sometimes he was maddeningly tire-
some. But whether he was being brilliant or dull, he had one sole
topic of conversation: himself. What *he* thought and what *he* did.

He had a mania for being in the right. The slightest hint of   3
disagreement, from anyone, on the most trivial point, was enough
to set him off on a harangue that might last for hours, in which he
proved himself right in so many ways, and with such exhausting
volubility, that in the end his hearer, stunned and deafened, would
agree with him, for the sake of peace.

It never occurred to him that he and his doings were not of   4
the most intense and fascinating interest to anyone with whom he
came in contact. He had theories about almost any subject under
the sun, including vegetarianism, the drama, politics, and music;
and in support of these theories he wrote pamphlets, letters, books
... thousands upon thousands of words, hundreds and hundreds
of pages. He not only wrote these things, and published them —
usually at somebody else's expense — but he would sit and read
them aloud, for hours, to his friends and his family.

He wrote operas; and no sooner did he have the synopsis of   5
a story, but he would invite — or rather summon — a crowd of his
friends to his house and read it aloud to them. Not for criticism.
For applause. When the complete poem was written, the friends
had to come again, and hear *that* read aloud. Then he would publish the poem, sometimes years before the music that went with it
was written. He played the piano like a composer, in the worst
sense of what that implies, and he would sit down at the piano
before parties that included some of the finest pianists of his time,
and play for them, by the hour, his own music, needless to say. He
had a composer's voice. And he would invite eminent vocalists to
his house, and sing them his operas, taking all the parts.

He had the emotional stability of a six-year-old child. When   6
he felt out of sorts, he would rave and stamp, or sink into suicidal
gloom and talk darkly of going to the East to end his days as a
Buddhist monk. Ten minutes later, when something pleased him,
he would rush out of doors and run around the garden, or jump
up and down on the sofa, or stand on his head. He could be grief-
stricken over the death of a pet dog, and he could be callous and

heartless to a degree that would have made a Roman emperor shudder.

He was almost innocent of any sense of responsibility. Not only did he seem incapable of supporting himself, but it never occurred to him that he was under any obligation to do so. He was convinced that the world owed him a living. In support of this belief, he borrowed money from everybody who was good for a loan — men, women, friends, or strangers. He wrote begging letters by the score, sometimes groveling without shame, at others loftily offering his intended benefactor the privilege of contributing to his support, and being mortally offended if the recipient declined the honor. I have found no record of his ever paying or repaying money to anyone who did not have a legal claim upon it.

What money he could lay his hands on he spent like an Indian rajah. The mere prospect of a performance of one of his operas was enough to set him running up bills amounting to ten times the amount of his prospective royalties. On an income that would reduce a more scrupulous man to doing his own laundry, he would keep two servants. Without enough money in his pocket to pay his rent, he would have the walls and ceiling of his study lined with pink silk. No one will ever know — certainly he never knew — how much money he owed. We do know that his greatest benefactor gave him 6,000 dollars to pay the most pressing of his debts in one city, and a year later had to give him 16,000 dollars to enable him to live in another city without being thrown into jail for debt.

He was equally unscrupulous in other ways. An endless procession of women marched through his life. His first wife spent twenty years enduring and forgiving his infidelities. His second wife had been the wife of his most devoted friend and admirer, from whom he stole her. And even while he was trying to persuade her to leave her first husband he was writing to a friend to inquire whether he could suggest some wealthy woman — *any* wealthy woman — whom he could marry for her money.

He was completely selfish in his other personal relationships. His liking for his friends was measured solely by the completeness of their devotion to him, or by their usefulness to him, whether financial or artistic. The minute they failed him — even by so much as refusing a dinner invitation — or began to lessen in usefulness, he cast them off without a second thought. At the end of his life he had exactly one friend left whom he had known even in middle age.

He had a genius for making enemies. He would insult a man   11
who disagreed with him about the weather. He would pull endless
wires in order to meet some man who admired his work, and was
able and anxious to be of use to him — and would proceed to make
a mortal enemy of him with some idiotic and wholly uncalled-for
exhibition of arrogance and bad manners. A character in one of
his operas was a caricature of one of the most powerful music
critics of his day. Not content with burlesquing him, he invited the
critic to his house and read him the libretto aloud in front of his
friends.

The name of this monster was Richard Wagner. Everything   12
that I have said about him you can find on record — in newspapers,
in police reports, in the testimony of people who knew him, in his
own letters, between the lines of his autobiography. And the curious thing about this record is that it doesn't matter in the least.

Because this undersized, sickly, disagreeable, fascinating little   13
man was right all the time. The joke was on us. He *was* one of the
world's great dramatists; he *was* a great thinker; he *was* one of the
most stupendous musical geniuses that, up to now, the world has
ever seen. The world did owe him a living. People couldn't know
those things at the time, I suppose; and yet to us, who know his
music, it does seem as though they should have known. What if he
did talk about himself all the time? If he talked about himself for
twenty-four hours every day for the span of his life he would not
have uttered half the number of words that other men have spoken
and written about him since his death.

When you consider what he wrote — thirteen operas and   14
music dramas, eleven of them still holding the stage, eight of them
unquestionably worth ranking among the world's great musico-
dramatic masterpieces — when you listen to what he wrote, the
debts and heartaches that people had to endure from him don't
seem much of a price. Eduard Hanslick, the critic whom he caricatured in *Die Meistersinger* and who hated him ever after, now lives
only because he was caricatured in *Die Meistersinger*. The women
whose hearts he broke are long since dead; and the man who could
never love anyone but himself has made them deathless atonement,
I think, with *Tristan und Isolde*. Think of the luxury with which
for a time, at least, fate rewarded Napoleon, the man who ruined

France and looted Europe; and then perhaps you will agree that a
few thousand dollars' worth of debts were not too heavy a price
to pay for the *Ring* trilogy.

What if he was faithless to his friends and to his wives? He   15
had one mistress to whom he was faithful to the day of his death:
music. Not for a single moment did he ever compromise with what
he believed, with what he dreamed. There is not a line of his music
that could have been conceived by a little mind. Even when he is
dull, or downright bad, he is dull in the grand manner. There is a
greatness about his worst mistakes. Listening to his music, one
does not forgive him for what he may or may not have been. It is
not a matter of forgiveness. It is a matter of being dumb with wonder that his poor brain and body didn't burst under the torment of
the demon of creative energy that lived inside him, struggling,
clawing, scratching to be released; tearing, shrieking at him to
write the music that was in him. The miracle is that what he did
in the little space of seventy years could have been done at all,
even by a great genius. Is it any wonder that he had no time to be
a man?

Meanings and Values

1. How much, if at all, does this selection's value and interest depend
   on the reader's being familiar with Wagner's music? Explain.

2a. Does Taylor seem guilty of sentimentality in the latter part of
    the essay? In what respect, if at all? (See Guide to Terms: *Sen-
    timentality.*)

 b. If it does appear sentimentalized to you, would qualification have
    helped? If so, how? (Guide: *Qualification.*)

3a. What presumably is meant by playing the piano "like a composer"
    (par. 5)?

 b. What do you think is meant by "a composer's voice"?

4. Evaluate this essay by use of our three-part system. (Guide: *Evaluation.*)

Expository Techniques

1a. Demonstrate the meaning of syntax by use of the introductory
    paragraph. (Guide: *Syntax.*)

 b. Is it an effective introduction? Why, or why not? (Guide: *Intro-
    duction.*)

2a. Of the two highly contrasting basic parts of this description, which is more impressionistic? Why?

b. What is the dominant impression?

c. What sort of details might have been included in this part which would have disrupted the dominant impression? Demonstrate how.

3. In what way does Taylor anticipate a possible charge of exaggeration in his descriptive details?

4. What is the structural function of paragraph 12?

5. Is withholding the monster's name until late in the essay entirely justified? Why, or why not?

Diction and Vocabulary

1a. How would it be possible for such a "monster" even to *have* any friends?

b. Does it seem to you that for Taylor the word "friends" (used no less than ten times!) may have a different connotation than it does for you? Explain. (Guide: *Connotation/Denotation*.)

2. You may have noticed a lack of figurative language in this essay, but figures of speech worth noting do occur in the last paragraph. Cite them and explain why you do, or do not, find them effective. (Guide: *Figures of Speech*.)

3. If you are unfamiliar with any of the following words, consult your dictionary as necessary: harangue, volubility (par. 3); eminent (5); groveling, recipient (7); scrupulous, benefactor (8); caricature, libretto (11); atonement (14).

Suggestions for Writing and Discussion

1. Do you agree with Wagner and Taylor that the world owes genius a handsome living? Consider various kinds of genius and develop your thesis carefully.

2. If you disagree with Taylor in his view that what a person is like is not important if his professional performance is excellent enough, explain your own reasoning and use examples as needed from the present and former times.

3. If you know of such a character/talent contrast currently in the arts, sports, science, or politics, explain why the discrepancy should, or should not, be publicized.

Writing Suggestions for Section 8
Description

1. Primarily by way of impressionistic description that focuses on a single dominant impression, show and explain the mood, or atmosphere of one of the following:

    a. A county fair.
    b. A ball game.
    c. A rodeo.
    d. A wedding.
    e. A funeral.
    f. A riot.
    g. A ghost town.

    h. A cave.
    i. A mine.
    j. An antique shop.
    k. A party.

    l. A family dinner.
    m. A traffic jam.
    n. Reveille.
    o. An airport (or bus depot).
    p. A drag race (or horse race).
    q. A home during one of its rush hours.
    r. The last night of Christmas shopping.
    s. A natural scene at a certain time of day.
    t. The campus at examination time.
    u. A certain person at a time of great emotion — e.g., joy, anger, grief.

2. Using objective description as your basic pattern, explain the functional qualities or the significance of one of the following:

    a. A house for sale.
    b. A public building.
    c. A dairy barn.
    d. An ideal workshop (or hobby room).

    e. An ideal garage.
    f. A commune.
    g. The layout of a town (or airport).
    h. The layout of a farm.
    i. A certain type of boat.

9

Using *Narration* as an Expository Technique

Attempts to classify the functions of narration seem certain to develop difficulties and end in arbitrary and sometimes fuzzy distinctions. These need not distress us, however, if we remember that narration remains narration — a factual or fictional report of a sequence of events — and that our only reason for trying to divide it into categories is to find some means of studying its uses.

In a sense, as we have already seen in Section 5, exposition by process analysis makes one important, if rather narrow, use of narration, since it explains in sequence how specific steps lead to completion of some process. But at the other extreme is narration that has very little to do with exposition: the story itself is the important thing, and instead of a series of steps leading obviously to a completed act, events *develop* out of each other and build suspense, however mild, through some kind of conflict. Here narration assumes importance in its own right as one of the four basic forms of prose, and it includes the novel and short story, as well as some news and sports reporting. Because we are studying exposition, however, we must avoid getting too involved with these uses of narration; they require special techniques, the study of which would require a whole course or, in fact, several courses.

Between the extremes of a very usable analysis of process and a very intriguing narration for the story's sake — and often seeming to blur into one or the other — is narration for *explanation's* sake, to explain a concept that is more than process and that might have been explained by one of the other patterns of exposition. Here only the form is narrative; the function is expository.

Fortunately, the average student seldom needs to use narration for major explanatory purposes, as it has been used in each of the following selections. But to learn the handling of even minor or localized narration, the best procedure (short of taking several college courses, or at least one that concentrates on the narrative form) is simply to observe how successful writers use it to perform various functions. Localized narration can sometimes be helpful as an aid in developing any of the other major patterns of exposition.

The most common problems can be summarized as follows:

1. *Selection of details.* As in writing description, the user of narration always has far more details available than he can or should use. Good unity demands that he select only those which are most relevant to his purpose and the effect he wants to create.

2. *Time order.* The writer can use straight chronology, relating events as they happen (the usual method in minor uses of narration); or he can use the flashback method, leaving the sequence temporarily in order to go back and relate some now-significant happening of a time prior to the main action. If flashback is used, it should be deliberate and for a valid reason — not merely because the episode was neglected at the beginning.

3. *Transitions.* The lazy writer of narration is apt to resort to the transitional style of a three-year-old: ". . . and then we . . . and then she . . . and then we. . . ." Avoiding this style may tax his ingenuity, but invariably the result is worth the extra investment of time and thought.

4. *Point of view.* This is a large and complex subject if dealt with fully, as a course in narration would do. Briefly, however, the writer should decide at the beginning whether the reader is to experience the action through a character's eyes (and ears and brain), or from an overall, objective view. This decision makes a difference in how much can be told, whose thoughts or secret actions can be included. The writer must be consistent throughout the narrative and include only information that could logically be known through the adopted point of view.

5. *Dialogue.* Presumably the writer already knows the mechanics of using quotations. Beyond these, his problems are to make conversation as natural-sounding as possible and yet to keep it from rambling through many useless details — to keep the narrative moving forward by *means* of dialogue.

As in most patterns of writing, the use of expository narration is most likely to be successful if the writer constantly keeps his purpose and his audience in mind, remembering that the only reason for using the method in the first place — for doing *any* writing — is to communicate ideas. Soundness, clarity, and interest are the best means of attaining this goal.

MARTIN GANSBERG

MARTIN GANSBERG, born in Brooklyn, N.Y., in 1920, received a
Bachelor of Social Sciences degree from St. John's University.
He has been an editor and reporter on *The New York Times*
since 1942, including a three-year period as editor of its inter-
national edition in Paris. He also served on the faculty of
Fairleigh Dickinson University for fifteen years. Gansberg has
written for many magazines, including *Diplomat, Catholic
Digest, Facts,* and *U.S. Lady.*

38 Who Saw Murder Didn't Call the Police

"38 Who Saw Murder . . ." was written for *The New York
Times* in 1964, and for obvious reasons it has been anthologized frequently since then. Cast in a deceptively simple news
style, it still provides material for serious thought, as well as a
means of studying the use and technique of narration.

For more than half an hour 38 respectable, law-abiding citizens in   1
Queens watched a killer stalk and stab a woman in three separate
attacks in Kew Gardens.

   Twice their chatter and the sudden glow of their bedroom   2
lights interrupted him and frightened him off. Each time he returned, sought her out, and stabbed her again. Not one person
telephoned the police during the assault; one witness called after
the woman was dead.

That was two weeks ago today.   3

Still shocked is Assistant Chief Inspector Frederick M. Lussen,   4
in charge of the borough's detectives and a veteran of 25 years of
homicide investigations. He can give a matter-of-fact recitation on
many murders. But the Kew Gardens slaying baffles him — not

because it is a murder, but because the "good people" failed to call the police.

"As we have reconstructed the crime," he said, "the assailant   5
had three chances to kill this woman during a 35-minute period.
He returned twice to complete the job. If we had been called when
he first attacked, the woman might not be dead now."

This is what the police say happened beginning at 3:20 A.M. in   6
the staid, middle-class, tree-lined Austin Street area:

Twenty-eight-year-old Catherine Genovese, who was called   7
Kitty by almost everyone in the neighborhood, was returning home
from her job as manager of a bar in Hollis. She parked her red
Fiat in a lot adjacent to the Kew Gardens Long Island Rail Road
Station, facing Mowbray Place. Like many residents of the neigh-
borhood, she had parked there day after day since her arrival from
Connecticut a year ago, although the railroad frowns on the prac-
tice.

She turned off the lights of her car, locked the door, and   8
started to walk the 100 feet to the entrance of her apartment at
82–70 Austin Street, which is in a Tudor building, with stores in
the first floor and apartments on the second.

The entrance to the apartment is in the rear of the building   9
because the front is rented to retail stores. At night the quiet neighborhood is shrouded in the slumbering darkness that marks most
residential areas.

Miss Genovese noticed a man at the far end of the lot, near a   10
seven-story apartment house at 82–40 Austin Street. She halted.
Then, nervously, she headed up Austin Street toward Lefferts
Boulevard, where there is a call box to the 102nd Police Precinct in
nearby Richmond Hill.

She got as far as a street light in front of a bookstore before   11
the man grabbed her. She screamed. Lights went on in the 10-story
apartment house at 82–67 Austin Street, which faces the bookstore.
Windows slid open and voices punctuated the early-morning stillness.

Miss Genovese screamed: "Oh, my God, he stabbed me!   12
Please help me! Please help me!"

From one of the upper windows in the apartment house, a   13
man called down: "Let that girl alone!"

The assailant looked up at him, shrugged and walked down   14

Austin Street toward a white sedan parked a short distance away. Miss Genovese struggled to her feet.

Lights went out. The killer returned to Miss Genovese, now   15 trying to make her way around the side of the building by the parking lot to get to her apartment. The assailant stabbed her again.

"I'm dying!" she shrieked. "I'm dying!"   16

Windows were opened again, and lights went on in many   17 apartments. The assailant got into his car and drove away. Miss Genovese staggered to her feet. A city bus, O–10, the Lefferts Boulevard line to Kennedy International Airport, passed. It was 3:35 A.M.

The assailant returned. By then, Miss Genovese had crawled   18 to the back of the building, where the freshly painted brown doors to the apartment house held out hope for safety. The killer tried the first door; she wasn't there. At the second door, 82–62 Austin Street, he saw her slumped on the floor at the foot of the stairs. He stabbed her a third time — fatally.

It was 3:50 by the time the police received their first call, from   19 a man who was a neighbor of Miss Genovese. In two minutes they were at the scene. The neighbor, a 70-year-old woman, and another woman were the only persons on the street. Nobody else came forward.

The man explained that he had called the police after much   20 deliberation. He had phoned a friend in Nassau County for advice and then he had crossed the roof of the building to the apartment of the elderly woman to get her to make the call.

"I didn't want to get involved," he sheepishly told the police.   21

Six days later, the police arrested Winston Moseley, a 29-year-   22 old business-machine operator, and charged him with homicide. Moseley had no previous record. He is married, has two children and owns a home at 133–19 Sutter Avenue, South Ozone Park, Queens. On Wednesday, a court committed him to Kings County Hospital for psychiatric observation.

When questioned by the police, Moseley also said that he had   23 slain Mrs. Annie May Johnson, 24, of 146–12 133d Avenue, Jamaica, on Feb. 29 and Barbara Kralik, 15, of 174–17 140th Avenue, Springfield Gardens, last July. In the Kralik case, the police are holding Alvin L. Mitchell, who is said to have confessed that slaying.

The police stressed how simple it would have been to have 24 gotten in touch with them. "A phone call," said one of the detectives, "would have done it." The police may be reached by dialing "O" for operator or SPring 7–3100.

Today witnesses from the neighborhood, which is made up of 25 one-family homes in the $35,000 to $60,000 range with the exception of the two apartment houses near the railroad station, find it difficult to explain why they didn't call the police.

A housewife, knowingly if quite casually, said, "We thought 26 it was a lover's quarrel." A husband and wife both said, "Frankly, we were afraid." They seemed aware of the fact that events might have been different. A distraught woman, wiping her hands in her apron, said, "I didn't want my husband to get involved."

One couple, now willing to talk about that night, said they 27 heard the first screams. The husband looked thoughtfully at the bookstore where the killer first grabbed Miss Genovese.

"We went to the window to see what was happening," he said, 28 "but the light from our bedroom made it difficult to see the street." The wife, still apprehensive, added: "I put out the light and we were able to see better."

Asked why they hadn't called the police, she shrugged and 29 replied: "I don't know."

A man peeked out from a slight opening in the doorway to his 30 apartment and rattled off an account of the killer's second attack. Why hadn't he called the police at the time? "I was tired," he said without emotion. "I went back to bed."

It was 4:25 A.M. when the ambulance arrived to take the body 31 of Miss Genovese. It drove off. "Then," a solemn police detective said, "the people came out."

Meanings and Values

1a. What is Gansberg's central (expository) theme?
 b. How might he have developed this theme without using narration at all? Specify what patterns of exposition he could have used instead.
 c. Would any of them have been as effective as narration *for the purpose*? Why, or why not?
2. Show how this selection could be used as an illustration in an ex-

planatory discussion of abstract and concrete writing. (See Guide to Terms: *Concrete/Abstract*.)

3a. Why has this narrative account of old news (the murder made its only headlines in 1964) retained its significance to this day?
 b. Are you able to see in this event a paradigm of any larger condition or situation? If so, explain, using examples as needed to illustrate your ideas.

4. If you have read the Toffler selection (Sec. 4), does it seem to you that the noninvolvement of Kitty Genovese's neighbors is an inevitable extension of urban "modularization"? Explain.

5. If you have read Wolfe's essay (Sec. 4), do you think Dr. Hall would have been very surprised at this New York case of noninvolvement? Why, or why not?

Expository Techniques

1a. What standard introductory technique is exemplified in paragraph 1? (Guide: *Introductions*.)
 b. How effective do you consider it?
 c. If you see anything ironic in the fact stated there, explain the irony. (Guide: *Irony*.)

2a. Where does the main narration begin?
 b. What, then, is the function of the preceding paragraphs?

3a. Study several of the paragraph transitions within the narration itself to determine Gansberg's method of advancing the time sequence (to avoid overuse of "and then"). What is the technique?
 b. Is another needed? Why, or why not?

4a. What possible reasons do you see for the predominant use of short paragraphs in this piece?
 b. Does this selection lose any effectiveness because of the short paragraphs?

5. Undoubtedly, the author selected with care the few quotations from witnesses that he uses. What principle, or principles, do you think applied to his selection?

6. Explain why you think the quotation from the "solemn police detective" was, or was not, deliberately and carefully chosen to conclude the piece. (Guide: *Closings*.)

7a. Briefly identify the point of view of the writing. (Guide: *Point of View*.)
 b. Is it consistent throughout?
 c. Show the relation, as you see it, between this point of view and the author's apparent attitude toward his subject matter.

8a. Does he permit himself any sentimentality? If so, where? (Guide: *Sentimentality*.)
   b. If not, specifically what might he have included that would have slipped into melodrama or sentimentality?

Diction and Vocabulary

1a. Why do you think the author used no difficult words in this narration?
   b. Do you find the writing at all belittling to college people because of this fact? Why, or why not?

Suggestions for Writing and Discussion

1. Use both developed and undeveloped examples to show the prevalence, among individuals, of an anti-involvement attitude today. Or, if you prefer, show that this accusation is unjustified.

2. If this narration can be regarded as a paradigm (see question 3b of "Meanings and Values"), select one example from the larger subject and develop it on whatever theme you choose. Your example could be from international affairs, if you like (and if you don't mind becoming the center of a controversy) — e.g., the recent cries of "murder!" from numerous small countries. If you prefer, go into more distant (and therefore less controversial) history for your example.

3. If such a crime as the Genovese murder were happening in an area or a situation where police were not so instantly available, what do you think an observer should do about it? What would *you* do? Justify your stand fully.

(NOTE: Suggestions for topics requiring development by NARRATION are on page 264, at the end of this section.)

HELEN KELLER

HELEN KELLER (1880–1968) was born in Tuscumbia, Alabama, and at the age of nineteen months lost both sight and hearing as a result of an illness. Because of the double disability there seemed no way even to teach her to speak; but in 1887 Anne Sullivan became her teacher-companion and by ingenuity and heroic patience overcame the obstacles. Helen Keller not only learned to speak fluently but also managed to earn a college diploma and to live a long and rewarding life. She was one of the most honored women of her time, famous throughout the world for her courage and charm, for her devotion to social causes and the inspiration she gave to handicapped people of all kinds. A frequent contributor to periodicals, she also wrote two popular books: *The Story of My Life* (1902) and *The World I Live In* (1908).

Three Days to See

"Three Days to See," as used here, is the greater portion of Helen Keller's essay by that title which was first published in *The Atlantic Monthly* in 1932. Since then it has been translated into numerous foreign languages and has always been popular in essay anthologies because of the unique quality of ideas and its distinctive style. For our purpose it also serves to illustrate again how narration can accomplish an expository purpose.

If I were the president of a university I should establish a compulsory course in "How To Use Your Eyes." The professor would try to show his pupils how they could add joy to their lives by really seeing what passes unnoticed before them. He would try to awake their dormant and sluggish faculties. 1

Perhaps I can best illustrate by imagining what I should most 2 like to see if I were given the use of my eyes, say, for just three days. And while I am imagining, suppose you, too, set your mind to work on the problem of how you would use your own eyes if you had only three more days to see. If with the oncoming darkness of the third night you knew that the sun would never rise for you again, how would you spend those three precious intervening days? What would you most want to let your gaze rest upon?

I, naturally, should want most to see the things which have 3 become dear to me through my years of darkness. You, too, would want to let your eyes rest long on the things that have become dear to you so that you could take the memory of them with you into the night that loomed before you.

If, by some miracle, I were granted three seeing days, to be 4 followed by a relapse into darkness, I should divide the period into three parts.

On the first day, I should want to see the people whose kind- 5 ness and gentleness and companionship have made my life worth living. First I should like to gaze long upon the face of my dear teacher, Mrs. Anne Sullivan Macy, who came to me when I was a child and opened the outer world to me. I should want not merely to see the outline of her face, so that I could cherish it in my memory, but to study that face and find in it the living evidence of the sympathetic tenderness and patience with which she accomplished the difficult task of my education. I should like to see in her eyes that strength of character which has enabled her to stand firm in the face of difficulties, and that compassion for all humanity which she has revealed to me so often.

I do not know what it is to see into the heart of a friend 6 through that "window of the soul," the eye. I can only "see" through my fingertips the outline of a face. I can detect laughter, sorrow, and many other obvious emotions. I know my friends from the feel of their faces. But I cannot really picture their personalities by touch. I know their personalities, of course, through other means, through the thoughts they express to me, through whatever of their actions are revealed to me. But I am denied that deeper understanding of them which I am sure would come through sight of them, through watching their reactions to various expressed thoughts and circumstances, through noting the immediate and fleeting reactions of their eyes and countenance.

Friends who are near to me I know well, because through the 7 months and years they reveal themselves to me in all their phases; but of casual friends I have only an incomplete impression, an impression gained from a handclasp, from spoken words which I take from their lips with my fingertips, or which they tap into the palm of my hand.

How much easier, how much more satisfying it is for you who can see to grasp quickly the essential qualities of another person by watching the subtleties of expression, the quiver of a muscle, the flutter of a hand. But does it ever occur to you to use your sight to see into the inner nature of a friend or acquaintance? Do not most of you seeing people grasp casually the outward features of a face and let it go at that? 8

For instance, can you describe accurately the faces of five good friends? Some of you can, but many cannot. As an experiment, I have questioned husbands of long standing about the color of their wives' eyes, and often they express embarrassed confusion and admit that they do not know. And, incidentally, it is a chronic complaint of wives that their husbands do not notice new dresses, new hats, and changes in household arrangements. 9

The eyes of seeing persons soon become accustomed to the routine of their surroundings, and they actually see only the startling and spectacular. But even in viewing the most spectacular sights the eyes are lazy. Court records reveal every day how inaccurately "eyewitnesses" see. A given event will be "seen" in several different ways by as many witnesses. Some see more than others, but few see everything that is within the range of their vision. 10

Oh, the things that I should see if I had the power of sight for just three days! 11

The first day would be a busy one. I should call to me all my dear friends and look long into their faces, imprinting upon my mind the outward evidences of the beauty that is within them. I should let my eyes rest, too, on the face of a baby, so that I could catch a vision of the eager, innocent beauty which precedes the individual's consciousness of the conflicts which life develops. 12

And I should like to look into the loyal, trusting eyes of my dogs — the grave, canny little Scottie, Darkie, and the stalwart, understanding Great Dane, Helga, whose warm, tender, and playful friendships are so comforting to me. 13

On that busy first day I should also view the small simple 14 things of my home. I want to see the warm colors in the rugs under my feet, the pictures on the walls, the intimate trifles that transform a house into home. My eyes would rest respectfully on the books in raised type which I have read, but they would be more eagerly interested in the printed books which seeing people can read, for during the long night of my life the books I have read and those which have been read to me have built themselves into a great shining lighthouse, revealing to me the deepest channels of human life and the human spirit.

In the afternoon of that first seeing day, I should take a long 15 walk in the woods and intoxicate my eyes on the beauties of the world of Nature, trying desperately to absorb in a few hours the vast splendor which is constantly unfolding itself to those who can see. On the way home from my woodland jaunt my path would lie near a farm so that I might see the patient horses plowing in the field (perhaps I should see only a tractor!) and the serene content of men living close to the soil. And I should pray for the glory of a colorful sunset.

When dusk had fallen, I should experience the double delight 16 of being able to see by artificial light, which the genius of man has created to extend the power of his sight when Nature decrees darkness.

In the night of that first day of sight, I should not be able to 17 sleep, so full would be my mind of the memories of the day.

The next day — the second day of sight — I should arise with 18 the dawn and see the thrilling miracle by which night is transformed into day. I should behold with awe the magnificent panorama of light with which the sun awakens the sleeping earth.

This day I should devote to a hasty glimpse of the world, past 19 and present. I should want to see the pageant of man's progress, the kaleidoscope of the ages. How can so much be compressed into one day? Through the museums, of course. Often I have visited the New York Museum of Natural History to touch with my hands many of the objects there exhibited, but I have longed to see with my eyes the condensed history of the earth and its inhabitants displayed there — animals and the races of men pictured in their native environment; gigantic carcasses of dinosaurs and mastodons which roamed the earth long before man appeared, with his tiny stature and powerful brain, to conquer the animal kingdom; realistic presentations of the processes of evolution in animals, in man,

and in the implements which man has used to fashion for himself
a secure home on this planet; and a thousand and one other aspects
of natural history.

I wonder how many readers of this article have viewed this   20
panorama of the face of living things as pictured in that inspiring
museum. Many, of course, have not had the opportunity, but I am
sure that many who *have* had the opportunity have not made use
of it. There, indeed, is a place to use your eyes. You who see can
spend many fruitful days there, but I, with my imaginary three
days of sight, could only take a hasty glimpse, and pass on.

My next stop would be the Metropolitan Museum of Art, for   21
just as the Museum of Natural History reveals the material aspects
of the world, so does the Metropolitan show the myriad facets of
the human spirit. Throughout the history of humanity the urge to
artistic expression has been almost as powerful as the urge for
food, shelter, and procreation. And here, in the vast chambers of
the Metropolitan Museum, is unfolded before me the spirit of
Egypt, Greece, and Rome, as expressed in their art. I know well
through my hands the sculptured gods and goddesses of the ancient Nile-land. I have felt copies of Parthenon friezes, and I have
sensed the rhythmic beauty of charging Athenian warriors. Apollos
and Venuses and the Winged Victory of Samothrace are friends of
my fingertips. The gnarled, bearded features of Homer are dear to
me, for he, too, knew blindness.

My hands have lingered upon the living marble of Roman   22
sculpture as well as that of later generations. I have passed my
hands over a plaster cast of Michelangelo's inspiring and heroic
Moses; I have sensed the power of Rodin; I have been awed by the
devoted spirit of Gothic wood carving. These arts which can be
touched have meaning for me, but even they were meant to be seen
rather than felt, and I can only guess at the beauty which remains
hidden from me. I can admire the simple lines of a Greek vase, but
its figured decorations are lost to me.

So on this, my second day of sight, I should try to probe into   23
the soul of man through his art. The things I knew through touch
I should now see. More splendid still, the whole magnificent world
of painting would be opened to me, from the Italian Primitives,
with their serene religious devotion, to the Moderns, with their
feverish visions. I should look deep into the canvases of Raphael,

Leonardo da Vinci, Titian, Rembrandt. I should want to feast my eyes upon the warm colors of Veronese, study the mysteries of El Greco, catch a new vision of Nature from Corot. Oh, there is so much rich meaning and beauty in the art of the ages for you who have eyes to see!

Upon my short visit to this temple of art I should not be able to review a fraction of that great world of art which is open to you. I should be able to get only a superficial impression. Artists tell me that for a deep and true appreciation of art one must educate the eye. One must learn through experience to weigh the merits of line, of composition, of form and color. If I had eyes, how happily would I embark upon so fascinating a study! Yet I am told that, to many of you who have eyes to see, the world of art is a dark night, un-explored and unilluminated.

It would be with extreme reluctance that I should leave the Metropolitan Museum, which contains the key to beauty — a beauty so neglected. Seeing persons, however, do not need a Metro-politan to find this key to beauty. The same key lies waiting in smaller museums, and in books on the shelves of even small li-braries. But naturally, in my limited time of imaginary sight, I should choose the place where the key unlocks the greatest trea-sures in the shortest time.

The evening of my second day of sight I should spend at a theater or at the movies. Even now I often attend theatrical per-formances of all sorts, but the action of the play must be spelled into my hand by a companion. But how I should like to see with my own eyes the fascinating figure of Hamlet, or the gusty Falstaff amid colorful Elizabethan trappings! How I should like to follow each movement of the graceful Hamlet, each strut of the hearty Falstaff! And since I could see only one play, I should be con-fronted by the many-horned dilemma, for there are scores of plays I should want to see. You who have eyes can see any you like. How many of you, I wonder, when you gaze at a play, a movie, or any spectacle, realize and give thanks for the miracle of sight which enables you to enjoy its color, grace, and movement?

I cannot enjoy the beauty of rhythmic movement except in a sphere restricted to the touch of my hands. I can vision only dimly the grace of a Pavlova, although I know something of the delight of rhythm, for often I can sense the beat of music as it vibrates through the floor. I can well imagine that cadenced motion must be one of the most pleasing sights in the world. I have been able to gather something of this by tracing with my fingers the lines in sculptured marble; if this static grace can be so lovely, how much more acute must be the thrill of seeing grace in motion.

One of my dearest memories is of the time when Joseph 28 Jefferson allowed me to touch his face and hands as he went through some of the gestures and speeches of his beloved Rip Van Winkle. I was able to catch thus a meager glimpse of the world of drama, and I shall never forget the delight of that moment. But, oh, how much I must miss, and how much pleasure you seeing ones can derive from watching and hearing the interplay of speech and movement in the unfolding of a dramatic performance! If I could see only one play, I should know how to picture in my mind the action of a hundred plays which I have read or had transferred to me through the medium of the manual alphabet.

So, through the evening of my second imaginary day of sight, 29 the great figures of dramatic literature would crowd sleep from my eyes.

The following morning, I should again greet the dawn, anxious 30 to discover new delights, for I am sure that, for those who have eyes which really see, the dawn of each day must be a perpetually new revelation of beauty.

This, according to the terms of my imagined miracle, is to be 31 my third and last day of sight. I shall have no time to waste in regrets or longings; there is too much to see. The first day I devoted to my friends, animate and inanimate. The second revealed to me the history of man and Nature. Today I shall spend in the workaday world of the present, amid the haunts of men going about the business of life. And where can one find so many activities and conditions of men as in New York? So the city becomes my destination.

I start from my home in the quiet little suburb of Forest Hills, 32 Long Island. Here, surrounded by green lawns, trees, and flowers, are neat little houses, happy with the voices and movements of wives and children, havens of peaceful rest for men who toil in the city. I drive across the lacy structure of steel which spans the East River, and I get a new and startling vision of the power and ingenuity of the mind of man. Busy boats chug and scurry about the river — racy speedboats, stolid, snorting tugs. If I had long days of sight ahead, I should spend many of them watching the delightful activity upon the river.

I look ahead, and before me rise the fantastic towers of New York, a city that seems to have stepped from the pages of a fairy story. What an awe-inspiring sight, these glittering spires, these vast banks of stone and steel — structures such as the gods might build for themselves! This animated picture is a part of the lives of millions of people every day. How many, I wonder, give it so much as a second glance? Very few, I fear. Their eyes are blind to this magnificent sight because it is so familiar to them. 33

I hurry to the top of one of those gigantic structures, the Empire State Building, for there, a short time ago, I "saw" the city below through the eyes of my secretary. I am anxious to compare my fancy with reality. I am sure I should not be disappointed in the panorama spread out before me, for to me it would be a vision of another world. 34

Now I begin my rounds of the city. First, I stand at a busy corner, merely looking at people, trying by sight of them to understand something of their lives. I see smiles, and I am happy. I see determination, and I am proud. I see suffering, and I am compassionate. 35

I stroll down Fifth Avenue. I throw my eyes out of focus so that I see no particular object but only a seething kaleidoscope of color. I am certain that the colors of women's dresses moving in a throng must be a gorgeous spectacle of which I should never tire. But perhaps if I had sight I should be like most other women — too interested in styles and the cut of individual dresses to give much attention to the splendor of color in the mass. And I am convinced, too, that I should become an inveterate window shopper, for it must be a delight to the eye to view the myriad articles of beauty on display. 36

From Fifth Avenue I make a tour of the city — to Park Avenue, to the slums, to factories, to parks where children play. I take a stay-at-home trip abroad by visiting the foreign quarters. Always my eyes are open wide to all the sights of both happiness and misery so that I may probe deep and add to my understanding of how people work and live. My heart is full of the images of people and things. My eye passes lightly over no single trifle; it strives to touch and hold closely each thing its gaze rests upon. Some sights are pleasant, filling the heart with happiness; but some are miser- 37 ably pathetic. To these latter I do not shut my eyes, for they, too, are part of life. To close the eye on them is to close the heart and mind.

My third day of sight is drawing to an end. Perhaps there are [38] many serious pursuits to which I should devote the few remaining hours, but I am afraid that on the evening of that last day I should again run away to the theater, to a hilariously funny play, so that I might appreciate the overtones of comedy in the human spirit.

At midnight my temporary respite from blindness would cease, [39] and permanent night would close in on me again. Naturally in those three short days I should not have seen all I wanted to see. Only when darkness had again descended upon me should I realize how much I had left unseen. But my mind would be so crowded with glorious memories that I should have little time for regrets. Thereafter the touch of every object would bring a glowing memory of how that object looked.

Perhaps this short outline of how I should spend three days of [40] sight does not agree with the program you would set for yourself if you knew that you were about to be stricken blind. I am, however, sure that if you actually faced that fate your eyes would open to things you had never seen before, storing up memories for the long night ahead. You would use your eyes as never before. Everything you saw would become dear to you. Your eyes would touch and embrace every object that came within your range of vision. Then, at last, you would really see, and a new world of beauty would open itself before you.

I who am blind can give one hint to those who see — one ad- [41] monition to those who would make full use of the gift of sight: Use your eyes as if tomorrow you would be stricken blind. And the same method can be applied to the other senses. Hear the music of voices, the song of a bird, the mighty strains of an orchestra, as if you would be stricken deaf tomorrow. Touch each object you want to touch as if tomorrow your tactile sense would fail. Smell the perfume of flowers, taste with relish each morsel, as if tomorrow you could never smell and taste again. Make the most of every sense; glory in all the facets of pleasure and beauty which the world reveals to you through the several means of contact which Nature provides. But of all the senses, I am sure that sight must be the most delightful.

Meanings and Values

1. Illustrate, by use of this essay, the meaning of "subjective writing." (See Guide to Terms: *Objective/Subjective.*)

2a. Aside from the pleasure of sharing the thoughts of a remarkable woman, what practical value should a seeing person be able to gain from reading this essay?
 b. Why is it "practical"?
 c. How would the value for a blind reader be entirely different?

3a. Illustrate the meaning of irony by use of Keller's basic assumption about people who can see. (Guide: *Irony.*)
 b. Do you think the assumption is correct?

4a. Do you find any evidence of sentimentality in this piece? (Guide: *Sentimentality.*)
 b. If so, is it justified, or perhaps even unavoidable? If not, how did you arrive at your decision?

5. Explain more fully the concept that artistic expression reveals the human spirit, that we may "probe into the soul of man through his art" (pars. 21–23).

6. If you have read "Reading as Narcotic" (Sec. 2), to which of Hall's types of reading does Keller seem to be referring in paragraph 14?

Expository Techniques

1a. Is this use of narrative form to develop the central theme more, or less, effective than would be some other method of fulfilling that expository purpose? (Guide: *Unity.*)
 b. Demonstrate how others might have been used.
 c. In view of the expository central theme, does the essay have good unity? Why, or why not?

2a. Which of the other patterns of exposition is constantly interwoven with the narrative development?
 b. Cite at least two examples of this method.

3a. If you were charged with the job of revising paragraphs 5–12, what would you regard as your basic challenge? Why?
 b. State briefly what you would include in each of your revised paragraph.
 c. Explain why this kind of revision would improve, or not improve, the writing.

4. What is the merit, if any, in the use of parallels in paragraph 35? (Guide: *Parallel Structures.*)

5a. Select three examples by which to illustrate typical aspects of Keller's style of syntax. (Guide: *Syntax* and *Style/Tone.*)

    b. Compare these with examples of syntax that are typical of two other selections in this book.

    c. Is Keller's style compatible with her subject and point of view? Why, or why not? (Guide: *Point of View*.)

Diction and Vocabulary

1a. To what extent is Keller's diction also a matter of style?

  b. How is it affected by metaphorical language? (Guide: *Figures of Speech*.) Use examples to illustrate.

2. What is a "many-horned dilemma (par. 26)?

3. Consult the dictionary as needed for an understanding of the following words: chronic (par. 9); canny (13); Parthenon, friezes (21); myriad (21,36); facets (21, 41); inveterate (36); respite (39); admonition, tactile (41).

Suggestions for Writing and Discussion

1. Develop the lighthouse metaphor in paragraph 14 (which already verges on analogy) into a full-scale analogy, showing the significance of good books.

2. Develop Keller's metaphor of the world of art as "a dark night" (par. 24) into a clear and meaningful analogy.

3. Illustrate by examples as specifically as possible, and in as many of its forms as possible, how artistic expression can be said to reveal the human spirit (pars. 21, 23). (Feel free to choose your examples from popular culture if you like.)

4. How is it possible, using the eyes, to "see into the inner nature" of another person (par. 8)? If you believe that even eyes have serious limitations in this respect, explain that too.

(NOTE: Suggestions for topics requiring development by NARRATION are on page 264, at the end of this section.)

ALEX HALEY

> Alex Haley, a native of Henning, Tennessee, began writing
> while enlisted in the U.S. Coast Guard. At 37 he turned to
> writing full-time and was coauthor of *The Autobiography of
> Malcolm X* (1965). His book *Roots* (1976) rapidly became one
> of the most famous books of modern times, and the American
> Broadcasting Company's eight-part television series based on
> it was a record-breaker for its wide appeal and tremendous
> viewer-audience.

My Furthest-Back Person—"The African"

> "My Furthest-Back Person — 'The African'" appeared in *The
> New York Times Magazine* four years prior to the publication
> of *Roots*. It is Haley's own condensed account of his almost
> incredible search for the roots of his origin; but its impor-
> tance, like that of the book, lies in a wider significance, the
> meaning others can care about and identify with. For our
> purposes, too, this essay will serve to illustrate most of the
> techniques readily available for use in narration.

My Grandma Cynthia Murray Palmer lived in Henning, Tenn.   1
(pop. 500), about 50 miles north of Memphis. Each summer as I
grew up there, we would be visited by several women relatives
who were mostly around Grandma's age, such as my Great Aunt
Liz Murray who taught in Oklahoma, and Great Aunt Till Merri-
wether from Jackson, Tenn., or their considerably younger niece,
Cousin Georgia Anderson from Kansas City, Kan., and some
others. Always after the supper dishes had been washed, they
would go out to take seats and talk in the rocking chairs on the
front porch, and I would scrunch down, listening, behind Grand-

ma's squeaky chair, with the dusk deepening into night and the lightning bugs flickering on and off above the now shadowy honeysuckles. Most often they talked about our family — the story had been passed down for generations — until the whistling blur of lights of the southbound Panama Limited train *whooshing* through Henning at 9:05 P.M. signaled our bedtime.

So much of their talking of people, places and events I didn't   2
understand: For instance, what was an "Ol' Massa," an "Ol' Missus" or a "plantation"? But early I gathered that white folks had done lots of bad things to our folks, though I couldn't figure out why. I guessed that all that they talked about had happened a long time ago, as now or then Grandma or another, speaking of someone in the past, would excitedly thrust a finger toward me, exclaiming, "Wasn't big as *this* young 'un!" And it would astound me that anyone as old and grey-haired as they could relate to my age. But in time my head began both a recording and picturing of the more graphic scenes they would describe, just as I also vis- ualized David killing Goliath with his slingshot, Old Pharaoh's army drowning, Noah and his ark, Jesus feeding that big multitude with nothing but five loaves and two fishes, and other wonders that I heard in my Sunday school lessons at our New Hope Methodist Church.

The furthest-back person Grandma and the others talked of —   3
always in tones of awe, I noticed — they would call "The African." They said that some ship brought him to a place that they pro- nounced "'Naplis." They said that then some "Mas' John Waller" bought him for his plantation in "Spotsylvania County, Va." This African kept on escaping, the fourth time trying to kill the "hate- ful po' cracker" slave-catcher, who gave him the punishment choice of castration or of losing one foot. This African took a foot being chopped off with an ax against a tree stump, they said, and he was about to die. But his life was saved by "Mas' John's" brother — "Mas' William Waller," a doctor, who was so furious about what had happened that he bought the African for himself and gave him the name "Toby."

Crippling about, working in "Mas' William's" house and yard,   4
the African in time met and mated with "the big house cook named Bell," and there was born a girl named Kizzy. As she grew up her African daddy often showed her different kinds of things, telling her what they were in his native tongue. Pointing at a banjo, for

example, the African uttered, *"ko"*; or pointing at a river near the plantation, he would say, *"Kamby Bolong."* Many of his strange words started with a *"k"* sound, and the little, growing Kizzy learned gradually that they identified different things.

When addressed by other slaves as "Toby," the master's name 5
for him, the African said angrily that his name was *"Kin-tay."* And as he gradually learned English, he told young Kizzy some things about himself — for instance, that he was not far from his village, chopping wood to make himself a drum, when four men had surprised, overwhelmed, and kidnaped him.

So Kizzy's head held much about her African daddy when at 6
age 16 she was sold away onto a much smaller plantation in North Carolina. Her new "Mas' Tom Lea" fathered her first child, a boy she named George. And Kizzy told her boy all about his African grandfather. George grew up to be such a gamecock fighter that he was called "Chicken George," and people would come from all over and "bet big money" on his cockfights. He mated with Matilda, another of Lea's slaves; they had seven children, and he told them the stories and strange sounds of their African great-grand-father. And one of those children, Tom, became a blacksmith who was bought away by a "Mas' Murray" for his tobacco plantation in Alamance County, N.C.

Tom mated there with Irene, a weaver on the plantation. She 7
also bore seven children, and Tom now told them all about their African great-great-grandfather, the faithfully passed-down knowledge of his sounds and stories having become by now the family's prideful treasure.

The youngest of that second set of seven children was a girl, 8
Cynthia, who became my maternal Grandma (which today I can only see as fated). Anyway, all of this is how I was growing up in Henning at Grandma's, listening from behind her rocking chair as she and the other visiting old women talked of that African (never then comprehended as *my* great-great-great-great-grandfather) who said his name was *"Kin-tay,"* and said *"ko"* for banjo, *"Kamby Bolong"* for river, and a jumble of other *"k"*-beginning sounds that Grandma privately muttered, most often while making beds or cooking, and who also said that near his village he was kidnaped while chopping wood to make himself a drum.

The story had become nearly as fixed in my head as in Grand- 9
ma's by the time Dad and Mama moved me and my two younger

brothers, George and Julius, away from Henning to be with them at the small black agricultural and mechanical college in Normal, Ala., where Dad taught.

To compress my next 25 years: When I was 17 Dad let me   10
enlist as a mess boy in the U.S. Coast Guard. I became a ship's cook out in the South Pacific during World War II, and at night down by my bunk I began trying to write sea adventure stories, mailing them off to magazines and collecting rejection slips for eight years before some editors began purchasing and publishing occasional stories. By 1949 the Coast Guard had made me its first "journalist"; finally with 20 years' service, I retired at the age of 37, determined to make a full time career of writing. I wrote mostly magazine articles; my first book was "The Autobiography of Malcolm X."

Then one Saturday in 1965 I happened to be walking past the   11
National Archives building in Washington. Across the interim years I had thought of Grandma's old stories — otherwise I can't think what diverted me up the Archives' steps. And when a main reading room desk attendant asked if he could help me, I wouldn't have dreamed of admitting to him some curiosity hanging on from boyhood about my slave forebears. I kind of bumbled that I was interested in census records of Alamance County, North Carolina, just after the Civil War.

The microfilm rolls were delivered, and I turned them through   12
the machine with a building sense of intrigue, viewing in different census takers' penmanship an endless parade of names. After about a dozen microfilmed rolls, I was beginning to tire, when in utter astonishment I looked upon the names of Grandma's parents: Tom Murray, Irene Murray . . . older sisters of Grandma's as well — every one of them a name that I'd heard countless times on her front porch.

It wasn't that I hadn't believed Grandma. You just *didn't* not   13
believe my Grandma. It was simply so uncanny actually seeing those names in print and in official U.S. Government records.

During the next several months I was back in Washington   14
whenever possible, in the Archives, the Library of Congress, the Daughters of the American Revolution Library. (Whenever black attendants understood the idea of my search, documents I requested reached me with miraculous speed.) In one source or another during 1966 I was able to document at least the highlights

of the cherished family story. I would have given anything to have told Grandma, but, sadly, in 1949 she had gone. So I went and told the only survivor of those Henning front-porch storytellers: Cousin Georgia Anderson, now in her 80's in Kansas City, Kan. Wrinkled, bent, not well herself, she was so overjoyed, repeating to me the old stories and sounds; they were like Henning echoes: "Yeah, boy, that African say his name was '*Kin-tay*'; he say the banjo was '*ko*,' and river '*Kamby-Bolong*,' an' he was off choppin some wood to make his drum when they grabbed 'im!" Cousin Georgia grew so excited we had to stop her, calm her down, "You go 'head, boy! Your grandma an' all of 'em — they up there watching what you do!"

That week I flew to London on a magazine assignment. Since   15
by now I was steeped in the old, in the past, scarcely a tour guide missed me — I was awed at so many historical places and treasures I'd heard of and read of. I came upon the Rosetta stone in the British Museum, marveling anew at how Jean Champollion, the French archeologist, had miraculously deciphered its ancient demotic and hieroglyphic texts . . .

The thrill of that just kept hanging around in my head. I was   16
on a jet returning to New York when a thought hit me. Those strange, unknown-tongue sounds, always part of our family's old story . . . they were obviously bits of our original African "*Kintay's*" native tongue. What specific tongue? Could I somehow find out?

Back in New York, I began making visits to the United Na-   17
tions Headquarters lobby; it wasn't hard to spot Africans. I'd stop any I could, asking if my bits of phonetic sounds held any meaning for them. A couple of dozen Africans quickly looked at me, listened, and took off — understandably dubious about some Tennesseean's accent alleging "African" sounds.

My research assistant, George Sims (we grew up together in   18
Henning), brought me some names of ranking scholars of African linguistics. One was particularly intriguing: a Belgian- and English-educated Dr. Jan Vansina; he had spent his early career living in West African villages, studying and tape-recording countless oral histories that were narrated by certain very old African men; he had written a standard textbook, "The Oral Tradition."

So I flew to the University of Wisconsin to see Dr. Vansina.   19
In his living room I told him every bit of the family story in the

fullest detail that I could remember it. Then, intensely, he queried me about the story's relay across the generations, about the gibberish of "*k*" sounds Grandma had fiercely muttered to herself while doing her housework, with my brothers and me giggling beyond her hearing at what we had dubbed "Grandma's noises."

Dr. Vansina, his manner very serious, finally said, "These   20
sounds your family has kept sound very probably of the tongue called 'Mandinka.' "

I'd never heard of any "Mandinka." Grandma just told of the   21
African saying "*ko*" for banjo, or "*Kamby Bolong*" for a Virginia river.

Among Mandinka stringed instruments, Dr. Vansina said, one   22
of the oldest was the "*kora*."

"*Bolong*," he said was clearly Mandinka for "river." Preceded   23
by "*Kamby*," it very likely meant "Gambia River."

Dr. Vansina telephoned an eminent Africanist colleague, Dr.   24
Philip Curtin. He said that the phonetic "*Kin-tay*" was correctly spelled "*Kinte*," a very old clan that had originated in Old Mali. The Kinte men traditionally were blacksmiths, and the women were potters and weavers.

I knew I must get to the Gambia River.   25

The first native Gambian I could locate in the U.S. was named   26
Ebou Manga, then a junior attending Hamilton College in upstate Clinton, N.Y. He and I flew to Dakar, Senegal, then took a smaller plane to Yundum Airport, and rode a van to Gambia's capital, Bathurst. Ebou and his father assembled eight Gambia government officials. I told them Grandma's stories, every detail I could remember, as they listened intently, then reacted. " 'Kamby Bolong' of course is Gambia River!" I heard. "But more clue is your forefather's saying his name was 'Kinte.' " Then they told me something I would never even have fantasized — that in places in the back country lived very old men, commonly called *griots*, who could tell centuries of the histories of certain very old family clans. As for *Kintes*, they pointed out to me on a map some family villages, Kinte-Kundah, and Kinte-Kundah Janneh-Ya, for instance.

The Gambian officials said they would try to help me. I re-   27
turned to New York dazed. It is embarrassing to me now, but despite Grandma's stories, I'd never been concerned much with Africa, and I had the routine images of African people living mostly in exotic jungles. But a compulsion now laid hold of me to

learn all I could, and I began devouring books about Africa, especially about the slave trade. Then one Thursday's mail contained a letter from one of the Gambian officials, inviting me to return there.

Monday I was back in Bathurst. It galvanized me when the   28
officials said that a *griot* had been located who told the *Kinte* clan history — his name was Kebba Kanga Fofana. To reach him, I discovered, required a modified safari: renting a launch to get upriver, two land vehicles to carry supplies by a roundabout land route, and employing finally 14 people, including three interpreters and four musicians, since a *griot* would not speak the revered clan histories without background music.

The boat Baddibu vibrated upriver, with me acutely tense: 29
Were these Africans maybe viewing me as but another of the pith-helmets? After about two hours, we put in at James Island, for me to see the ruins of the once British-operated James Fort. Here two centuries of slave ships had loaded thousands of cargoes of Gambian tribespeople. The crumbling stones, the deeply oxidized swivel cannon, even some remnant links of chain seemed all but impossible to believe. Then we continued upriver to the left-bank village of Albreda, and there put ashore to continue on foot to Juffure, village of the *griot*. Once more we stopped, for me to see *toubob kolong*, "the white man's well," now almost filled in, in a swampy area with abundant, tall, saw-toothed grass. It was dug two centuries ago to "17 men's height deep" to insure survival drinking water for long-driven, famishing coffles of slaves.

Walking on, I kept wishing that Grandma could hear how her   30
stories had led me to the "*Kamby Bolong*." (Our surviving storyteller Cousin Georgia died in a Kansas City hospital during this same morning, I would learn later.) Finally, Juffure village's playing children, sighting us, flashed an alert. The 70-odd people came rushing from their circular, thatch-roofed, mud-walled huts, with goats bounding up and about, and parrots squawking from up in the palms. I sensed him in advance somehow, the small man amid them, wearing a pillbox cap and an off-white robe – the *griot*. Then the interpreters went to him, as the villagers thronged around me.

And it hit me like a gale wind: every one of them, the whole   31
crowd, was *jet black*. An enormous sense of guilt swept me — a sense of being some kind of hybrid . . . a sense of being impure among the pure. It was an awful sensation.

The old *griot* stepped away from my interpreters and the ^{32} crowd quickly swarmed around him — all of them buzzing. An interpreter named A. B. C. Salla came to me; he whispered: "Why they stare at you so, they have never seen here a black American." And that hit me: I was symbolizing for them twenty-five millions of us they had never seen. What did they think of me — of us?

Then abruptly the old *griot* was briskly walking toward me. ^{33} His eyes boring into mine, he spoke in Mandinka, as if instinctively I should understand — and A. B. C. Salla translated:

"Yes . . . we have been told by the forefathers . . . that many ^{34} of us from this place are in exile . . . in that place called America . . . and in other places."

I suppose I physically wavered, and they thought it was the ^{35} heat; rustling whispers went through the crowd, and a man brought me a low stool. Now the whispering hushed — the musicians had softly begun playing *kora* and *balafon*, and a canvas sling lawn seat was taken by the *griot*, Kebba Kanga Fofane, aged 75 "rains" (one rainy season each year). He seemed to gather himself into a physical rigidity, and he began speaking the *Kinte* clan's ancestral oral history; it came rolling from his mouth across the next hours . . . 17th- and 18th-century *Kinte* lineage details, predominantly what men took wives; the children they "begot," in the order of their births; those children's mates and children.

Events frequently were dated by some proximate singular ^{36} physical occurrence. It was as if some ancient scroll were printed indelibly within the *griot's* brain. Each few sentences or so, he would pause for an interpreter's translation to me. I distill here the essence:

The *Kinte* clan began in Old Mali, the men generally black- ^{37} smiths ". . . who conquered fire," and the women potters and weavers. One large branch of the clan moved to Mauretania from where one son of the clan, Kairaba Kunta Kinte, a Moslem Marabout holy man, entered Gambia. He lived first in the village of Pakali N'Ding; he moved next to Jiffarong village; ". . . and then he came here, into our own village of Juffure."

In Juffure, Kairaba Kunta Kinte took his first wife, ". . . a ^{38} Mandinka maiden, whose name was Sireng. By her, he begot two sons, whose names were Janneh and Saloum. Then he got a second wife, Yaisa. By her, he begot a son, Omoro."

The three sons became men in Juffure. Janneh and Saloum ^{39}

went off and founded a new village, Kinte-Kundah Janneh-Ya. "And then Omoro, the youngest son, when he had 30 rains, took as a wife a maiden, Binta Kebba.

"And by her, he begot four sons — Kunta, Lamin, Suwadu, and Madi . . ."

Sometimes, a "begotten," after his naming, would be accompanied by some later-occurring detail, perhaps as ". . . in time of big water (flood), he slew a water buffalo." Having named those four sons, now the *griot* stated such a detail.

"About the time the king's soldiers came, the eldest of these fours sons, Kunta, when he had about 16 rains, went away from this village, to chop wood to make a drum . . . and he was never seen again . . ."

Goose-pimples the size of lemons seemed to pop all over me. In my knapsack were my cumulative notebooks, the first of them including how in my boyhood, my Grandma, Cousin Georgia and the others told of the African *"Kin-tay"* who always said he was kidnapped near his village — while chopping wood to make a drum . . .

I showed the interpreter, he showed and told the *griot*, who excitedly told the people; they grew very agitated. Abruptly then they formed a human ring, encircling me, dancing and chanting. Perhaps a dozen of the women carrying their infant babies rushed in toward me, thrusting the infants into my arms — conveying, I would later learn, "the laying on of hands . . . through this flesh which is us, we are you, and you are us." The men hurried me into their mosque, their Arabic praying later being translated outside: "Thanks be to Allah for returning the long lost from among us." Direct descendants of Kunta Kinte's blood brothers were hastened, some of them from nearby villages, for a family portrait to be taken with me, surrounded by actual ancestral sixth cousins. More symbolic acts filled the remaining day.

When they would let me leave, for some reason I wanted to go away over the African land. Dazed, silent in the bumping Land Rover, I heard the cutting staccato of talking drums. Then when we sighted the next village, its people came thronging to meet us. They were all — little naked ones to wizened elders — waving, beaming, amid a cacophony of crying out; and then my ears identified their words: *"Meester Kinte! Meester Kinte!"*

Let me tell you something: I am a man. But I remember the

sob surging up from my feet, flinging up my hands before my face and bawling as I had not done since I was a baby . . . the jet-black Africans were jostling, staring . . . I didn't care, with the feelings surging. If you really knew the odyssey of us millions of black Americans, if you really knew how we came in the seeds of our forefathers, captured, driven, beaten, inspected, bought, branded, chained in foul ships, if you really knew, you needed weeping . . .

Back home, I knew that what I must write, really, was our   47
black saga, where any individual's past is the essence of the millions'. Now flat broke, I went to some editors I knew, describing the Gambian miracle, and my desire to pursue the research; Doubleday contracted to publish, and Reader's Digest to condense the projected book; then I had advances to travel further.

What ship brought Kinte to Grandma's " 'Naplis" (Annapolis,   48
Md., obviously)? The old *griot's* time reference to "king's soldiers" sent me flying to London. Feverish searching at last identified, in British Parliament records, "Colonel O'Hare's Forces," dispatched in mid-1767 to protect the then British-held James Fort whose ruins I'd visited. So Kunta Kinte was down in some ship probably sailing later that summer from the Gambia River to Annapolis.

Now I feel it was fated that I had taught myself to write in   49
the U.S. Coast Guard. For the sea dramas I had concentrated on had given me years of experience searching among yellowing old U.S. maritime records. So now in English 18th Century marine records I finally tracked ships reporting themselves in and out to the Commandant of the Gambia River's James Fort. And then early one afternoon I found that a Lord Ligonier under a Captain Thomas Davies had sailed on the Sabbath of July 5, 1767. Her cargo: 3,265 elephants' teeth, 3,700 pounds of beeswax, 800 pounds of cotton, 32 ounces of Gambian gold, and 140 slaves; her destination: "Annapolis."

That night I recrossed the Atlantic. In the Library of Congress   50
the Lord Ligonier's arrival was one brief line in "Shipping In The Port Of Annapolis — 1748–1775." I located the author, Vaughan W. Brown, in his Baltimore brokerage office. He drove to Historic Annapolis, the city's historical society, and found me further documentation of her arrival on Sept. 29, 1767. (Exactly two centuries later, Sept. 29, 1967, standing, staring seaward from an Annapolis pier, again I knew tears). More help came in the Maryland Hall of Records. Archivist Phebe Jacobsen found the Lord Ligonier's ar-

riving customs declaration listing, "98 Negroes" — so in her 86-day crossing, 42 Gambians had died, one among the survivors being 16-year-old Kunta Kinte. Then the microfilmed Oct. 1, 1767, Maryland Gazette contained, on page two, an announcement to prospective buyers from the ship's agents, Daniel of St. Thos. Jenifer and John Ridout (the Governor's secretary): "from the River GAMBIA, in AFRICA . . . a cargo of choice, healthy SLAVES . . ."

Meanings and Values

1. In one or more places Haley indicates that he considers this narrative to be more than just a slice of family history. Cite at least one such passage and put into your own words what he does consider it to be.

2. What irony, if any, do you find in paragraph 31? (See Guide to Terms: *Irony.*) Explain.

3. How can this essay best be classified — as formal, informal, or familiar? (Guide: *Essay.*) Why do you so classify it?

4. Demonstrate how it would have been a different narrative entirely if written by someone with a different point of view. (Guide: *Point of View.*)

5a. Do you consider the essay primarily objective or subjective? (Guide: *Objective/Subjective.*) Why?

   b. What, if anything, is the relationship between your answers to questions 4 and 5a?

6. As Haley is writing about extremely personal and, to him, important and sometimes emotional experiences, it could be expected that he might slip into sentimentality. (Guide: *Sentimentality.*) To what extent, if at all, does this happen? Cite specific passages to illustrate your opinion.

Expository Techniques

1a. What is the primary time order of this narrative?

   b. By what simple means is the secondary time order woven into the primary so that the reader is scarcely aware of any changes?

2. Cite three examples of Haley's handling of time lapses in the chronological portions of the story, showing how effectively transitions were made.

3a. Cite patterns of exposition other than narration in paragraph 2.

b. Does this mixture of patterns help or hinder the progress of the narrative? Why?

4a. Comment on the choice of details in any one portion of the essay, from the hundreds of details that must have ben available to the author.

b. Does it seem that the author could have made more effective choices for his purpose? If so, explain what kind they would be.

5a. Some writers would have included considerably more dialogue than Haley did. What technique did he frequently use to merely imply conversations?

b. Did you find it effective? Why, or why not?

6a. What seems to be the purpose of paragraph 8?

b. Is it worthwhile?

7a. What effect is achieved by the brevity of paragraph 25?

b. What principles are involved in gaining this effect? (Remember that such things don't just happen: the author *makes* them happen.) What are the dangers in overuse of the technique?

8a. Select any three suitable consecutive paragraphs — paragraphs 45–47 would be suitable, for instance — by which to demonstrate Haley's distinctive syntax. (Guide: *Syntax*.) What are its distinctive characteristics?

b. Explain how, if at all, this is also a matter of style. (Guide: *Style/Tone*.)

Diction and Vocabulary

1a. What does the author mean (par. 29) when he says the natives may have been viewing him as another of the pith-helmets?

b. Could pith-helmets be regarded in this connection as symbolic? (See Fromm's "Symbolic Language," or Guide: *Symbol*.) Why, or why not?

2a. You could probably find very few colloquialisms in this selection, but two of those are in the first two paragraphs. What are they? (Guide: *Colloquial Expressions*.)

b. Does their use in this portion seem inconsistent with the generally pure quality of Haley's prose? Why, or why not?

3. If you are unfamiliar with any of the following words, consult your dictionary: intrigue (par. 12); uncanny (13); steeped (15); alleging (17); phonetic (17, 24); linguistics (18); gibberish (19); eminent, colleague (24); compulsion (27); galvanized, revered (28); coffles (29); lineage (35); proximate (36); staccato, wizened, cacophony (45); odyssey (46); saga (47).

Suggestions for Writing and Discussion

1. To be especially memorable as literature, a biography or auto-biography needs to be more than *just* the story of an individual or his family. Does Haley's personal narrative qualify in this respect? Explain fully.

2. In view of the short life of most family legends, which seldom endure for more than two or three generations, how can the longevity and accuracy of details in Kinte's story be explained?

3. For Gambia tribesmen, the "laying on of hands" (par. 44) was obviously a symbolic act. In your own family, neighborhood, or sub-culture, what symbolic acts are practiced? Of what value are they?

4. In what respects, if any, can your family's history be regarded as a "saga" in that it is the "essence" of a whole people's story (par. 47)?

5. If you have read the book *Roots* and seen the TV movie version, prepare a well-developed comparison/contrast of the two. In order to do a thorough study of whatever you attempt, it may be best to restrict the analysis to one aspect for comparison.

Writing Suggestions for Section 9
Narration

Use narration as at least a partial pattern (e.g., in developed examples or in comparison) for one of the following expository themes or another suggested by them. You should avoid the isolated personal account that has little broader significance. Remember, too, that development of the essay should itself make your point, without excessive moralizing.

1. People can still succeed without a college education.
2. The frontiers are not all gone.
3. When people succeed in communicating, they can learn to get along with each other.
4. Even with "careful" use of capital punishment, innocent people can be executed.
5. Homosexuals can't always be recognized by appearance and mannerisms.
6. True courage is different from boldness in time of sudden danger.
7. Conditioning to the realities of his job is as important to the policeman as professional training.
8. It is possible for the employee himself to determine when he has reached his highest level of competence.
9. Wartime massacres are not a new development.
10. Worn-out land can be restored without chemicals to its original productivity.
11. Back-to-the-earth, "family" style communes can be made to work.
12. Such communes (as in 11 above) are a good (or poor) place to raise children.
13. Both heredity and environment shape personality.

Reasoning by Use of *Induction* and *Deduction*

Induction and deduction, important as they are in argumentation, may also be useful methods of exposition. They are often used simply to explain a stand or conclusion, without any effort or need to win converts.

Induction is the process by which we accumulate evidence until, at some point, we can make the "inductive leap" and thus reach a useful *generalization*. The science laboratory employs this technique; hundreds of tests and experiments and analyses may be required before the scientist will generalize, for instance, that polio is caused by a certain virus. It is also the primary technique of the prosecuting attorney who presents pieces of inductive evidence, asking the jury to make the inductive leap and conclude that the accused did indeed kill the victim. On a more personal level, of course, we all learned to use induction at a very early age. We may have disliked the taste of orange juice, winter squash, and carrots, and we were not too young to make a generalization: orange-colored food tastes bad.

Whereas induction is the method of reaching a potentially useful generalization (for example, Professor Melville always gives an "F" to students who cut his class three times), *deduction* is the method of *using* such a generality, now accepted as a fact (for example, if we cut this class again today, we will get an "F"). Working from a generalization already formulated — by ourselves, by someone else, or by tradition — we may deduce that a specific thing or circumstance that fits into that generality will act the same. Hence, if convinced that orange-colored food tastes bad, we will be reluctant to try pumpkin pie.

A personnel manager may have discovered over the years that electronics majors from Central College are invariably well trained in their field. His induction may have been based on the evidence of observations, records, and the opinions of fellow Rotary members; and, perhaps without realizing it, he has made the usable generalization about the training of Central College electronics majors. Later, when he has an application from Nancy Poe, a graduate of Central College, his *deductive* process will probably work as follows: Central College turns out well-trained electronics majors; Poe was trained at Central; therefore, Poe must be well trained. Here he has used a generalization to apply to a specific case. (We can also see both kinds of reasoning at work in Pirsig's "Mechanics' Logic" in Section 5.)

Put in this simplified form (which, in writing, it seldom is),[1] the deductive process is also called a "syllogism" — with the beginning generality known as the "major premise" and the specific that fits into the generality known as the "minor premise." For example:

>*Major premise* — Orange-colored food is not fit to eat.
>*Minor premise* — Pumpkin pie is orange-colored.
>*Conclusion* — Pumpkin pie is not fit to eat.

Frequently, however, the validity of one or both of the premises may be questionable, and here is one of the functions of *induction*: to give needed support — with evidence such as opinions of experts, statistics, and results of experiments or surveys — to the *deductive* syllogism, whether stated or implied. Deductive reasoning, in whatever form presented, is only as sound as both its premises. The child's conviction that orange-colored food is not fit to eat was not necessarily true; therefore his conclusion about

---

[1] Neither induction nor deduction is confined even to a particular order of presentation. If we use specific evidence to *reach* a generalization, it is induction regardless of which part is stated first in a written or spoken account. (Very likely, both the prosecutor's opening remarks and Dr. Salk's written reports first presented their generalizations and then the inductive evidence by which they had been reached.) But if we use a generality in which to *place* a specific, it is still deduction, however stated. (Hence, the reasoning of the personnel manager might be: "Poe must be well trained because she was educated at C.C., and there's where they really know how to do it.")

pumpkin pie is not very trustworthy. The other conclusions, that we will automatically get an "F" by cutting Melville's class and that Poe is well trained in electronics, can be only as reliable as the original generalizations that were used as deductive premises. If the generalizations themselves were based on flimsy or insufficient evidence, any future deduction using them is likely to be erroneous.

These two faults are common in induction: (1) the use of *flimsy* evidence — mere opinion, hearsay, or analogy, none of which can support a valid generalization — instead of verified facts or opinions of reliable authorities; and (2) the use of *too little* evidence, leading to a premature inductive leap.

The amount of evidence needed in any situation depends, of course, on purpose and audience. The success of two Central College graduates might be enough to convince some careless personnel director that all Central electronics graduates would be good employees, but two laboratory tests would not have convinced Dr. Salk, or any of his colleagues, that he had learned anything worthwhile about the polio virus. The authors of the Declaration of Independence, in explaining to a wide variety of readers and listeners why they considered the king tyrannical, listed twenty-eight despotic acts of his government, each of which was a verifiable fact, a matter of public record.

Induction and deduction are highly logical processes, and any trace of weakness can seriously undermine an exposition that depends on their reasonableness. (Such weakness can, of course, be even more disastrous in argument.) Although no induction or deduction ever reaches absolute, 100 per cent certainty, we should try to get from these methods as high a degree of *probability* as possible. (We can never positively prove, for instance, that the sun will rise in the east tomorrow, but thousands of years of inductive observation and theorizing make the fact extremely probable — and certainly sound enough for any working generalization.)

The student using induction and deduction in compositions, essay examinations, or term papers — showing that Stephen Crane was a naturalistic writer, or that our national policies are unfair to revolutionary movements — should always assume that he will have a skeptical audience that wants to know the logical basis for *all* generalizations and conclusions.

BENJAMIN FRANKLIN

BENJAMIN FRANKLIN (1706–1790) was born in Boston, but lived most of his life in Philadelphia. His versatility as statesman and diplomat, author, scientist, and inventor is well known, both in this country and abroad, and his biography is a rags-to-riches classic. Many people of his time agreed with the noted French economist, Robert Jacques Turgot, who stated, "He snatched the lightning from the skies and the sceptre from tyrants." Franklin's interest in an astonishing variety of fields remained acute until his death at eighty-four. To quote from the *Encyclopaedia Britannica:* "Of all the founding fathers of the United States, Franklin, were there such a thing as reincarnation, would adapt himself most readily to the complexities of the latter half of the 20th century."

On the Choice of a Mistress

"On the Choice of a Mistress" (editor's title) has had a unique history under many titles, but its existence was not even known to the public until many years after Franklin's death. Three versions of it were found in 1850 among the papers of his then deceased grandson, William Temple Franklin. Thereafter it passed through a variety of ownerships and was occasionally printed, but furtively and in limited editions — once under the title "A Philosopher in Undress." Although the piece had enjoyed a sort of locker-room fame for some time, not until 1926 was it published in a widely read biography, written by Phillips Russell, who called Benjamin Franklin "the first civilized American."

June 25, 1745

My dear Friend,[1]

I know of no Medicine fit to diminish the violent natural   1
Inclinations you mention; and if I did, I think I should not com-

Reprinted by permission of Yale University Press from *The Papers of Benjamin Franklin*, Volume 3, edited by Leonard W. Labaree (1961).

[1] The addressee is unknown; the letter may in fact be an essay in the form of a letter.

municate it to you. Marriage is the proper Remedy. It is the most
natural State of Man, and therefore the State in which you are
most likely to find solid Happiness. Your Reasons against entring
into it at present, appear to me not well-founded. The circum-
stantial Advantages you have in View by postponing it, are not
only uncertain, but they are small in comparison with that of the
Thing itself, the being *married and settled*. It is the Man and
Woman united that make the compleat human Being. Separate, she
wants his Force of Body and Strength of Reason; he, her Softness,
Sensibility and acute Discernment. Together they are more likely to
succeed in the World. A single Man has not nearly the Value he
would have in that State of Union. He is an incomplete Animal.
He resembles the odd Half of a Pair of Scissars. If you get a prudent healthy Wife, your industry in your Profession, with her
good Economy, will be a Fortune sufficient.

But if you will not take this Counsel, and persist in thinking   2
a Commerce with the Sex inevitable, then I repeat my former
Advice, that in all your Amours you should *prefer old Women* to
young ones. You call this a Paradox, and demand my Reasons.
They are these:

1. Because as they have more Knowledge of the World and   3
their Minds are better stor'd with Observations, their Conversation
is more improving and more lastingly agreeable.

2. Because when Women cease to be handsome, they study to   4
be good. To maintain their Influence over Men, they supply the
Diminution of Beauty by an Augmentation of Utility. They learn
to do a 1000 Services small and great, and are the most tender
and useful of all Friends when you are sick. Thus they continue
amiable. And hence there is hardly such a thing to be found as an
old Woman who is not a good Woman.

3. Because there is no hazard of Children, which irregularly   5
produc'd may be attended with much Inconvenience.

4. Because thro' more Experience, they are more prudent and   6
discrete in conducting an Intrigue to prevent Suspicion. The Commerce with them is therefore safer with regard to your Reputation.
And with regard to theirs, if the Affair should happen to be known,
considerate People might be rather inclin'd to excuse an old Woman
who would kindly take care of a young Man, form his Manners

by her good Counsels, and prevent his ruining his Health and Fortune among mercenary Prostitutes.

5. Because in every Animal that walks upright, the Deficiency   7
of the Fluids that fill the Muscles appears first in the highest Part:
The Face first grows lank and wrinkled; then the Neck; then the
Breast and Arms; the lower Parts continuing to the last as plump
as ever: So that covering all above with a Basket, and regarding
only what is below the Girdle, it is impossible of two Women to
know an old from a young one. And as in the dark all Cats are
grey, the Pleasure of corporal Enjoyment with an old Woman is
at least equal, and frequently superior, every Knack being by
Practice capable of Improvement.

6. Because the Sin is less. The debauching a Virgin may be   8
her Ruin, and make her for Life unhappy.

7. Because the Compunction is less. The having made a young   9
Girl *miserable* may give you frequent bitter Reflections; none of
which can attend the making an old Woman *happy*.

8[thly and Lastly] They are so *grateful!!*   10

Thus much for my Paradox. But still I advise you to marry directly;   11
being sincerely Your affectionate Friend.

Meanings and Values

1. The author refers to his thesis as a paradox. Explain how it does, or does not, fit our own definition of paradox. (See Guide to Terms: *Paradox*.)

2. What is to be gained and/or lost by learning that great men, past or present, are not always perfect models of propriety (contrary, of course, to what we are sometimes led to believe as small children)?

3. How seriously do you think Franklin meant this to be taken? Why?

4a. Why do you suppose Franklin's grandson, having changed his mind at least once about publication, kept the letter's existence a secret from the public until his death?

  b. Would you do the same today, in similar circumstances? Why, or why not?

Expository Techniques

1. Is the reasoning of this piece inductive or deductive? Explain your reasons carefully, as though to a person who was not aware of any difference between the two.

2. Is the numbering of parts in exposition such as this a good technique, or not? Why?

3. If this, as many believe, was really not a letter at all, but an essay intended for public readership, what is gained by framing it in the form of a letter?

Diction and Vocabulary

1. Writing styles change with the years and centuries. Identify the elements of diction and syntax in this writing which you think distinguish it from the style of modern authors. Use examples from the essay to clarify. (Guide: *Diction* and *Syntax*.)

2. What kind of figure of speech, if any, is the reference to "Scissars" in paragraph 1? (Guide: *Figures of Speech*.)

3. The words "commerce" (pars. 2, 6) and "want" (par. 1) are used here with somewhat different meanings than are common today. What do they mean in this writing?

4. Use your dictionary as necessary to be sure of the meanings of the following words: discernment (par. 1); amours (2); diminution, augmentation, amiable (4); corporal (7); debauching (8); compunction (9).

Suggestions for Writing and Discussion

1. Develop your answer to question 2 of "Meanings and Values" into a full-scale composition or discussion, using examples for illustration. State your purpose clearly, show effects, and avoid a mere cataloging of sins and foibles.

2. If you have experienced or seriously observed the women's liberation movement, use its viewpoint to comment on one or more of Franklin's "Reasons" or on his argument for marrying. (You might assume this essay to have been published in a modern advice column, perhaps in *Playboy* or *Esquire*.)

(NOTE: Suggestions for topics requiring development by INDUCTION and DEDUCTION are on page 288, at the end of this section.)

THOMAS JEFFERSON

THOMAS JEFFERSON (1743–1826) was born in Virginia, where he lived during his childhood and later attended William and Mary College. He became a lawyer, a member of the Virginia House of Burgesses and of the Continental Congress in 1775. His influence as a liberal democrat was always aided by his prolific and forceful writing. During the Revolutionary War he became Governor of Virginia. After the war he served the new government in various capacities, including those of special minister to France, Secretary of State under Washington, Vice-President, and, for two terms, the country's third President. He died on July 4, the fiftieth anniversary of the signing of the Declaration of Independence.

The Declaration of Independence

The Declaration of Independence, written and revised by Jefferson, was later further revised by the Continental Congress, meeting then in Philadelphia. In this way, as Jefferson later remarked, it drew its authority from "the harmonizing sentiments of the day"; it was, when signed on July 4, 1776, "an expression of the American mind." However, the document still retained much of the form and style of Jefferson's writing, and as literature it has long been admired for its lean and forthright prose. We can find no clearer example of the practical combination of deductive and inductive writing.

When in the course of human events, it becomes necessary for one people to dissolve the political bands which have connected them with another, and to assume among the Powers of the earth, the separate and equal station to which the Laws of Nature and of Nature's God entitle them, a decent respect to the opinions of mankind requires that they should declare the causes which impel them to the separation. 1

We hold these truths to be self-evident, that all men are created equal, that they are endowed by their Creator with certain 2 unalienable Rights, that among these are Life, Liberty and the pursuit of Happiness. That to secure these rights, Governments are instituted among Men, deriving their just powers from the consent of the governed. That whenever any Form of Government becomes destructive of these ends, it is the Right of the People to alter or to abolish it, and to institute new Government, laying its foundation on such principles and organizing its powers in such form, as to them shall seem most likely to effect their Safety and Happiness. Prudence, indeed, will dictate that Governments long established should not be changed for light and transient causes; and accordingly all experience hath shown, that mankind are more disposed to suffer, while evils are sufferable, than to right themselves by abolishing the forms to which they are accustomed. But when a long train of abuses and usurpations pursuing invariably the same Object evinces a design to reduce them under absolute Despotism, it is their right, it is their duty, to throw off such government, and to provide new Guards for their future security. Such has been the patient sufferance of these Colonies; and such is now the necessity which constrains them to alter their former Systems of Government. The history of the present King of Great Britain is a history of repeated injuries and usurpations, all having in direct object the establishment of an absolute Tyranny over these States. To prove this, let Facts be submitted to a candid world.

He has refused his Assent to Laws, the most wholesome and 3 necessary for the public good.

He has forbidden his Governors to pass Laws of immediate 4 and pressing importance, unless suspended in their operation till his Assent should be obtained; and when so suspended, he has utterly neglected to attend to them.

He has refused to pass other Laws for the accommodation of 5 large districts of people, unless those people would relinquish the right of Representation in the Legislature, a right inestimable to them and formidable to tyrants only.

He has called together legislative bodies at places unusual, un- 6 comfortable, and distant from the depository of their Public Records, for the sole purpose of fatiguing them into compliance with his measures.

He has dissolved Representative Houses repeatedly, for op- 7 posing with manly firmness his invasions on the rights of the people.

He has refused for a long time, after such dissolutions, to 8
cause others to be elected; whereby the Legislative Powers, incapable of Annihilation, have returned to the People at large for
their exercise; the State remaining in the mean time exposed to all
the dangers of invasion from without, and convulsions within.

He has endeavoured to prevent the population of these States; 9
for that purpose obstructing the Laws of Naturalization of Foreign-
ers; refusing to pass others to encourage their migration hither, and
raising the conditions of new Appropriations of Lands.

He has obstructed the Administration of Justice, by refusing 10
his Assent to Laws for establishing Judiciary Powers.

He has made Judges dependent on his Will alone, for the 11
tenure of their offices, and the amount and payment of their
salaries.

He has erected a multitude of New Offices, and sent hither 12
swarms of Officers to harass our People, and eat out their substance.

He has kept among us, in time of peace, Standing Armies 13
without the Consent of our Legislature.

He has affected to render the Military independent of and 14
superior to the Civil Power.

He has combined with others to subject us to jurisdictions 15
foreign to our constitution, and unacknowledged by our laws;
giving his Assent to their acts of pretended Legislation:

For quartering large bodies of armed troops among us: 16

For protecting them, by a mock Trial, from Punishment for 17
any Murders which they should commit on the Inhabitants of
these States:

For cutting off our Trade with all parts of the world: 18

For imposing Taxes on us without our Consent: 19

For depriving us in many cases, of the benefits of Trial by 20
Jury:

For transporting us beyond Seas to be tried for pretended 21
offenses:

For abolishing the free System of English Laws in a Neigh- 22
bouring Province, establishing therein an Arbitrary government,
and enlarging its boundaries so as to render it at once an example
and fit instrument for introducing the same absolute rule into these
Colonies:

For taking away our Charters, abolishing our most valuable 23
Laws, and altering fundamentally the Forms of our Governments:

For suspending our own Legislatures, and declaring themselves 24
invested with Power to legislate for us in all cases whatsoever.

He has abdicated Government here, by declaring us out of his 25
Protection and waging War against us.

He has plundered our seas, ravaged our Coasts, burnt our 26
towns and destroyed the Lives of our people.

He is at this time transporting large Armies of foreign Mer- 27
cenaries to compleat the works of death, desolation and tyranny,
already begun with circumstances of Cruelty & perfidy scarcely
paralleled in the most barbarous ages, and totally unworthy the
Head of a civilized nation.

He has constrained our fellow Citizens taken Captive on the 28
high Seas to bear Arms against their Country, to become the ex-
ecutioners of their friends and Brethren, or to fall themselves by
their Hands.

He has excited domestic insurrections amongst us, and has en- 29
deavoured to bring on the inhabitants of our frontiers, the merciless
Indian Savages, whose known rule of warfare, is an undistinguished
destruction of all ages, sexes and conditions.

In every stage of these Oppressions We have Petitioned for 30
Redress in the most humble terms: Our repeated petitions have
been answered only by repeated injury. A Prince, whose character
is thus marked by every act which may define a Tyrant, is unfit to
be the ruler of a free People.

Nor have We been wanting in attention to our British brethren. 31
We have warned them from time to time of attempts by their
legislature to extend an unwarrantable jurisdiction over us. We
have reminded them of the circumstances of our emigration and
settlement here. We have appealed to their native justice and magnanimity and we have conjured them by the ties of our common
kindred to disavow these usurpations, which would inevitably
interrupt our connections and correspondence. They too have been
deaf to the voice of justice and of consanguinity. We must, therefore acquiesce in the necessity, which denounces our Separation,
and hold them, as we hold the rest of mankind, Enemies in War, in
Peace Friends.

We, therefore, the Representatives of the United States of 32
America, in General Congress, Assembled, appealing to the Su-
preme Judge of the world for the rectitude of our intentions, do, in
the Name, and by Authority of the good People of these Colonies,

solemnly publish and declare, That these United Colonies are, and of Right ought to be Free and Independent States; that they are Absolved from all Allegiance to the British Crown, and that all political connection between them and the State of Great Britain, is and ought to be totally dissolved; and that as Free and Independent States, they have full power to levy War, conclude Peace, contract Alliances, establish Commerce, and to do all other Acts and Things which Independent States may of right do. And for the support of this Declaration, with a firm reliance on the protection of Divine Providence, we mutually pledge to each other our lives, our Fortunes and our sacred Honor.

Meaning and Values

1. For what practical reasons (other than the "decent respect to the opinions of mankind") did the Founding Fathers need to explain so carefully their reasons for declaring independence?
2a. By what justification can this selection be considered expository?
   b. Why might it also be classified as argument? (See Guide to Terms: *Argument*.)
   c. Except for study purposes, is there any reason to categorize it at all? Explain.
3. Many American colonials opposed the break with England and remained loyal to the Crown throughout the struggle for independence. What do you suppose could inspire such loyalty to a king whom most of them had never seen and who had shown little concern for their welfare?

Expository Techniques

1. The basis of the Declaration of Independence is deduction and can therefore be stated as a logical syllogism. The major premise, stated twice in the second paragraph, may be paraphrased as follows: When a government proves to be despotic, it is the people's right and duty to get rid of it.
   a. What, then, is the minor premise of the syllogism?
   b. Where is the syllogism's conclusion set forth? Restate it concisely in your own words.
   c. Write this resulting syllogism in standard form.
2. Twenty-eight pieces of inductive evidence are offered as support for one of the deductive premises.
   a. Which premise is thus supported?

b. Demonstrate the meaning of "inductive leap" by use of materials from this selection. (Remember that the order of presentation in inductive or deductive writing is merely an arrangement for *telling*, not necessarily that of the original reasoning.)

3a. Why, according to the document itself, is the other premise not supported by any inductive reasoning?

b. Would everyone agree with this premise? If not, why do you suppose the Founding Fathers did not present inductive evidence to support it?

4. What benefits are gained in the Declaration by the extensive use of parallel structures? (Guide: *Parallel Structure*.)

5. Show as specifically as possible the effects that a "decent respect to the opinions of mankind" apparently had on the selection and use of materials in the Declaration of Independence.

Diction and Vocabulary

1. Select five words or phrases from the Declaration of Independence to demonstrate the value of an awareness of connotation. (Guide: *Connotation/Denotation*.)

2. If not already familiar with the following words as they are used in this selection, consult your dictionary for their meanings: impel (par. 1); transient, usurpations, evinces, sufferance, constrains (2); inestimable (5); depository (6); dissolutions (8); mercenaries, perfidy (27); redress (30); magnanimity, conjured, consanguinity, acquiesce (31); rectitude, absolved (32).

Suggestions for Writing and Discussion

1. George Santayana, an American writer and expatriate, called the Declaration of Independence "a salad of illusion." Develop this metaphor into a full-scale analogy to explain his meaning. Without arguing the matter, attempt to assess the truth of his allegation.

2. Select one important similarity or difference between the rebellion of the American colonials and that of some other country in recent history. Use comparison or contrast to develop a theme on this subject.

3. Compare or contrast any of the Declaration signers with one of the leaders of some other country's more recent severance of ties with a colonial power.

4. Give evidence from your knowledge of history to support, or to negate, the following statement by Patrick Henry, one of the signers of the Declaration: "It is impossible that a nation of in-

fidels or idolators should be a nation of freemen. It is when a people forget God, that tyrants forge their chains. A vitiated state of morals, a corrupted public conscience, is incompatible with freedom."

(NOTE: Suggestions for topics requiring development by INDUCTION and DEDUCTION are on page 288, at the end of this section.)

ARTHUR C. CLARKE

ARTHUR C. CLARKE (b. 1917) was born and educated in England and served in the Royal Air Force during World War II. His varied early career included underwater photography in Ceylon and Australia, editing *Physics Abstracts*, and auditing. He has served as chairman of the Royal Astronomical Society and is recipient of many awards and honors including the Stuart Ballantine Medal of the Franklin Institute (1963) "for his soundly based and prophetic early concept of the application of satellites in the primary human endeavor of communication." Clarke is perhaps best known for his novel and screenplay *2001: A Space Odyssey*. A prolific science-fiction writer, he has also published numerous nonfiction and juvenile books. Some of his latest are *Earthlight, Expedition to Earth,* and *Reach for Tomorrow* (1975), and *Prelude to Space* and *Rendezvous with Rama* (1976).

We'll Never Conquer Space

"We'll Never Conquer Space," as presented here, is the major portion of an essay by that title first published in 1960. To develop his complex and nearly incomprehensible subject, Clarke makes liberal use of most of the basic patterns of exposition, as well as various other rhetorical techniques with which we are already familiar. The result, like most of his writing, is not just comprehensible but fascinating to most readers.

Psychologically as well as physically, there are no longer any remote places on earth. When a friend leaves for what was once a far country, even if he has no intention of returning, we cannot feel that same sense of irrevocable separation that saddened our forefathers. We know that he is only hours away by jet liner, and that we have merely to reach for the telephone to hear his voice. 1

In a very few years, when the satellite communication net- 2
work is established, we will be able to see friends on the far side of
the earth as easily as we talk to them on the other side of the town.
Then the world will shrink no more, for it will have become a di-
mensionless point.

But the new stage that is opening up for the human drama 3
will never shrink as the old one has done. We have abolished space
here on the little earth; we can never abolish the space that yawns
between the stars. Once again we are face to face with immensity
and must accept its grandeur and terror, its inspiring possibilities
and its dreadful restraints. From a world that has become too small,
we are moving out into one that will forever be too large, whose
frontiers will recede from us always more swiftly than we can
reach out towards them.

Consider first the fairly modest solar, or planetary, distances 4
which we are now preparing to assault. The very first Lunik made a
substantial impression upon them, traveling more than 200 million
miles from the earth — six times the distance to Mars. When we
have harnessed nuclear energy for spaceflight, the solar system will
contract until it is little larger than the earth today. The remotest
of the planets will be perhaps no more than a week's travel from
the earth, while Mars and Venus will be only a few hours away.

This achievement, which will be witnessed within a century, 5
might appear to make even the solar system a comfortable, homely
place, with such giant planets as Saturn and Jupiter playing much
the same role in our thoughts as do Africa or Asia today. (Their
qualitative differences of climate, atmosphere and gravity, fundamental though they are, do not concern us at the moment.) To
some extent this may be true, yet as soon as we pass beyond the
orbit of the moon, a mere quarter-million miles away, we will meet
the first of the barriers that will separate the earth from her scattered children.

The marvelous telephone and television network that will 6
soon enmesh the whole world, making all men neighbors, cannot
be extended into space. It will never be possible to converse with
anyone on another planet.

Do not misunderstand this statement. Even with today's radio 7
equipment, the problem of sending speech to the other planets is
almost trivial. But the messages will take minutes — sometimes
hours — on their journey, because radio and light waves travel at
the same limited speed of 186,000 miles a second.

Twenty years from now you will be able to listen to a friend   8
on Mars, but the words you hear will have left his mouth at least
three minutes earlier, and your reply will take a corresponding
time to reach him. In such circumstances, an exchange of verbal
messages is possible — but not a conversation.

Even in the case of the nearby moon, the 2½-second time lag   9
will be annoying. At distances of more than a million miles, it will
be intolerable.

To a culture which has come to take instantaneous communi-   10
cation for granted, as part of the very structure of civilized life, this
"time barrier" may have a profound psychological impact. It will
be a perpetual reminder of universal laws and limitations against
which not all our technology can ever prevail. For it seems as certain as anything can be that no signal — still less any material object — can ever travel faster than light.

The velocity of light is the ultimate speed limit, being part of   11
the very structure of space and time. Within the narrow confines
of the solar system, it will not handicap us too severely, once we
have accepted the delays in communication which it involves. At
the worst, these will amount to twenty hours — the time it takes
a radio signal to span the orbit of Pluto, the outermost planet.

Between the three inner worlds, the earth, Mars, and Venus,   12
it will never be more than twenty minutes — not enough to interfere seriously with commerce or administration, but more than sufficient to shatter those personal links of sound or vision that can
give us a sense of direct contact with friends on earth, wherever
they may be.

It is when we move out beyond the confines of the solar sys-   13
tem that we come face to face with an altogether new order of
cosmic reality. Even today, many otherwise educated men — like
those savages who can count to three but lump together all numbers beyond four — cannot grasp the profound distinction between
solar and stellar space. The first is the space enclosing our neigh-
boring worlds, the planets; the second is that which embraces those
distant suns, the stars, and it is literally millions of times greater.

There is no such abrupt change of scale in terrestrial affairs.   14
To obtain a mental picture of the distance to the nearest star, as
compared with the distance to the nearest planet, you must imagine
a world in which the closest object to you is only five feet away —
and then there is nothing else to see until you have traveled a thousand miles.

Many conservative scientists, appalled by these cosmic gulfs,   15
have denied that they can ever be crossed. Some people never
learn; those who sixty years ago scoffed at the possibility of flight,
and ten (even five!) years ago laughed at the idea of travel to the
planets, are now quite sure that the stars will always be beyond
our reach. And again they are wrong, for they have failed to grasp
the great lesson of our age — that if something is possible in theory, and no fundamental scientific laws oppose its realization, then
sooner or later it will be achieved.

One day, it may be in this century, or it may be a thousand   16
years from now, we shall discover a really efficient means of pro-
pelling our space vehicles. Every technical device is always developed to its limit (unless it is superseded by something better) and
the ultimate speed for spaceships is the velocity of light. They will
never reach that goal, but they will get very close to it. And then
the nearest star will be less than five years' voyaging from the
earth.

Our exploring ships will spread outwards from their home   17
over an ever-expanding sphere of space. It is a sphere which will
grow at almost — but never quite — the speed of light. Five years
to the triple system of Alpha Centauri, ten to the strangely-matched
doublet Sirius A and B, eleven to the tantalizing enigma of 61
Cygni, the first star suspected to possess a planet. These journeys
are long, but they are not impossible. Man has always accepted
whatever price was necessary for his explorations and discoveries,
and the price of Space is Time.

Even voyages which may last for centuries or millennia will   18
one day be attempted. Suspended animation has already been
achieved in the laboratory, and may be the key to interstellar
travel. Self-contained cosmic arks which will be tiny traveling
worlds in their own right may be another solution, for they would
make possible journeys of unlimited extent, lasting generation after
generation.

The famous Time Dilation effect predicted by the Theory of   19
Relativity, whereby time appears to pass more slowly for a traveler
moving at almost the speed of light, may be yet a third. And there
are others.

Looking far into the future, therefore, we must picture a slow   20
(little more than half a billion miles an hour!) expansion of human
activities outwards from the solar system, among the suns scat-

tered across the region of the galaxy in which we now find ourselves. These suns are on the average five light-years apart; in
other words, we can never get from one to the next in less than
five years.

To bring home what this means, let us use a down-to-earth   21
analogy. Imagine a vast ocean, sprinkled with islands — some desert, others perhaps inhabited. On one of these islands an energetic
race has just discovered the art of building ships. It is preparing to
explore the ocean, but must face the fact that the very nearest
island is five years' voyaging away, and that no possible improvement in the technique of shipbuilding will ever reduce this time.

In these circumstances (which are those in which we will soon   22
find ourselves) what could the islanders achieve? After a few centuries, they might have established colonies on many of the nearby
islands and have briefly explored many others. The daughter colonies might themselves have sent out further pioneers, and so a
kind of chain reaction would spread the original culture over a
steadily expanding area of the ocean.

But now consider the effects of the inevitable, unavoidable time   23
lag. There could be only the most tenuous contact between the
home island and its offspring. Returning messengers could report
what had happened on the nearest colony — five years ago. They
could never bring information more up to date than that, and dis-
patches from the more distant parts of the ocean would be from
still further in the past — perhaps centuries behind the times.
There would never be news from the other islands, but only history.

All the star-borne colonies of the future will be independent,   24
whether they wish it or not. Their liberty will be inviolably protected by Time as well as Space. They must go their own way and
achieve their own destiny, with no help or hindrance from Mother
Earth.

At this point, we will move the discussion on to a new level   25
and deal with an obvious objection. Can we be sure that the velocity of light is indeed a limiting factor? So many "impassible" barriers have been shattered in the past; perhaps this one may go the
way of all the others.

We will not argue the point, or give the reasons why scien-   26
tists believe that light can never be outraced by any form of radia-
tion or any material object. Instead, let us assume the contrary and

see just where it gets us. We will even take the most optimistic possible case and imagine that the speed of transportation may eventually become infinite.

Picture a time when, by the development of techniques as far 27 beyond our present engineering as a transistor is beyond a stone axe, we can reach anywhere we please instantaneously, with no more effort than by dialing a number. This would indeed cut the universe down to size and reduce its physical immensity to nothingness. What would be left?

Everything that really matters. For the universe has two aspects — its scale, and its overwhelming, mind-numbing complexity. Having abolished the first, we are now face-to-face with the second. 28

What we must now try to visualize is not size, but quantity. 29 Most people today are familiar with the simple notation which scientists use to describe large numbers; it consists merely of counting zeroes, so that a hundred becomes 10^2, a million, 10^6, a billion, 10^9 and so on. This useful trick enables us to work with quantities of any magnitude, and even defense-budget totals look modest when expressed as $\$5.76 \times 10^9$ instead of $5,760,000,000.

The number of other suns in our own galaxy (that is, the whirl- 30 pool of stars and cosmic dust of which our sun is an out-of-town member, lying in one of the remoter spiral arms) is estimated at about 10^{11} — or written in full, 100,000,000,000. Our present telescopes can observe something like 10^9 other galaxies, and they show no sign of thinning out even at the extreme limit of vision.

There are probably at least as many galaxies in the whole of 31 creation as there are stars in our own galaxy, but let us confine ourselves to those we can see. They must contain a total of about 10^{11} times 10^9 stars, or 10^{20} stars altogether. One followed by twenty other digits is, of course, a number beyond all understanding.

Before such numbers, even spirits brave enough to face the 32 challenge of the light-years must quail. The detailed examination of all the grains of sand on all the beaches of the world is a far smaller task than the exploration of the universe.

And so we return to our opening statement. Space can be 33 mapped and crossed and occupied without definable limit; but it can never be conquered. When our race has reached its ultimate achievements, and the stars themselves are scattered no more widely than the seed of Adam, even then we shall still be like ants crawling on the face of the earth. The ants have covered the world, but have they conquered it — for what do their countless colonies know of it, or of each other?

So it will be with us as we spread outwards from Mother 34 Earth, loosening the bonds of kinship and understanding, hearing faint and belated rumors at second — or third — or thousandth hand of an ever-dwindling fraction of the entire human race.

Though Earth will try to keep in touch with her children, in 35 the end all the efforts of her archivists and historians will be defeated by time and distance, and the sheer bulk of material. For the number of distinct societies or nations, when our race is twice its present age, may be far greater than the total number of all the men who have ever lived up to the present time.

We have left the realm of human comprehension in our vain 36 effort to grasp the scale of the universe, so it must always be, sooner rather than later.

When you are next outdoors on a summer night, turn your 37 head toward the zenith. Almost vertically above you will be shining the brightest star of the northern skies — Vega of the Lyre, twenty-six years away at the speed of light, near enough to the point of no return for us short-lived creatures. Past this blue-white beacon, fifty times as brilliant as our sun, we may send our minds and bodies, but never our hearts.

For no man will ever turn homewards from beyond Vega, to 38 greet again those he knew and loved on the earth.

Meanings and Values

   1a. In which paragraph do we first read the author's statement of his central theme? (See Guide to Terms: *Unity*.)
   b. How, if at all, did we already know what it is?
   c. Do any portions of the selection not serve as tributaries into this theme? If any, state why they are disunifying.
   2. Why does Clarke put aside the "qualitative differences of climate, atmosphere and gravity" as of no concern to us at the moment (par. 5)?
   3. Clarify further how the "time barrier" effect on conversation would have a "profound psychological impact" (par. 8–10).
   4a. How does Clarke anticipate the probable criticism of conservative scientists?

b. How does he answer the probable objection that the speed of transportation may not be limited to the speed of light?

c. Are both of these countermeasures handled in a completely logical and satisfying manner? Why, or why not?

5. If you read the Rettie piece in Section 4, does the shocking implication of its last paragraph seem more absurd, or less so, after being reminded of the unimaginable number of "worlds" in the universe? Why?

Expository Techniques

1a. At what part of his inductive analysis does Clarke first state for us his inductive conclusion, or generalization?

b. Would the statement have been better placed somewhere else? Why, or why not?

2. Where, if at all, is there a major use of deduction?

3a. In the first three paragraphs, what is the primary pattern of exposition?

b. Why is its use important early in the writing?

4a. Cite the various uses of analogy.

b. Explain why analogy is needed to do the jobs Clarke assigned to them.

c. How effectively do they perform their functions?

5. Most of the other patterns of exposition are also employed, to some extent, in the course of the inductive process. Cite at least one example of each and show why it is needed.

6a. On what did the author apparently base his arrangement of materials? (It is not likely that they just arranged themselves: *he* had to do it — as, of course, we all do.)

b. What then, other than closing, was the purpose of the last three paragraphs?

c. Does it also effectively close the essay — i.e., tie up the composition into a neat package? Why, or why not? (Guide: *Closings*.)

7a. What mechanical devices of emphasis can we illustrate in paragraphs 17 and 20? (Guide: *Emphasis*.)

b. Does Clarke overuse these devices, thus wasting their effectiveness?

8. By what means does the author achieve clarity, enabling even non-scientific readers to read with interest and understanding?

9a. Although the inductive process used comprehensively here is a fundamental technique of argument, this selection does not really qualify as argument. Why not? (Guide: *Argument*.)

b. On what grounds does it qualify as exposition?

Diction and Vocabulary

1a. Cite examples of figurative language which will illustrate one distinctive element of Clarke's style. (Guide: *Figures of Speech* and *Style/Tone*.)

b. Cite examples of nonfigurative diction and syntax which also seem to be important elements of his style. (Guide: *Diction* and *Syntax*.)

2. Study the author's uses of the following words, consulting the dictinary as needed: irrevocable (par. 1); stellar, literally (13); superseded (16); enigma (17); millennia (18); tenuous (23); inviolably (24); quail (32).

Suggestions for Writing and Discussion

1. Preferably developing a central theme of your own, base your discussion on some topic suggested by the last sentence either of paragraph 15 or paragraph 18.

2. Examine in detail the nature of a person (and what would have to be exceptionally strong motivations) who would be willing to leave home and friends to go into space knowing that he would never return.

Writing Suggestions for Section 10
Induction and Deduction

Choose one of the following unformed topics and shape your central theme from it. This could express the view you prefer or an opposing view. Develop your composition primarily by use of induction, alone or in combination with deduction. But unless otherwise directed by your instructor, be completely objective and limit yourself to exposition, rather than engaging in argumentation.

1. Little League Baseball (or the activities of 4-H clubs, Boy Scouts, Girl Scouts, etc.) as a molder of character.
2. Conformity as an expression of insecurity.
3. The display of *non*conformity as an expression of insecurity.
4. The status symbol as a motivator to success.
5. The liberal arts curriculum and its relevance to "real life."
6. Student opinion as the guide to better educational institutions.
7. College education as a prerequisite for worldly success.
8. The values of education, beyond dollars and cents.
9. Knowledge and its relation to wisdom.
10. The right of the individual to select the laws he obeys.
11. Television commercials as a molder of morals.
12. The "other" side of one ecological problem.
13. The value of complete freedom from worry.
14. Decreased effectiveness of the home as an influence in adolescent development.

Further Readings

PLATO (about 427–347 B.C.), an early Greek philosopher, was a younger friend and perhaps student of Socrates. In Athens Plato founded and administered the first university, the Academy, which continued operation until 529 A.D. One of the most brilliant figures in the history of Western philosophy, his ideas are still reflected in much modern thought. He was a prolific writer (his works include *The Symposium, Phaedrus,* and *The Republic*), and frequently employed dialogue to reproduce conversations between Socrates (who had written nothing himself) and his students. While Plato was still a young man, Socrates had been condemned to death for "impiety" and "corruption of youth," trumped-up political charges brought by a hostile new democratic regime which feared that he was teaching his students disrespect for state authority and religious dogma. At the trial he defended himself, but his "defense" amounted more to avowal and justification, and he was executed — i.e., he "drank the hemlock" in the traditional manner. Plato later recorded his friend's defense as "The Apology of Socrates," of which the following is an excerpt.

Socrates "Defends" Himself

Someone will say: And are you not ashamed, Socrates, of a course   1
of life which is likely to bring you to an untimely end? To him I may fairly answer: There you are mistaken: a man who is good for anything ought not to calculate the chance of living or dying; he ought only to consider whether in doing anything he is doing right or wrong — acting the part of a good man or of a bad. . . .

Strange, indeed, would be my conduct, O men of Athens, if I,   2
who when I was ordered by the generals whom you chose to command me at Potidaea[1] and Amphipolis and Delium, remained where they placed me, like any other man, facing death — if now, when,

---

[1] Socrates had served in the Athenian infantry during some of the northern campaigns of the Peloponnesian War.

as I conceive and imagine, God orders me to fulfill the philosopher's mission of searching into myself and other men, I were to
desert my post through fear of death, or any other fear; that would
indeed be strange, and I might justly be arraigned in court for
denying the existence of the gods, if I disobeyed the oracle because
I was afraid of death, fancying that I was wise when I was not
wise. For the fear of death is indeed the pretense of wisdom, and
not real wisdom, being a pretense of knowing the unknown; and
no one knows whether death, which men in their fear apprehend
to be the greatest evil, may not be the greatest good. Is not this
ignorance of a disgraceful sort, the ignorance which is the conceit
that a man knows what he does not know? And in this respect
only I believe myself to differ from men in general, and may perhaps claim to be wiser than they are: that whereas I know but little
of the world below, I do not suppose that I know: but I do know
that injustice and disobedience to a better, whether God or man,
is evil and dishonorable, and I will never fear or avoid a possible
good rather than a certain evil. And therefore if you let me go
now, and are not convinced by Anytus,[2] who said that since I had
been prosecuted I must be put to death (or if not, that I ought
never to have been prosecuted at all); and that if I escape now,
your sons will all be utterly ruined by listening to my words — if
you say to me, Socrates, this time we will not mind Anytus, and
you shall be let off, but upon one condition, that you are not to
inquire and speculate in this way any more, and that if you are
caught doing so again you shall die; if this was the condition on
which you let me go, I should reply: Men of Athens, I honor and
love you; but I shall obey God rather than you, and while I have
life and strength I shall never cease from the practice and teaching
of philosophy, exhorting anyone whom I meet and saying to him
after my manner: "You my friend — a citizen of the great and
mighty and wise city of Athens — are you not ashamed of heaping
up the greatest amount of money and honor and reputation, and
caring so little about wisdom and truth and the greatest improvement of the soul, which you never regard or heed at all?" And if
the person with whom I am arguing, says: "Yes, but I do care";
then I do not leave him or let him go at once; but I proceed to
interrogate and examine and cross-examine him, and if I think that
he has no virtue in him, but only says that he has, I reproach him

[2] Instigator of the proceedings.

with undervaluing the greater and overvaluing the less. And I shall repeat the same words to everyone whom I meet, young and old, citizen and alien, but especially to the citizens, inasmuch as they are my brethren. For know that this is the command of God; and I believe that no greater good has ever happened in the state than my service to the God. For I do nothing but go about persuading you all, old and young alike, not to take thought for your persons or your properties, but first and chiefly to care about the greatest improvement of the soul. I tell you that virtue is not given by money, but that from virtue comes money and every other good of man, public as well as private. This is my teaching, and if this is the doctrine which corrupts the youth, I am a mischievous person. But if anyone says that this is not my teaching, he is speaking an untruth. Wherefore, O men of Athens, I say to you, do as Anytus bids or not as Anytus bids, and either acquit me or not; but whichever you do, understand that I shall never alter my ways, not even if I have to die many times.

Men of Athens, do not interrupt, but hear me; there was an understanding between us that you should hear me to the end; I have something more to say, at which you may be inclined to cry out; but I believe that to hear me will be good for you, and therefore I beg that you will not cry out. I would have you know that if you kill such an one as I am, you will injure yourselves more than you will injure me. Nothing will injure me, not Meletus[3] nor yet Anytus — they cannot, for a bad man is not permitted to injure a better than himself. I do not deny that Anytus may, perhaps, kill him, or drive him into exile, or deprive him of civil rights; and he may imagine, and others may imagine, that he is inflicting a great injury upon him: but there I do not agree. For the evil of doing as he is doing — the evil of unjustly taking away the life of another — is greater far.

And now, Athenians, I am not going to argue for my own sake, as you may think, but for yours, that you may not sin against the God by condemning me, who am his gift to you. For if you kill me you will not easily find a successor to me, who, if I may use such a ludicrous figure of speech, am a sort of gadfly, given to the state by God; and the state is a great and noble steed who is tardy in his motions owing to his very size, and requires to be stirred into

[3] The prosecutor.

life. I am that gadfly which God has attached to the state, and all day long and in all places am always fastening upon you, arousing and persuading and reproaching you. You will not easily find another like me, and therefore I would advise you to spare me. I dare say that you may feel out of temper (like a person who is suddenly awakened from sleep), and you think that you might easily strike me dead as Anytus advises, and then you would sleep on for the remainder of your lives, unless God in his care of you sent you another gadfly. When I say that I am given to you by God, the proof of my mission is this: if I had been like other men, I should not have neglected all my own concerns or patiently seen the neglect of them during all these years, and have been doing yours, coming to you individually like a father or elder brother, exhorting you to regard virtue; such conduct, I say, would be unlike human nature. If I had gained anything, or if my exhortations had been paid, there would have been some sense in my doing so; but now, as you will perceive, not even the impudence of my accusers dares to say that I have ever exacted or sought pay of anyone; of that they have no witness. And I have a sufficient witness to the truth of what I say — my poverty.

Someone may wonder why I go about in private giving advice 5 and busying myself with the concerns of others, but do not venture to come forward in public and advise the state. I will tell you why. You have heard me speak at sundry times and in divers places of an oracle or sign which comes to me, and is the divinity which Meletus ridicules in the indictment. This sign, which is a kind of voice, first began to come to me when I was a child; it always forbids but never commands me to do anything which I am going to do. This is what deters me from being a politician. And rightly, as I think. For I am certain, O men of Athens, that if I had engaged in politics, I should have perished long ago, and done no good either to you or to myself. And do not be offended at my telling you the truth: for the truth is, that no man who goes to war with you or any other multitude, honestly striving against the many lawless and unrighteous deeds which are done in a state, will save his life; he who will fight for the right, if he would live even for a brief space, must have a private station and not a public one. . . .

JONATHAN SWIFT

JONATHAN SWIFT (1667–1745), an Anglican clergyman whose English family were long-time residents of Ireland, was Dean of Saint Patrick's in Dublin and also a poet and political pamphleteer. The greatest satirist of his period, Swift was noted for his clear, sharp prose and his effective indignation at social injustices of the day. His best-known works are *The Battle of the Books, Gulliver's Travels, The Tale of a Tub,* and *A Modest Proposal.* The latter, written in 1729, remains one of the world's greatest satires[1] and is almost certainly the most vitriolic, grotesque in its details. It was aimed directly at his fellow Englishmen for their oppression of the Irish people. Writing students should remember, however, that effective as satire can be as a rouser of emotions (i.e., as persuasion), it is not a reliable tool of logic (e.g., as in argument).

A Modest Proposal

FOR PREVENTING THE CHILDREN OF POOR PEOPLE IN IRELAND FROM BEING A BURDEN TO THEIR PARENTS OR COUNTRY, AND FOR MAKING THEM BENEFICIAL TO THE PUBLIC

It is a melancholy object to those who walk through this great town[2] or travel in the country, when they see the streets, the roads, and cabin doors, crowded with beggars of the female sex, followed by three, four, or six children, all in rags and importuning every passenger for an alms. These mothers, instead of being able to work for their honest livelihood, are forced to employ all their time in strolling to beg sustenance for their helpless infants, who, as they grow up, either turn thieves for want of work, or leave their dear native country to fight for the Pretender in Spain, or sell themselves to the Barbadoes.[3]   1

I think it is agreed by all parties that this prodigious number   2
of children in the arms, or on the backs, or at the heels of their

---

[1] See Guide to Terms: *Satire.*
[2] Dublin.
[3] That is, bind themselves to work for a period of years, in order to pay for their transportation to a colony.

294

mothers, and frequently of their fathers, is in the present deplorable state of the kingdom a very great additional grievance; and therefore whoever could find out a fair, cheap, and easy method of making these children sound, useful members of the commonwealth would deserve so well of the public as to have his statue set up for a preserver of the nation.

But my intention is very far from being confined to provide 3 only for the children of professed beggars; it is of a much greater extent, and shall take in the whole number of infants at a certain age who are born of parents in effect as little able to support them as those who demand our charity in the streets.

As to my own part, having turned my thoughts for many 4 years upon this important subject, and maturely weighed the several schemes of other projectors, I have always found them grossly mistaken in their computation. It is true, a child just dropped from its dam may be supported by her milk for a solar year, with little other nourishment; at most not above the value of two shillings, which the mother may certainly get, or the value in scraps, by her lawful occupation of begging; and it is exactly at one year old that I propose to provide for them in such a manner as instead of being a charge upon their parents or the parish, or wanting food and raiment for the rest of their lives, they shall on the contrary contribute to the feeding, and partly to the clothing, of many thousands.

There is likewise another great advantage in my scheme, that 5 it will prevent those voluntary abortions, and that horrid practice of women murdering their bastard children, alas, too frequent among us, sacrificing the poor innocent babes, I doubt, more to avoid the expense than the shame, which would move tears and pity in the most savage and inhuman breast.

The number of souls in this kingdom being usually reckoned 6 one million and a half, of these I calculate there may be about two hundred thousand couples whose wives are breeders; from which number I subtract thirty thousand couples who are able to maintain their own children, although I apprehend there cannot be so many under the present distress of the kingdom; but this being granted, there will remain an hundred and seventy thousand breeders. I again subtract fifty thousand for those women who miscarry, or whose children die by accident or disease within the year. There only remain an hundred and twenty thousand children of poor parents annually born. The question therefore is, how this number shall be reared and provided for, which, as I have already said, under the present situation of affairs, is utterly impossible by all the methods hitherto proposed. For we can neither employ them in handicraft or agriculture; we neither build houses (I mean in the country) nor cultivate land. They can very seldom pick up a livelihood by stealing till they arrive at six years old, except where they are of towardly parts; although I confess they learn the rudiments much earlier, during which time they can however be looked upon only as probationers, as I have been informed by a principal gentleman in the country of Cavan, who protested to me that he never knew above one or two instances under the age of six, even in a part of the kingdom so renowned for the quickest proficiency in that art.

I am assured by our merchants that a boy or a girl before   7
twelve years old is no salable commodity; and even when they come to this age they will not yield above three pounds, or three pounds and half a crown at most on the Exchange; which cannot turn to account either to the parents or the kingdom, the charge of nutriment and rags having been at least four times that value.

I shall now therefore humbly propose my own thoughts,   8
which I hope will not be liable to the least objection.

I have been assured by a very knowing American of my ac-   9
quaintance in London, that a young healthy child well nursed is at a year old a most delicious, nourishing, and wholesome food, whether stewed, roasted, baked, or boiled; and I make no doubt that it will equally serve in a fricassee or a ragout.

I do therefore humbly offer it to public consideration that of   10
the hundred and twenty thousand children, already computed, twenty thousand may be reserved for breed, whereof only one fourth part to be males, which is more than we allow to sheep, black cattle, or swine; and my reason is that these children are seldom the fruits of marriage, a circumstance not much regarded by our savages, therefore one male will be sufficient to serve four females. That the remaining hundred thousand may at a year old be offered in sale to the persons of quality and fortune through the kingdom, always advising the mother to let them suck plentifully in the last month, so as to render them plump and fat for a good table. A child will make two dishes at an entertainment for friends; and when the family dines alone, the fore or hind quarter

will make a reasonable dish, and seasoned with a little pepper or salt will be very good boiled on the fourth day, especially in winter.

I have reckoned upon a medium that a child just born will   11
weigh twelve pounds, and in a solar year if tolerably nursed increaseth to twenty-eight pounds.

I grant this food will be somewhat dear, and therefore very   12
proper for landlords, who, as they have already devoured most of the parents, seem to have the best title to the children.

Infant's flesh will be in season throughout the year, but more   13
plentiful in March, and a little before and after. For we are told by a grave author, an eminent French physician,[4] that fish being a prolific diet, there are more children born in Roman Catholic countries about nine months after Lent than at any other season; therefore, reckoning a year after Lent, the markets will be more glutted than usual, because the number of popish infants is at least three to one in this kingdom; and therefore it will have one other collateral advantage, by lessening the number of Papists among us.

I have already computed the charge of nursing a beggar's   14
child (in which list I reckon all cottagers, laborers, and four fifths of the farmers) to be about two shillings per annum, rags included; and I believe no gentleman would repine to give ten shillings for the carcass of a good fat child, which, as I have said, will make four dishes of excellent nutritive meat, when he hath only some particular friend or his own family to dine with him. Thus the squire will learn to be a good landlord, and grow popular among the tenants; the mother will have eight shillings net profit, and be fit for work till she produces another child.

Those who are more thrifty (as I must confess the times re-   15
quire) may flay the carcass; the skin of which artificially dressed will make admirable gloves for ladies, and summer boots for fine gentlemen.

As to our city of Dublin, shambles may be appointed for this   16
purpose in the most convenient parts of it, and butchers we may be assured will not be wanting; although I rather recommend buying the children alive, and dressing them hot from the knife as we do roasting pigs.

A very worthy person, a true lover of his country, and whose   17

[4] François Rabelais.

virtues I highly esteem, was lately pleased in discoursing on this matter to offer a refinement upon my scheme. He said that many gentlemen of his kingdom, having of late destroyed their deer, he conceived that the want of venison might be well supplied by the bodies of young lads and maidens, not exceeding fourteen years of age nor under twelve, so great a number of both sexes in every county being now ready to starve for want of work and service; and these to be disposed of by their parents, if alive, or otherwise by their nearest relations. But with due deference to so excellent a friend and so deserving a patriot, I cannot be altogether in his sentiments; for as to the males, my American acquaintance assured me from frequent experience that their flesh was generally tough and lean, like that of our schoolboys, by continual exercise, and their taste disagreeable; and to fatten them would not answer the charge. Then as to the females, it would, I think with humble submission, be a loss to the public, because they soon would become breeders themselves: and besides, it is not improbable that some scrupulous people might be apt to censure such a practice (although indeed very unjustly) as a little bordering upon cruelty; which, I confess, hath always been with me the strongest objection against any project, how well soever intended.

But in order to justify my friend, he confessed that this expe- 18 dient was put into his head by the famous Psalmanazar, a native of the island Formosa, who came from thence to London above twenty years ago, and in conversation told my friend that in his country when any young person happened to be put to death, the executioner sold the carcass to persons of quality as a prime dainty; and that in his time the body of a plump girl of fifteen, who was crucified for an attempt to poison the emperor, was sold to his Imperial Majesty's prime minister of state, and other great mandarins of the court, in joints from the gibbet, at four hundred crowns. Neither indeed can I deny that if the same use were made of several plump young girls in this town, who without one single groat to their fortunes cannot stir abroad without a chair, and appear at the playhouse and assemblies in foreign fineries which they never will pay for, the kingdom would not be the worse.

Some persons of a desponding spirit are in great concern 19 about that vast number of poor people who are aged, diseased, or maimed, and I have been desired to employ my thoughts what course may be taken to ease the nation of so grievous an encumbrance. But I am not in the least pain upon that matter, because it is very well known that they are every day dying and rotting by cold and famine, and filth and vermin, as fast as can be reasonably expected. And as to the younger laborers, they are now in almost as hopeful a condition. They cannot get work, and consequently pine away for want of nourishment to a degree that if at any time they are accidentally hired to common labor, they have not strength to perform it; and thus the country and themselves are happily delivered from the evils to come.

I have too long digressed, and therefore shall return to my 20 subject. I think the advantages by the proposal which I have made are obvious and many, as well as of the highest importance.

For first, as I have already observed, it would greatly lessen 21 the number of Papists, with whom we are yearly overrun, being the principal breeders of the nation as well as our most dangerous enemies; and who stay at home on purpose to deliver the kingdom to the Pretender, hoping to take their advantage by the absence of so many good Protestants, who have chosen rather to leave their country than to stay at home and pay tithes against their conscience to an Episcopal curate.

Secondly, the poorer tenants will have something valuable of 22 their own, which by law may be made liable to distress, and help to pay their landlord's rent, their corn and cattle being already seized and money a thing unknown.

Thirdly, whereas the maintenance of an hundred thousand 23 children, from two years old and upwards, cannot be computed at less than ten shillings a piece per annum, the nation's stock will be thereby increased fifty thousand pounds per annum, besides the profit of a new dish introduced to the tables of all gentlemen of fortune in the kingdom who have any refinement in taste. And the money will circulate among ourselves, the goods being entirely of our own growth and manufacture.

Fourthly, the constant breeders, besides the gain of eight shil- 24 lings sterling per annum by the sale of their children, will be rid of the charge of maintaining them after the first year.

Fifthly, this food would likewise bring great custom to tav- 25 erns, where the vintners will certainly be so prudent as to procure the best receipts for dressing it to perfection, and consequently have their houses frequented by all the fine gentlemen, who justly value themselves upon their knowledge in good eating; and a skill-

ful cook, who understands how to oblige his guests, will contrive
to make it as expensive as they please.

Sixthly, this would be a great inducement to marriage, which   26
all wise nations have either encouraged by rewards or enforced by
laws and penalties. It would increase the care and tenderness of
mothers toward their children, when they were sure of a settlement
for life to the poor babes, provided in some sort by the public, to
their annual profit instead of expense. We should see an honest
emulation among the married women, which of them could bring
the fattest child to the market. Men would become as fond of their
wives during the time of their pregnancy as they are now of their
mares in foal, their cows in calf, or sows when they are ready to
farrow; nor offer to beat or kick them (as is too frequent a practice) for fear of a miscarriage.

Many other advantages might be enumerated. For instance,   27
the addition of some thousand carcasses in our exportation of bar-
reled beef, the propagation of swine's flesh, and improvements in
the art of making good bacon, so much wanted among us by the
great destruction of pigs, too frequent at our tables, which are no
way comparable in taste or magnificence to a well-grown, fat, year-
ling child, which roasted whole will make a considerable figure at a
lord mayor's feast or any other public entertainment. But this and
many others I omit, being studious of brevity.

Supposing that one thousand families in this city would be   28
constant customers for infants' flesh, besides others who might
have it at merry meetings, particularly weddings and christenings,
I compute that Dublin would take off annually about twenty thousand carcasses, and the rest of the kingdom (where probably they
will be sold somewhat cheaper) the remaining eighty thousand.

I can think of no one objection that will possibly be raised   29
against this proposal, unless it should be urged that the number of
people will be thereby much lessened in the kingdom. This I freely
own, and it was indeed one principal design in offering it to the
world. I desire the reader will observe, that I calculate my remedy
for this one individual kingdom of Ireland and for no other that
ever was, is, or I think ever can be upon earth. Therefore let no
man talk to me of other expedients: of taxing our absentees at five
shillings a pound: of using neither clothes nor household furniture
except what is of our own growth and manufacture: of utterly re-
jecting the materials and instruments that promote foreign luxury:

of curing the expensiveness of pride, vanity, idleness, and gaming in our women: of introducing a vein of parsimony, prudence, and temperance: of learning to love our country, in the want of which we differ even from Laplanders and the inhabitants of Topinamboo[5]: of quitting our animosities and factions, nor acting any longer like the Jews, who were murdering one another at the very moment their city was taken: of being a little cautious not to sell our country and conscience for nothing: of teaching landlords to have at least one degree of mercy toward their tenants: lastly, of putting a spirit of honesty, industry, and skill into our shopkeepers; who, if a resolution could now be taken to buy only our native goods, would immediately unite to cheat and exact upon us in the price, the measure, and the goodness, nor could ever yet be brought to make one fair proposal of just dealing, though often and earnestly invited to it.[6]

Therefore I repeat, let no man talk to me of these and the like   30
expedients, till he hath at least some glimpse of hope that there will ever be some hearty and sincere attempt to put them in practice.

But as to myself, having been wearied out for many years   31
with offering vain, idle, visionary thoughts, and at length utterly despairing of success, I fortunately fell upon this proposal, which, as it is wholly new, so it hath something solid and real, of no expense and little trouble, full in our own power, and whereby we can incur no danger in disobliging England. For this kind of commodity will not bear exportation, the flesh being of too tender a consistence to admit a long continuance in salt, although perhaps I could name a country which would be glad to eat up our whole nation without it.

After all, I am not so violently bent upon my own opinion as   32
to reject any offer proposed by wise men, which shall be found equally innocent, cheap, easy, and effectual. But before something of that kind shall be advanced in contradiction to my scheme, and offering a better, I desire the author or authors will be pleased maturely to consider two points. First, as things now stand, how they will be able to find food and raiment for an hundred thousand useless mouths and backs. And secondly, there being a round mil-

[5] A district in Brazil.
[6] Swift himself has made these various proposals in previous works.

lion of creatures in human figure throughout this kingdom, whose sole subsistence put into a common stock would leave them in debt two millions of pounds sterling, adding those who are beggars by profession to the bulk of farmers, cottagers, and laborers, with their wives and children who are beggars in effect; I desire those politicians who dislike my overture, and may perhaps be so bold to attempt an answer, that they will first ask the parents of these mortals whether they would not at this day think it a great happiness to have been sold for food at a year old in this manner I prescribe, and thereby have avoided such a perpetual scene of misfortunes as they have since gone through by the oppression of landlords, the impossibility of paying rent without money or trade, the want of common sustenance, with neither house nor clothes to cover them from the inclemencies of the weather, and the most inevitable prospect of entailing the like or greater miseries upon their breed forever.

I profess, in the sincerity of my heart, that I have not the least   33 personal interest in endeavoring to promote this necessary work, having no other motive than the public good of my country, by advancing our trade, providing for infants, relieving the poor, and giving some pleasure to the rich. I have no children by which I can propose to get a single penny; the youngest being nine years old, and my wife past childbearing.

JIMMY CARTER

JIMMY CARTER, an eighth-generation Georgian (born in 1924)
and former governor of Georgia, in 1977 became the 39th
President of the United States. In 1974, two years before his
nomination, Governor Carter delivered a rather unusual and
informal address before a group of largely conservative lawyers convening at the University of Georgia Law School. No
doubt expecting a standard praise-and-welcome speech by the
host-state governor, the visiting lawyers may have been
startled by what they got. But Hunter Thompson, covering
the event for *Rolling Stone,* was highly impressed and reported accordingly, noting that he could tell by "the rising
anger in Carter's voice that we were in for an interesting
ride." When Carter won the presidential election in 1976,
Rolling Stone published the following text of the address,
which has become known as the "Law Day Speech."

To Establish Justice in a Sinful World

One of the sources for my understanding about the proper applica-   1
tion of criminal justice and the system of equity is from reading
Reinhold Niebuhr. The other source is from a friend of mine, a
poet named Bob Dylan. After listening to his records about "The
Lonesome Death of Hattie Carroll" and "Like a Rolling Stone"
and "The Times They Are A-Changin'," I've learned to appreciate
the dynamism of change in a modern society.

One of the things that Niebuhr says is that the said duty of   2
the political system is to establish justice in a sinful world. I would
like to talk to you for a few moments about some of the practical
aspects of being a governor who is still deeply concerned about the

inadequacies of a system of which it is obvious that you're so patently proud.

I don't know exactly how to say this, but I was thinking just 3 a few moments ago about some of the things that are of deep concern to me as governor. As a scientist, I was working constantly, along with almost everyone who professes that dedication of life, to probe, probe every day of my life for constant change for the better. As a farmer, the same motivation persists.

In my opinion, it's different in the case of lawyers. And maybe 4 this is a circumstance that is so inherently true that it can't be changed.

In general, the powerful and the influential in our society 5 shape the laws and have a great influence on the legislature or the Congress. This creates a reluctance to change, because the powerful and the influential have carved out for themselves or have inherited a privileged position in society. I remember when I was a child, I lived on a farm about three miles from Plains, and we didn't have electricity or running water. We lived on the railroad. Like all farm boys I had a flip, a slingshot. They had stabilized the railroad bed with little white round rocks, which I used for ammunition. I would go out frequently to the railroad and gather the most perfectly shaped rocks of proper size.

One day I was leaving the railroad track with my pockets full 6 of rocks and hands full of rocks, and my mother came out on the front porch — this is not a very interesting story but it illustrates a point — and she had in her hands a plate full of cookies that she had just baked for me. She called me, I am sure with love in her heart, and said, "Jimmy, I've baked some cookies for you." I remember very distinctly walking up to her and standing there for 15 or 20 seconds, in honest doubt about whether I should drop those rocks which were worthless and take the cookies that my mother had prepared for me, which between her and me were very valuable.

Quite often we have the same inclination in our everyday 7 lives. We don't recognize that change can sometimes be very beneficial although we fear it. Anyone who lives in the South looks back on the last 15 to 20 years with some degree of embarrassment, including myself. The first speech I ever made in the Georgia Senate, representing the most conservative district in Georgia, was concerning the abolition of 30 questions that we had so proudly evolved as a subterfuge to keep black citizens from voting and which we used with a great deal of smirking and pride for decades or generations ever since the War between the States — questions that nobody could answer in this room. I spoke in that chamber, fearful of the news media reporting it back home, but overwhelmed with a commitment to the abolition of that artificial barrier to the rights of an American citizen. I remember the thing that I used in my speech, that a black pencil salesman on the outer door of the Sumter County courthouse could make a better judgment about who ought to be sheriff than two highly educated professors at Georgia Southwestern College.

The point I want to make to you is that we still have a long way to go. But who's going to search the heart and the soul of an organization like yours, or a law school, or state or nation, and say, "What can we still do to restore equity and justice, or to preserve it, or to enhance it in this society?" 8

I was in the Governor's Mansion for two years, enjoying the services of a very fine cook, who was a prisoner — a woman. One day she came to me, after she got over her two years of timidity, and said, "Governor, I would like to borrow $250 from you." I said, "I'm not sure that a lawyer would be worth that much." She said, "I don't want to hire a lawyer; I want to pay the judge." 9

I thought it was a ridiculous statement for her; I felt that she was ignorant. But I found out she wasn't. She had been sentenced by a superior court judge in the state, who still serves, to seven years or $750. I had Bill Harper, my legal aide, look into it. She was quickly released under a recent court ruling. 10

My heart feels and cries out that something ought to be analyzed, not just about the structure of government, judicial qualification councils and judicial appointment committees and eliminating the unsworn statement — those things are important. But they don't reach the crux of the point — that now we assign punishment to fit the criminal and not the crime. 11

You can go in the prisons of Georgia, and I don't know, it may be that poor people are the only ones who commit crimes, but I do know they are the only ones who serve prison sentences. 12

We had an ethics bill in the state legislature this year. Half of it passed — to require an accounting for contributions during a campaign — but the part that applied to people after the campaign failed. We couldn't get through a requirement for revelation of 13

payments or gifts to officeholders after they are in office. The   14
largest force against that ethics bill was the lawyers.

The regulatory agencies in Washington are made up, not of
people to regulate industries, but of representatives of the industries that are regulated. Is that fair and right and equitable? I don't
think so.

I see the lobbyists in the state capitol filling the halls on occa-   15
sions. Good people, competent people, the most pleasant, person-
able, extroverted citizens of Georgia. But I tell you that when a
lobbyist goes to represent the Peanut Warehouseman's Association
of the Southeast, which I helped to organize, they go there to represent the peanut warehouseman. They don't go there to represent
the customers of the peanut warehouseman.

When your own organization is interested in some legislation   16
there in the capitol, they're interested in the welfare or prerogatives
or authority of the lawyers. They are not there to represent in any
sort of exclusive way the client of the lawyers.

This bothers me; and I know that if there was a commitment   17
on the part of the attorneys in this state to eliminate many of the
inequities I've just described, our state could be transformed in the
attitude of its people toward the government.

When I was about 12 years old, I liked to read, and I had a   18
school principal named Miss Julia Coleman. She forced me pretty
much to read, read, read classical books. One day, she called me in
and she said, "Jimmy, I think it's time for you to read *War and
Peace*." I was completely relieved because I thought it was a book
about cowboys and Indians.

What Tolstoy points out in the epilogue is that he didn't write   19
the book about Napoleon or the czar of Russia or even the generals,
except in a rare occasion. He wrote it about the students and the
housewives and the barbers and the farmers and the privates in
the army. And the point of the book is that the course of human
events, even the greatest historical events, are not determined by
the leaders of a nation or a state. They are controlled by the combined wisdom and courage and commitment and discernment and
unselfishness and compassion and love and idealism of the common
ordinary people.

I've read parts of the embarrassing [White House] transcripts,   20
and I've seen the proud statement of a former attorney general who
protected his boss and now brags on the fact that he tiptoed

through a mine field and came out, quote, clean, unquote. I can't imagine somebody like Thomas Jefferson tiptoeing through a mine field on the technicalities of the law, and then bragging about being clean afterwards.

I think our people demand more than that. Everyone in this 21 room ought to remember the oath that Thomas Jefferson and others took when they practically signed their own death warrant, writing the Declaration of Independence. To preserve justice and equality and freedom and fairness, they pledged their lives, their fortunes and their sacred honor.

Thank you very much. 22

GEORGE ORWELL

GEORGE ORWELL (1903–1950), whose real name was Eric Blair, was a British novelist and essayist, well known for his satire. He was born in India and educated at Eton in England; he was wounded while fighting in the Spanish Civil War. Later he wrote the books *Animal Farm* (1945), a satire on Soviet history, and *1984* (1949), a vivid picture of life in a projected totalitarian society. He was, however, also sharply aware of injustices in democratic societies and was consistently socialistic in his views. Many of Orwell's essays are collected in *Critical Essays* (1946), *Shooting an Elephant* (1950), and *Such, Such Were the Joys* (1953). "Politics and the English Language," published in 1945, is one of his most famous essays.

Politics and the English Language

Most people who bother with the matter at all would admit that   1
the English language is in a bad way, but it is generally assumed that we cannot by conscious action do anything about it. Our civilization is decadent and our language — so the argument runs — must inevitably share in the general collapse. It follows that any struggle against the abuse of language is a sentimental archaism, like preferring candles to electric light or hansom cabs to aeroplanes. Underneath this lies the half-conscious belief that language is a natural growth and not an instrument which we shape for our own purpose.

Now, it is clear that the decline of a language must ultimately   2
have political and economic causes: it is not due simply to the bad influence of this or that individual writer. But an effect can become a cause, reinforcing the original cause and producing the same

effect in an intensified form, and so on indefinitely. A man may take to drink because he feels himself to be a failure, and then fail all the more completely because he drinks. It is rather the same thing that is happening to the English language. It becomes ugly and inaccurate because our thoughts are foolish, but the slovenliness of our language makes it easier for us to have foolish thoughts. The point is that the process is reversible. Modern English, especially written English, is full of bad habits which spread by imitation and which can be avoided if one is willing to take the necessary trouble. If one gets rid of these habits one can think more clearly, and to think clearly is a necessary first step towards political regeneration: so that the fight against bad English is not frivolous and is not the exclusive concern of professional writers. I will come back to this presently, and I hope that by that time the meaning of what I have said here will have become clearer. Meanwhile, here are five specimens of the English language as it is now habitually written.

These five passages have not been picked out because they are especially bad — I could have quoted far worse if I had chosen — but because they illustrate various of the mental vices from which we now suffer. They are a little below the average, but are fairly representative samples. I number them so that I can refer back to them when necessary: 3

"(1) I am not, indeed, sure whether it is not true to say that the Milton who once seemed not unlike a seventeenth-century Shelley had not become, out of an experience ever more bitter in each year, more alien [sic] to the founder of that Jesuit sect which nothing could induce him to tolerate."

Professor Harold Laski (Essay in *Freedom of Expression*)

"(2) Above all, we cannot play ducks and drakes with a native battery of idioms which prescribes such egregious collocations of vocables as the Basic *put up with* for *tolerate* or *put at a loss* for *bewilder*."

Professor Lancelot Hogben (*Interglossa*).

"(3) On the one side we have the free personality: by definition it is not neurotic, for it has neither conflict nor dream. Its desires, such as they are, are transparent, for they are just what institutional approval keeps in the forefront of consciousness; another institutional pattern would alter their number and intensity; there is little in them that is natural, irreducible, or culturally dangerous. But *on the other side*, the social bond itself is nothing but the mutual reflection of these self-secure integrities. Recall the definition of love. Is not this the very picture of a small academic? Where is there a place in this hall of mirrors for either personality or fraternity?"

Essay on psychology in *Politics* (New York).

"(4) All the 'best people' from the gentlemen's clubs, and all the frantic fascist captains, united in common hatred of Socialism and bestial horror of the rising tide of the mass revolutionary movement, have turned to acts of provocation, to foul incendiarism, to medieval legends of poisoned wells, to legalize their own destruction of proletarian organizations, and rouse the agitated petty-bourgeoisie to chauvinistic fervour on behalf of the fight against the revolutionary way out of the crisis."

Communist pamphlet.

"(5) If a new spirit *is* to be infused into this old country, there is one thorny and contentious reform which must be tackled, and that is the humanization and galvanization of the B.B.C. Timidity here will bespeak cancer and atrophy of the soul. The heart of Britain may be sound and of strong beat, for instance, but the British lion's roar at present is like that of Bottom in Shakespeare's *Midsummer Night's Dream* — as gentle as any sucking dove. A virile new Britain cannot continue indefinitely to be traduced in the eyes or rather ears, of the world by the effete languors of Langham Place, brazenly masquerading as 'standard English'. When the Voice of Britain is heard at nine o'clock, better far and infinitely less ludicrous to hear aitches honestly dropped than the present priggish, inflated, inhibited, school-ma'amish arch braying of blameless bashful mewing maidens!"

Letter in *Tribune*.

Each of these passages has faults of its own, but, quite apart from avoidable ugliness, two qualities are common to all of them. The first is staleness of imagery: the other is lack of precision. The writer either has a meaning and cannot express it, or he inadvertently says something else, or he is almost indifferent as to whether his words mean anything or not. This mixture of vagueness and sheer incompetence is the most marked characteristic of modern English prose, and especially of any kind of political writing. As soon as certain topics are raised, the concrete melts into the abstract and no one seems to think of turns of speech that are not hackneyed: prose consists less and less of *words* chosen for the sake of their meaning, and more and more of *phrases* tacked together like the sections of a prefabricated hen-house. I list below, with notes and examples, various of the tricks by means of which the work of prose-construction is habitually dodged:

DYING METAPHORS

A newly invented metaphor assists thought by evoking a visual 5
image, while on the other hand a metaphor which is technically
"dead" (e.g. *iron resolution*) has in effect reverted to being an ordinary word and can generally be used without loss of vividness. But
in between these two classes there is a huge dump of worn-out
metaphors which have lost all evocative power and are merely used
because they save people the trouble of inventing phrases for themselves. Examples are: *Ring the changes on, take up the cudgels for,
toe the line, ride roughshod over, stand shoulder to shoulder with,
play into the hands of, no axe to grind, grist to the mill, fishing in
troubled waters, on the order of the day, Achilles' heel, swan song,
hotbed.* Many of these are used without knowledge of their meaning (what is a "rift", for instance?), and incompatible metaphors
are frequently mixed, a sure sign that the writer is not interested in
what he is saying. Some metaphors now current have been twisted
out of their original meaning without those who use them even
being aware of the fact. For example, *toe the line* is sometimes
written *tow the line.* Another example is *the hammer and the anvil,*
now always used with the implication that the anvil gets the worst
of it. In real life it is always the anvil that breaks the hammer,
never the other way about: a writer who stopped to think what he
was saying would be aware of this, and would avoid perverting the
original phrase.

OPERATORS OR VERBAL FALSE LIMBS

These save the trouble of picking out appropriate verbs and nouns, 6
and at the same time pad each sentence with extra syllables which
give it an appearance of symmetry. Characteristic phrases are:
*render inoperative, militate against, make contact with, be sub-
jected to, give rise to, give grounds for, have the effect of, play a
leading part (role) in, make itself felt, take effect, exhibit a tendency to, serve the purpose of, etc., etc.* The keynote is the elimination of simple verbs. Instead of being a single word, such as
break, stop, spoil, mend, kill, a verb becomes a *phrase,* made up of
a noun or adjective tacked on to some general-purpose verb such
as *prove, serve, form, play, render.* In addition, the passive voice
is wherever possible used in preference to the active, and noun
constructions are used instead of gerunds (*by examination of* in-

stead of *by examining*). The range of verbs is further cut down by means of the *-ize* and *de-* formation, and the banal statements are given an appearance of profundity by means of the *not un-* formation. Simple conjunctions and prepositions are replaced by such phrases as *with respect to, having regard to, the fact that, by dint of, in view of, in the interests of, on the hypothesis that;* and the ends of sentences are saved from anticlimax by such resounding commonplaces as *greatly to be desired, cannot be left out of account, a development to be expected in the near future, deserving of serious consideration, brought to a satisfactory conclusion,* and so on and so forth.

PRETENTIOUS DICTION

Words like *phenomenon, element, individual* (as noun), *objective,*   7
categorical, effective, virtual, basic, primary, promote, constitute, exhibit, exploit, utilize, eliminate, liquidate, are used to dress up simple statements and give an air of scientific impartiality to biased judgments. Adjectives like *epoch-making, epic, historic, unforgettable, triumphant, age-old, inevitable, inexorable, veritable,* are used to dignify the sordid processes of international politics, while writing that aims at glorifying war usually takes on an archaic colour, its characteristic words being: *realm, throne, chariot, mailed fist, trident, sword, shield, buckler, banner, jackboot, clarion.* Foreign words and expressions such as *cul de sac, ancien régime, deus ex machina, mutatis mutandis, status quo, gleichschaltung, weltanschauung,* are used to give an air of culture and elegance. Except for the useful abbreviations *i.e., e.g.,* and *etc.,* there is no real need for any of the hundreds of foreign phrases now current in English. Bad writers, and especially scientific, political and sociological writers, are nearly always haunted by the notion that Latin or Greek words are grander than Saxon ones, and unnecessary words like *expedite, ameliorate, predict, extraneous, deracinated, clandestine, subaqueous* and hundreds of others constantly gain ground from their Anglo-Saxon opposite numbers.[1] The jargon peculiar to

[1] An interesting illustration of this is the way in which the English flower names which were in use till very recently are being ousted by Greek ones, *snapdragon* becoming *antirrhinum, forget-me-not* becoming *myosotis,* etc. It is hard to see any practical reason for this change of fashion: it is probably due to an instinctive turning-away from the more homely word and a vague feeling that the Greek word is scientific.

Marxist writing (*hyena, hangman, cannibal, petty bourgeois, these gentry, lacquey, flunkey, mad dog, White Guard,* etc.) consists largely of words and phrases translated from Russian, German or French; but the normal way of coining a new word is to use a Latin or Greek root with the appropriate affix and, where necessary, the *-ize* formation. It is often easier to make up words of this kind (*deregionalize, impermissible, extramarital, nonfragmentatory* and so forth) than to think up the English words that will cover one's meaning. The result, in general, is an increase in slovenliness and vagueness.

MEANINGLESS WORDS

In certain kinds of writing, particularly in art criticism and literary criticism, it is normal to come across long passages which are almost completely lacking in meaning.[2] Words like *romantic, plastic, values, human, dead, sentimental, natural, vitality,* as used in art criticism, are strictly meaningless in the sense that they not only do not point to any discoverable object, but are hardly ever expected to do so by the reader. When one critic writes, "The outstanding feature of Mr. X's work is its living quality", while another writes, "The immediately striking thing about Mr. X's work is its peculiar deadness", the reader accepts this as a simple difference of opinion. If words like *black* and *white* were involved, instead of the jargon words *dead* and *living,* he would see at once that language was being used in an improper way. Many political words are similarly abused. The word *Fascism* has now no meaning except in so far as it signifies "something not desirable". The words *democracy, socialism, freedom, patriotic, realistic, justice,* have each of them several different meanings which cannot be reconciled with one another. In the case of a word like *democracy,* not only is there no agreed definition, but the attempt to make one is resisted from all sides. It is almost universally felt that when we call a country democratic we are praising it: consequently the defenders of every

8

[2] Example: "Comfort's catholicity of perception and image, strangely Whitmanesque in range, almost the exact opposite in aesthetic compulsion, continues to evoke that trembling atmospheric accumulative hinting at a cruel, an inexorably serene timelessness ... Wrey Gardiner scores by aiming at simple bull's-eyes with precision. Only they are not so simple, and through this contented sadness runs more than the surface bitter-sweet of resignation." (*Poetry Quarterly.*)

kind of régime claim that it is a democracy, and fear that they might have to stop using the word if it were tied down to any one meaning. Words of this kind are often used in a consciously dishonest way. That is, the person who uses them has his own private definition, but allows his hearer to think he means something quite different. Statements like *Marshal Pétain was a true patriot, The Soviet Press is the freest in the world, The Catholic Church is opposed to persecution,* are almost always made with intent to deceive. Other words used in variable meanings, in most cases more or less dishonestly, are: *class, totalitarian, science, progressive, reactionary, bourgeois, equality.*

Now that I have made this catalogue of swindles and perver- 9
sions, let me give another example of the kind of writing that they lead to. This time it must of its nature be an imaginary one. I am going to translate a passage of good English into modern English of the worst sort. Here is a well-known verse from *Ecclesiastes:*

"I returned and saw under the sun, that the race is not to the swift, nor the battle to the strong, neither yet bread to the wise, nor yet riches to men of understanding, nor yet favour to men of skill; but time and chance happeneth to them all."

Here it is in modern English:

"Objective consideration of contemporary phenomena compels the conclusion that success or failure in competitive activities exhibits no tendency to be commensurate with innate capacity, but that a considerable element of the unpredictable must invariably be taken into account."

This is a parody, but not a very gross one. Exhibit (3), above, 10
for instance, contains several patches of the same kind of English. It will be seen that I have not made a full translation. The beginning and ending of the sentence follow the original meaning fairly closely, but in the middle the concrete illustrations — race, battle, bread — dissolve into the vague phrase "success or failure in competitive activities". This had to be so, because no modern writer of the kind I am discussing — no one capable of using phrases like "objective consideration of contemporary phenomena" — would ever tabulate his thoughts in that precise and detailed way. The

whole tendency of modern prose is away from concreteness. Now analyse these two sentences a little more closely. The first contains forty-nine words but only sixty syllables, and all its words are those of everyday life. The second contains thirty-eight words of ninety syllables: eighteen of its words are from Latin roots, and one from Greek. The first sentence contains six vivid images, and only one phrase ("time and chance") that could be called vague. The second contains not a single fresh, arresting phrase, and in spite of its ninety syllables it gives only a shortened version of the meaning contained in the first. Yet without a doubt it is the second kind of sentence that is gaining ground in modern English. I do not want to exaggerate. This kind of writing is not yet universal, and outcrops of simplicity will occur here and there in the worst-written page. Still, if you or I were told to write a few lines on the uncertainty of human fortunes, we should probably come much nearer to my imaginary sentence than to the one from *Ecclesiastes.*

As I have tried to show, modern writing at its worst does not 11 consist in picking out words for the sake of their meaning and inventing images in order to make the meaning clearer. It consists in gumming together long strips of words which have already been set in order by someone else, and making the results presentable by sheer humbug. The attraction of this way of writing is that it is easy. It is easier — even quicker, once you have the habit — to say *In my opinion it is a not unjustifiable assumption that* than to say *I think.* If you use ready-made phrases, you not only don't have to hunt about for words, you also don't have to bother with the rhythms of your sentences, since these phrases are generally so arranged as to be more or less euphonious. When you are composing in a hurry — when you are dictating to a stenographer, for instance, or making a public speech — it is natural to fall into a pretentious, Latinized style. Tags like *a consideration which we should do well to bear in mind* or *a conclusion to which all of us would readily assent* will save many a sentence from coming down with a bump. By using stale metaphors, similes and idioms, you save much mental effort, at the cost of leaving your meaning vague, not only for your reader but for yourself. This is the significance of mixed metaphors. The sole aim of a metaphor is to call up a visual image. When these images clash — as in *The Fascist octopus has sung its swan song, the jackboot is thrown into the melting pot* — it can be taken as certain that the writer is not seeing a mental image of the objects he is naming; in other words he is not really thinking. Look again at the examples I gave at the beginning of this essay. Professor Laski (1) uses five negatives in fifty-three words. One of these is superfluous, making nonsense of the whole passage, and in addition there is the slip *alien* for akin, making further nonsense, and several avoidable pieces of clumsiness which increase the general vagueness. Professor Hogben (2) plays ducks and drakes with a battery which is able to write prescriptions, and, while disapproving of the everyday phrase *put up with*, is unwilling to look *egregious* up in the dictionary and see what it means. (3), if one takes an uncharitable attitude towards it, is simply meaningless: probably one could work out its intended meaning by reading the whole of the article in which it occurs. In (4), the writer knows more or less what he wants to say, but an accumulation of stale phrases chokes him like tea leaves blocking a sink. In (5), words and meaning have almost parted company. People who write in this manner usually have a general emotional meaning — they dislike one thing and want to express solidarity with another — but they are not interested in the detail of what they are saying. A scrupulous writer, in every sentence that he writes, will ask himself at least four questions, thus: What am I trying to say? What words will express it? What image or idiom will make it clearer? Is this image fresh enough to have an effect? And he will probably ask himself two more: Could I put it more shortly? Have I said anything that is avoidably ugly? But you are not obliged to go to all this trouble. You can shirk it by simply throwing your mind open and letting the ready-made phrases come crowding in. They will construct your sentences for you — even think your thoughts for you, to a certain extent — and at need they will perform the important service of partially concealing your meaning even from yourself. It is at this point that the special connection between politics and the debasement of language becomes clear.

In our time it is broadly true that political writing is bad   12
writing. Where it is not true, it will generally be found that the writer is some kind of rebel, expressing his private opinions and not a "party line". Orthodoxy, of whatever colour, seems to demand a lifeless, imitative style. The political dialects to be found in pamphlets, leading articles, manifestos, White Papers and the speeches of under-secretaries do, of course, vary from party to party, but they are all alike in that one almost never finds in them

a fresh, vivid, home-made turn of speech. When one watches some tired hack on the platform mechanically repeating the familiar phrases — *bestial atrocities, iron heel, bloodstained tyranny, free peoples of the world, stand shoulder to shoulder* — one often has a curious feeling that one is not watching a live human being but some kind of dummy: a feeling which suddenly becomes stronger at moments when the light catches the speaker's spectacles and turns them into blank discs which seem to have no eyes behind them. And this is not altogether fanciful. A speaker who uses that kind of phraseology has gone some distance towards turning himself into a machine. The appropriate noises are coming out of his larynx, but his brain is not involved as it would be if he were choosing his words for himself. If the speech he is making is one that he is accustomed to make over and over again, he may be almost unconscious of what he is saying, as one is when one utters the responses in church. And this reduced state of consciousness, if not indispensable, is at any rate favourable to political conformity.

In our time, political speech and writing are largely the defence of the indefensible. Things like the continuance of British rule in India, the Russian purges and deportations, the dropping of the atom bombs on Japan, can indeed be defended, but only by arguments which are too brutal for most people to face, and which do not square with the professed aims of political parties. Thus political language has to consist largely of euphemism, question-begging and sheer cloudy vagueness. Defenseless villages are bombarded from the air, the inhabitants driven out into the countryside, the cattle machine-gunned, the huts set on fire with incendiary bullets: this is called *pacification*. Millions of peasants are robbed of their farms and sent trudging along the roads with no more than they can carry: this is called *transfer of population* or *rectification of frontiers*. People are imprisoned for years without trial, or shot in the back of the neck or sent to die of scurvy in Arctic lumber camps: this is called *elimination of unreliable elements*. Such phraseology is needed if one wants to name things without calling up mental pictures of them. Consider for instance some comfortable English professor defending Russian totalitarianism. He cannot say outright, "I believe in killing off your opponents when you can get good results by doing so". Probably, therefore, he will say something like this:

"While freely conceding that the Soviet régime exhibits cer- 14
tain features which the humanitarian may be inclined to deplore,
we must, I think, agree that a certain curtailment of the right to
political opposition is an unavoidable concomitant of transitional
periods, and that the rigours which the Russian people have been
called upon to undergo have been amply justified in the sphere of
concrete achievement."

The inflated style is itself a kind of euphemism. A mass of 15
Latin words falls upon the facts like soft snow, blurring the outlines and covering up all the details. The great enemy of clear
language is insincerity. When there is a gap between one's real and
one's declared aims, one turns as it were instinctively to long words
and exhausted idioms, like a cuttlefish squirting out ink. In our
age there is no such thing as "keeping out of politics". All issues
are political issues, and politics itself is a mass of lies, evasions,
folly, hatred and schizophrenia. When the general atmosphere is
bad, language must suffer. I should expect to find — this is a guess
which I have not sufficient knowledge to verify — that the German,
Russian and Italian languages have all deteriorated in the last ten
or fifteen years, as a result of dictatorship.

But if thought corrupts language, language can also corrupt 16
thought. A bad usage can spread by tradition and imitation, even
among people who should and do know better. The debased language that I have been discussing is in some ways very convenient.
Phrases like *a not unjustifiable assumption, leaves much to be
desired, would serve no good purpose, a consideration which we
should do well to bear in mind,* are a continuous temptation, a
packet of aspirins always at one's elbow. Look back through this
essay, and for certain you will find that I have again and again
committed the very faults I am protesting against. By this morning's post I have received a pamphlet dealing with conditions in
Germany. The author tells me that he "felt impelled" to write it. I
open it at random, and here is almost the first sentence that I see:
"(The Allies) have an opportunity not only of achieving a radical
transformation of Germany's social and political structure in such a
way as to avoid a nationalistic reaction in Germany itself, but at
the same time of laying the foundations of a co-operative and unified Europe." You see, he "feels impelled" to write — feels, presumably, that he has something new to say — and yet his words,
like cavalry horses answering the bugle, group themselves auto-

matically into the familiar dreary pattern. This invasion of one's mind by ready-made phrases *(lay the foundations, achieve a radical transformation)* can only be prevented if one is constantly on guard against them, and every such phrase anaesthetizes a portion of one's brain.

I said earlier that the decadence of our language is probably 17 curable. Those who deny this would argue, if they produced an argument at all, that language merely reflects existing social conditions, and that we cannot influence its development by any direct tinkering with words and constructions. So far as the general tone or spirit of a language goes, this may be true, but it is not true in detail. Silly words and expressions have often disappeared, not through any evolutionary process but owing to the conscious action of a minority. Two recent examples were *explore every avenue* and *leave no stone unturned*, which were killed by the jeers of a few journalists. There is a long list of flyblown metaphors which could similarly be got rid of if enough people would interest themselves in the job; and it should also be possible to laugh the *not un-* formation out of existence,[3] to reduce the amount of Latin and Greek in the average sentence, to drive out foreign phrases and strayed scientific words, and, in general, to make pretentiousness unfashionable. But all these are minor points. The defence of the English language implies more than this, and perhaps it is best to start by saying what it does *not* imply.

To begin with it has nothing to do with archaism, with the 18 salvaging of obsolete words and turns of speech, or with the setting up of a "standard English" which must never be departed from. On the contrary, it is especially concerned with the scrapping of every word or idiom which has outworn its usefulness. It has nothing to do with correct grammar and syntax, which are of no importance so long as one makes one's meaning clear, or with the avoidance of Americanisms, or with having what is called a "good prose style". On the other hand it is not concerned with fake simplicity and the attempt to make written English colloquial. Nor does it even imply in every case preferring the Saxon word to the Latin one, though it does imply using the fewest and shortest words that will cover

---

[3] One can cure oneself of the *not un-* formation by memorizing this sentence: *A not unblack dog was chasing a not unsmall rabbit across a not ungreen field.*

one's meaning. What is above all needed is to let the meaning choose the word, and not the other way about. In prose, the worst thing one can do with words is to surrender to them. When you think of a concrete object, you think wordlessly, and then, if you want to describe the thing you have been visualizing you probably hunt about till you find the exact words that seem to fit. When you think of something abstract you are more inclined to use words from the start, and unless you make a conscious effort to prevent it, the existing dialect will come rushing in and do the job for you, at the expense of blurring or even changing your meaning. Probably it is better to put off using words as long as possible and get one's meaning as clear as one can through pictures or sensations. Afterwards one can choose — not simply *accept* — the phrases that will best cover the meaning, and then switch round and decide what impression one's words are likely to make on another person. This last effort of the mind cuts out all stale or mixed images, all prefabricated phrases, needless repetitions, and humbug and vagueness generally. But one can often be in doubt about the effect of a word or a phrase, and one needs rules that one can rely on when instinct fails. I think the following rules will cover most cases:

(i) Never use a metaphor, simile or other figure of speech which you are used to seeing in print.

(ii) Never use a long word where a short one will do.

(iii) If it is possible to cut a word out, always cut it out.

(iv) Never use the passive where you can use the active.

(v) Never use a foreign phrase, a scientific word or a jargon word if you can think of an everyday English equivalent.

(vi) Break any of these rules sooner than say anything outright barbarous.

These rules sound elementary, and so they are, but they demand a deep change of attitude in anyone who has grown used to writing in the style now fashionable. One could keep all of them and still write bad English, but one could not write the kind of stuff that I quoted in those five specimens at the beginning of this article.

I have not here been considering the literary use of language, but merely language as an instrument for expressing and not for concealing or preventing thought. Stuart Chase and others have come near to claiming that all abstract words are meaningless, and have used this as a pretext for advocating a kind of political quietism. Since you don't know what Fascism is, how can you struggle against Fascism? One need not swallow such absurdities as this, but one ought to recognize that the present political chaos is connected with the decay of language, and that one can probably bring about some improvement by starting at the verbal end. If you simplify your English, you are freed from the worst follies of orthodoxy. You cannot speak any of the necessary dialects, and when you make a stupid remark its stupidity will be obvious, even to yourself. Political language — and with variations this is true of all political parties, from Conservatives to Anarchists — is designed to make lies sound truthful and murder respectable, and to give an appearance of solidity to pure wind. One cannot change this all in a moment, but one can at least change one's own habits, and from time to time one can even, if one jeers loudly enough, send some worn-out and useless phrase — some *jackboot, Achilles' heel, hotbed, melting pot, acid test, veritable inferno* or other lump of verbal refuse — into the dustbin where it belongs.

IRVING KRISTOL

IRVING KRISTOL, a New Yorker born in 1920, graduated as a history major from New York University, where he is now Henry Luce Professor of Urban Studies. A fellow of the American Academy of Arts and Sciences, he has been awarded numerous honors and university degrees. Kristol has served as editor of *Commentary*, *Encounter*, and *Reporter* magazines and is founder and coeditor of the quarterly journal *The Public Interest*. A collection of his essays, *On the Democratic Idea in America*, was published in 1972. In his early career Kristol was a highly vocal liberal, but he has gradually become more moderate in his views, convinced that many of our reforms are concocted too fast and with too little regard for tradition. One such tendency, he thinks, has been the rapid liberalizing of antipornography laws, and he takes on this eminently controversial subject in "Censorship: Where Do We Draw the Line?"

Censorship: Where Do We Draw the Line?

Being frustrated is disagreeable, but the real disasters in life begin   1
when you get what you want. For almost a century now, a great many intelligent, well-meaning and articulate people have argued eloquently against any kind of censorship of art and entertainment. Within the past ten years, courts and legislatures have found these arguments so persuasive that censorship is now a relative rarity in most states.

Is there triumphant exhilaration in the land? Hardly. Some-   2
how, things have not worked out as they were supposed to, and many civil-libertarians have said this was not what they meant. They wanted a world in which Eugene O'Neill's *Desire Under the Elms* could be produced, or James Joyce's *Ulysses* published, with-

As condensed in *Reader's Digest*, January 1975, from "The Case for Liberal Censorship," *The New York Times*, March 28, 1971. Copyright © 1971 by Irving Kristol. Reprinted by permission.

out interference. They got that, of course; but they also got a world in which homosexual rape is simulated on the stage, in which the public flocks to witness professional fornication, in which New York's Times Square has become a hideous marketplace for printed filth.

But does this really matter? Might not our disquiet be merely a cultural hangover? Was anyone ever corrupted by a book?   3

This last question, oddly enough, is asked by the same people who seem convinced that advertisements in magazines or displays of violence on television *do* have the power to corrupt. It is also asked, incredibly enough and in all sincerity, by university professors and teachers whose very lives provide the answer. After all, if you believe that no one was ever corrupted by a book, you have also to believe that no one was ever improved by a book. You have to believe, in other words, that art is morally trivial and that education is morally irrelevant.   4

To be sure, it is extremely difficult to trace the effects of any single book (or play or movie) on any reader. But we all know that the ways in which we use our minds and imaginations do shape our characters and help define us as persons. That those who certainly know this are moved to deny it merely indicates how a dogmatic resistance to the idea of censorship can result in a mindless insistence on the absurd.   5

For the plain fact is that we all believe that there is some point at which the public authorities ought to step in to limit the "self-expression" of an individual or a group. A theatrical director might find someone willing to commit suicide on the stage. We would not allow that. And I know of no one who argues that we ought to permit public gladiatorial contests, even between consenting adults.   6

No society can be utterly indifferent to the ways its citizens publicly entertain themselves. Bearbaiting and cockfighting are prohibited only in part out of compassion for the animals; the main reason is that such spectacles were felt to debase and brutalize the citizenry who flocked to witness them. The question with regard to pornography and obscenity is whether they will brutalize and debase our citizenry. We are, after all, not dealing with one book or one movie. We are dealing with a general tendency that is suffusing our entire culture.   7

Pornography's whole purpose, it seems to me, is to treat human beings obscenely, to deprive them of their specifically human   8 dimension. Imagine a well-known man in a hospital ward, dying an agonizing death. His bladder and bowels empty themselves of their own accord. His consciousness is overwhelmed by pain, so that he cannot communicate with us, nor we with him. Now, it would be technically easy to put a television camera in his room and let the whole world witness this spectacle. We don't do it — at least not yet — because we regard this as an obscene invasion of privacy. And what would make the spectacle obscene is that we would be witnessing the extinguishing of humanity in a human animal.

Sex — like death — is an activity that is both animal and hu- 9
man. There are human sentiments and human ideals involved in this animal activity. But when sex is public, I do not believe the viewer can see the sentiments and the ideals, but sees only the animal coupling. And that is why when most men and women make love, they prefer to be alone — because it is only when you are alone that you can make love, as distinct from merely copulating. When sex is a public spectacle, a human relationship has been debased into a mere animal connection.

But even if all this is granted, it doubtless will be said that we 10
ought not to be unduly concerned. Free competition in the cultural marketplace, it is argued by those who have never otherwise had a kind word to say for laissez-faire, will dispose of the problem; in the course of time, people will get bored with pornography and obscenity.

I would like to be able to go along with this reasoning, but I 11
think it is false, and for two reasons. The first reason is psychological; the second, political.

In my opinion, pornography and obscenity appeal to and pro- 12
voke a kind of sexual regression. The pleasure one gets from pornography and obscenity is infantile and autoerotic; put bluntly, it is a masturbatory exercise of the imagination. Now, people who masturbate do not get bored with masturbation, just as sadists don't get bored with sadism, and voyeurs don't get bored with voyeurism. In other words, like all infantile sexuality, it can quite easily become a permanent self-reinforcing neurosis. And such a neurosis, on a mass scale, is a threat to our civilization and humanity, nothing less.

I am already touching upon a political aspect of pornography 13
when I suggest that it is inherently subversive of civilization. But

there is another political aspect, which has to do with the relationship of pornography and obscenity to democracy, and especially to the quality of public life on which democratic government ultimately rests.

Today a "managerial" conception of democracy prevails — 14 wherein democracy is seen as a set of rules and procedures, and *nothing but* a set of rules and procedures, by which majority rule and minority rights are reconciled into a state of equilibrium. Thus, the political system can be fully reduced to its mechanical arrangements.

There is, however, an older idea of democracy — fairly com- 15 mon until about the beginning of this century — for which the conception of the quality of public life is absolutely crucial. This idea starts from the proposition that democracy is a form of self-government, and that you are entitled to it only if that "self" is worthy of governing. Because the desirability of self-government depends on the character of the people who govern, the older idea of democracy was very solicitous of the condition of this character. This older democracy had no problem in principle with pornography and obscenity; it censored them; it was not about to permit people to corrupt themselves.

But can a liberal — today — be for censorship? Yes, but he 16 ought to favor a liberal form of censorship.

I don't think this is a contradiction in terms. We have no 17 problem contrasting *repressive* laws governing alcohol, drugs and tobacco with laws *regulating* (that is, discouraging the sale of) alcohol, drugs and tobacco. We have not made smoking a criminal offense. We have, however, and with good liberal conscience, prohibited cigarette advertising on television. The idea of restricting individual freedom, in a liberal way, is not at all unfamiliar to us.

I therefore see no reason why we should not be able to dis- 18 tinguish repressive censorship from liberal censorship of the written word. In Britain, until a few years ago, you could perform almost any play you wished — but certain plays, judged to be obscene, had to be performed in private theatrical clubs. In the United States, all of us who grew up using public libraries are familiar with the circumstances under which certain books could be circulated only to adults, while still other books had to be read in the library. In both cases, a small minority that was willing to make a serious effort to see an obscene play or book could do so.

But the impact of obscenity was circumscribed, and the quality of public life was only marginally affected.

It is a distressing fact that any system of censorship is bound,   19
upon occasion, to treat unjustly a particular work of art — to find pornography where there is only gentle eroticism, to find obscenity where none really exists, or to find both where the work's existence ought to be tolerated because it serves a larger moral purpose. That is the price one has to be prepared to pay for censorship — even liberal censorship.

But if you look at the history of American or English litera-   20
ture, there is precious little damage you can point to as a consequence of the censorship that prevailed throughout most of that history. I doubt that many works of real literary merit ever were suppressed. Nor did I notice that hitherto suppressed masterpieces flooded the market when censorship was eased.

I should say, to the contrary, that literature has lost quite a   21
bit now that so much is permitted. It seems to me that the cultural market in the United States today is awash in dirty books, dirty movies, dirty theater. Our cultural condition has not improved as a result of the new freedom.

I'll put it bluntly: if you care for the quality of life in our   22
American democracy, then you have to be for censorship.

ALEKSANDR SOLZHENITSYN

Aleksandr Solzhenitsyn, Nobel Prize winning Russian author born in 1918, was exiled from his native country in 1974 and now lives in the United States. In 1975 under the auspices of the AFL-CIO, Solzhenitsyn delivered two speeches, one in Washington and the other in New York, in which he challenged the wisdom of the U.S. policy of détente with the Soviet Union. The addresses were noteworthy not only for their clear and somber message, but also for the commanding credentials of the speaker. Solzhenitsyn — whose works include *One Day in the Life of Ivan Denisovich, Cancer Ward, The First Circle,* and *August 1914* — is not only the greatest Russian novelist of this century, but also the world's most eloquent former political prisoner; *The Gulag Archipelago,* which has attracted still further acclaim throughout the world than his fiction, is his searing account of the Soviet prison system. Following is a condensation of the New York speech, delivered July 9, 1975. It carries a disturbing warning even today, and should be especially interesting to students of composition for its basic organization, which can be seen as a kind of *layering* of logical and emotional elements.

Wake Up, America!

Is it possible to transmit the experience of those who have suffered   1
to those who have yet to suffer? Can one part of humanity learn from the bitter experience of another? Is it possible to warn someone of danger?

How many witnesses have been sent to the West in the last   2
60 years? How many millions of persons? You know who they are: if not by their spiritual disorientation, their grief, then by their accents, by their external appearance. Waves of immigrants, coming from different countries, have warned you of what is happen-

ing. But your proud skyscrapers point to the sky and say: It will never happen here. It's not possible here.

It can happen. It is possible. As a Russian proverb says: 3 "When it happens to you, you'll know it's true."

Do we have to wait until the knife is at our throats? Isn't it 4 possible to assess the menace that threatens to swallow the whole world? I was swallowed myself. I have been in the red burning belly of the dragon. He wasn't able to digest me. He threw me up. I come to you as a witness to what it's like there.

Communism has been writing about itself in the most open 5 way for 125 years. It is perfectly amazing. The whole world can read but somehow no one wants to understand what communism is. Communism is as crude an attempt to explain society and the individual as if a surgeon were to perform his delicate operations with a meat-ax. All that is subtle in human psychology and the structure of society (which is even more delicate) is reduced to crude economic processes. This whole created being — man — is reduced to matter.

Communism has never concealed the fact that it rejects all 6 absolute concepts of morality. It scoffs at "good" and "evil" as indisputable categories. Communism considers morality to be relative. Depending upon circumstances, any act, including the killing of thousands, could be good or bad. It all depends upon class ideology, defined by a handful of people. In this respect, communism has been most successful. Many people are carried away by this idea today. It is considered rather awkward to use seriously such words as "good" and "evil." But if we are to be deprived of these concepts, what will be left? We will decline to the status of animals.

Freedom's Tax. But what is amazing is that, apart from all the 7 books, communism has offered a multitude of examples for modern man to see. The tanks have rumbled through Budapest and into Czechoslovakia. Communists have erected the Berlin Wall. For 14 years people have been machine-gunned there. Has the wall convinced anyone? No. We'll never have a wall like that. And the tanks in Budapest and Prague, they won't come here either. In the communist countries they have a system of forced treatment in insane asylums. Three times a day the doctors make rounds and inject substances into people's arms that destroy their brains. Pay no attention to it. We'll continue to live in peace and quiet here.

What's worst in the communist system is its unity, its cohe-   8
sion. All the seeming differences among the communist parties of
the world are imaginary. All are united on one point: *your social
order must be destroyed.*

All of the communist parties, upon achieving power, have be-   9
come completely merciless. But at the stage before they achieve
power, they adopt disguises. Sometimes we hear words such as
"popular front" or "dialogue with Christianity." *Communists* have
a dialogue with Christianity? In the Soviet Union this dialogue was
a simple matter: they used machine guns. And last August, in
Portugal, unarmed Catholics were fired upon by the communists.
This is dialogue? And when the French and the Italian communists
say that they are going to have a dialogue, let them only achieve
power and we shall see what this dialogue will look like.

As long as in the Soviet Union, in China and in other com-   10
munist countries there is no limit to the use of violence, how can
you consider yourselves secure or at peace? I understand that you
love freedom, but in our crowded world you have to pay a tax for
freedom. You cannot love freedom just for yourselves and quietly
agree to a situation where the majority of humanity is being sub-
jected to violence and oppression.

The communist ideology is to destroy your society. This has   11
been their aim for 125 years and has never changed; only the
methods have changed. When there is détente, peaceful coexistence
and trade, they will still insist: The ideological war must continue!
And what is ideological war? It is a focus of hatred, a continued
repetition of the oath to destroy the Western world.

I understand, it's only human that persons living in prosperity   12
have difficulty understanding the necessity of taking steps — here
and now — to defend themselves. When your statesmen sign a
treaty with the Soviet Union or China, you want to believe that it
will be carried out. But the Poles who signed a treaty in Riga in
1921 with the communists also wanted to believe that the treaty
would be carried out; they were stabbed in the back. Estonia, Lat-
via and Lithuania signed treaties of friendship with the Soviet
Union and wanted to believe that they would be carried out; these
countries were swallowed.

And those who sign treaties with you now, at the same time   13
give orders for sane and innocent people to be confined in mental
hospitals and prisons. Why should they be different? Do they have
any love for you? Why should they act honorably toward you

while they crush their own people? The advocates of détente have never explained this.

You want to believe, and you cut down on your armies. You cut down on your research. You eliminate the Institute for the Study of the Soviet Union — the last genuine institute which actually could study Soviet society — because there wasn't enough money to support it. But the Soviet Union is studying you. They follow what's going on in your institutions. They visit Congressional committees; they study everything.   14

Nuclear Checkmate. The principal argument of the advocates of détente is that détente is necessary to avoid nuclear war. But I think I can set your minds at ease: there will not be any nuclear war. Why should there be a nuclear war if for the last 30 years the communists have been breaking off as much of the West as they wanted, piece after piece? In 1975 alone, three countries in Indochina were broken off.   15

You have theoreticians who say: "The United States has enough nuclear weapons to destroy the other half of the world. Why should we need more?" Let the American nuclear specialists reason this way if they want, but the leaders of the Soviet Union think differently. In the SALT talks, your opponent is continually deceiving you. Either he is testing radar in a way which is forbidden by the agreement; or he is violating the limitations on the dimensions of missiles; or he is violating the conditions on multiple warheads.   16

Once there was no comparison between the strength of the U.S.S.R. and yours. Now theirs is becoming superior to yours. Soon the ratio will be 2 to 1. Then 5 to 1. With such a nuclear superiority it will be possible to block the use of your weapons, and on some unlucky morning they will declare: "Attention. We're marching our troops to Europe and, if you make a move, we will annihilate you." And this ratio of 2 to 1 or 5 to 1 will have its effect. You will not make a move.   17

A World of Crisis. In addition to the grave political situation in the world today, we are approaching a major turning point in history. I can compare it only with the turning point from the Middle Ages to the modern era, a shift of civilizations. It is the sort of turning point at which the hierarchy of values to which we have   18 been dedicated all our lives is starting to waver, and may collapse.

These two crises — the political and spiritual — are occurring   19
simultaneously. It is our generation that will have to confront
them. The leadership of your country will have to bear a burden
greater than ever before. Your leaders will need profound intuition,
spiritual foresight, high qualities of mind and soul. May God grant
that you will have at the helm personalities as great as those who
created your country.

Those men never lost sight of their moral bearings. They did   20
not laugh at the absolute nature of the concepts of "good" and
"evil." Their policies were checked against a moral compass. They
never said, "Let slavery reign next door, and we will enter into
détente with this slavery so long as it doesn't come over to us."

I have traveled enough through your country to have become   21
convinced that the American heartland is healthy, strong, and
broad in its outlook. And when one sees your free and independent
life, all the dangers which I talk about indeed seem imaginary; in
your wide-open spaces, even I get infected. But this carefree life
cannot continue in your country or in ours. A concentration of
world evil, of hatred for humanity is taking place, and it is fully
determined to destroy your society. Must you wait until it comes
with a crowbar to break through your borders?

No More Shovels! We in the Soviet Union are born slaves. You   22
were born free. Why then do you help our slaveowners? When
they bury us in the ground alive, please do not send them shovels.
Please do not send them the most modern earth-moving equipment.

The existence of our slaveowners from beginning to end de-   23
pends upon Western economic assistance. What they need from
you is absolutely indispensable. The Soviet economy has an extremely low level of efficiency. What is done here by a few people,
by a few machines, in our country takes tremendous crowds of
workers and enormous masses of materials. Therefore, the Soviet
economy cannot deal with every problem at once: war, space,
heavy industry, light industry, and at the same time feed and
clothe its people. The forces of the entire Soviet economy are concentrated on war, where you won't be helping them. But everything that is necessary to feed the people, or for other types of
industry, they get from you. You are helping the Soviet police
state.

Our country is taking your assistance, but in the schools they   24
teach and in the newspapers they write, "Look at the Western
world, it's beginning to rot. Capitalism is breathing its last. It's
already dead. And our socialist economy has demonstrated once
and for all the triumph of communism." I think that we should at
last permit this socialist economy to prove its superiority. Let's
allow it to show that it is advanced, that it is omnipotent, that it
has overtaken you. Let us not interfere with it. Let us stop selling
to it and giving it loans. Let it stand on its own feet for 10 or 15
years. Then we will see what it looks like.

I can tell you what it will look like. It will have to reduce its   25
military preparations. It will have to abandon the useless space
effort, and it will have to feed and clothe its own people. And the
system will be forced to relax.

The Cold War — the war of hatred — is still going on, but   26
only on the communist side. What is the Cold War? It's a war of
abuse. They trade with you, they sign agreements and treaties, but
they still abuse you, they still curse you. In the depths of the Soviet
Union, the Cold War has never stopped for one second. They never
call you anything but "American imperialists." Do I call upon you
to return to the Cold War? By no means, Lord forbid! What for?
The only thing I'm asking you to do is to stop helping the Soviet
economy.

In ancient times, trade began with the meeting of two persons   27
who would show each other that they were unarmed. As a sign of
this each extended an open hand. This was the beginning of the
handclasp. Today's word "détente" means a relaxation of tension.
But I would say that what we need is rather this image of the open
hand.

Relations between the Soviet Union and the United States   28
should be such that there would be no deceit in the question of
armaments, that there would be no concentration camps, no psychiatric wards for healthy people. Relations should be such that
there would be an end to the incessant ideological warfare waged
against you and that an address such as mine today would in no
way be an exception. People would be able to come to you from
the Soviet Union and from other communist countries and tell you
the truth about what is going on. This would be, I say, a period in
which we would truly be able to present "open hands" to each
other.

E. B. WHITE

E. B. White, distinguished essayist, was born in Mount Vernon, New York, in 1899. A graduate of Cornell University, White has worked as reporter and advertising copywriter, and in 1926 he joined the staff of *The New Yorker* magazine. Since 1937 he has done most of his writing at his farm in Maine, for many years contributing a regular column, "One Man's Meat," for *Harper's* magazine and free-lance editorials for the "Notes and Comments" column of *The New Yorker*. White has also written children's books, two volumes of verse, and, with James Thurber, *Is Sex Necessary?* (1929). With his wife he compiled *A Subtreasury of American Humor* (1941). Collections of his own essays include *One Man's Meat* (1942), *The Second Tree from the Corner* (1953), and *The Points of My Compass* (1962). In 1959 he revised and enlarged William Strunk's *The Elements of Style*, a textbook still widely used in college classrooms. White has been recipient of many honors and writing awards as he gained renown for his crisp, highly individual style and his sturdy independence of thought. These qualities are evident in the following unit, complete with editorial notations, from *Letters of E. B. White* (collected and edited by Dorothy Lobrano Guth, 1976), in which he starts (and wins) a controversy over what he could see, as few others had at the time, a serious threat to an independent press in America.

Letters on the "Xerox–Esquire–Salisbury Axis"

To THE EDITOR OF THE ELLSWORTH (MAINE) AMERICAN

[North Brooklin, Me.]
January 1, 1976

To the Editor:

I think it might be useful to stop viewing fences for a moment   1
and take a close look at Esquire magazine's new way of doing busi-

From *Letters of E. B. White,* collected and edited by Dorothy Lobrano Guth: "Letter to the Editor of the Ellsworth (Maine) *American* — North Brooklin, January 1, 1976," "Letter to W. B. Jones — North Brooklin, January 30, 1976," (pp. 657–661). Copyright © 1976 by E. B. White. Reprinted by permission of Harper & Row, Publishers, Inc.

ness. In February, Esquire will publish a long article by Harrison E. Salisbury, for which Mr. Salisbury will receive no payment from Esquire but will receive $40,000 from the Xerox Corporation — plus another $15,000 for expenses. This, it would seem to me, is not only a new idea in publishing, it charts a clear course for the erosion of the free press in America. Mr. Salisbury is a former associate editor of the New York Times and should know better. Esquire is a reputable sheet and should know better. But here we go — the Xerox–Salisbury–Esquire axis in full cry!

A news story about this amazing event in the December 14th issue of the Times begins: "Officials of Esquire magazine and of the Xerox Corporation report no adverse reactions, so far, to the announcement that Esquire will publish a 23-page article [about travels through America] in February 'sponsored' by Xerox." Herewith I am happy to turn in my adverse reaction even if it's the first one across the line.

Esquire, according to the Times story, attempts to justify its new payment system (get the money from a sponsor) by assuring us that Mr. Salisbury will not be tampered with by Xerox; his hand and his pen will be free. If Xerox likes what he writes about America, Xerox will run a "low keyed full-page ad preceding the article" and another ad at the end of it. From this advertising, Esquire stands to pick up $115,000 and Mr. Salisbury has already picked up $40,000, traveling, all expenses paid, through this once happy land. . . .

Apparently Mr. Salisbury had a momentary qualm about taking on the Xerox job. The Times reports him as saying, "At first I thought, gee whiz, should I do this?" But he quickly conquered his annoying doubts and remembered that big corporations had in the past been known to sponsor "cultural enterprises," such as opera. The emergence of a magazine reporter as a cultural enterprise is as stunning a sight as the emergence of a butterfly from a cocoon. Mr. Salisbury must have felt great, escaping from his confinement.

Well, it doesn't take a giant intellect to detect in all this the shadow of disaster. If magazines decide to farm out their writers to advertisers and accept the advertiser's payment to the writer and to the magazine, then the periodicals of this country will be far down the drain and will become so fuzzy as to be indistinguishable from the controlled press in other parts of the world.

E. B. White

[Some weeks after his letter on the Xerox–Esquire–Salisbury   6
arrangement was published, White received a letter of inquiry from
W. B. Jones, Director of Communications Operations at Xerox Cor-
poration, outlining the ground rules of the corporation's sponsor-
ship of the Salisbury piece and concluding: "With these ground
rules, do you still see something sinister in the sponsorship? The
question is put seriously, because if a writer of your achievement
and insight — after considering the terms of the arrangement —
still sees this kind of corporate sponsorship as leading the periodi-
cals of this country toward the controlled press of other parts of
the world, then we may well reconsider our plans to underwrite
similar projects in the future." White's reply follows.]

To w. b. jones

North Brooklin
January 30, 1976
Dear Mr. Jones:

In extending my remarks on sponsorship, published in the   7
Ellsworth *American*, I want to limit the discussion to the press —
that is, to newspapers and magazines. I'll not speculate about television, as television is outside my experience and I have no ready
opinion about sponsorship in that medium.

In your recent letter to me, you ask whether, having studied   8
your ground rules for proper conduct in sponsoring a magazine
piece, I still see something sinister in the sponsorship. Yes, I do.
Sinister may not be the right word, but I see something ominous
and unhealthy when a corporation underwrites an article in a magazine of general circulation. This is not, essentially, the old familiar
question of an advertiser trying to influence editorial content; almost everyone is acquainted with that common phenomenon.
Readers are aware that it is always present but usually in a rather
subdued or non-threatening form. Xerox's sponsoring of a specific
writer on a specific occasion for a specific article is something quite
different. No one, as far as I know, accuses Xerox of trying to influence editorial opinion. But many people are wondering why a
large corporation placed so much money on a magazine piece, why
the writer of the piece was willing to get paid in so unusual a fashion, and why Esquire was ready and willing to have an outsider
pick up the tab. These are reasonable questions.

The press in our free country is reliable and useful not be- 9
cause of its good character but because of its great diversity. As
long as there are many owners, each pursuing his own brand of
truth, we the people have the opportunity to arrive at the truth and
to dwell in the light. The multiplicity of ownership is crucial. It's
only when there are few owners, or, as in a government-controlled
press, one owner, that the truth becomes elusive and the light fails.
For a citizen in our free society, it is an enormous privilege and a
wonderful protection to have access to hundreds of periodicals, each
peddling its own belief. There is safety in numbers: the papers expose each other's follies and peccadillos, correct each other's mistakes, and cancel out each other's biases. The reader is free to range
around in the whole editorial bouillabaisse and explore it for the
one clam that matters — the truth.

When a large corporation or a rich individual underwrites an 10
article in a magazine, the picture changes: the ownership of that
magazine has been diminished, the outline of the magazine has
been blurred. In the case of the Salisbury piece, it was as though
Esquire had gone on relief, was accepting its first welfare payment,
and was not its own man anymore. The editor protests that he accepts full responsibility for the text and that Xerox had nothing to
do with the whole business. But the fact remains that, despite his
full acceptance of responsibility, he somehow did not get around
to paying the bill. This is unsettling and I think unhealthy. Whenever money changes hands, something goes along with it — an in-
tangible something that varies with the circumstances. It would be
hard to resist the suspicion that *Esquire* feels indebted to Xerox,
that Mr. Salisbury feels indebted to both, and that the ownership,
or sovereignty, of *Esquire* has been nibbled all around the edges.

Sponsorship in the press is an invitation to corruption and 11
abuse. The temptations are great, and there is an opportunist behind every bush. A funded article is a tempting morsel for any
publication — particularly for one that is having a hard time making ends meet. A funded assignment is a tempting dish for a writer,
who may pocket a much larger fee than he is accustomed to getting. And sponsorship is attractive to the sponsor himself, who, for
one reason or another, feels an urge to penetrate the editorial columns after being so long pent up in the advertising pages. These
temptations are real, and if the barriers were to be let down I believe corruption and abuse would soon follow. Not all corporations

would approach subsidy in the immaculate way Xerox did or in the same spirit of benefaction. There are a thousand reasons for someone's wishing to buy his way into print, many of them unpalatable, all of them to some degree self-serving. Buying and selling space in news columns could become a serious disease of the press. If it reached epidemic proportions, it could destroy the press. I don't want IBM or the National Rifle Association providing me with a funded spectacular when I open my paper. I want to read what the editor and the publisher have managed to dig up on their own — and paid for out of the till. . . .

My affection for the free press in a democracy goes back a   12
long way. My love for it was my first and greatest love. If I felt a shock at the news of the Salisbury–Xerox–Esquire arrangement, it was because the sponsorship principle seemed to challenge and threaten everything I believe in: that the press must not only be free, it must be fiercely independent — to survive and to serve. Not all papers are fiercely independent, God knows, but there are always enough of them around to provide a core of integrity and an example that others feel obliged to steer by. The funded article is not in itself evil, but it is the beginning of evil and it is an invitation to evil. I hope the invitation will not again be extended, and, if extended, I hope it will be declined.

About a hundred and fifty years ago, Tocqueville wrote: "The   13
journalists of the United States are generally in a very humble position, with a scanty education and a vulgar turn of mind." Today, we chuckle at this antique characterization. But about fifty years ago, when I was a young journalist, I had the good fortune to encounter an editor who fitted the description quite closely. Harold Ross, who founded the *New Yorker*, was deficient in education and had — at least to all outward appearances — a vulgar turn of mind. What he did possess, though, was the ferocity of independence. He was having a tough time finding money to keep his floundering little sheet alive, yet he was determined that neither money nor influence would ever corrupt his dream or deflower his text. His boiling point was so low as to be comical. The faintest suggestion of the shadow of advertising in his news and editorial columns would cause him to erupt. He would explode in anger, the building would reverberate with his wrath, and his terrible swift sword would go flashing up and down the corridors. For a young man, it was an impressive sight and a memorable one. Fifty years have not dimmed

for me either the spectacle of Ross's ferocity or my own early convictions — which were identical with his. He has come to my mind
often while I've been composing this reply to your inquiry.

I hope I've clarified by a little bit my feelings about the anat-   14
omy of the press and the dangers of sponsorship of articles. Thanks
for giving me the chance to speak my piece.

Sincerely,
E. B. White

[*Mr. Jones wrote and thanked White for "telling me what I didn't*   15
want to hear." In May another letter arrived from Jones saying
that Xerox had decided not to underwrite any more articles in the
press and that they were convinced it was "the right decision."]

A Guide to Terms

Abstract   (See *Concrete/Abstract.*)
Allusion   (See *Figures of Speech.*)
Analogy   (See *Section 4.*)
Argument is one of the four basic forms of prose. It usually employs one or all of the other forms — exposition, narration, description — sometimes becoming difficult to distinguish from them. The difference is in its basic motivation: argument assumes that there are two sides to the matter under discussion, but it aims to resolve the conflict by influencing the reader to favor one side.

    A distinction is ordinarily made between *logical argument* (usually called simply "argument") and *persuasive argument* (usually termed "persuasion"). Whereas logical argument appeals to reason, persuasion appeals to the emotions. The aim of both, however, is to convince, and they are nearly always blended into whatever mixture seems most likely to do the convincing. After all, reason and emotion are both important human elements — and we may have to persuade someone even to listen to our logic. The emphasis on one or the other, of course, should depend on the subject and the audience.

    Some authorities make a somewhat different distinction: we argue merely to get someone to change his mind; we use persuasion to get him to *do* something about it — e.g., to vote a Republican ticket, not just agree with the party platform. But this view is not entirely inconsistent with the other. We can hardly expect to change a *mind* by emotional appeal, but we can hope to get someone to *act* because of it, whether or not his mind has been changed.

Cause   (See *Section 6.*)
Central Theme   (See *Unity.*)
Classification   (See *Section 2.*)
Clichés are tired expressions, perhaps once fresh and colorful, that
   have been overused until they have lost most of their effectiveness and become trite or hackneyed. The term is also applied,
   less commonly, to trite ideas or attitudes.

   We may need to use clichés in conversation, of course,
where the quick and economical phrase is an important and
useful tool of expression — and where no one expects us to be
constantly original. We are fortunate, in a way, to have a large
accumulation of clichés from which to draw. To describe
someone, without straining our originality very much, we can
always declare that he is *as innocent as a lamb, as thin as a
rail,* or *as fat is a pig;* that he is *as dumb as an ox, as sly as a
fox,* or *as wise as an owl;* that he is *financially embarrassed* or
has a fly in the ointment or *his ship has come in;* or that, *last
but not least, in this day and age,* the *Grim Reaper* has taken
him to *his eternal reward.* There is indeed *a large stockpile*
from which we can draw for ordinary conversation.

   But the trite expression, written down on paper, is a permanent reminder that the writer is either lazy or not aware of
the dullness of stereotypes — or, even more damaging, it is a
clue that his ideas themselves may be threadbare, and therefore can be adequately expressed in threadbare language.

   Occasionally, of course, a writer can use obvious clichés
deliberately, for his own purposes. (See Roiphe, par. 4; Sheehy,
12; Allen, 14; B. Lawrence, 1.) But usually to be fully effective, writing must be fresh and should seem to have been
written specifically for the occasion. Clichés, however fresh
and appropriate at one time, have lost these qualities.
Closings are almost as much of a problem as introductions, and
   they are fully as important. The function of a closing is simply
   "to close," of course; but this implies somehow tying the entire writing into a neat package, giving the final sense of unity
   to the whole endeavor, and thus leaving the reader with a
   sense of satisfaction instead of an uneasy feeling that he ought
   to be looking around for another page.

   There is no standard length for closings. A short composition may be effectively completed with one sentence — or even without any real closing at all, if the last point discussed is a strong or climactic one. A longer piece of writing, however, may end more slowly, perhaps through several paragraphs.

A few types of weak endings are so common that warnings are in order here. The careful writer will avoid these faults: (1) giving the effect of having suddenly become tired and quit; (2) ending on a minor detail or an apparent afterthought; (3) bringing up a new point in the closing; (4) using any new qualifying remark in the closing (if he wants his opinions to seem less dogmatic or generalized, he should go back to do his qualifying where the damage was done); (5) ending with an apology of any kind (if the author is not interested enough to become at least a minor expert in his subject, he should not be wasting the reader's time).

Of the several acceptable ways of giving the sense of finality to a paper, the easiest is the *summary,* but it is also the least desirable for most short papers. If the reader has read and understood something only a page or two before, he probably does not need to have it reviewed for him. It is apt to seem merely repetitious. Longer writings, of course, such as research or term papers, may require thorough summaries.

Several other closing techniques are available to the writer. The following, which do not represent all the possibilities, are useful in many situations, and they can frequently be employed in combination:

1. *Using word signals* — e.g., *finally, at last, thus, and so, in conclusion,* as well as more original devices suggested by the subject itself. (See Thurber, Robinson.)

2. *Changing the tempo* — usually a matter of sentence length or pace. This is a very subtle indication of finality, and it is difficult to achieve. (For examples of modified use, see Masters/Johnson, Hall, Asimov, Clarke.)

3. *Restating the central idea* of the writing — sometimes a "statement" so fully developed that it practically becomes a summary itself. (See Catton, Mead/Metraux.)

4. *Using climax* — a natural culmination of preceding points or, in some cases, the last major point itself. This is

suitable, however, only if the materials have been so arranged that the last point is noticeably outstanding. (See Catton, B. Lawrence, Haley, Rettie.)

5. *Making suggestions,* perhaps mentioning a possible solution to the problem being discussed — a useful technique for exposition as well as for argument, and a natural signal of the end. (See Peter/Hull, Allen, Asimov, Keller, Clarke.)

6. *Showing the topic's significance,* its effects, or the universality of its meaning — a commonly used technique that, if carefully handled, is an excellent indication of closing. (See Masters/Johnson, B. Lawrence, Rettie, Asimov, Keller.)

7. *Echoing the introduction* — a technique that has the virtue of improving the effect of unity by bringing the development around full circle, so to speak. The echo may be a reference to a problem posed or a significant expression, quotation, analogy, or symbol used in the introduction or elsewhere early in the composition. (See Thurber, Sheehy, Franklin, Plimpton.)

8. *Using some rhetorical device* — a sort of catchall category, but a good supply source that includes several very effective techniques: pertinent quotations, anecdotes and brief dialogues, metaphors, allusions, ironic comments, and various kinds of witty or memorable remarks. All, however, run the risk of seeming forced, and hence amateurish; but properly handled they make for an effective closing. (See Sheehy, B. Lawrence, Rettie.)

Coherence is the quality of good writing that results from the presentation of all parts in logical and clear relations.

Coherence and unity are usually studied together and, indeed, are almost inseparable. But whereas unity refers to the relation of parts to the central theme (see *Unity*), coherence refers to their relations with each other. In a coherent piece of writing, each sentence, each paragraph, each major division seems to grow out of those preceding it.

Several transitional devices (see *Transition*) help to make these relations clear, but far more fundamental to coherence is the sound organization of materials. From the moment he first begins to visualize his subject materials in patterns, the writer's goal must be clear and logical development. If it is, coherence is almost assured.

Colloquial Expressions are characteristic of conversation and informal writing, and they are normally perfectly appropriate in those contexts. However, most writing done for college, business, or professional purposes is considered "formal" writing; and for such usage colloquialisms are too informal, too *folksy* (a word itself which most dictionaries label "colloq.").

Some of the expressions appropriate only for informal usage are *kid* (for child), *boss* (for employer), *flunk, buddy, snooze, gym, a lot of, phone, skin flicks, porn.* In addition, contractions such as *can't* and *I'd* are usually regarded as colloquialisms and are never permissible in, for instance, a research or term paper.

Slang is defined as a low level of colloquialism, but it is sometimes placed "below" colloquialism in respectability; even standard dictionaries differ as to just what the distinction is. (Some of the examples in the preceding paragraph, if included in dictionaries at all, are identified both ways.) At any rate, slang generally comprises words either coined or given novel meanings in an attempt at colorful or humorous expression. Slang soon becomes limp with overuse, however, losing whatever vigor it first had. In time, slang expressions either disappear completely or graduate to more acceptable colloquial status and thence, possibly, into standard usage. (That is one way in which our language is constantly changing.) But until their "graduations," slang and colloquialism have an appropriate place in formal writing only if used sparingly and for special effect. Because dictionaries frequently differ in matters of usage, the student should be sure he is using a standard edition approved by his instructor. (For further examples, see Plimpton, pars. 2, 3; Elbow, 1, 6; Pirsig; Roiphe; Wolfe; Sheehy; Masters/Johnson, 9; Allen, 10, 13, 22; Haley, 1, 11.)

Comparison (See *Section 3.*)

Conclusions (See *Closings.*)

Concrete and **Abstract** words are both indispensable to the language, but a good rule in most writing is to use the concrete whenever possible. This policy also applies, of course, to sentences that express only abstract ideas, which can often be made clearer, more effective, by use of concrete examples. Many expository paragraphs are constructed with an abstract topic sentence and its concrete support. (See *Unity.*)

A concrete word names something that exists as an entity in itself, something that can be perceived by the human senses. We can see, touch, hear, and smell a horse — hence *horse* is a concrete word. But a horse's *strength* is not. We have no reason to doubt that strength exists, but it does not have an independent existence: something else must *be* strong or there is no strength. Hence, *strength* is an abstract word.

Purely abstract reading is difficult for the average reader; with no concrete images provided for him, he is constantly forced to make his own. Concrete writing helps the reader to visualize and is therefore easier and faster to read.

(See *Specific/General* for further discussion.)

Connotation and **Denotation** both refer to the meanings of words. Denotation is the direct, literal meaning as it would be found in a dictionary, whereas connotation refers to the response a word *really* arouses in the reader or listener. (See Wolfe, 14; B. Lawrence.)

There are two types of connotation: personal and general. Personal connotations vary widely, depending on the experiences and moods that an individual associates with the word. (This corresponds with personal symbolism; see *Symbol*.) *Waterfall* is not apt to have the same meaning for the happy young honeymooners at Yosemite as it has for the grieving mother whose child has just drowned in a waterfall. But general connotations are those shared by many people. *Fireside*, far beyond its obvious dictionary definition, generally connotes warmth and security and good companionship. *Mother*, which denotatively means simply "female parent," means much more connotatively.

A word or phrase considered less distasteful or offensive than a more direct expression is called a *euphemism,* and this is also a matter of connotation. (See Mitford.) The various expressions used instead of the more direct "four-letter words" referring to daily bathroom events are examples of euphemisms. (See Wolfe's "mounting" or D. H. Lawrence's "dirt.") *Remains* is often used instead of *corpse,* and a few newspapers still have people *passing away* and being *laid to rest,* rather than *dying* and being *buried.*

But a serious respect for the importance of connotations goes far beyond euphemistic practices. The young writer can hardly expect to know all the different meanings of words for all his potential readers, but he can at least be aware that they do *have* different meanings. Of course, this is most important in persuasive writing — in political speeches, in advertising copywriting, and in any endeavor where some sort of public image is being created. When President Franklin Roosevelt began his series of informal radio talks, he called them "fireside chats," thus putting connotation to work. An advertising copywriter trying to evoke the feeling of love and tenderness associated with motherhood is not seriously tempted to use *female parent* instead of *mother*.

In exposition, however, where the primary purpose is to explain, the writer ordinarily tries to avoid words that may have emotional overtones, unless these can somehow be used to increase understanding.

Contrast (See *Section 3.*)

Deduction (See *Section 10.*)

Denotation (See *Connotation/Denotation.*)

Description (See *Section 8.*)

Diction refers simply to "choice of words," but, not so simply, it involves many problems of usage, some of which are explained under several other headings in this guide, e.g., *Clichés, Colloquial Expressions, Connotation/Denotation, Concrete/Abstract* — anything, in fact, which pertains primarily to word choices. But the characteristics of good diction may be more generally classified as follows:

1. *Accuracy* — the choice of words that mean exactly what the author intends.

2. *Economy* — the choice of the simplest and fewest words that will convey the exact shade of meaning intended.

3. *Emphasis* — the choice of fresh, strong words, avoiding clichés and unnecessarily vague or general terms.

4. *Appropriateness* — the choice of words that are appropriate to the subject matter, to the prospective reader-audience, and to the purpose of the writing.

(For contrasts of diction see Thurber, Fromm, Rettie, Wolfe, Allen, Clarke, Keller.)

Division (See *Section 2.*)

Effect (See *Section 6.*)

Emphasis is almost certain to fall *somewhere*, and the author should be the one to decide where. He should make certain that a major point, not some minor detail, is emphasized.

Following are the most common ways of achieving emphasis. Most of them apply to the sentence, the paragraph, or the overall writing — all of which can be seriously weakened by emphasis in the wrong places.

1. By *position*. The most emphatic position is usually at the end, the second most emphatic at the beginning. (There are a few exceptions, including news stories and certain kinds of scientific reports.) The middle, therefore, should be used for materials that do not deserve special emphasis. (See Peter/ Hull, for the order of examples; Catton, par. 16; Franklin; Haley's cargo list, 49; and Rettie, for the long withheld revelation of real central theme.)

A sentence in which the main point is held until the last is called a *periodic sentence*, e.g., "After a long night of suspense and horror, the cavalry arrived." In a *loose sentence*, the main point is disposed of earlier and followed by dependencies, e.g., "The cavalry arrived after a long night of suspense and horror."

2. By *proportion*. Ordinarily, but not necessarily, important elements are given the most attention and thus automatically achieve a certain emphasis. (See Hall, for his special treatment of his narcotic type of reading; Elbow, for his disproportionate attention to justification; and Rettie, for a unique kind of *reverse* application of this method.)

3. By *repetition*. Words and ideas may sometimes be given emphasis by reuse, usually in a different manner. If not cautiously handled, however, this method can seem merely repetitious, not emphatic. (See Thurber, Peter/Hull, D. H. Lawrence, Keller.)

4. By *flat statement*. Although an obvious way to achieve emphasis is simply to *tell* the reader what is most important, it is often least effective, at least when used as the only method. Readers have a way of ignoring such pointers as "most important of all" and "especially true." (See Catton, par. 16; Keller.)

5. By *mechanical devices*. Emphasis can be achieved by using italics (underlining), capital letters, or exclamation points. But too often these devices are used, however uninten-

tionally, to cover deficiencies of content or style. Their employment can quickly be overdone and their impact lost. (For very limited and therefore especially emphatic use of italics, see Lawrence; Franklin; Clarke, par. 17; Taylor, 2, 13. Notice that Mitford, with a more emphatic style than most, uses none of these devices.)

6. By *distinctiveness of style*. The author can emphasize subtly with fresh and concrete words or figures of speech, crisp or unusual structures, and careful control of paragraph or sentence lengths. (These methods are used in many essays in this book: see Catton; Rettie, par. 19; Wolfe; Allen; Curtin, 7–15; Asimov; Clarke; Haley; and Twain who changes style radically for the second half of his essay.) *Verbal irony* (see *Irony*), including *sarcasm* (see Hall) and the rather specialized form known as *understatement*, if handled judiciously, is another valuable means of achieving distinctiveness of style and increasing emphasis. (See Wolfe, Mitford, D. H. Lawrence.)

Essay refers to a brief prose composition on a single topic, usually, but not always, communicating the author's personal ideas and impressions. Beyond this, because of the wide and loose application of the term, no really satisfactory definition has been arrived at.

Classifications of essay types have also been widely varied and sometimes not very meaningful. One basic and useful distinction, however, is between *formal* and *informal* essays, although many defy classification even in such broad categories as these. It is best to regard the two types as opposite ends of a continuum, along which most essays may be placed.

The formal essay usually develops an important theme through a logical progression of ideas, with full attention to unity and coherence, and in a serious tone. Although the style is seldom completely impersonal, it is literary rather than colloquial. (For examples of essays that are somewhere near the "formal" end of the continuum, see Fromm, Greenfield, Catton, Masters/Johnson, Mead/Metraux, B. Lawrence. The Declaration of Independence, a completely formal document, is not classifiable as an "essay" at all.)

The informal, or personal, essay is less elaborately organized and more chatty in style. First-person pronouns, contractions, and other colloquial or even slang expressions are often freely used. Informal essays are less serious in apparent purpose than formal essays. Although most do contain a worthwhile message or observation of some kind, an important purpose of many is to entertain. (See Thurber, Wolfe, Allen.)

The more personal and intimate informal essays may be classifiable as *familiar* essays, although, again, there is no well-established boundary. Familiar essays pertain to the author's own experience, ideas, or prejudices, frequently in a light and humorous style. (See Plimpton, Roiphe, Curtin, Keller.)

Evaluation of a literary piece, like that of any other creative endeavor, is meaningful only when based somehow on the answers to three questions: (1) What was the author's purpose? (2) How successfully does he fulfill it? (3) How worthwhile was it?

An architect could hardly be blamed for designing a poor gymnasium if his commission had been to design a library. Similarly, if an author is trying to sort out for us the qualities that determine a president's character (as is Barber), he cannot be faulted for failing to make the reader laugh. However, if his purpose is simply to amuse (a worthy enough goal, by the way), he should not be condemned for teaching little about melatonin. (Nothing prevents his trying to explain pornography through the use of humor, or trying to amuse by comparing two Civil War generals, but in these situations his purpose has changed — and grown almost unbearably harder to achieve.)

If the architect was commissioned to design a gymnasium, however, he could be justifiably criticized on whether the building is successful and attractive *as a gymnasium*. If an author is trying to explain symbolism (as is Fromm) the reader has a right to expect sound reasoning and clear expository prose.

Many things are written and published that succeed very well in carrying out the author's intent — but simply are not worthwhile. Although this is certainly justifiable ground for unfavorable criticism, the reader should first make full allowance for his own limitations and perhaps his narrow range of interests, evaluating the work as nearly as possible from the standpoint of the average reader for whom the writing was intended.

Figures of Speech are short, vivid comparisons, either stated or implied; but they are not literal comparisons (e.g., "Your car is like my car," which is presumably a plain statement of fact). Figures of speech are more imaginative. They imply analogy but, unlike analogy, are used less to inform than to make quick and forceful impressions. All figurative language is a comparison of unlikes, but the unlikes do have some interesting point of likeness, perhaps one never noticed before.

A *metaphor* merely suggests the comparison and is worded as if the two unlikes were the same thing — e.g., "the language of the river" and "was turned to blood" (Twain, par. 1) and "a great chapter in American life" (Catton, 1). For some of the many other examples in this book, see Roiphe; Hall; Mitford; Masters/Johnson; Mead/Metraux, 3; D. H. Lawrence; Asimov, 4; Keller; Clarke, 2–4.

A *simile* (which is sometimes classified as a special kind of metaphor) expresses a similarity directly, usually with the word *like* or *as* — e.g., "like marionette strings" (Roiphe, par. 2). (For further illustrations, see Barber, 2; Rettie, 6; Toynbee, 4; Robinson, 13.)

A *personification*, which is actually a special type either of metaphor or simile, is usually classified as a "figure" in its own right. In personification, inanimate things are treated as if they had the qualities or powers of a person — e.g., "our sun is an out-of-town member" (Clarke, par. 30) or "concepts clothed in character" (Hall, 5). Some people would also label as personification any characterization of inanimate objects as animals, or of animals as humans — as in the descriptions and "love displays" of the Thurber piece.

An *allusion* is literally any casual reference, any alluding, to something; but rhetorically it is limited to a figurative reference to a famous or literary person, event, or quotation, and it should be distinguished from the casual reference that has a literal function in the subject matter. Hence, casual mention of Judas Iscariot's betrayal of Jesus is merely a reference, but calling a modern traitor a "Judas" is an allusion. A rooster might be referred to as "the Hitler of the barnyard," or a lover as a "Romeo." Many allusions refer to mythological or biblical persons or places. (See Barber, par. 16; Wolfe, title and par. 1; Rettie, title; Petrunkevitch, 9.)

Irony and paradox (both discussed under their own headings) and analogy (see *Section 4*) are also frequently classed as figures of speech, and there are several other, less common types that are really subclassifications of those already discussed.

General   (See *Specific/General.*)

Illustration   (See *Section 1.*)

Impressionistic Description   (See *Section 8.*)

Induction   (See *Section 10.*)

Introductions give readers their first impressions, which often turn out to be the lasting ones. In fact, unless an introduction succeeds in somehow attracting a reader's interest, he probably will go no further. Its importance is one reason that writing it is nearly always difficult.

Sometimes, when the writer remains at a loss to know how to begin, he should forget about the introduction for a while and go ahead with the main body of his writing. Later he may find that a suitable introduction has suggested itself or even that the way he did start is actually introduction enough.

Introduction may vary in length from one sentence in a short composition to several paragraphs or even several pages in longer and more complex expositions, such as research papers and reports of various kinds.

Good introductions in expository writing have at least three and sometimes four functions:

1. *To identify the subject and set its limitations,* thus building a solid foundation for unity. This function usually includes some indication of the central theme, letting the reader know what point is to be made about the subject. Unlike the other forms of prose, which can often benefit by some degree of mystery, exposition has the primary purpose of explaining, so the reader has a right to know from the beginning just *what* is being explained.

2. *To interest the reader,* and thus ensure his attention. To be sure of doing this, the writer must analyze his prospective readers and their interest in his subject. The account of a new X-ray technique would need an entirely different kind of

introduction if written for doctors than if written for the campus newspaper.

3. *To set the tone* of the rest of the writing. (See *Style/Tone.*) Tone varies greatly in writing, just as the tone of a person's voice varies with his mood. One function of the introduction is to let the reader know the author's attitude since it may have a subtle but important bearing on the communication.

4. *Frequently*, but not always, *to indicate the plan of organization*. Although seldom important in short, relatively simple compositions and essay examinations, this function of introductions can be especially valuable in more complex papers.

These are the necessary functions of an introduction. For best results, keep these guidelines in mind: (1) Avoid referring to the title, or even assuming that the reader has seen it. Make the introduction do all the introducing. (2) Avoid crude and uninteresting beginnings, such as "This paper is about. . . ." (3) Avoid going too abruptly into the main body — smooth transition is at least as important here as anywhere else. (4) Avoid overdoing the introduction, either in length or in extremes of style.

Fortunately, there are many good ways to introduce expository writing, and several of the most useful are illustrated by the selections in this book. Many writings, of course, combine two or more of the following techniques for interesting introductions.

1. *Stating the central theme*, which is sometimes fully enough explained in the introduction to become almost a preview-summary of the exposition to come. (See Thurber, Petrunkevitch.)

2. *Showing the significance of the subject*, or stressing its importance. (See Catton, Wolfe.)

3. *Giving the background of the subject*, usually in brief form, in order to bring the reader up to date as early as possible for a better understanding of the matter at hand. (See Peter/Hull, Hall, Greenfield, Mead/Metraux, Haley.)

4. *"Focusing down"* to one aspect of the subject, a technique similar to that used in some movies, showing first a broad scope (of subject area, as of landscape) and then pro-

gressively narrowing views until the focus is on one specific thing (perhaps the name "O'Flinnigan Jones" on a mailbox by a gate — or the specific aspect of Hesse that is worthy of discussion, as in the selection by Huxley. (See also Toffler, Rettie, Haley.)

5. *Using a pertinent rhetorical device* that will attract interest as it leads into the main exposition — e.g., an anecdote, analogy, allusion, quotation, or paradox. (See Sheehy, Plimpton.)

6. *Using a short but vivid comparison or contrast* to emphasize the central idea. (See Thurber, Petrunkevitch, Greenfield.)

7. *Posing a challenging question*, the answering of which the reader will assume to be the purpose of the writing. (See B. Lawrence, Greenfield, Mead/Metraux.)

8. *Referring to the writer's experience with the subject*, perhaps even giving a detailed account of that experience. Some writings, of course, especially descriptive or narrative essays, are simply continuations of experience so introduced, perhaps with the expository purpose of the telling made entirely evident only at the end or slowly unfolding as the account progresses. (See Peter/Hull, Roiphe.)

9. *Presenting a startling statistic or other fact* that will indicate the nature of the subject to be discussed. (See Thurber.)

10. *Making an unusual statement* that can intrigue as well as introduce. (See Thurber, Berne, Roiphe, Wolfe, Sheehy, Gansberg, Asimov.)

11. *Making a commonplace remark* that can draw interest because of its very commonness in sound or meaning. (See Peter/Hull, Berne, Haley, Taylor.)

Irony, in its verbal form sometimes classed as a figure of speech, consists of saying one thing on the surface but meaning exactly (or nearly) the opposite — e.g., "this beautiful neighborhood of ours" may mean that it is a dump. (For other illustrations, see Thurber, Wolfe, Mitford.)

Verbal irony has a wide range of tones, from the gentle, gay, or affectionate to the sharpness of outright *sarcasm* (see Hall), which is always intended to cut. It may consist of only a word or phrase, it may be a simple *understatement* (see Mitford), or it may be sustained as one of the major components of satire.

Irony can be an effective tool of exposition if its tone is consistent with the overall tone and if the writer is sure that his audience is bright enough to recognize it. In speech, a person usually indicates by voice or eye-expression that he is not to be taken literally; in writing, the words on the page have to speak for themselves.

In addition to verbal irony, there is also an *irony of situation*, in which there is a sharp contradiction between what is logically expected to happen and what does happen — e.g., a man sets a trap for an obnoxious neighbor and then gets caught in it himself. Or the ironic situation may simply be some discrepancy that an outsider can see, while those involved cannot. (The principle itself in "The Peter Principle" can illustrate irony of situation, as can the "situation" discussed in many of the other essays: e.g., Huxley; Plimpton; Thurber; Roiphe, par. 2; Toffler, 7; Sheehy, 9; Masters/Johnson, 16; B. Lawrence, 11–12; Keller, 8–10.)

Logical Argument   (See *Argument*.)

Loose Sentences   (See *Emphasis*.)

Metaphor   (See *Figures of Speech*.)

Narration   (See *Section 9*.)

Objective writing and **Subjective** writing are distinguishable by the extent to which they reflect the author's personal attitudes or emotions. The difference is usually one of degree, as few writing endeavors can be completely objective or subjective.

Objective writing, seldom used in its pure form except in business or scientific reports, is impersonal and concerned almost entirely with straight narration, with logical analysis, or with the description of external appearances. (For somewhat objective writing, see Berne, Toffler, Fromm, Barber, Pirsig, Clarke.)

Subjective writing (in description usually called "impressionistic" — see *Section 8*) is more personalized, more expressive of the beliefs, ideals, or impressions of the author. Whereas in objective writing the emphasis is on the object being written about, in subjective writing the emphasis is on the way the author sees and interprets the object. (For some of the many examples in this book, see Thurber, Twain,

Plimpton, Hall, Wolfe, Roiphe, Toynbee, Mitford, B. Lawrence, D. H. Lawrence, Keller, Haley.)

Paradox is a statement or remark that, although seeming to be contradictory or absurd, actually contains some truth. Many paradoxes are ironical. The Masters/Johnson reference to "married celibacy" (par. 16) very likely seems both paradoxical and ironical to some readers, as might Henry L. Stimson's indirect assertion that some men are "made free" by responsibility (Barber, par. 3).

Paragraph Unity (See *Unity*.)

Parallel Structure refers in principle to the same kind of "parallelism" that is studied in grammar: the principle that coordinate elements should have coordinate presentation, as in a pair or a series of verbs, prepositional phrases, gerunds. It is often as much a matter of "balance" as it is of parallelism.

But the principle of parallel structure, far from being just a negative "don't mix" set of rules, is also a positive rhetorical device. Many writers use it as an effective means of stressing variety or profusion in a group of nouns or modifiers, or of emphasizing parallel ideas in sentence parts, in two or more sentences, or even in two or more paragraphs. At times it can also be useful stylistically, to give a subtle poetic quality to the prose.

(For illustrations of parallel parts within a sentence: see Berne, par. 5; Roiphe, 2, 14; Toffler, 8; Wolfe, 1, 4; Asimov, 7, 9. Of sentences themselves: Peter/Hull; Berne, 4; Catton, 14; Allen, 15, 18–22; Franklin, Jefferson. Of both parts and sentences: Twain. Of paragraphs: Jefferson; Allen, 18–22; and the beginnings of Rettie's paragraphs 6–14 and most of Taylor's first eleven paragraphs.)

Periodic Sentence (See *Emphasis*.)

Personification (See *Figures of Speech*.)

Point of view is simply the position of the author in relation to his subject matter. Rhetorical point of view, our only concern here, has little in common with the grammatical sort and differs somewhat from point of view in fiction.

A ranch in a mountain valley is seen differently by the practical stockman working at the corral, by his wife deciding where to plant her petunias, by the artist or poet viewing the ranch from the mountainside, and by the careful geographer in a plane above, map-sketching the valley in relation to the entire range. It is the same ranch, but the positions and attitudes of the viewers are varied.

So it is with expository prose. The position and attitude of the author are the important lens through which the reader sees the subject. Consistency is important, because if the lens is changed without sufficient cause and explanation, the reader will become disconcerted, if not annoyed.

Obviously, since the point of view is partially a matter of attitude, the tone and often the style of writing are closely linked to it. (See *Style/Tone*.)

The selections in this book provide examples of numerous points of view. Barber's and Twain's are those of authority in their own fields of experience; Huxley is the student of human nature; Mitford is the debunking prober, Asimov the prober of futures, and Keller the blind person wistfully longing to see. In each of these (and the list could be extended to include all the selections in the book), the subject would seem vastly different if seen from some other point of view.

Process Analysis   (See *Section 5*.)

Purpose that is clearly understood by the author before he starts to write is essential to both unity and coherence. A worthwhile practice, certainly in the training stages, is to write down the controlling purpose before even beginning the outline. Some instructors require both a statement of purpose and a statement of central theme. (See *Unity*.)

The most basic element of a statement of purpose is the commitment to "explain," or perhaps for some assignments to "convince" (argument), to "relate" (narration), or to "describe." But the statement of purpose, whether written down or only decided upon, goes further — e.g., "to explain that most employees are promoted until they are on their level of incompetence, where they remain" (Peter/Hull) or "to explain that 'dirty words' are logically offensive because of the sources and connotations of the words themselves" (B. Lawrence).

Qualification is the tempering of broad statements to make them more valid and acceptable, the author himself admitting the probability of exceptions. This qualifying can be done inconspicuously, to whatever degree needed, by the use of *possibly, nearly always* or *most often, usually* or *frequently, sometimes* or *occasionally*. Instead of saying that "freshman composition is the most valuable course in college," it may be more accurate and defensible to say that it is for *some people* or that *it can be* the most valuable.

Masters and Johnson repeatedly use such qualifiers. Peter/Hull's "principle" states that "every employee *tends* to rise to his level of incompetence," and Robinson states that *most* who have had experience in meditation disagree with the cynics. (You may decide that some of the authors should have made greater use of qualification than they did.)

A **Rhetorical question** is posed with no expectation of receiving an answer; it is used solely as a structural device to launch or further a discussion, or to achieve emphasis. (See Berne's title; Rettie's last sentence; Toynbee, par. 4; Roiphe, 4, 6; Mead/Metraux, 1; Sheehy; B. Lawrence; D. H. Lawrence; Keller; Clarke, 33.)

Sarcasm   (See *Irony*.)

Satire, sometimes called "extended irony," is a literary form that brings wit and humor to the serious task of pointing out frailties or evils of human institutions. It has thrived in Western literature since the time of the ancient Greeks, and English literature of the eighteenth century was particularly noteworthy for the extent and quality of its satire. Broadly, two types are recognized: *Horatian satire* that is gentle, smiling, and aims to correct by invoking laughter and sympathy; and *Juvenalian satire*, which is sharper and which points with anger, contempt, moral indignation, to corruption and evil. (Swift's "A Modest Proposal" belongs in the latter category.)

Sentimentality, also called *sentimentalism,* is an exaggerated show of emotion, whether intentional or caused by lack of restraint. An author can oversentimentalize almost any situation, but the trap is most dangerous when he writes of timeworn emotional symbols or scenes — e.g., a broken heart, mother love, a lonely death, the conversion of a sinner. However sincere the author may be, if his reader is not fully oriented to the worth and uniqueness of the situation described, he may be either resentful or amused at any attempt to play on his emotions. Sentimentality is, of course, one of the chief characteristics of melodrama. (For examples of writing that, less adeptly handled, could easily have slipped into sentimentality, see

Twain, Greenfield, Catton, Curtin, Gansberg. The Keller essay, were it not for the highly unique viewpoint of the author, would no doubt seem hopelessly sentimentalized to most readers.)

Simile   (See *Figures of Speech*.)

Slang   (See *Colloquial Expressions*.)

Specific and **General** terms, and the distinctions between the two, are similar to concrete and abstract terms (as discussed under their own heading), and for our purpose there is no real need to keep the two sets of categories separated. Whether *corporation* is thought of as "abstract" and *Ajax Motor Company* as "concrete," or whether they are assigned to "general" and "specific" categories, the principle is the same: in most writing, *Ajax Motor Company* is better.

But "specific" and "general" are relative terms. For instance, the word *apple* is more specific than *fruit* but less so than *Winesap*. And *fruit*, as general as it certainly is in one respect, is still more specific than *food*. Such relationships are shown more clearly in a series, progressing from general to specific: *food, fruit, apple, Winesap;* or *vehicle, automobile, Ford, Mustang*. Modifiers and verbs can also have degrees of specificity: *bright, red, scarlet;* or *moved, sped, careened*. It is not difficult to see the advantages to the reader — and, of course, to the writer who needs to communicate an idea clearly: in "the scarlet Mustang careened through the pass," instead of "the bright-colored vehicle moved through the pass."

Obviously, however, there are times when the general or the abstract term or statement is essential — e.g., "a balanced diet includes some fruit," or "there was no vehicle in sight." But the use of specific language whenever possible is one of the best ways to improve diction and thus clarity and forcefulness in writing.

(Another important way of strengthening general, abstract writing is, of course, to use examples or other illustrations. See *Section 1*.)

Style and **Tone** are so closely linked and so often even elements of each other, that it is best to consider them together.

But there is a difference. Think of two young men, each with his girl friend on separate moonlight dates, whispering in nearly identical, tender and loving tones of voice. One young man says, "Your eyes, dearest, reflect a thousand sparkling candles of heaven," and the other says, "Them eyes of yours — in this light — they really bug me." Their *tones* were the same; their *styles* considerably different.

The same distinction exists in writing. But naturally, with more complex subjects than the effect of moonlight on a maiden's eyes, there are more complications in separating the two qualities, even for the purpose of study.

The tone is determined by the *attitude* of the writer toward his subject and toward his audience. He, too, may be tender and loving, but he may be indignant, solemn, playful, enthusiastic, belligerent, contemptuous — the list could be as long as a list of the many "tones of voice." (In fact, wide ranges of tone may be illustrated by essays of this book. Compare, e.g., those of the two parts of Twain; Barber and Mitford; or B. Lawrence and Hall.)

Style, on the other hand, expresses the author's individuality through his choices of word (see *Diction*), his sentence patterns (see *Syntax*), and his selection and arrangement of details and basic materials. (All these elements of style are illustrated in the contrasting statements of the moonstruck lads.) These matters of style are partially prescribed, of course, by the adopted tone, but they are still bound to reflect the writer's personality and mood, his education and general background.

(Some of the more distinctive styles — partially affected by and affecting tone — represented by selections in this book are those of Thurber, Wolfe, D. H. Lawrence, Hall, Rettie, Pirsig, Keller.)

Subjective Writing   (See *Objective/Subjective.*)

Symbol refers to anything that, although real itself, also suggests something broader or more significant — not just in greater numbers, however, as a man would not symbolize a group or even mankind itself, although he might be typical or representative in one or more abstract qualities. On the most elementary level, even words are symbols — e.g., *bear* brings to mind the furry beast itself. But more important is that things, persons, or even acts may also be symbolic, if they invoke abstract concepts, values, or qualities apart from themselves or their own kind. Such symbols, in everyday life as well as in literature and the other arts, are generally classifiable according to three types, which, although terminology differs, we may label *natural, personal,* and *conventional.* (Erich Fromm, in his "Symbolic Language," uses the same classification system but with somewhat different labels: universal, accidental, and conventional.)

In a natural symbol, the symbolic meaning is inherent in the thing itself. The sunrise naturally suggests new beginnings to most people, an island is almost synonymous with isolation, a cannon automatically suggests war; hence these are natural symbols. It does not matter that some things, by their nature, can suggest more than one concept; although a valley may symbolize security to one person and captivity to another, both meanings, contradictory as they might seem, are inherent, and in both respects the valley is a natural symbol.

The personal symbol, depending as it does on private experience or perception, is meaningless to others unless they are told about it or allowed to see its significance in context (as in literature). Although the color green may symbolize the outdoor life to the farm boy trapped in the gray city (in this respect perhaps a natural symbol), it can also symbolize romance to the girl proposed to while wearing her green blouse, or dismal poverty to the woman who grew up in a weathered green shanty; neither of these meanings is suggested by something *inherent* in the color green, so they are personal symbols. Anything at all could take on private symbolic meaning, even the odor of marigolds or the sound of a lawnmower. The sunrise itself could mean utter despair, instead of fresh opportunities, to the man who has long despised his daily job and cannot find another.

Conventional symbols usually started as personal symbols, but continued usage in life or art permits them to be generally recognized for their broader meanings, which depend on custom rather than any inherent quality — e.g., the olive branch for peace, the flag for love of country, the cross for Christianity, the raised fist for black power.

Symbols are used less in expository writing than in fic-

tion and poetry, but a few authors represented in this book
have either referred to the subtle symbolism of others or made
use of it in developing their own ideas — all without ever
mentioning the term. For the early Hessians (Huxley essay)
the waterworks evidently symbolized royal power; Plimpton
mentions the fans' raised forefinger (symbolizing their team's
number one position); Hall believes that in earlier and harder-
working days, reading came to symbolize wealth and leisure;
in Asimov's view of 1977, cars had come to symbolize "filthy"
riches; and apparently even the pith-helmet seemed, at least
to Haley, a conventional symbol in the native society of the
Gambia River jungle.

Syntax is a very broad term — too broad, perhaps, to be very useful — referring to the arrangement of words in a sentence.
Good syntax implies the use not only of correct grammar but
also of effective patterns. These patterns depend on sentences
with good unity, coherence, and emphasis, on the use of sub-
ordination and parallel construction as appropriate, on economy, and on a consistent and interesting point of view. A
pleasing variety of sentence patterns is also important in
achieving effective syntax.

Theme   (See *Unity.*)

Thesis   (See *Unity.*)

Tone   (See *Style/Tone.*)

Transition is the relating of one topic to the next, and smooth
transition is an important aid to the coherence of a sentence,
a paragraph, or an entire piece of writing. (See *Coherence.*)

The most effective coherence, of course, comes about naturally with sound development of ideas, one growing logically
into the next — and that virtue depends on sound organization. But sometimes beneficial even in this situation, particularly in going from one paragraph to the next, is the use of
appropriate transitional devices.

Readers are apt to be sensitive creatures, easy to lose.
(And, of course, the writer is the real loser since he is the
one who presumably has something he wants to communicate.) If the reader gets into a new paragraph and the territory
seems familiar, chances are that he will continue. But if there
are no identifying landmarks, he will often begin to feel un-

easy and will either start worrying about his slow comprehension or take a dislike to the author and subject matter. Either way, a communication block arises, and very likely the author will soon have one less reader.

A good policy, then, unless the progression of ideas is exceptionally smooth and obvious, is to provide some kind of familiar identification early in the new paragraph, to keep the reader feeling at ease with the different ideas. The effect is subtle but important. These familiar landmarks or transitional devices are sometimes applied deliberately but more often come naturally, especially when the prospective reader is kept constantly in mind at the time of writing.

An equally important reason for using some kinds of transitional devices, however, is a logical one: while functioning as bridges between ideas, they also assist the basic organization by pointing out the *relationship* of the ideas — and thus contributing still further to readability.

Transitional devices useful for bridging paragraph changes (and, some of them, to improve transitional flow within paragraphs) may be roughly classified as follows:

1. *Providing an "echo"* from the preceding paragraph. This may be the repetition of a key phrase or word, or a pronoun referring back to such a word, or a casual reference to an idea. (See Thurber; Fromm, par. 6; Mitford; Wolfe, especially from 1 to 2, and 4 to 5.) Such an echo cannot be superimposed on new ideas, but must, by careful planning be made an organic part of them.

2. *Devising a whole sentence or paragraph* to bridge between other important paragraphs or major divisions. (See Peter/Hull, par. 30; Barber, 6; Pirsig, 3; Taylor, 12; Keller, 11; Clarke, 36.)

3. *Using parallel structure* between an important sentence of one paragraph and the first sentence of the next. This is a subtle means of making the reader feel at ease in the new surroundings, but it is seldom used because it is much more limited in its potential than the other methods of transition. (See B. Lawrence, pars. 1 to 2.)

4. *Using standard transitional expressions,* most of which have the additional advantage of indicating relationship of

ideas. Only a few of those available are classified below, but nearly all the reading selections of this book can amply illustrate such transitional expressions:

Time — soon, immediately, afterward, later, meanwhile, after a while.

Place — nearby, here, beyond, opposite.

Result — as a result, therefore, thus, consequently, hence.

Comparison — likewise, similarly, in such a manner.

Contrast — however, nevertheless, still, but, yet, on the other hand, after all, otherwise.

Addition — also, too, and, and then, furthermore, moreover, finally, first, third.

Miscellaneous — for example, for instance, in fact, indeed, on the whole, in other words.

Trite   (See *Clichés*.)

Unity in writing is the same as unity in anything else — in a picture, a musical arrangement, a campus organization — and that is a *one*ness, in which all parts contribute to an overall effect.

Many elements of good writing contribute in varying degrees to the effect of unity. Some of these are properly designed introductions and closings; consistency of point of view, tone, and style; sometimes the recurring use of analogy or thread of symbolism; occasionally the natural time boundaries of an experience or event, as in the Mitford, Masters and Johnson, Rettie, Pirsig, Keller, Gansberg, and Haley selections.

But in most expository writing the only dependable unifying force is the *central theme*, which every sentence, every word, must somehow help to support. (The central theme is also called the *central idea* or the *thesis* when pertaining to the entire writing. In an expository paragraph it is the same as the *topic sentence*, which may be implied or, if stated, may be located anywhere in the paragraph, but is usually placed first.) As soon as anything appears which is not related to the central idea, then there are *two* units instead of one. Hence, unity is basic to all other virtues of good writing, even to coherence and emphasis, the other two organic essentials. (See *Coherence* and *Emphasis*.)

An example of unity may be found in a single river system (for a practical use of analogy), with all its tributaries, big or little, meandering or straight, flowing into the main stream and making it bigger — or at least flowing into another tributary that finds its way to the main stream. This is *one* river system, an example of unity. But now also picture another, nearby stream that does not empty into the river but goes off in some other direction. There are now two systems, not one, and there is no longer unity.

It is the same way with writing. The central theme is the main river, flowing along from the first capital letter to the very last period. Every drop of information must find its way into this theme-river, or it is not a part of the system at all. It matters not even slightly if the water is good, the idea-stream perhaps deeper and finer than any of the others: if it is not a tributary, it has no business pretending to be relevant to *this* theme of writing.

And that is why most students are required to state their central idea, usually in solid sentence form, before even starting to organize their ideas. If the writer can use only tributaries, it is very important to know from the start just what the river is.

To the Student:

If we are to make *Patterns of Exposition 6* a better book next time, we must know what students think of what we've done this time. Please help us by filling out this questionnaire and returning it to: Little, Brown and Co., College English, 34 Beacon Street, Boston, Mass. 02106.

School:_____ Course title:_____

Instructor's name:_____

Please give us your reaction to the selections:

		Keep	Drop	Didn't Read
Huxley	Waterworks and Kings	___	___	___
Plimpton	The American Tradition of Winning	___	___	___
Thurber	Courtship Through the Ages	___	___	___
Peter & Hull	The Peter Principle	___	___	___
Berne	Can People Be Judged by Their Appearance?	___	___	___
Hall	Reading Tastes and Habits	___	___	___
Fromm	Symbolic Language	___	___	___
Barber	Four Types of President	___	___	___
Twain	Two Ways of Seeing a River	___	___	___
Greenfield	Uncle Tom's Roots	___	___	___
Catton	Grant and Lee: A Study in Contrasts	___	___	___
Roiphe	Confessions of a Female Chauvinist Sow	___	___	___
Toffler	Modular Man	___	___	___
Rettie	But a Watch in the Night	___	___	___
Wolfe	O Rotten Gotham	___	___	___
Elbow	Freewriting	___	___	___
Pirsig	Mechanics' Logic	___	___	___
Petrunkevitch	The Spider and the Wasp	___	___	___
Mitford	To Dispel Fears of Live Burial	___	___	___
Toynbee	Intellectual Suicide at Puberty	___	___	___
Sheehy	$70,000 a Year, Tax Free	___	___	___
Robinson	Recharging Yourself Through Meditation	___	___	___
Masters & Johnson	Touching — and Being Touched	___	___	___
Allen	A Brief, Yet Helpful, Guide to Civil Disobedience	___	___	___

		Keep	Drop	Didn't Read
Mead & Metraux	The Egalitarian Error	___	___	___
B. Lawrence	Four-Letter Words Can Hurt You	___	___	___
D. H. Lawrence	Pornography	___	___	___
Curtin	Aging in the Land of the Young	___	___	___
Asimov	The Nightmare Life Without Fuel	___	___	___
Taylor	The Monster	___	___	___
Gansberg	38 Who Saw Murder Didn't Call the Police	___	___	___
Keller	Three Days to See	___	___	___
Haley	My Furthest-Back Person — "The African"	___	___	___
Franklin	On the Choice of a Mistress	___	___	___
Jefferson	The Declaration of Independence	___	___	___
Clarke	We'll Never Conquer Space	___	___	___
Plato	Socrates "Defends" Himself	___	___	___
Swift	A Modest Proposal	___	___	___
Carter	To Establish Justice in a Sinful World	___	___	___
Orwell	Politics and the English Language	___	___	___
Kristol	Censorship: Where Do We Draw the Line?	___	___	___
Solzhenitsyn	Wake Up, America!	___	___	___
White	Letters on the "Xerox–Esquire–Salisbury Axis"	___	___	___

1. Are there any authors not included whom you would like to see represented? _____

2. Were the biographical sketches useful? _____ How might they be improved? _____

3. Were the introductions helpful? _____ How might they be improved? _____

4. Will you keep this book for your library? _____

5. Please add any comments or suggestions. _____

_____

_____

_____

6. May we quote you in our promotional efforts for this book? _____ Yes _____ No

_____	_____
date	signature

_____

mailing address